Analysing Religious Discourse

AF166681

Language plays a key role in religion, framing how people describe spiritual experience and giving structure to religious beliefs and practices. Bringing together work from a team of world-renowned scholars, this volume introduces contemporary research on religious discourse from a variety of theoretical and methodical perspectives. It introduces methods for analysis of a range of different kinds of text and talk, including institutional discourse within organised religions, discourse around spirituality and spiritual experience within religious communities, media discourse about the role of religion and spirituality in society, translations of sacred texts, political discourse, and ritual language. Engaging and easy to read, it is accessible to researchers across linguistics, religious studies, and other related disciplines. A comprehensive introduction to all the major research approaches to religious language, it will become a key resource in the emerging interdisciplinary field of language and religion.

STEPHEN PIHLAJA is the author of three books about Language and Religion including *Religious Talk Online* (Cambridge University Press, 2018), and *Talk about Faith* (Cambridge University Press, 2021).

Analysing Religious Discourse

Edited by

Stephen Pihlaja

Newman University

Shaftesbury Road, Cambridge CB2 8EA, United Kingdom

One Liberty Plaza, 20th Floor, New York, NY 10006, USA

477 Williamstown Road, Port Melbourne, VIC 3207, Australia

314–321, 3rd Floor, Plot 3, Splendor Forum, Jasola District Centre, New Delhi – 110025, India

103 Penang Road, #05–06/07, Visioncrest Commercial, Singapore 238467

Cambridge University Press is part of Cambridge University Press & Assessment, a department of the University of Cambridge.

We share the University's mission to contribute to society through the pursuit of education, learning and research at the highest international levels of excellence.

www.cambridge.org
Information on this title: www.cambridge.org/9781108799386

DOI: 10.1017/9781108863957

First published 2021
First paperback edition 2025

A catalogue record for this publication is available from the British Library

ISBN   978-1-108-83613-5   Hardback
ISBN   978-1-108-79938-6   Paperback

Contents

Figures

Tables

Contributors

ZAYNEB AL-BUNDAWI is a lecturer at the department of Translation, college of Arts, Al-Mustansiriya University in Baghdad, Iraq. She holds her PhD from the School of English, Communication and Philosophy, Cardiff University. She works on the role of sacred texts in the identity construction of Shi'i Muslim women who live in the diaspora.

DAVID CRYSTAL is known chiefly for his research work in English language studies, in such fields as intonation and stylistics, and in the application of linguistics to religious, educational, and clinical contexts, notably in the development of a range of linguistic profiling techniques for diagnostic and therapeutic purposes. He held a chair at the University of Reading for ten years, and is now Honorary Professor of Linguistics at the University of Bangor.

FRANCESCO DE TONI is Honorary Research Fellow at the University of Western Australia. His research interests include the historical evolution of the linguistic expression of emotions in European languages, emotions and letter writing, the role of emotion language in religious contexts, and the history of emotions in zones of cultural and linguistic contact. As part of his research, he employs computational-linguistic methods to investigate large collections of historical texts.

ALETTA G. DORST is Assistant Professor in English Linguistics and Translation at Leiden University. Her research interests include metaphor in fiction, metaphor and translation, and metaphor and health communication.

XIN GAO is Assistant Professor in the School of Education, University of Nottingham. Her research interests are social psychological process of instructed SLA, especially L2 motivation, Chinese women professionals with advanced English and cultural development, students' experience in the international higher education, and creative qualitative and mixed methods research.

WEI-LUN LU is Assistant Professor and Language Program Coordinator in the Language Center and Department of Chinese Studies of Masaryk University. He adopts a linguistic (discourse-analytic) approach to the Chinese culture and thinking. The types of discourse he is interested in working with include translated world masterpieces (contrasting Chinese and English), religious discourse, and leadership discourse.

VALLY LYTRA is Reader in Languages in Education in the Department of Educational Studies at Goldsmiths, University of London. Her research and practice investigates bilingualism and biliteracy in homes, schools, and communities that have experienced diverse migration flows. She is the author of *Play Frames and Social Identities: Contact Encounters in a Greek Primary School* and has edited *Multilingualism and Identities across Contexts: Cross-disciplinary Perspectives on Turkish-speaking Youth in Europe* (with Jens Normann Jørgensen) (2008, University of Copenhagen), *Sites of Multilingualism Complementary Schools in Britain Today* (with Peter Martin) (2010, Trentham), and *When Greeks and Turks Meet: Interdisciplinary Perspectives on the Relationship since 1923* (2014, Routledge). Her most recent book is *Navigating Languages, Literacies and Identities: Religion in Young Lives* (2016, Routledge).

BEAU PIHLAJA is Assistant Professor of Technical Communication and Rhetoric in the Department of English at Texas Tech University. He received his PhD in Rhetoric and Composition from the Department of English, University of Texas at El Paso, investigating cross-cultural, technologically mediated interaction on the US–Mexico border. Additionally, he holds a Masters of Divinity and a Masters in Systematic Theology from Trinity International University, and has experience teaching theology in ecclesial schools in international contexts, most extensively in southeast Asia.

STEPHEN PIHLAJA is Reader in Stylistics at Newman University (Birmingham). He has published broadly in the field of religious discourse including *Antagonism on YouTube* (2013, Bloomsbury), *Religious Talk Online* (2018, Cambridge University Press), and *Talk About Faith* (2021, Cambridge University Press). He is the book reviews editor for *The Journal of Language and Discrimination*.

KATE POWER is a critical discourse analyst whose research focuses on religious discourse, gender/sexuality, and interdisciplinary approaches to contemporary social issues. She has published on using linguistic tools for religious studies inquiries, as well as media representations of powerful religious women, and has collaborated with economists on the analysis of development and austerity discourses. She is currently a Lecturer in Communication at the University of Queensland Business School, Australia, where she uses Systemic Functional Linguistics and genre theory to teach graduate-level academic and professional writing. She was twice elected as Secretary for the International Gender and Language Association (IGALA) and is currently Managing Editor for the online, open-access journal *Secularism and Nonreligion*.

PETER RICHARDSON is a lecturer in English Language in the Research Faculty of Media and Communication at Hokkaido University, Japan. He completed his PhD related to applying cognitive linguistics to the analysis of religious language at the University of Birmingham in the UK in 2013 and has previously taught English in Taiwan, Thailand, and Turkey. His most recent research project, an analysis of the discourse of three conversations between Christian and Muslim believers, culminated in an article in the 2017 issue of *Metaphor and the Social World*.

HELEN RINGROW is Senior Lecturer in Communication Studies and Applied Linguistics at the University of Portsmouth. She holds a PhD from Queen's University Belfast. She is the author of *The Language of Cosmetics Advertising* (2016, Palgrave). She is co-editor of the special issue of *TranscUlturAl* on "Translation and Borders" (2017) and co–book reviews editor for *Critical Approaches to Discourse Analysis Across Disciplines*.

MARIANA ROCCIA is the co-editor of the book series Bloomsbury Advances in Ecolinguistics and co-convenes the International Ecolinguistics Association (IEA). She is a qualified English–Spanish translator and EFL teacher. Though her research interests are varied, she is particularly drawn to the emerging field of the environmental humanities and its articulation to other disciplines, such as literary studies, ecolinguistics, and religious studies. Her work featured in *Discurso & Sociedad* focused on examining commonalities and differences between Pope Francis and Benedict XVI's discourses regarding homosexuality, abortion, and child abuse.

ANDREY ROSOWSKY is Senior Lecturer at the University of Sheffield. His research explores literacy and language practices of faith-based supplementary schools. He has an interest in Qur'anic literacy and its relationship to notions of performance and how poetry and song in both heritage languages and English support devotional religious and linguistic practices. He recently led an AHRC international interdisciplinary research project on performance and religious practice, "Heavenly Acts: Aspects of performance through an interdisciplinary lens." He is the author of (2008) *Heavenly Readings: Liturgical Literacy in a Multilingual Context* and editor of (2017) *Faith and Language Practices in Digital Spaces* (both Multilingual Matters).

SVITLANA SHURMA is Associate Professor at the Faculty of Humanities of Tomas Bata University in Zlín and Associate Professor at Borys Grinchenko Kyiv University. She adopts rhetoric and critical discourse-analytic approaches to Ukrainian, Czech, and Anglophone cultures. The types of discourse she is interested in working with include translated world masterpieces, violence, and propaganda discourses, as well as multimodal discourses.

JULIET THONDHLANA is Associate Professor in Education and Migration, School of Education, University of Nottingham. Her research interests are in the area of higher education, employability and migration; sociolinguistics and intercultural communication; and teamwork and academic literacies.

SARAH TURNER is Lecturer in English (Stylistics) at Coventry University, with a specific interest in figurative language. Her main research interest lies in the analysis of figurative language production to provide insights into physical, psychological and social experiences, with a current focus on the experience of grief and bereavement.

KAROLIEN VERMEULEN is a postdoctoral researcher at the Institute of Jewish Studies, University of Antwerp. Her research interests include wordplay and related textual features, cognitive-stylistic approaches to the Hebrew Bible, the book of Genesis, and ancient conceptions of (urban) space. Recent publications include "The Body of Nineveh: The Conceptual Image of the City in Nahum 2–3," *Journal of Hebrew Scriptures* 17 (2017) and "Home in Biblical and Antwerp City Poems: A Journey," *Arcadia* 52, 1 (2017). She is also the editor of *Doubling and Duplicating in the Book of Genesis: Literary and Stylistic Approaches to the Text* (with Elizabeth Hayes, 2016, Eisenbrauns).

SHAWN WARNER is a sociocultural linguist who specializes in the study of language, sexuality, and religion. Her current research focuses on the discourses of sexual ethics among Baptists in the United States. Her work has appeared in peer-reviewed journals such as *Pragmatics*, *Gender and Language*, and *Language Policy*, and has been covered by media outlets such as Baptist News Global. In addition to her academic work, she directs a collaborative outreach project that promotes conversations around sexuality and sexual ethics in Baptist communities by providing free online, research-based educational materials related to the intersections of faith and sexuality.

PHILIP WILSON is Lecturer in Philosophy at the University of East Anglia, Norfolk, UK, where he teaches literature and philosophy after teaching at İnönü University, Turkey. Publications include *The Luther Breviary* (translated with John Gledhill, 2007, Wartburg); *Literary Translation: Redrawing the Boundaries* (edited with Jean Boase-Beier and Antoinette Fawcett, 2014, Palgrave Macmillan); *The Bright Rose: German Verse 800–1280* (translated and edited, 2015, Arc); *Translation after Wittgenstein* (2015, Routledge). He has edited *The Routledge Handbook of Translation and Philosophy* (with Piers Rawling, 2019).

ALAIN WOLF is a Lecturer in translation studies and intercultural communication at the University of East Anglia, Norfolk, UK. He has written on interreligious dialogue, the translation of literary and sacred texts and queer intercultural identity. His period of training for the priesthood in the Church of England has also led him to explore the place of a religious ethics in all forms of translated discourse. He is the author of *A Religious Ethics of Translation: The Love Command*: *Queer Intercultural Relationships: Translating the Polyphonic Self*; the co-author of *Researching across Languages and Cultures: A Guide to Doing Research Interculturally*; and the translator of other essays and academic articles.

1 Analysing Religious Discourse: Introduction

Stephen Pihlaja

1.1 Background, History, and Key Terms

When you think about *religious discourse*, you probably think of some kind of institutional text or talk – sermons and catechisms, sacred books, prayers, and hymns. Institutions dominate what we think religions are, how we think about them, and how religious belief is established and develops. The people writing religious texts are often revered and seen to be holding special knowledge – prophets and theologians and the enlightened. They might wear clothes to set them apart. They might write or stand and speak to religious believers from a physical distance. Their words can be seen as inspired or infallible, or even the very words of the divine.

The texts themselves also have power. They can invoke a reality beyond what we can see and they connect the hearer to something beyond themselves, to something ineffable. The words of these texts have power even when they are referred to in passing. The very mention of them has meaning, like a sport fan holding a sign that simply says 'John 3:16'. They have power to make believers act, like when the call to prayer draws people to the neighbourhood mosque. The language of religion, when it is used, changes things.

Sacred texts, sermons, hadiths, and catechisms are, indeed, important for how individuals and communities come to understand and follow religions. They lay the foundation for religious belief and practice and can be the definitive authorities. However, they are only part of the story of religious discourse. Official documents and sacred books are read and used by real people in real, dynamic contexts. Believers listen to the words of theologians and teachers and then go on to live their own lives, talking about and interpreting these texts in their own communities. Everyday interaction, where institutional discourse is worked out and used in real life, is harder to track and trace, but its position within religious belief is essential for understanding how religions emerge, develop, and change over time.

Even though we use the world *religion* in day-to-day life, thinking about what should or should not count as a religion can be quite difficult. Durkheim's (2008 [1915]) classic conception of religion is a 'unified system of beliefs and practices' (p. 47), which is a helpful starting point to think about what we mean: religion has something to do with what we believe and what we do in response to that belief. Hjarvard (2008) describes religion as 'human actions, beliefs and symbols related to supernatural agencies' (quoted in English by Lövheim, 2011, p. 154). The beliefs in religion often include something about the 'supernatural', while others refer to the 'ineffable' qualities of religion and religious experience (McNamara and Giordano, 2018). Religious belief often includes not only the belief in the supernatural but beliefs about how that supernatural being or beings interacts with the world around us.

Belief, however, is also a problematic thing to define. What a person believes, or says they believe, is simpler to define in some confessional faiths, like Judaism and Islam, where there is an explicit statement that believers say with intention to affirm their faith. However, as Harrison (2006) shows in a useful review of the topic, religion is never 'one thing' and essentialist approaches to the category are unlikely to capture the diversity of the ways people believe and act within religions, or create useful boundaries between what should or shouldn't be included. Instead, Harrison (2006) categorises three approaches to religion: intellectual, focusing on belief; affective, focusing on emotions; and functional, focusing on practice.

Each of these approaches foregrounds particular religions over others and have implicit strengths and weaknesses. Analysis of Christianity and Islam in terms of beliefs and practices might be useful, but Jainism, Hinduism, Buddhism, and Shintoism treat belief in a vastly different way. Certain religions might not necessarily foreground belief in the supernatural. In many situations, focusing on practice could be much more useful in explaining how religion functions in social contexts.

Named religions are also not the only places where people hold beliefs about the supernatural or divine. People may claim to be, for example, 'spiritual, not religious' and explicitly reject elements of a structured sense of spirituality in day-to-day life. The spiritual is internal and focused on one's own experiences of the world, while the religious is focused on organised practice. That isn't to say that one excludes the other: in Ammerman's (2013) study, the 'spiritual, but not religious' were not necessarily unaffiliated – they often still attended religious services and could describe themselves with categorical religious labels. The rejection of being 'religious' may be less about the beliefs that an individual holds and more about the perception of their beliefs by others and their own felt experience of their belief.

Like religion, *discourse* can be understood in many ways. The Foucauldian understanding of *discourse* as describing larger social systems of ordering knowledge and power (Foucault, 1971) has had an important influence on how the word is conceived in the contemporary academic world. For Foucault, discourse is more than just the language or interaction in a particular context, but everything that comes to bear on the production of language at a particular point in time – the ideology of the speaker, the social history, the culture, the power structures. However, Foucault didn't look closely at specifics of interaction the way that a linguist might. For researchers who want to do empirical research on religious language as it occurs in the real world, understanding language as it is being used in a real situation by people practising religion, is fundamental to understanding how that religion works.

If we would like to take a more language-focused approach, *discourse* could be simply a way of describing 'language used to do something and mean something, language produced and interpreted in a real-world context' (Cameron, 2001, p. 13). Discourse is more than language as an abstract system of signs captures – it captures how language is used at specific times in specific spaces and encompasses interaction. This is not a new idea, of course: Saussure's (1916) distinction between *langue* and *parole* – language as a system vs language in use – shows that scholars have long realised the difference between thinking about language as an abstract collection of signs and language as it is used in day-to-day interaction. Of course, grammar structures and individual words are important for the meaning of any individual utterance, but how that meaning emerges in an utterance requires looking beyond just the words and the order in which they are said.

Once we start to look at language in context and consider the different components of a specific interaction, things can become quite complicated. The elements that make up any individual interaction are numerous, and many different elements might have some impact on why any given interaction develops in the way it does. Larsen-Freeman and Cameron (2008) use complex systems theory to help describe and map the development of language in use, drawing on the physical principles of the biological systems in which human animals interact. In Complex Systems Theory, a key concept is *emergence*; that is, patterns and order come naturally into existence from the repeated interaction of individuals over time.

Discourse is then not the result of central planning but rather, it comes about when all the components of the system interact with one another, along with the time and space in which they occur. These components might include important figures like imams or priests or gurus, or important sacred texts or unwritten doctrines, but these components are not necessarily determinative. The patterns that emerge in the ways that people interact with one another around religious issues are also scalable. Phenomena that emerge in individual interactions, can also emerge as consistent discourse practices on larger scales, the way that certain ways of praying or metaphors for religious experience become common among many believers in a particular religious tradition.

Discourse from this perspective can then be treated in a variety of different ways. We could think about how religious discourse is embedded or 'nested' in larger systems. One could also think about how discourse exists in time. What occurs before and after any individual interaction can be incredibly important, with things said or written thousands of years ago being repeated in the contemporary discourse and, in turn, the things religious believers say and write now, affecting how religious belief will develop going forward. Timescales can be considered on many different levels, from the moment-by-moment interaction of people to the discourse event as one in a series of discourse events, and over years.

Discourse, particularly in religious contexts like rituals, can be quite stable over time, with the same words being uttered again and again. Those same rituals can also change, depending on the context and who is speaking. Throughout this book are examples of rituals being played out in different context, both establishing a relationship with the past and creating new contexts for faith. These relationships between past utterances and new contexts, with new conditions for production are ultimately the focus of much religious discourse analysis, with rich histories and complex contexts for interaction resulting in interaction that can reveal the relationships between language and religious belief and practice.

Conversation analysts like Sacks, Jefferson, and Schegloff (Sacks, 1992; Sacks, Schegloff, and Jefferson, 1974; Schegloff, 1972) show that the patterns which occur in discourse often operate without the speakers themselves being explicitly aware of them. Instead, they are accepted as common sense, just the things that humans naturally do. Language use and interaction are also important sites of meaning making and identity construction, as work by Labov (1972; Labov and Waletzky, 1967) established early in the history of conversation analysis. Patterns, beliefs, or regularities in social interaction have a recursive relationship with the social world. Individual utterances reflect what has been said in the past and affect what will be said in the future.

Discourse analysts can also focus on patterns in interaction like conversation analysts might, revealing how everyday life creates and maintains norms. Linguistic ethnographers, on the other hand, may place more focus on the context of interaction and use longitudinal observation and ask people about their experience to help make explicit insider and outsider perspectives on religious discourse. These methods make clear the different findings and insights can be gained from approaching different data sources from different perspectives.

Analysing Religious Discourse showcases a range of tools different analysts might employ in looking at language and religion, from a focus on the processes of cognition to the study of the translation of sacred texts, to the emergence of metaphor in talk about religious experiences and the ineffable. These methods are diverse, but they all are built on valid, reliable frameworks for thinking about language in use, grounded in theories and methods that have been applied to ranges of different texts. The way any single utterance, or interaction, or text should be analysed is up to you, the analyst, and this book intends to help you think through the range of different possibilities that are out there for you to find the answers to the questions you might ask about religious discourse.

1.2   Key Topics, Questions, and Debates

Along with the difficulty of describing religion comes the question of whether *religious language* is a category of discourse that should be treated in a different way than other forms of discourse (see Hobbs, 2021 for a full discussion). Of course, most language analysts would be happy to differentiate kinds of institutional discourse, and language that occurs in sermons could be treated as distinct from other kinds of informal interaction without much disagreement. There's no question that prayer, particularly across different traditions, represents particular ways of communicating. The trouble, however, comes with how researchers and analysts should treat the belief that prayers are, indeed, interaction with something or someone that exists beyond the natural, empirical language that is observable. Religious discourse forces several uncomfortable decisions on the researcher, both in deciding from an etic perspective what religious is, exactly, and what people are doing when they talk about their faith.

In considering the boundaries of religious discourse, different approaches can be seen both in work looking at language around experiences of the so-called 'ineffable' (Chilton and Kopytowska, 2018) or in work that looks more at the sociolinguistic elements of religious language (Omoniyi and Fishman, 2006) or practices around texts (Rosowsky, 2008, 2017). All these works have key differences, of course, in the kinds of discourse that they consider, but the research they include does not always occur in religious contexts even if it is explicitly religious in some way. What is religious for one person might not be religious for another.

Along with the problem of deciding where the boundaries of religious discourse are, there is the problem of deciding that the religious aspect of the interaction is the most important element to focus on. Religious belief or practice is not explicitly the topic of discussion in some discourse where religion plays an important role, as in, for example, a discussion of the US President George W Bush's speeches about the invasion of Iraq in 2003. Researchers might foreground religion in relation to Bush's statements, as van Noppen (2012) does in his work, but this decision is not necessarily straightforward. To foreground an individual's religious identity, particularly when they themselves might not explicitly be doing so, is an important ethical decision that discourse analysts must consider.

Conversely, in analysis of explicitly religious discourse, where the speakers are focused on issues of religious belief and practice, doing analysis of the talk with a focus on religion might be misleading. For example, in analysis in conversations about institutional religion and shifts in belief in a Christian podcast, my own research (Pihlaja, 2021) has shown that issues like gender and race may be more salient than religious belief and practice, even when the focus is about religious belief. Other cultural, sociopolitical issues may be more salient even when a religious person is claiming to be speaking primarily about a religious topic.

Another key issue for researchers working in religious discourse is how to treat truth claims with religion and respect the beliefs and practices of religious adherents while describing their interaction in an empirical way. These issues can be particularly problematic when analysing the truth claims speakers make that might be viewed from a variety of different perspectives. In a charismatic prayer service, a Christian might describe themselves as having the Spirit of God 'in' their body, a description that an analyst might describe as being metaphorical. The believer themselves, however, may claim that the phrase is not metaphorical, that the Spirit of God is actually inhabiting the body in a way that should not be understood metaphorically.

And although Complex Systems Theory describes the emergence of particular patterns of speaking and belief, for those who believe in the a higher power or God or gods actively engaging with the physical world, the analysis of interaction without taking into account the will or plan of supernatural powers will be necessarily limited and not provide an accurate description of why things are the way they are. A linguistic analysis of the Qur'an, for example, might be understood to be challenging the assertion that it was dictated to the Prophet Mohammed word-for-word, and could be seen by some Muslims as offensive.

The examples are problematic because they show a difference in beliefs about causation. For the analyst, the explanation for the patterns in speech and writing can be traced using empirical linguistic analysis that takes into account a range of elements and agents that can be observed or whose presence can be extrapolated from the evidence. With a range of different truth claims about supernatural realities and the ways that the divine interacts with reality taking care to both recognise and respect those beliefs, while at the same time avoid making claims that can't be supported by empirical evidence, is a key ethical obligation. Discourse analysis is not theology and its usefulness and limitations should be acknowledged, while taking care to show respect for the beliefs of the religious believers who are often the focus of analysis, whether the analyst shares their beliefs or not.

The researchers in this book have their own religious beliefs and practices and represent a variety of different cultural and religious backgrounds, including researchers of no religious faith. However, the analysis in this book is presented from an agnostic position. This does limit the possible outcomes of the analysis – for example, no one will claim that their research is evidence of the reality of the divine or supernatural. This approach does also not exclude the possibility that some religious believers may find discourse analysis to be useful in understanding their own faith and faith communities. Religious believers may, for example, benefit from analysing the use of metaphor in their own religious texts to better understand and deepen their own faith.

Rather than attempt to resolve the key questions and debates that emerge in the discussion of religious discourse, the chapters in this book offer different perspectives for readers to consider for themselves, to use or disregard as is appropriate in each project. Ultimately, given the range of perspectives on language and religion, generosity towards others and a recognition that different perspectives will lead to different approaches is the goal of this book.

1.3   Book Contents

This book is meant to be read however you want to read it. You can, of course, read it cover to cover, but more likely you will find yourself dipping in and out of chapters that you find interesting. Each chapter follows the same structure to make it easier to find key information about different chapter themes and compare chapters quickly and easily. The chapters all begin with a presentation of *background, history, and key terms*. This section gives a basic sense of the context of the theme, with the necessary vocabulary used by scholars working on the theme. Next, the *key topics, questions, and debates* section describes the current state of the field, with a sense for how scholars are doing research, what questions they are pursuing, the conflicts that might be arising, and the debates that conflicts might expose. Each chapter then includes a *case study*, providing an example of the how the author's own research is addressing the questions that have been brought up in the previous sections, and showing how they investigate the theme. The chapters include some of the most recent discourse analysis of religious discourse as well, with the researchers presenting innovative and creative analyses. Finally, the *future directions* sections discuss how the field is likely to look like going forward, providing researchers the chance to think about how their own work might benefit from issues discussed in each chapter.

The book begins with a chapter by Shawn Warner on *Interaction*, focused on highlighting the tools of conversation analysis, a long-standing staple in discourse analysis, to understand how religious doctrine is worked out in interaction.

Vally Lytra examines *Ethnography* as an approach to understanding language and literacy practices of particular religious communities, with researchers living and working among religious believers to gain important insider insights about how religious practice and belief is enacted in believers' lives.

Zayneb Al-Bundawi shows how *Narrative* approaches and storytelling within communities can be an important way of tracing how community and individual identity are tied to interaction around sacred texts and rituals, even in informal settings.

Sarah Turner's chapter on *Multimodality* looks beyond spoken and written language to how people communicate about their religious experiences using other resources, like gesture, showing how insights can be gleaned about how people think and talk about their experiences by specifically looking at how they gesture.

Beau Pihlaja introduces *Rhetoric*, discussing how the long history of the study of rhetoric from Plato to the present day has developed tools that can be used to understand contemporary readings and uses of sacred texts, specifically as a part of political speech.

Philip Wilson describes the key issue of *Translation* in religious discourse, including not only the translation of religious texts, but other important documents for the development of doctrine, touching on issues of grammar, lexis, and sociohistorical context.

Kate Power discusses the role of *Institutions* in the development of religious belief and practice, discussing how power operates in different ways, and how models of governance, like elections, mix both secular and religious politics, with broader social contexts influencing who comes to power within an individual institution.

Stephen Pihlaja looks at *Media*, and the ways that technology in the recent past has changed how people talk about religious belief and practice, and the consequences of those changes on how people think, believe, and act.

Andrey Rosowsky introduces the concept of *Community* and the role of ritual language and interpersonal interaction in creating and maintaining religious communities, in terms of passing on rituals and practices using sacred, liturgical language.

Xin Gao and Juliet Thondhlana discuss *Education*, looking specifically at how religious language interacts with educational settings where a teacher's religious identity is a key part of their motivation for their work: Christians teaching English as a second or additional language in contexts where teachers are explicitly motivated by their religious beliefs.

Alain Wolf describes *Inter-religious Dialogue*, focusing on the issue of speaking across religious traditions as a kind of translation and looking specifically at how institutional religious documents deal with the issue of other religious traditions and what this shows about the nature of religious belief.

Wei-lun Lu and Svitlana Shurma then discuss *Ritual*, using the concept of pragamemes to discuss idiomatic eulogies in Taiwanese funerals. The analysis looks specifically at how religious beliefs influence the construction of Buddhist and Christian phrases, with important difference in the conceptual metaphors the idioms employ.

Aletta Dorst expands on *Metaphor*, which has long been a key issue for scholars of religious language and discourse, given its prevalence across traditions and religions in religious text and talk relating to the ineffable. The chapter unpacks theories of metaphor that understand it both as a cognitive function and as emerging in the dynamic interaction of individuals.

Francesco de Toni then discusses *Emotion,* introducing appraisal theory to show how emotions and emotional language can be analysed, with a case study looking at multilingual correspondence within a community of European Catholic missionaries in nineteenth-century Australia.

Helen Ringrow discusses *Identity*, focusing specifically on issues around individual and social identity in the presentation of self, and how religious believers use language to present themselves as members of communities and holding specific beliefs, often implicitly, with particular language.

Peter Richardson then outlines the broad topic of *Cognition*, focusing on several key concepts driving research in the study of language in the mind: conceptual metaphor, metonymy, blending, and force-dynamics.

Karolien Vermeulen introduces the key concept of *Sacred Texts* and their role in religious belief and practice, focusing specifically on how the reading of sacred texts can create a spatial and temporal experience of the divine for readers.

Mariana Roccia discusses *Ecology* and the role of natural environments in religious discourse, looking specifically at how religious institutions talked about the environment and conceive of it in relation to religious doctrine and belief and practice.

Finally, David Crystal draws the book to its conclusion, considering the main themes in light of the history of research into language and religion, and offering suggestions for several main streams of research going forward.

Among these different chapters, you will undoubtedly see useful connections. For example, the cognition, metaphor, and multimodality chapters all relate to similar issues; the ethnography, community, and identity chapters highlight some of the concerns at different scales. You'll see connections between the interreligious dialogue chapter and the translation one, as well as between the discussion of narrative and interaction. Discussions about the importance of metaphor are included in many different chapters.

Religious discourse – its role in social and cultural futures, its presence in day-to-day life, its emergent behaviours and structures – has always been and will continue to be a fundamental part of how humans understand their own lived experiences. How you choose to look at those experiences and how people think and talk about them will depend on your own questions, the data that you have and that you can collect, and what the ultimate goal of your work is. *Analysing Religious Discourse* is meant to introduce you to new ideas about discourse or old ideas that you might think about in a new way. Whether you decide to follow one approach over another, there is something to be learned from every one.

1.4   References

Ammerman, N. T. (2013). Spiritual but not religious? Beyond binary choices in the study of religion. *Journal for the Scientific Study of Religion*, *52*(2), 258–78.

Cameron, D. (2001). *Working with Spoken Discourse*. London: SAGE.

Chilton, P., and Kopytowska, M. (2018). *Religion, Language, and the Human Mind*. Oxford: Oxford University Press.

Durkheim, E. (2008 [1915]). *The Elementary Forms of the Religious Life*. Oxford: Oxford University Press.

Foucault, M. (1971). The orders of discourse. *Social Science Information*, *10*(2), 7–30.

Harrison, V. S. (2006). The pragmatics of defining religion in a multi-cultural world. *International Journal for Philosophy of Religion*, *59*(3), 133–152.

Hjarvard, S. (2008). The mediatization of religion: A theory of the media as agents of religious change. *Northern Lights: Film and Media Studies Yearbook*, *6*(1), 9–26.

Hobbs, V. (2021). *An Introduction to Religious Language: Exploring Theolinguistics in Contemporary Contexts*. London: Bloomsbury.

Labov, W. (1972). *Sociolinguistic Patterns*. Philadelphia: University of Pennsylvania Press.

Labov, W., and Waletzky, J. (1967). Narrative analysis: Oral versions of personal experience. In J. Helm (ed.), *Essays on the Verbal and Visual Arts*. Seattle and Washington, DC: University of Washington Press.

Larsen-Freeman, D., and Cameron, L. (2008). *Complex Systems and Applied Linguistics*. Oxford: Oxford University Press.

Lövheim, M. (2011). Mediatisation of religion: A critical appraisal. *Culture and Religion*, *12*(2), 153–166.

McNamara, P., and Giordano, M. (2018). Cognitive neuroscience and religious language: A working hypothesis. In P. Chilton and M. Kopytowska (eds.), *Religion, Language, and the Human Mind*. Oxford: Oxford University Press.

Omoniyi, T., and Fishman, J. A. (2006). *Explorations in the Sociology of Language and Religion*. Amsterdam: John Benjamins.

Pihlaja, S. (2021). *Talk about Faith: How Conversation Shapes Belief*. Cambridge: Cambridge University Press.

Rosowsky, A. (2008). *Heavenly Readings: Liturgical Literacy in a Multilingual Context*, Vol. 9. Bristol: Multilingual Matters.

Rosowsky, A. (ed.). (2017). *Faith and Language Practices in Digital Spaces*. Bristol: Multilingual Matters.

Sacks, H. (1992). *Lectures on Conversation*. London: Blackwell.

Sacks, H., Schegloff, E. A., and Jefferson, G. (1974). A simplest systematics for the organization of turn-taking for conversation. *Language*, *50*(4), 696–735.

Saussure, F. D. (2011 [1916]). *Course in General Linguistics*. New York: Columbia University Press.

Schegloff, E. A. (1972). Notes on a conversational practice: Formulating place. In D. N. Sudnow (ed.), *Studies in Social Interaction* (pp. 75–119). Cambridge: The Free Press.

van Noppen, J. P. (2012). *God in George W. Bush's Rhetoric*. www.o-re-la.org/index .php/analyses/item/175-god-in-george-w-bush%E2%80%99s-rhetoric.

2   Interaction

Shawn Warner

2.1   Background, History, and Key Terms

When thinking about the intersections of language and religion, the enshrined structures that create the history and ritual of religious practice are likely the first that come to mind. However, religion is very much a dynamic entity, and it is always changing through the ways that people experience it. It exists in the bedroom as much as on bookshelves. It is discussed as much at supper as in the sanctuary. It is crystallized over coffee as much as in catacombs.

Communication scholars have long studied the patterns of *social interaction* among humans, especially as it relates to how we organize our communication in different contexts. While some have focused on the observable language practices of people engaging with one another, others have focused on the underlying psychology or the symbolism of interaction. The ways we study interaction often have much to do with the contexts we want to know more about. Social interaction has been investigated in family systems, healthcare settings, small groups, large groups, corporations, intimate relationships, human–computer interactions, and the global tourism industry, to name a few. In addition to where we find social interaction, we have also studied what we find when we look there: communication without words (nonverbal), communication about conflict, communication across cultures.

Not surprisingly, scholars have studied social interaction in many ways, not least because social interaction – like many of the things that humans do – is quite complex. Some researchers ask people to describe what they do in social inter-action in a process known as self-reporting, while others directly observe and sometimes record it with methodologies like conversation analysis. Still others embed themselves in the interactional context itself using methodologies such as ethnography and participant observation (e.g. Atkinson et al., 2001). Sometimes, researchers even set up experimental situations to see whether people will react in certain ways to particular types of interactions (e.g. Drager, 2013). A handful of approaches also emphasize that the researcher is not simply an outside observer to social interaction but an active participant in it – whether directly by engaging with participants or indirectly by setting up a situation where interaction can be studied in the first place (e.g. Cukor-Avila, 2000). And, like many phenomena, social interaction can be studied from a quantitative perspective (by counting things) or a qualitative perspective (by describing things) or sometimes a mix of both. All these approaches help us understand what social interaction looks like and why certain patterns emerge.

Another aspect that scholars are interested in is what social interaction means to the people engaged in it. One useful way of looking at this has been through the concept of *social construction*, which has widespread usage among scholars in the social sciences. Social construction is the idea that people create their own understanding of the world and the meanings assigned to particular things, experiences, and people. Crucially, they do this with other people and always as part of some larger social context. There are several ways that people do social construction, such as through language and interaction, and there are lots of things that they create in the process – everything from identities and relationships to memories and institutions.

Functional approaches to studying language often include some assumptions or discussions of social construction, starting from the premise that language is used by people to create their world. Indeed, many scholars take language to be the most central and significant tool in social construction since words define and are defined by our social reality. Hall and Bucholtz (1995) present research that examines how language can be used not only to create but also to control, appropriate, and remix the ways in which people move through and experience the world, particularly as it relates to gender. Crucially, this work debunks the idea that social identities are inherent or static, and they demonstrate the pivotal role that interaction plays in the construction and negotiation of identity. This element of creating social worlds together is also highlighted in Jacoby and Ochs (1995), who argue that even though language is the primary way we construct our world, the context in which it occurs is often what brings things into focus. That is, we are always doing social construction with others; it never occurs in a vacuum.

Another vein of scholarly inquiry that has focused a great deal on the contexts – both past and present – in which co-construction occurs is called *interdiscursivity* (or sometimes, intertextuality). This is the idea that words and texts are always grounded in and inextricably linked to other words and texts. The concept of interdiscursivity is especially useful for understanding the social construction of religion in interaction because religions have rich histories of words and texts that most adherents are intimately familiar with. The integration of these words and texts into everyday religious practice – through hymns and devotions and sermons – brings to the fore questions about who is speaking, where particular beliefs come from, and what authority is being invoked. An area where the process of interdiscursivity can be seen fairly clearly is in the translation or interpretation of sacred texts. Linguistic anthropologist Handman (2010) provides an illustrative exploration of biblical translations among Christians in Papua New Guinea showing that when religious practitioners interact with words and texts such as scripture, it is not just about finding the best or the most correct understanding of something in the past; rather, it is about how people use these words and texts to understand their current experiences.

Two additional approaches to studying interaction that also draw our attention to elements beyond what is simply said are *conversation analysis* (Schegloff, 2007) and *multimodal discourse analysis* (O'Halloran, 2004). Conversation analysis is primarily focused on studying the sequential arrangement of interaction, and it takes the interactional turn as the basic unit of analysis. This methodology offers a way to study how the unfolding of interaction through time gives rise to particular types of meaning. Multimodal discourse analysis is a term that covers a multitude of different approaches, but the primary focus is on contextualizing language as occurring in the midst of other modes of communicating. This can include observable concrete elements like gesture, gaze, and physical space, but also more abstract concepts like historical timescales and virtual discourse spaces. Both of these approaches to studying interaction demonstrate the importance of recognizing that talk does not exist in a vacuum – it is situated in time and space, and all of these elements work together to create meaning in interaction.

Given that language is central to the study of interaction, and that people are central to the production of language, it is no wonder that a broad analytical approach becomes necessary to adequately study all these elements. The field of *linguistic anthropology* offers one such holistic and interdisciplinary framework, providing a high-level focus on cultures and systems and an in-depth focus on linguistic form and participant identity. In particular, linguistic anthropologists home in on the importance of discourse for understanding what is meaningful for participants.

As a large focus of this book, discourse provides a useful starting point in how we approach the study of religion in interactional settings. Discourse can be understood as the construction of meaning by social actors using communicative systems that are embedded in sociocultural contexts. This definition addresses the "what," "how," and "where" of interaction between people.

The first element is related to the "what" of discourse and draws on interdiscursivity; that is, the construction of meaning does not happen in isolation but in relation to prior texts and the ever-evolving social influences of culture and ideology. Although some scholars might consider a speech utterance or a bounded event as the primary unit of analysis, focusing on discourse prompts us to think about and account for the ways in which interaction is situated within larger systems, histories, and contexts.

The second element relates to the "how" of discourse and involves two parts: social actors and communicative systems. The constructed meaning of discourse does not exist apart from the entities that create it. Most of the time, we assume these entities are human beings, though sometimes even dogs and deities can be deputized as social actors (see Tannen 2004; Titon 1988), and this blurs the lines on who or what is understood to participate in meaning-making processes. What counts as a communicative system is not always a straightforward matter either. The resources of embodiment, multimodality, and technology may also be employed in the construction of meaning in addition to linguistic systems.

The third element of the definition focuses on the "where" of discourse as being situated in a particular time and place. Looking at the contexts in which discourse occurs provides a way to analyze phenomena that may be felt by participants to be singular or constant and yet are contextualized by complex histories and activated in dynamic ways.

2.2   Key Topics, Questions, and Debates

A lot of scholarly attention has been paid to how religion is constituted through ritual language, sacred texts, and esoteric practices (see Chilton and Kopytowska, 2018). These studies have noted that language often holds a unique status in religious contexts. For example, it can be constructed as a holy artifact such as a sacred text. It can be enshrined as a means to salvation such as a prayer of repentance. It can be used to create and disseminate religious tradition and doctrine through the production of instructive texts such as a catechism. While these studies show the critical role that language plays in the social construction of religion, they often neglect to show how religion is a lived entity built through everyday interaction by religious practitioners.

In fact, interaction is fundamental to religion. Many sacred texts are filled with accounts of pivotal interactions between humans and deities, or humans with each other, and these stories form the backbone of many belief systems. Moreover, religious doctrine does not simply come to be out of thin air but is often worked out through interaction in religious communities.

Sociolinguists have long shown that the stories we tell create our identities and our world (Labov, 1972; Schiffrin, 1996). It is in interactions with each other that we shape who we are, what we value, and – of course – what we believe. These beliefs are indeed codified and enshrined and passed down, but we cannot overlook the interactional spaces in which they come to be and are continually transformed. Take, for example, a Bible study class in a Christian church. Here, practitioners engage in depth with a sacred text (the Bible) that has been studied for millennia. The leader of the group may or may not have any formal theological training. Some of the attendees may have been active in the church for decades, while others may have shown up on the church's doorstep for the first time. In all likelihood, no doctrinal documents will come out of this Bible study gathering, but belief systems will be molded, stories will gain new meaning, and the iteration of a religious system will continue. These liminal settings that uniquely blend the formal characteristics of codified religion with the informal aspects of people's day-to-day lives reveal to us the dynamic and ever-changing nature of religion that would be missed if we only ever look at rituals and sacred texts.

Interaction is also a place where we can see not only how religious systems internally shift over time but also how people engage with them from the edges. Proselytism in various religions, from Christian street evangelism to Islamic da'wah, demonstrates how interactional contexts expand the boundaries of religious participation. Distinct from traditional missionization efforts that are largely steeped in colonialism, these interactional sites show how education and apologetics can exist alongside spirited debate and even religious transformation.

Although interaction provides the potential for rich analysis in the study of religion, it can also present unique challenges as well. Two seminal works on religious language, Keane (1997 and 2004) remind us that many of the basic assumptions we have about language and interaction – including identity, agency, authorship, genre, and register – are often called into question in religious contexts. For example, consider the setting of a ritual prayer led by a priest in the presence of other religious practitioners. The priest may speak words and perform actions that have been prescribed by tradition or sacred texts, so where do we locate agency and authority in those words and actions? How do we determine the participant roles of others who are physically present? What kinds of social actors are the invisible or unobservable beings such as deities and ancestors? Moreover, Keane points out, while some might equate religion with holding beliefs, in actuality, it is because these beliefs are mediated through linguistic practices that we can ascribe meaning and validity to them in the first place. Therefore, to understand religion, we must investigate the observable social practices that constitute it.

These interactions can take a variety of forms as well. To study language and religion, we have to look beyond just situations where primarily religious folks are talking exclusively about religious things and only in religious spaces. There is a lot of fluidity in the topics, participants, and settings that constitute the practice of religion. In fact, it is often in these informal and "unofficial" contexts where we see the crux of how religious beliefs are forged. In understanding these contexts, we are better able to understand how religious systems are made and remade.

2.3   Case Study

To see how religion is negotiated in the everyday lives of practitioners, we have to go to the places where their everyday lives happen. In this case study, that happens to be the dining room of a woman who has been deeply embedded in the life of her Christian community for many years. The others people that she invites into this space are fellow members of her church but also friends and confidants. The space is warm and inviting, with children's religious-themed artwork hanging on the walls. The topics they address in their conversation are sprawling yet intimate – from the challenges of parenting, to the evolution of their personal faith stories, to the possibilities and pitfalls of pornography. The auspices under which they are gathered are likely familiar to many: a book club meeting to discuss an emergent pop culture zeitgeist.

The four women in the data presented here are connected by their involvement in the same Baptist church located in southern California. They are between the ages of twenty-eight and forty and are middle to upper-middle class. Kasey is hosting the gathering in her home, is married with three children, is a stay-at-home mom, and is active as a laymember in the church. Beth is married with no children, is training to be a counselor, and is an active attendant at the church. Donna is married with two children and is on staff at the church as their children's minister. Autumn is married with three children and is also on staff at the church as their associate pastor. Three of the four women (Kasey, Donna, and Beth) identify as white and one woman (Autumn) identifies as Hispanic. Figure 2.1 shows the arrangement for the book club meeting and I will be referring back to the material realities it captures throughout the analysis.

The books they are discussing – the *50 Shades of Grey* trilogy by E. L. James – are also notable for a number of reasons. In 2012, when this data was collected, the book series had taken the literary world – as well as the bookshelves and bedrooms of many middle-class women – by storm. Dubbed "mommy porn," the trilogy follows a young woman's initiation into the world of BDSM (bondage, discipline, sadism, and masochism) and became a worldwide bestseller as well as a series of feature-length films within the span of a few years. The provocative material in the series caused many communities – scholarly, secular, and religious among them – to debate the merits and missteps of the books' representations of sexual desire, erotic expression, and consent. Many American Christian communities at the time debated whether the books should be viewed as cautionary tales or prompts for discussion. Nonetheless, the staggering popularity of the *50 Shades* books has prompted many Christians, and especially Christian women, to examine the role of erotica and sexuality in their lives more broadly.

Figure 2.1 Anonymized drawing of the book club gathering, illustration by Rosemary Jones

The book series has inspired a number of productive veins of scholarly inquiry, including psychological analysis of safewording and kinkphobia, communication studies on the discourses of female submission as seen in the books, and public health examinations on the impact of intimate-partner violence. In discourse-analysis circles, several scholars have focused on not necessarily the content of the books but rather the conversations that happen around the books themselves. Many of these analyses home in on the concept of *agency* – which is defined by Ahearn (2001) as the socioculturally mediated capacity to act – and explore the ways that people both exert and constrain their sexual agency in response to the books (e.g. Mills and Jones, 2014). Crucially, these negotiations of agency happen in the context of interaction. In the analysis here, I focus on the topic of agency as it provides a multitude of opportunities for exploring the negotiation of identity through discourse.

The data presented in this section are drawn from a 1.5-hour video recording collected in 2012. Throughout the duration of the recording, the four women participants are gathered in Kasey's home and discuss a wide range of topics including the *50 Shades* books but also other broader issues such as sexual ethics, religious identity, media consumption, and family dynamics. Due to the nature of their occupations, as well as the nature of their conversations, the participants requested I use pseudonyms instead of their real names and that I obscure their likenesses to remove the element of identifiability. As an ethnographer, one of the important parts of my methodology is to talk explicitly about my access to and involvement in the communities with whom I work. In

2012, when this data was collected, I was somewhat tangentially involved in the Baptist community in question, primarily through family ties. I had attended services on occasion, was familiar with all the women who participated in the data, and was even related to one (Autumn) as an in-law through marriage at the time. Though Kasey was the host of the gathering, Autumn was the convener and had arranged for me to capture the interaction on video. I was only present at the beginning and the end of the recording to set up and take down equipment. These details of my involvement, as well as the details of these women's lives and identities, are not simply a supplement to the analysis of interaction but rather an integral part to understanding how it unfolds.

All four women were actively involved in their church community in various capacities. In fact, Donna and Autumn were both in leadership positions where they regularly served as disseminators for the official religious discourses of their institution. However, their gathering for breakfast book club represented a markedly different context than that in which they typically found themselves, and this context allowed for different kinds of discussions to take place. The participants themselves note this in their interaction. In Example 1, Donna has been talking about how different people in her life have reacted to talking about the *50 Shades* series with her. She launches into a story about running into a pastor's wife at the store where the two of them began whispering about the books, presumably because they are both in church leadership positions and their discussion of the books might be frowned upon if observed by others. (NB: see the end of this chapter for a summary of transcription notation conventions.)

Example 1   "I appreciate opportunities to talk about sexuality"

1	Donna:	So I was,	
2		talking to a pastor's wife in Target yesterday.	
3		(1.2)	
4		A:nd she mentioned,	
5		(2.2)	
6		that she had heard somebody talking about Fifty Shades of Gray and,	*Donna cocks head to the side*
7		(0.7)	
8		I said <VOX> yeah I'm,	*Donna raises right hand in front of her*
9		(0.2)	
10		I'm actually going to a thing I'm going to talk about it tomorrow morning </VOX> and,	*Donna adjusts drinking glass in front of her*
11		(0.4)	
12		I,	
13		(1.9)	
14		not <u>like</u> but I,	*Donna raises right hand in front of her*

15		(0.3)	
16		appreciate opportunities to talk about sexuality.	*Donna rotates right hand palm up*
17		(0.3)	
18	Beth:	Mhm.	*Beth nods*
19		(0.1)	
20	Donna:	And faith,	
21		<u>because</u>,	
22		(0.8)	
23		u:m,	*Donna rests right hand on side of face*
24		(0.7)	
25		I think it ought to happen more often.	
26		(1.8)	*Beth and Autumn nod*
27		And,	
28		(0.4)	
29		that with such a popular book,	
30		(0.5)	
31		I think a lot more of us should be talking about it.	
32		(0.2)	*Beth nods*
33		When you don't talk a@bout @it @it's @a @problem.	
34		(H)	*Kasey rests left hand on side of face*
35		Um,	
36		(1.9)	
37		and,	
38		(0.9)	
39		so in the middle of Target with my mom a couple of rows away,	*Donna waves right hand off to the side*
40		(0.1)	
41	Beth:	@@[@@@]@	*Kasey reaches toward food in the middle of the table*
42	Donna:	[kinda,]	
43		(0.4)	
44		whispering about,	
45		(0.4)	
46	Kasey:	(H)	
47	Beth:	@@@@@	
48		(0.1)	
49	Donna:	this book.	
50		(0.2)	
51		@	
52	Autumn:	@@@@	
53	Donna:	And,	
54		(0.2)	

55	um,
56	(1.3)
57	so she was really interested in knowing, *Autumn adjusts in her seat*
58	(1.2)
59	what other people think of it.
60	She hadn't read it,
61	but she's heard so many people talking
	about it.

Example 1 shows how many view religion and sexuality as mutually exclusive, or at least are uncomfortable when they do intersect. Donna describes her interaction with the pastor's wife as somewhat salacious, noting that they were "kinda whispering about this book" (lines 42–49) and that Donna's mom was just a few aisles away and could potentially overhear them (line 39). Donna also recounts how she delicately situated her participation in the book club gathering to the pastor's wife, casting the conversation about the book – as well as her interest in it – as educational and even a moral duty. In lines 10–25, she describes her interest in the book club as an opportunity to talk about two things that rarely get discussed together (faith and sexuality), but she is careful not to insinuate that she might have other interests in the topic, though it's unclear what precisely she might be alluding to (line 14). In lines 27–33, she also notes that *not* talking about a book like *50 Shades* could be problematic, given its ubiquity in pop culture. Beth and Autumn nod along to these accounts justifying Donna's interest, indicating perhaps that they also identify with these reasons or they see them as acceptable motivations for participation.

These delicate conversations where people navigate the waters of faith and sexuality are commonplace in many religious communities, though the settings in which they occur are somewhat rare. There seem to be two notable characteristics of the book club setting that provide for a more intimate context. The first has to do with the institutional roles of the women present. When Autumn and Donna are in their official roles as ministers of their church, there are certain constraints on what they can say and do. In this more informal setting, they are simply among friends and those official identities become less salient. This allows them a space to "try on" different identities and ideologies without enshrining them as dogma or doctrine (cf. Warner-Garcia, 2015). The second has to do with the conversational nature of their interaction. There is no designated leader of the group, though as mentioned before, Autumn is the convener and Kasey is the host. Each of the women contributes in substantive ways to the conversation, and there are often differences of opinions and divergences in experiences. For example, throughout the interaction, Autumn often cites that the books have had an overwhelmingly positive impact on her and her sex life, but she also expresses profound reticence in talking about this in a public setting or with other religious leaders. In stark contrast, Kasey notes that while in general she is comfortable discussing sexuality openly with others, the books have had a pervasively negative impact on her for a variety of reasons, which are discussed in the next example.

The analytic lens of agency can be helpful in examining how the women in this group talk about the impact of the book series on their lives. Agency is something that is constructed by both people and social structures, but it is also constrained by these things as well (see *Cognition* chapter, this volume). These dual processes of construction and constraint can be seen especially clearly when considering the ways in which people impose constraints on themselves, particularly due to moral or religious convictions. Such situations prompt us to inquire whether the self-imposition of constraints is an act of agency, and also whether the location of agency is inside or outside of the individual.

Examples 2 and 3 feature an extended interaction focused on Kasey. They provide a good demonstration of how close analysis of an interactional setting can yield valuable insights into the religious experiences of individuals. In these examples, Kasey recounts her religious conversion experience and how it prompted her to reimagine her personal sexual ethics and practices. Immediately preceding Example 2, Kasey has been discussing some of her past sexual experiences, which she characterizes as promiscuous, experimental, and unhealthy. Throughout this and other examples, Kasey also references shared knowledge with the other women about her husband Vic's sexual history. Based on information gained through my larger ethnographic project, I learned that Vic had engaged in same-sex sexual practices prior to his relationship with Kasey, and he now speaks semi-publicly about his past. Some of Vic's discourses about what he calls his "struggle" with homosexuality are reminiscent of ex-gay ministries, but it is not clear whether Vic views homosexuality as inherently sinful. The discussion of and prior knowledge of both Kasey and Vic's sexual histories form the contextual backdrop for Example 2. Here, Kasey shares a portion of her religious conversion story and how that has impacted her views and practices regarding her own sexuality. She presents her conversion experience as a transformative – yet agentive – act of constraining.

Example 2 "Recommitted my life"

1	Kasey:	And so,	
2		(0.2)	
3		Then,	
4		you know,	
5		after Don left,	
6		and I kind of recommitted my life to Jesus,	*Kasey circles hands in front of self*

7		in a <u>huge</u> way,
8		(0.5)
9		u:m,	*Kasey drops hands in lap and slouches*
10		(0.5)
11		and then,
12		(0.2)
13		wasn't dating,	*Kasey shakes head*
14		and then dated Vic,	*Kasey tucks hair behind ear*
15		and,
16		decided to approach,
17		(0.5)
18		my:,
19		(0.2)
20		sexuality in a different way,	*Kasey slides vertical hand along table*
21		because I [reali]zed that uh,
22	Beth:	[Mhm.]
23	Kasey:	so much of that was coming from,
24		a place of brokenness,	*Donna, Autumn, and Beth nod*
25		and,
26		(0.7)
27		I was so sad,	*Kasey shakes head*
28		that I was just giving myself away,
29		[in that] way.
30	Beth:	[Mhm.]
31		(0.7)
32	Kasey:	And so,
33		(0.3)
34		um,
35		Vic and I waited until we were,	*Kasey lifts palm*
36		(0.5)
37		married to have sex,	*Donna nods*
38		and,
39		(0.3)
40		you guys know-
41		part of his background [too,]	*Kasey places palm on table*
42	Beth:	[Mhm.]	*Beth smiles and nods*
43	Kasey:	and so,
44		it was just kind of a complicat[ed,]	*Kasey swirls hands in front of self*
45	Donna:	[M]m.	*Donna drinks from glass*
46		(0.7)
47	Kasey:	blend.	*Autumn and Beth nod*
48		(0.5)
49		Of,	*Kasey lifts both palms up*
50		(0.4)
51		experiences.	*Donna nods*

52	And needs,
53	and_desires,
54	and_stuff.

In this example, Kasey juxtaposes her sexual history with a spiritual turning point in her life. When talking about her past sexual experiences in lines 27–29, Kasey characterizes herself as the agent of her own prior sexual exploitation ("I was so sad that I was just giving myself away in that way"). That is, she made personal choices that in effect reduced her own ability to find happiness and fulfillment. By contrast, she characterizes her conversion moment in lines 6–7 with an assertion of agency by grammatically expressing herself as the initiator of this recommitment ("I kind of recommitted my life to Jesus in a huge way"). However, she also uses linguistic devices that both mitigate ("kind of") and intensify ("in a huge way") her agentive action in her conversion experience. She is thus setting up her conversion narrative as being characterized by a concurrent foregrounding and backgrounding of her agency.

In some respects, Kasey's conversion narrative involves a reclamation of her own agency by making more intentional decisions about her sexuality, such as not dating for a period of time following her conversion (line 13) and then waiting until marriage to have sex again (lines 32–37). However, the new relationships she has forged with God and her husband also involve a radical self-constraining of her agency. Not only is she submitting her own will and desires to God through her recommitment to Jesus, she is also constraining her sexuality to be confined within a marriage relationship with her husband. In the recounting of both her sexual history and her religious conversion, Kasey casts herself as performing an agentive act of self-constraining. In her past sexual experiences, she chose to 'give herself away' to other individuals in ways that constrained her ability to find happiness. In her religious conversion, she chose to constrain her sexual will and desires. For Kasey, this submission was a type of liberation that prompted her to engage in sexual practices that were more healthy and positive for her.

After the previous example, Kasey continues the story of her and Vic's sexual lives together, from having three kids and nursing (which caused a large drop in her sex drive) to now not nursing and ovulation causing a large surge in her sex drive. She then turns to the subject of the *50 Shades* books and how they have caused problems for her marriage. In the previous example, Kasey characterizes her act of constraint – of choosing not to choose certain sexual acts – as leading to personal happiness and fulfilment. In Example 3, however, her agentive act of constraint is the source of her dissatisfaction. While a modernist view would typically correlate agency with the ability to achieve self-actualization, Kasey complicates this in the ways that she characterizes the effects that erotic media have had on her sexual relationship with her husband.

Example 3   **"Really dissatisfied"**

1	Kasey:	And so then I read these ((*50 Shades* books)),	
2		I-	
3		truthfully just on accident.	*Kasey lifts palm up, Beth nods*
4		Because I didn't even know what it was.	*Kasey lifts both palms up*
5	Beth:	Yeah.	*Donna nods*
6		(0.5)	
7	Kasey:	An-	
8		but then when I started,	*Beth nods*
9		you know,	
10		yes I chose to keep reading them,	*Kasey wipes under eye*
11		ob[viously.]	*Beth smiles*
12	Autumn:	[@@@]	*Autumn smiles and nods*
13	Kasey:	And,	
14		(0.4)	
15		um,	
16		(0.7)	
17		and,	
18		(0.6)	
19		it's made me really dissatis[fied,]	*Autumn nods*
20	Beth:	[Mm.]	*Beth raises eyebrows*
21	Kasey:	with our [₂sex life.]	
22	Autumn:	[₂ Mm.]	*Donna raises eyebrows*
23		(0.4)	
24	Kasey:	Because,	*Kasey brings hand to chin*
25		(0.5)	
26		not because I wanna do all of that stuff,	*Kasey raises both hands in front of self*
27		because,	*Donna and Beth nod, Autumn shakes head*
28		I <u>don't</u>.	*Autumn nods*
29		And I don't think that,	
30		some-	
31		even some of the stuff that I did in the past,	*Kasey shakes head, closes fists*
32		does <u>not</u> need to be a part of our relationship.	*Kasey swipes both bands in front of self*
33		(0.9)	*Autumn shakes head, Beth nods*
34		But,	*Kasey folds arms, tilts head*
35		(1.7)	
36		I want it to be something more.	
37		(0.3)	*Autumn and Beth nod*
38		And,	
39		and I'm not sure that it will be.	*Autumn nods*
40		(0.2)	

41	Beth:	Mhm.	
42		(0.5)	
43	Kasey:	I'm not sure that,	
44		(0.3)	
45		that it will be,	
46		(0.7)	
47		you know,	
48		with Vic.	*Kasey lifts right palm up*
49	Beth:	[Yeah.]	*Beth nods*
50	Kasey:	[And so,]	*Kasey folds arms*
51		and that's terrible.	*Autumn and Beth nod*
52		That's a terrible,	*Kasey pushes right hand away from self*
53	Beth:	Mhm.	
54	Kasey:	thing to have set up.	
55		You know is,	*Beth nods*
56		is a sense of,	
57		(0.7)	
58		dissatisfaction.	
59	Autumn:	[Mhm.]	*Autumn nods*
60	Beth:	[Mhm.]	*Beth nods*
61		(0.2)	
62	Kasey:	Like a really deep one.	*Kasey holds right palm vertical, Beth nods*
63	Autumn:	Yeah.	
64	Kasey:	And,	
65		you know we've discussed it,	*Beth adjusts in chair*
66		and stuff,	
67		and,	
68		(0.2)	
69		but it's-	*Autumn tilts head*
70		(0.7)	
71		it sucks.	
72		And I wish I hadn't read them.	*Kasey brings hand to chin*

In this example, Kasey oscillates between foregrounding and backgrounding her agency in relation to her encounter with the *50 Shades* books. In line 3, she says that she initially read these books "on accident," before she really knew what kind of material they contained. However, she does claim responsibility for continuing to read the books in lines 8–11 ("But then when I started, you know, yes I chose to keep reading them"). The introduction of erotic material into Kasey's life then becomes a source of sexual dissatisfaction (lines 19–21), as the books generate sexual desires in Kasey that she cannot act upon. This tension between Kasey's desire and agency is especially apparent in lines 36–48 when she says "I want it to be something more … and I'm not sure that it will be with Vic." Kasey's sexual relationship is beholden to a person who cannot (or will not) accommodate her desires, and this causes disappointment for her. However, her relationship not only provides constraints on her possible actions, it also makes other actions possible – such as talking with her husband about her struggles as she mentions in lines 64–66 ("we've discussed it and stuff"). Kasey's religious identity therefore affords a space within which she can make sense of her experiences and work out issues of agency and desire.

Although constraints on agency might be seen as inherently negative, this assumption is a value judgment that is based in modernist understandings of individuation and autonomy. Modernism presumes that every instance of individual freedom is a moral good and that all people and institutions should strive for expanding this freedom. The analysis here shows that agentive acts of constraint such as the ones Kasey describes can lead to either self-fulfillment or discontent, and sometimes both at the same time. Therefore, it is important to understand local systems of moral value and the different ways that agency can take shape. Moreover, in many religious communities, a distribution of agency among internal and external forces does not necessarily indicate a fragmentation of the self. Rather, the presence of paradoxical tensions is often considered a marker of spiritual authenticity. By taking participants at their word in their discussion of religious beliefs and experiences, a better understanding emerges of how those beliefs and experiences influence the social construction of selves and their lived realities.

2.4   Future Directions

Neither religion nor interaction are static entities, and this fact is what makes them both fascinating and challenging to study. Often, it requires a lot of different tools in our analytic toolbox to make sense of these phenomena, and we must maintain an openness and curiosity throughout. Traditionally, what 'counts' as interaction has been presumed to include multiple participants engaging in real time and most likely in person. This is what has often been referred to by discourse analysts as "naturally occurring interaction," and it has both dominated the scope of what scholars study and created some false dichotomies between types of discourse. Conversation analysts often point to specific characteristics that make institutional discourses different from 'everyday' or 'mundane' conversations (Heritage 2005). This can include things like conversational goals, institutional identities, and constraints on what counts as allowable contributions. 'Conversation,' on the other hand, is thought to be a more basic or unmarked form of interaction (Goodwin and Heritage 1990) since it involves an element of casualness and equality of speaker rights.

However, Gaudio (2003) complicates this notion by pointing out that these characteristics of conversation are actually the result of interactional and ideological 'work' by participants rather than being inherent or default. He notes that the strict separation of institutional and informal discourse is also problematic since it "fails to account for the many conversational interactions that combine some structural informality with adherence to ritual or institutional constraints" (Gaudio 2003, p. 664). This is particularly true in religious settings, where the lines between institutional and informal are often blurred. Moreover, we miss a lot of rich detail if we overlook the ways participants are actively creating the contexts in which they are operating. While the case study presented here looks at interactional spaces in a Christian community in the United States, future research would benefit from exploring interactional contexts within other religious and cultural traditions as well. Issues of agency, authority, identity, and participation frameworks will likely vary widely from place to place.

Whenever researchers endeavor to study phenomena that occur in such tightly regulated spaces or esoteric communities, a host of methodological issues can come up. Of note are the types of interactions scholars are able to gain access to in the first place, and then subsequently what we are able to observe and understand once we inhabit those spaces. Labov (1966) noted that researchers frequently face the 'observer's paradox,' which essentially states that by observing a particular type of behavior, we inevitably change that which we are observing. This can therefore limit what researchers are able to directly access to begin with (e.g. participants of a particular social category may not engage in certain types of behaviors if the researcher is seen as an outsider). It can also change the entire nature of the interaction, as participants will often unknowingly alter their behavior when they are being observed. Many of the spaces where religious practices happen have limited access for outsiders or are even wholly inaccessible to researchers. Or, if researchers are able to gain access, the nature of the interaction is fundamentally altered. These issues raise not only practical implications on what researchers can study but also ethical implications on who gets to control discourse spaces and for what purposes.

For example, I was able to gain access to the data presented in this chapter because of a number of personal factors such as my upbringing in a Baptist community, my familiarity with the participants involved, and my understanding of the history and practice of Christianity. One might also factor in the similarities in my age, gender, race, geographic location, and socioeconomic status with the members of this community of practice. While these areas of overlap no doubt influenced my ability to interface with this community, there is also always the risk of falling into the pitfalls of "mesearch" (e.g. Edward 2018), where researchers develop a research agenda that is closely tied to their personal identity, values, and goals.

On the other hand, it is difficult (though not impossible) to imagine how a complete outsider to a religious community would be able to gain access to do research there. Consider a young white American woman such as myself traveling to southeast Asia to study Islamic spiritual practices. The barriers to participation, not to mention the challenges in accessing sensitive or personal or controversial parts of the religious community, would be substantial. To start, there is language to consider – both the local tongue(s) and the language(s) of religious practice, which are not always the same. Additional factors might include citizenship (many countries have tight controls over visitors entering the country to study religion), race/ethnicity (many religions have strong ties to particular racial and ethnic groups and might be inaccessible to those who are seen as outsiders), age (religious communities with a strong hierarchical system of elders may preclude access for younger researchers), and gender (often the level and type of religious participation allowed are dictated by a person's perceived gender), to name a few. Studying interactional contexts depends on the researcher's ability not only to get access to the contexts in which interaction occurs but also their ability to actively participate and understand the nuances of them as well.

Additionally, consideration should be paid to the triangulation of power between the researcher, community participants, and community leaders. This is the case when doing ethnographic or interactional fieldwork in any setting, but these issues may take a unique shape in religious communities where power and authority are sometimes obscured by the community's understanding of deities, ancestors, and spirits. Given all of these considerations, future research on religious discourse must provide nuanced and reflective accounts of the researcher's access to, participation in, and influence on the interactions they are studying.

Transcription Conventions

Intonation unit	{line break}
Final intonation	.
Continuing intonation	,
High-rising intonation	?
Speech overlap	[ ]
Truncated intonation unit	–
Elongated speech	:
Connected speech	_
Voice of another	<VOX> </VOX>
Laughter pulse	@
Timed pause (in seconds)	(0.0)
Contextual information	(( ))
Emphatic speech	Underline
Embodied action	*Italics*

2.5   References

Ahearn, L. M. (2001). Language and agency. *Annual Review of Anthropology, 30*(1), 109–137.

Atkinson, P., Coffey, A., Delamont, S., Lofland, J., and Lofland, L. (eds.). (2001). *Handbook of Ethnography.* London: SAGE.

Chilton, P. A., and Kopytowska, M. W. (eds.). (2018). *Religion, Language, and the Human Mind.* Oxford: Oxford University Press.

Cukor-Avila, P. (2000). Revisiting the observer's paradox. *American Speech, 75*(3), 253–254.

Drager, K. (2013). Experimental methods in sociolinguistics. In J. Holms and K. Hazen (eds.), *Research Methods in Sociolinguistics: A Practical Guide* (pp. 58–73). Chichester: Wiley.

Du Bois, J. W. (2009). Interior dialogues. In G. Senft and E.B. Basso (eds.), *Ritual Communication* (pp. 317–340). Oxford: Berg.

Edward, M. (2018). Between dance and detention: Ethical considerations of 'mesearch' in performance. In Iphofen, R., and Tolich, M. (eds.), *The SAGE Handbook of Qualitative Research Ethics* (pp. 161–173). London: SAGE.

Foucault, M. (1978). *The History of Sexuality: An Introduction*, Vol. 1. New York: Vintage.

Gaudio, R. P. (2003). Coffeetalk: Starbucks™ and the commercialization of casual conversation. *Language in Society, 32*(5), 659–691.

Goddard, V. A. (2000). *Gender, Agency, and Change: Anthropological Perspectives.* East Sussex, UK: Psychology Press.

Goodwin, C., and Heritage, J. (1990). Conversation analysis. *Annual Review of Anthropology, 19*(1), 283–307.

Hall, D. D. (1997). *Lived Religion in America: Toward a History of Practice.* Princeton, NJ: Princeton University Press.

Hall, K., and Bucholtz, M. (eds.). (1995). *Gender Articulated: Language and the Socially Constructed Self.* London: Routledge.

Handman, C. (2010). Events of translation: Intertextuality and Christian ethnotheologies of change among Guhu-Samane, Papua New Guinea. *American Anthropologist, 112*(4), 576–588.

Heritage, J. (2005). Conversation analysis and institutional talk. *Handbook of Language and Social Interaction, 103*, 47.

Jacoby, S., and Ochs, E. (1995). Co-construction: An introduction. *Research on Language and Social Interaction, 28*(3), 171–183.

Keane, W. (1997). Religious language. *Annual Review of Anthropology, 26*, 47–71.

Keane, W. (2004). Language and religion. In A. Duranti (ed.), *A Companion to Linguistic Anthropology* (pp. 431–448). Malden: Blackwell.

Labov, W (1966). *The Social Stratification of English in New York City.* Washington, DC: Center for Applied Linguistics.

Labov, W. (1972). *Language in the Inner City: Studies in the Black English Vernacular*, Vol. 3. Philadelphia: University of Pennsylvania Press.

McElhinny, B. (1997). Ideologies of public and private language in sociolinguistics. In R. Wodak (ed.), *Gender and Discourse* (pp. 106–139). London: SAGE.

McGuire, M. B. (2008). *Lived Religion: Faith and Practice in Everyday Life.* Oxford: Oxford University Press.

Mills, S., and Jones, L. (2014). Analysing agency: Reader responses to *Fifty Shades of Grey. Gender and Language, 8*(*2*), 225–244.

O'Halloran, K. (ed.). (2004). *Multimodal Discourse Analysis: Systemic Functional Perspectives*. London: A & C Black.

Schegloff, E. A. (2007). *Sequence Organization in Interaction: A Primer in Conversation Analysis I*, Vol. 1. Cambridge: Cambridge University Press.

Schiffrin, D. (1996). Narrative as self-portrait: Sociolinguistic constructions of identity. *Language in Society, 25*(2), 167–203.

Tannen, D. (2004). Talking the dog: Framing pets as interactional resources in family discourse. *Research on Language and Social Interaction, 37*(*4*), 399–420.

Tannen, D., Hamilton, H. E., and Schiffrin, D. (eds.). (2015). *The Handbook of Discourse Analysis*, Vol. 1. Chicester: Wiley.

Titon, J. T. (1988). *Powerhouse for God: Speech, Chant, and Song in an Appalachian Baptist Church*. Austin: University of Texas Press.

Voloshinov, V. (1986). *Marxism and the Philosophy of Language*. Boston: Harvard University Press.

Warner-Garcia, S. (2015). 'His belly dancer': Young women's interactional negotiation of sexual bodies and desire at a Baptist university. *Gender and Language 9*(2), 255–277.

3 Ethnography

Vally Lytra

3.1 Background, History, and Key Terms

Religion is central to the everyday experiences of many individuals and communities worldwide. As a force for learning and socialisation and as an important marker of identity, it can provide a sense of membership and belonging within and across generations. The social and cultural practices in religions are shaped by individual as well as institutional, social, and ideological forces and processes, instantiated locally, translocally, and globally. Specific ways of utilising language and literacy can also be seen as a social practice that individuals draw upon for meaning making and building social relationships. Language and literacy practices are then historically situated and embedded within power relations and societal discourses of distinction, where some languages and literacies become dominant and others are frequently silenced or considered irrelevant or problematic.

An emergent body of interdisciplinary scholarship has examined the intersection of language, literacy, and religion from a social and cultural practice perspective. Methodologically, this body of research uses ethnography as a key conceptual approach to understanding social interaction for systematic knowledge building and the generation of theory. Although recognising the intellectual antecedents of ethnography in anthropology and sociology, there is no consensus about what counts as ethnography (Hammersley, 2018). Simply put, ethnography refers to the description and interpretation of people's behaviours and attitudes to make sense of the world from their perspectives. Hammersley and Atkinson (1983, p. 2) observe, 'the ethnographer participates, overtly or covertly, in people's lives for an extended period of time, watching what happens, listening to what is said, asking questions; in fact collecting whatever data is available to throw light on the issues with which he or she is concerned.'

Ethnography goes beyond merely describing people's social and cultural practices, but captures the complexity and multilayeredness of social experience, and social rules and patterns. In this respect, ethnography 'describe[s] the apparently messy and complex activities that make up social action, not to reduce their complexity but to describe and explain it' (Blommaert and Jie

2010, p. 11–12). Doing ethnography is, thus, an interpretivist and inductive process: the empirical data guide the ethnographer to the application of particular theories rather than the other way round. Ethnography is also reflexive; ethnographers are part of the social world they are studying and they actively shape that world.

The following excerpt is from a six-page narrative documenting my second visit to the Sri Murugan Temple in Newham, East London. My visit to the Temple was part of a multisited, three-year collaborative team ethnography entitled 'Becoming Literate in Faith Settings: Language and Literacy Learning in the Life of New Londoners' (the BeLiFS project), supported by the Economic and Social Research Council, UK. The study investigated how sixteen children aged between four and twelve develop their language and literacy learning and belonging through religious activities in London, UK. The children and their families were part of the Bangladeshi Muslim, Ghanaian Pentecostal, Polish Catholic, and Tamil Hindu/Saiva religious communities that have grown in numbers from the 1950s onwards. The research team consisted of eleven researchers sharing a wide range of linguistic, cultural, and ethnic backgrounds, age, gender, professional and educational circumstances, research experience, and religious and non-religious beliefs and worked with four families from each community, their religious leaders, teachers, and older community members.

Taking a case-study approach, four research pairs were formed where a new researcher who was a member of the ethno-linguistic community (and, in three out of the four case studies, of the faith community) was paired with a more established researcher who was not (in three out of the four case studies). Arani Ilankuberan (who was visiting the Temple with me that day) and I formed a research pair working with the children and the families from the Tamil Hindu/Saiva faith community.

When I enter the Temple, I am immediately struck by how busy it is even though the Temple has just opened its doors. I can hear chanting coming from the loudspeakers. It sounds like a woman chanting solo. Arani explains that it's a *suprabhatham*, a devotional song typically sung early in the morning. It is believed that listening to the chanting confers a positive vibration for the whole day. The chanting is pervasive almost drowning out all other human voices and activity. You almost feel transported into a spiritual realm and I come to appreciate what I read some time ago about the divine character of Hindu temples enabling people to feel the presence of God. This feeling of being transported into a spiritual realm is compounded by the intense smell of incense burning. I am overwhelmed and I seek refuge in the chairs lined up on the left side of the Temple, close to the temple of Ganesh (also referred to as the elephant god). I wonder if regular worshippers feel the same way every time they enter the Temple and whether a non Greek-Orthodox would feel the same way when entering a Greek-Orthodox church, for instance, and being confronted with a huge dome with the depiction of Christ the Saviour and the intricate frescos, mosaics and icons lining the walls from top to bottom. (Tamil Temple, 6.10.2009).

This extract is an example of a field narrative crafted by the researchers visiting and engaging in participant observations in their own research site as well as the sites of other project members. The field narratives were written during the first year of the ethnography and aligned with our aim 'to produce rich descriptions of ceremonies, rituals and events in the places of worship across settings' (Gregory and Lytra, 2012, p. 200). Keeping the field narratives allowed the researchers to make their experience explicit and accessible to others. Drafting the field narratives allowed the project team members to reflect upon their own research site, compare it with that of others, and ultimately develop a deeper awareness and understanding of both their own site and that of others. Moreover, it supported the creation of more multi-voiced ethnographic accounts that better represented the multiple perspectives of project team members.

Participant observation is the scholarly term for researchers observing, talking, and listening to the research participants as the former try to make sense of the lives and social activities of the latter. Ethnographers write up accounts of their observations either during or soon after the events and activities they have observed in the form of field notes. Like field notes, field narratives are a form of representation of participant observations. The project team conceived field narratives as 'a written dialogue, an interactive way of teaching and learning from each other, and a way of sharing emotions with those who have deeply held belief in their faith' (Gregory and Lytra, 2012, p. 197). Like all forms of representation, field narratives are partial accounts that are generated through processes of selection. Field narratives were shared, discussed, and commented on online and during pair and team meetings as the research team members with different backgrounds and degrees of knowledge of the religious practices under study sought to understand the role of religion in children's learning and identity affirmation within and across the different faith communities.

Hymes' (1996, p. 13) asserts that 'our ability to learn ethnographically is an extension of what every human being must do, that is learn the meanings, norms, patterns of everyday life.' In the previous field narrative excerpt, I am trying to make sense of a new and largely unfamiliar religion and some of the faith literacies of Hindu/Saiva Temple. By observing, reflecting upon and documenting some of the routines and activities, I am trying to gain insights into the religious setting, make explicit the assumptions taken for granted by members of the community and share these insights with my co-researcher and the other members of the team. My account represents my encounter with the Temple first and foremost as a sensorial, embodied, and affective experience (Lytra, Gregory, and Ilankuberan, 2016). I comment on the buzz of activity even though the Temple has just opened its doors to devotees, the chanting of a devotional song that can be heard from the loudspeakers and the intense smell of incense burning. I also share the feelings of wonder and awe this encounter generates which forces me to sit down in one of the chairs at the side of the Temple and contemplate whether similar feelings might be experienced when others unfamiliar with my own faith enter a Greek-Orthodox church for the first time.

The field narrative field narratives crafted allowed us to make explicit our own long-held assumptions, stances, and positionings. They demonstrated how our researcher identities were interconnected with other identity aspects and our lived experience, mediated via language and literacy as well as other communicative resources. They also illustrated the learning process an ethnographer undertakes as they enter a new setting and become socialised into its norms and routines. This learning process is essential, especially in the case of a researcher who is not a member of the religious community under study.

3.2   Key Topics, Questions, and Debates

3.2.1   Knowledge Construction and Representation

Early ethnographic descriptions of religion as situated cultural practice have drawn upon social psychology, anthropology, and literacy studies, in particular New Literacy Studies: see, for instance, the seminal studies by Scribner and Cole (1981) among the Vai in Liberia, Street (1984) in Iran, and Heath (1983) in the USA. These studies questioned traditional conceptualisations of literacy as a set of neutral skills and competences, developing instead a sustained analytical focus on the relationship between situated interaction and practice and macro-level structures and ideologies. They foregrounded the entanglement of the cognitive with the sociocultural, historical, and ideological dimensions of language and literacy learning through religious practice. Moreover, they examined literacies in everyday life, extending the investigation of language and literacy learning beyond schools and classrooms to include religious contexts as rich sites for teaching and learning in their own right, thereby challenging dichotomies between learning in religious settings and learning in other settings.

In a comparative ethnography of children's early language socialisation in two communities, Heath (1983) demonstrated how children from white and black working class communities become socialised in and through language in different ways in their home and respective communities, including places of worship and religious education classes. Children fused elements from religious narratives, vocabulary and modes of discourse learned in religious settings with broader repertoires of everyday, social, and cultural practice and verbal activities with the purpose of sustaining their moral and spiritual development. Equally importantly, Heath's study alerted language and literacy researchers to the discrepancy between the sense of validation, expertise, and belonging that children experienced within their homes and communities and the low academic expectations of their mainstream schools and teachers who often framed their competences in deficit terms. From an ethnographic perspective, it exemplified how general claims about macro-level structures and processes such as challenging teachers' deficit perspectives of working class students' abilities are anchored onto the close examination of micro-level data, such as specific language and literacy activities, or linguistic and cultural features.

Indeed, religious learning is unique in that the language and literacy practices practised, performed, and perfected over time are a means to build a relationship with a higher and eternal being. Learning in and through religious practice entails not only acquiring symbolic knowledge, moral and spiritual beliefs, language skills, and interaction patterns to participate in religious ritual but also becoming socialised into religious frames of making sense of the self and the world often mediated intergenerationally (Heath 1983; also see studies in Lytra, Volk, and Gregory 2016). At the same time, it acknowledges that each person may experience and engage in religious practice in deeply personal and theological ways.

Language socialisation and sociocultural approaches have been frequently drawn upon as influential frameworks for studying the intersection of language, literacy, and religion from a social and cultural practice perspective. The *language socialisation paradigm* has as its starting point that social actors are socialised through and to language (Schieffelin and Ochs, 1986); it is concerned with how 'through the process of learning with and from others, we learn through language but also acquire relevant language forms,' both synchronically and across the lifespan (Baquedano-López, 2016, p. 71). Language is key resource for meaning making and for the development of membership in religious communities and has been central to the maintenance, development, and spread of religion and religious practices.

Religion and religious practices have also affected language maintenance, shift and change across generations, time, and space. Studies deploying a *language socialisation* lens have examined the interrelationship between languages, literacies, interaction, and learning in a range of diverse and stratified minority and migrant contexts. For instance, Avni (2012) explored the intertwining of learning different varieties of Hebrew with English and the articulation of multiple identity options in a Jewish (secular) primary school in New York. In another study of Hasidic (non-liberal) Jewish girls' language socialisation across home, school, and community, Fader (2009) illustrated that language use is linked to the development of modes of thinking, interpreting, feeling, and behaving, including religious beliefs and practices, in culturally appropriate ways. In particular, her study revealed how the learning of different forms of Biblical Hebrew, Yiddish, English, and Hasidic English was connected to the girls' acquisition and display of gendered roles and identities that were infused by a Hasidic form of femininity. Baquedano-López (2000) demonstrated how the ideological orientation of using Spanish in religious education classes reinforced the link between language, religion, and ethnicity among school-age Mexican immigrant children in a majority English diasporic context. Knowledge and practice from home and community settings, including faith settings, went largely unrecognized in supporting language proficiency and identity affirmation in mainstream school contexts.

Sociocultural approaches start from the learning contexts in which a sense of belonging are developed and sustained through participation, apprenticeship, and appropriation with the support of more experienced group or community members. Learning thus takes place between individuals (interpersonal) through situated interaction and practices and within the individual (intrapersonal) through internalised cognitive processes (Vygotsky, 1978). While recognising the importance of language in learning and identity construction, using a sociocultural lens urges us to investigate language as one of a wealth of mediational tools, focusing instead on the role of cultural contexts and practices, the breadth of mediational tools and mediators for learning across families and communities (Rogoff, 1990). In this sense, it examines the interconnection of language with other repertoires of semiotic resources, for instance gesture, posture, music and rhythm, dance and movement as well as images and artefacts, to uncover how sociocultural contexts impact on what is learned and how that is learned.

In our longitudinal ethnography in religious settings (the BeLiFS project), Kenner and colleagues (2016) illustrated how children developed successful learner identities and a sense of agency with the expert mediation of supportive parents, faith teachers, and other faith community members. The dispositions, abilities, and positive expectations cultivated could then be leveraged within and beyond the Bangladeshi Muslim and Ghanaian Pentecostal religious settings respectively to sustain children's learning in mainstream schools. Souza, Barradas, and Woodham (2016, p. 52) illustrated this by describing how Adam, a nine-year-old Polish boy, developed symbolic knowledge and 'multiple layers of his identity as a member of the Polish community and as a member of a faith community' through his participation in Easter celebrations at home under the purposeful guidance of family and friends. Gregory, Lytra and Ilankuberan (2015) similarly showed how two siblings internalised knowledge of Hindu/Saiva rituals and symbols and transformed plastic building blocks and other everyday objects into important religious artefacts through play.

Both language socialization and sociocultural approaches to the study of religion as social and cultural practice can be seen as complementary. As Lytra, Volk, and Gregory (2016, p. 6) have argued, 'the language and texts of an individual religious practice are actually inseparable from the practice itself and an in depth account of the learning taking place by young people needs to account equally for both language and context.' In their ethnographic accounts of children's language and literacy learning through religious practices, the authors sought to capture the emic perspectives of the religious community members themselves; that is, select, categorise, identify, and represent some of the patterns of religious practices, beliefs, and interpretations of cultural and contextual meaning that were salient to the participants. Getting at the perspectives of community members is a challenging task for ethnographers who at the same time infuse their ethnographic accounts with their own particular, etic, perspectives. These include orientating theories and analytic procedures as well as previous research in the area of study (Hammersley and Atkinson, 1983).

3.2.2   Researcher Reflexivity and Religious Practice Exclusivity

The continual dialogue between *emic* and *etic* perspectives foreground the researchers' own subjectivities and the role they play in shaping the understandings and interpretations of the social and cultural practices they study. Ethnographers must then acknowledge the 'joint responsibility for the knowledge construction process in which they participate when doing ethnography' (Patiño-Santos, 2019, p. 213). The partiality and context-sensitivity of ethnographic understandings and interpretations and the dynamic process of knowledge gathering and sense making must also be acknowledged. Moreover, they must be constantly aware that ethnographic research is dynamic, subjective, and context-sensitive and that the object of study is nested within specific micro-level contexts and macro-level structures and processes. Indeed, participants are often not actively aware of particular social and cultural practices and their own behaviours. Ethnographers uncover these implicit practices and behaviours through fieldwork that involves sustained participation and observation over long periods of time rather than solely asking participants questions about their conduct and beliefs, for example, in the form of interviews.

In this respect, fieldwork is closely linked to the ethnographer's personal journey of knowledge generation as they reconstruct different participants' worldviews. Because the ethnographer captures and represents the various voices of the participants, including their own accounts, ethnographic narratives are by nature dialogical and polyphonic (Heller 2009). Yet, processes of selection and representation of different perspectives in ethnographic accounts raise issues of whose voices get included and whose get silenced or ignored as well as the ethnographer's stance towards these voices. Therefore, developing researcher reflexivity that is carefully thinking about 'the politics of identity and positioning in the field' (Patiño-Santos, 2019, p. 217) throughout the different research stages is a crucial endeavour for the ethnographer and a precondition for building respectful and equitable relationships with research participants.

Engaging in researcher reflexivity is especially pertinent when investigating religious settings. Religion is often regarded as a very private and personal matter which inevitably raises issues of exclusiveness and exclusion of those who are not members of the religious community, thereby adding further layers of complexity when documenting religious practices and beliefs. Fader (2009) and Sarroub (2005), among others, have critically discussed the challenges in researching religious settings where the ethnographer is not perceived as a member of the religious community. Although Jewish, Fader's Jewishness was monitored and scrutinised during and after the fieldwork as she was not an Orthodox Jew and was positioned as an 'outsider' to the Hasidic Jewish community she studied. Additionally, this positioning had material conse-quences for the fieldwork too, as it confined her access to and engagement with women and girls' lived experiences only. In a similar vein, Sarroub carefully considered the interplay of ethnic, religious, and gender identity aspects and how they prompted the Yemeni-American high school students in her study to position her in particular ways: 'The underlying assumption among my informants was that I would not understand them if I was not really Muslim as they were. As an outsider I could never capture their reality' (Sarroub, 2005, p. 17). Other ethnographers researching religious settings have argued that being a member of the religious community is crucial for acceptance by participants (Rosowsky, 2008).

Nevertheless, Gregory and Ruby (2011), in their work with children and families learning in homes and schools in cross-cultural contexts, have questioned the binaries of 'insider' and 'outsider' roles. They have showed that such dichotomies may oversimplify the process of researching cultural practices and behaviours, as issues of accountability and problems of transla-tion may arise for both 'insider' and 'outsider' ethnographers. In fact, they highlighted how their own backgrounds (for one very similar to the children and the families they studied and for the other very different) afforded them with different degrees of insiderness and outsiderness, and how they negoti-ated and transformed their personal and social identities throughout the research process. However, in most cases, the ethnographer enters the field as an 'outsider', with limited knowledge of the social environment, its cultural practices, and social norms. They must gradually learn the tacit rules and conventions and move from peripheral participation to a more central position, adapting their conduct according to the group's expectations. Even when the ethnographer is a member of the group, they still need to call into question their prior assumptions and established cultural practices and norms as they inquire into their 'own' cultural practices and beliefs in their researcher capacity.

The tension in negotiating researcher and religious identities in particular is encapsulated in the question raised by Arani Ilankuberan, my co-researcher in the BeLiFS project: 'When I'm in the Temple, how can I manage to pray and do research at the same time' (Gregory and Lytra 2012, p. 197). Arani's questions reminds us that becoming a researcher in religious settings, especially in one's own place of worship, 'may easily appear intrusive, insensitive, or even disrespectful' (p. 197). It can pose additional dilemmas: 'if one is a known member of the congregation, how can one take on the role of researcher instead of worshipper? How does one balance the different roles?' (p. 197). Recognizing these challenges further alerts us to the importance of building relationships of collaboration and trust with participants in the field.

Although the ethnographer has traditionally been thought of as the lone researcher in the pursuit of knowledge, collaboration is in fact at the heart of ethnographic research. As Wasser and Bresler (1996, p. 5) argue, 'this image of the independent scholar, however, glosses over the very social nature of the research process, making invisible the researcher's connections to the participants of the study and those numerous others with whom the researcher worked during the course of a study and who made important contributions to his/her interpretation.' Collaboration also takes the form of ethnographers working together in interdisciplinary research teams and with stakeholders from non-academic institutions and increasingly engaging in impact activities for a range of academic and non-academic audiences.

3.3   Case Study

From 2009 to 2013, the 'Becoming Literate in Faith Settings: Language and Literacy Learning in the Life of New Londoners' BeLiFS (BeLiFS) project team of eleven researchers engaged in a multisited ethnography in places of worship, religious education classes, and homes in London. We sought to investigate the following questions using a multi-method approach to data collection: (1) What is the scope and nature of literacy practices in each faith setting? (2) How do teaching and learning take place during faith literacy activities across different settings? (3) In what ways have faith literacy activities changed over time in the London setting and across generations? and (4) How does participation in faith literacies contribute to individual and collective identities? During the first year of the ethnography, the research team investigated the breadth of children's faith literacy learning and socialisation by collecting demographic and historical data about each faith and the area around each site of worship. We then drafted field narratives based on our participant observations in the places of worship, religious education classes, and during other cultural activities as well as during our visits to each other's place of worship. In collaboration with faith leaders and faith teachers, we identified sixteen families we would work with for the next two years.

In the second and third year of the project, each research pair worked closely with the four children and their families in each faith community. At the beginning of the second year, we gave all participant children an A4-size scrapbook with multicolored pages and asked them to write, draw, and stick in it what they considered important about their faith and they wanted to share with the researchers. During home visits, researchers leafed through the scrapbooks, discussed their content, and shared their responses with the children and the other family members who were present. The researchers then discussed the scrapbooks page by page with the children and with siblings who had co-authored them. In the Tamil Hindu/Saiva case study, these conversations were video-recorded and additionally, we gave each family a digital tape-recorder, a camera, and a light-weight, easy-to-use video camera and asked the children and other family members to record daily faith rituals and special religious celebrations and take photographs of religious and other cultural artefacts at home and in the places of worship. We also shadowed and recorded the children at their religious education classes. Finally, we interviewed the children, the parents, faith leaders, and faith teachers. For our interviews with the children, we adapted the 'draw and talk' method (Coates and Coates, 2006) where the children made drawings, including mind maps, as they were talking with the researcher about their language use and literacy practices associated with faith. In the project's third year, the children themselves became researchers and, with the help of the project team, prepared questions to ask either a grandparent or an older member of the community about how the faith had changed across time, space, and generations.

Throughout the research process, we engaged in methodological reflexivity with the purpose of monitoring, clarifying, and adjusting accordingly 'the epistemological, methodological and analytical decisions taken' (Patiño-Snatos 2019, p. 214). Doing research with children required developing child-friendly methodologies that positioned children as knowledgeable and active meaning makers in their own right and captured and represented their perspectives and experiences. Moreover, previous research with children has documented the value of using visual and multimodal modes of representation, such as photography, drawing, and scrapbooks (Kenner et al., 2016; Lytra et al., 2016; Souza et al., 2016). These methodologies have the potential to uncover children's creativity, intentionality, and expertise because they exercise agency over how they share and co-construct knowledge with the researchers as well as with family members, religious leaders, teachers, and community members who support their learning and identity affirmation in and through religious practice and belief.

Ethical issues are equally very important and inevitably influenced the methodological decisions made before, during, and after the fieldwork has been completed. Researchers have a duty of care towards all research participants, ensuring their safety and well-being. This is especially true when working with children. Project team members cultivated a good working relationship with the families, faith leaders, faith teachers, and other community members who participated in the project. Although participants were briefed about the research project and gave their informed consent, at each stage of the project, they were consulted about their right to withdraw. In fact, our decision to select four families from each faith community was motivated by our concern that some families might withdraw from the project given the complex and sensitive nature of researching faith settings and the project's long-term commitment: neither the families nor any of the other participants withdrew. Permission for filming, photographing, and audio- and video-recording children was obtained from parents at the beginning and throughout the course of the longitudinal study. To address the sensitive nature of faith literacy practices, the participants were given recording equipment to document the faith practices they decided to share. At the end of the study, all participants signed letters of agreement, allowing project team members to use the data gathered for public dissemination, including uploading a selection of the data on the project website (www.belifs.co.uk). We also asked all participants to decide on the use of pseudonyms and where requested we have used those pseudonyms.

For this case study, I will discuss specifically an annual special celebration, the celebration of the *Pongal* festival at the home of Thiani. The aim of the analysis is to illustrate what Thiani and her older brother Tianan might be learning by partaking in this special celebration and how their learning might be supported by their parents and maternal grandmother. The analysis draws upon insights to learning from sociocultural and language socialisation approaches and combines data from home video-recording and photography with children's scrapbooks.

The analysis is multilayered with separate foci on the outer, middle, and inner layers. However, the layers are not separate or discrete entities, but rather interconnected, shaping one another. Starting with the outer layer, the analysis explores the broader historical and cultural contexts in which the festival is situated in the country of origin and in the diaspora. It then moves on to the middle layer and zooms in the celebration as it takes place at Thiani's home with the participation of her parents, older brother, and maternal grandmother in the early morning before the children go the school. The analysis includes the activity, the mediational tools (including the languages being used during the celebration), and the mediators of learning and illustrates how the celebration supports the children's faith learning and is reinforced by a wider web of valued faith literacy practices. The examination of the middle layer also alerts us to how the family has adapted the festival to the London setting while keeping its core elements the same across continents. Finally, the analysis concentrates on

Figure 3.1 Happy Pongal

the inner layer, the interaction patterns among family members, the language and literacy abilities developed, and strategies employed.

3.3.1   Outer Layer: The Broader Historical and Cultural Contexts

Pongal is an important festival for Tamils and is observed in Tamil communities in South India, Sri Lanka, and in the diaspora worldwide. The purpose of the festival is to give thanks to the Sun God for a successful harvest and it is celebrated over four days during the Tamil month of Thai (January 15–18). The main event consists of observing the ritual boiling and spilling over of the milk, which symbolises abundance and prosperity for the household. Once the milk has boiled and spilt, brown rice, sugar, jaggery, cashew nuts, raisins, and ghee are added to the milk to turn the mixture into pongal, a thick brown sweet dish that is then shared with family and friends. The word 'pongal', therefore, refers to both the festival and the dish. The *Pongal* festival emerged as a recurring theme in the children's scrapbooks too. Children drew images of the pot with milk spilling over in abundance and wrote 'Happy Pongal' messages. Hajipan (age eight, at the beginning of the fieldwork) crafted the following description of Pongal in the scrapbook he co-created with his younger sister, Tanja (age six, at the beginning of the fieldwork):

We celebrate Pongal because to say thank you for growing plants and vegetables for us. It is on January 18th. We cook pongal and eat it. We have fun together and every year you have to cook in a new pot. You can do it before the Sun rises because you have to say thank you for the SUN.

The description was accompanied by a pencil line drawing of a traditional clay pot with milk spilling over and of the Sun (image 3.1). Above the text-making, Hajipan stuck a drawing of another bigger, more colourful clay pot with traditional patterns and with milk overflowing in large quantities, and wrote the message 'Happy Pongal' in equally colourful block letters. The colourful drawing and message are reminiscent of the *Pongal* cards families routinely receive every year from friends and relatives in Sri Lanka and the children had shown to us. Both the images Hajipan drew and those of other children sought to capture the most auspicious moment of the event that is the overflow of the milk in abundance, indicating that they have come to recognise and have internalised its importance and symbolism.

In their text-making, the siblings demonstrate their developing cultural knowledge and religious understanding: the purpose of the celebration (to give thanks for the harvest), the date (January 18), the main artefact required (a new pot every year), the social and communal nature (having fun and consuming the dish together), and the religious dimension of the celebration which is linked to giving thanks to the Sun God for the successful harvest. Their text-making reveals how their faith literacy learning supports the development of their multimodal literacies drawing on a combination of written text, images, colour, and spatial arrangements (Lytra, Gregory, and Ilankuberan, 2017). It illustrates how children capitalise on their 'funds of knowledge' that is 'the historically accumulated and culturally developed bodies of knowledge and skills' (Gonzalez, Moll, and Amanti, 2005, p. 133) that can be found within families and communities and are very often made invisible in mainstream schools and classroom; religious practices, values and beliefs.

3.3.2   Middle Layer: Activity, Mediational Tools and Mediators of Learning

We asked each family to record important religious celebrations they participated in. Thiani's family chose to record the *Pongal* celebration in their home. The father, mother, and children took turns to film key moments of the celebration, which lasted over two and a half hours in total. Arani Ilankuberan then edited the clips to create an eight-minute film with the highlights of the celebration in chronological order and added English subtitles as most of the interaction in the film takes place in Tamil. Arani shared the edited film she created with the family for feedback and got their verbal consent to upload it on the project website alongside videos taken by other participating families documenting religious celebrations across the four faith communities in homes and places of worship. Additionally, Thiani was tasked by the family with taking photographs of the most important rituals during the celebration.

In Sri Lanka, the *Pongal* celebration traditionally takes place at dawn at the threshold of the house. In London, Thiani and her family moved the celebration indoors and drew a *kolam* (a form of geometric line drawing typically created on the threshold of one's home) in the middle of the living room. The design of the *kolam* is a perfect square with openings in the middle of each side made of rice powder. On the top corner, the mother drew the image of the Sun. A portable cooker heating the pot with the milk and the other ingredients rests on a brick block in the middle of the square. Surrounding the image of the Sun, the family placed several religious artefacts to be used in the rituals: a silver decorative oil lamp, a coconut placed on leaves on a silver pot on a large green leaf, a bell, small containers with white and red holy ash, bananas, oranges, a bottle of oil for the oil lamp, and a matchbox.

The edited film captures the main events of the activity: it opens with Thiani (age seven at the beginning of the fieldwork) and her brother, Tianan, (age ten at the beginning of the fieldwork) observing the milk boiling as their mother brings the container with the soaked brown rice to be added to the milk. The family carefully watch and comment on the milk boiling and overflowing, a mop in hand to deal with any spillage. The mother alerts the grandmother to the directionality of the overflow: 'Mother come and see it's boiling over on the east side!' which is ostensibly an auspicious sign (image 3.2). Once the milk has overflowed, the father takes a handful of brown rice and squats over the pot making sure he does not touch the pot with his knees. He moves his hands clockwise circling the pot three times before gently putting the rice in the pot. He repeats the action three times before inviting the other family members one by one to repeat the action. The other ingredients are added in the mixture and family members are invited to take turns stirring the mixture so that it doesn't stick to the bottom of the pot under the watchful eye of the father and the grandmother.

Once the pongal has been cooked, the mother takes a prayerful position. She brings her two palms together, closes her eyes, bows her head, and starts

Figure 3.2 The overflowing of the milk, photo by Thiani

singing a *Thevaram* (a Tamil hymn) to Lord Ganesh. She then starts singing the first verse of the next *Thevaram* to Lord Shiva and nods to Thiani to continue. Modelling her mother's actions, Thiani stands upright in a prayerful position and sings the hymn in a loud, clear voice. The other family members stand by observing. After the singing of the hymns, the father takes the sacred oil lamp and asks each family member to touch and pray to the flame, as Thiani rings the bell with a big smile on her face. The father takes the sacred oil lamp upstairs to the family prayer shelf containing images of Gods and sacred objects and circles the sacred flame clockwise in front of the deities while Thiani continues ringing the bell. The mother invites family members to apply white holy ash across their forehead and to their neck. They make three horizontal lines with white holy ash across the forehead and a dot in the middle of the forehead using red holy ash.

3.3.3   Inner Layer: Interaction Patterns, Skills and Strategies

The interaction patterns among the family members, the language and literacy abilities developed, and the strategies employed are the focus of the inner-layer analysis. Thiani takes responsibility to lead the collective prayer for the family by closely modelling her mother's prayerful position and attitude. As she sings the *Thevaram*, she engages in the use of sophisticated language forms in archaic Tamil, which differ from vernacular forms of Tamil she uses everyday with her family. At the same time, Thiani practises and performs the main act of praying for Saivites (Saivaism is a devotional branch of Hinduism. Saivaites believe that Lord Shiva is the ultimate deity). Her performance reveals the importance placed on correct enunciation and clear pronunciation in singing the devotional hymns and the deployment of a respectful embodied stance, what Ochs and Capps (2002, p. 40) have referred to as 'a prayerful attitude'.

Throughout her religious socialisation, Thiani has had many opportunities to listen to, practise, perform, and learn about *Thevarams*. At home, her mother regularly plays devotional hymns in the mornings, as the family members prepare themselves to go to school and work. Thiani has also sung *Thevarams*, individually and collectively at the Temple. In the religious education classes, she attends on Sundays after Tamil school, at the beginner's class, Thiani learned to repeat, memorise, and practise devotional hymns. In the intermediate class, she was introduced to the social, cultural, and historical contexts in which the devotional hymns were created. Viewed within a sociocultural frame, by actively participating in the *Pongal* festival at home under the guidance of more knowledgeable family members, the children are socialised into developing membership and a sense of belonging to the Hindu/Saiva faith community. Membership identity is not fixed but achieved interactionally through engaging in and sometimes leading religious practice, as in the case of Thiani's prayer. Through 'guided participation' (Rogoff 1990) in faith activities, children learn to take up roles and perform religious rituals that also help them build their self-esteem and self-confidence, important resources that can be transferred to learning in other contexts, including the mainstream school.

The multilayered analysis demonstrates how children's participation in iterative religious celebrations allows them to co-construct culturally valued practices and routines mediated by symbols and sacred objects and forge enduring relationships with family members and the broader faith community. It also illustrates how faith learning provides a bridge between past, present, and future of cultural practices. As cultural practices travel across continents and generations, they create a rich tapestry that weaves together different threads of religious experience, locally, nationally, and transnationally, attesting to the enduring relationship between Tamil ethnicity, language, and faith in a diasporic setting.

3.4   Future Directions

The aim of our three-year, multisited team ethnography was to document the significance of religious contexts in many children's lives; the breadth and scope of teaching and the range of skills learnt, including languages and literacies; and the development of identities, knowledge, and abilities. Concurring with Long (2016, p 227), it sprang from 'a sense of urgency', an acknowledgement that 'schooling and the wider society can isolate, ignore, and create taboos that keep us from recognising the rich learning, teaching, heritage, histories and literacies, and a sense of community and belonging that define many faith contexts'. Previous ethnographic work by Heath (1983), Gonzalez, Moll, and Amanti (2005), among others cited earlier in this chapter, has demonstrated the importance of investigating teaching and learning in out-of-school contexts for the development children's abilities, potential, and positive learner identities in mainstream schools and classrooms.

Educators and policy makers in particular would benefit from insights from teaching and learning in faith settings. Given the growing diversity of the student population in schools and classrooms around the world, further ethnographic studies need to explore to what extent and in what ways the wealth of knowledge, skills, and expertise, as well as high standards and expectations, nourished in a faith setting can be utilised for thinking and learning and can contribute to children's academic success (this investigation was beyond the scope of the BeLiFS project). To date, very few studies have explored the possibilities and limitations of mobilising children's religious knowledge and understanding for literacy instruction (but see Damico and Hall, 2014 and LeBlanc, 2017, for notable exceptions).

Yet, if, as educators, we wish to honour all children's languages, literacies, heritages, and histories, and we are committed to supporting and sustaining inclusive and pluralistic pedagogies, then more attention needs to be given to children's religious practices and identities. To this end, ethnography can provide a powerful epistemological, ontological, and methodological frame.

Another area of future ethnographic research involves the mediation of religious belief and practice via new and traditional media. A recent edited collection of studies by Rosowsky (2018) has aptly illustrated the increased significance of digital technologies in sustaining and transforming language use and in creating new religious practices and identity options. These studies have pointed to the development of more individualised forms of religious expression and the concomitant fragmentation of traditional religious authority and have raised questions regarding what might count as authentic religious practice in the twenty-first century. The focus on more individualised forms of religious expression was explored in Ilankuberan's (2021) longitudinal ethnography of three second-generation British Sri Lankan Hindu Saiva Tamil teenagers engaging with the canon of 1960s Tamil Hindu mythological film. Participants engaged in film viewing with the researcher as an embodied and affective experience. They utilised films as a means to support and enhance their spiritual, theological, and moral development and to express their emergent faith identities in highly personalised and unique ways. The emphasis on more individualised forms of religious expression is in tune with what is sometimes referred to as the 'biographical turn' in ethnography. This turn has also meant the recognition of the importance of biographical experiences in shaping participants' heteroglossic language practices and linguistic repertoires.

While ethnographic research in faith settings has demonstrated the strong link between language and ethno-religious identity (Souza 2016), at the same time, it has alerted language researchers to the socially and culturally situated ways language resources circulate across time, space, and generations. Rather than construing linguistic fixity and fluidity as dichotomous, it has pointed to the need to examine under what conditions and with what consequences participants orient to fixed and fluid language practices to construct their (religious) identities. The analytical focus on the interplay between linguistic fixity and fluidity has coincided with a conceptual shift within sociolinguistics and applied linguistics from a view of languages as discrete and autonomous entities to languages as social and ideological constructs and from a focus on code to a focus on language users, their multilingual repertoires, and biographical trajectories (Heller 2007).

Indeed, there is growing consensus among language researchers of the analytical value of a view of language as resource, part and parcel of participants' full communicative repertoires, online and offline (Busch 2012). This rethinking of repertoire departs from Gumperz's (1964) original formulation of linguistic repertoire tied to membership in relatively stable speech communities. Instead, global conditions of migration and new communication technologies may allow (or constrain) participants in moving between various more or less short-term group formations across the lifespan. This conceptual shift has further alerted us to the unequal distribution of knowledge and access to linguistic and other communicative resources within and across multilingual settings, religious settings being one such case; to issues of power and control, competing language ideologies and language hierarchies, the privileging of particular linguistic resources and their speakers, as well as of particular roles and identity ascriptions over others. These topics can provide fruitful avenues for future ethnographic research at the intersection of language, literacy, and religion too, as ethnographers seek to capture the complexity and unpredictability of contemporary everyday communication as well as new and more established (religious) identity options.

Acknowledgements

Author note: A special thanks to the participating children and their families for sharing their religious experiences, practices, and beliefs, and to my co-researcher, Arani Ilankuberan, for her insights into the data analysis.

3.5   References

Avni, S. (2012). Translation as a site of language policy negotiation in jewish day school education. *Current Issues in Language Planning*, 13, 76–104.

Baquedano-López, P. (2016). Socialisation into religious sensation in children's Catholic religious instruction. In V. Lytra, D. Volk, and E. Gregory (eds.), *Navigating Languages, Literacies and Identities: Religion in Young Lives* (pp. 71–84). New York: Routledge.

Baquedano-López, P. (2000). Narrating community in doctrina classes. *Narrative Inquiry*, 10(2), 429–52.

Blommaert, J., and Jie, D. (2010). *Ethnographic Fieldwork: A Beginner's Guide*. Bristol: Multilingual Matters.

Busch, B. (2012). The linguistic repertoire revisited. *Applied Linguistics*, 33, 503–23.

Coates, E., and Coates, A. (2006). Young children talking and drawing. *International Journal of Early Years Education*, 14(3), 221–41.

Damico, J. S., and Hall, T. (2014) The cross and the lynching tree: Exploring religion and race in the elementary classroom. *Language Arts*, 92(3), 187–98.

Fader, A. (2009). *Mitzvah Girls: Bringing Up the Next Generation of Hasidic Jews in Brooklyn*. Princeton, NJ: Princeton University Press.

González, N., Moll, L. C., and Amanti, C. (eds.). (2005). *Funds of Knowledge: Theorizing Practices in Households, Communities, and Classrooms*. Mahwah, NJ: Lawrence Erlbaum Associates Publishers.

Gregory, E., and Lytra, V., with Ilankuberan, A., Choudhury, H., and Woodham, M. (2012). Translating faith: Field narratives as a means of dialogue in collaborative ethnographic research. *International Journal of Qualitative Methods*, *11*(3), 196–213.

Gregory, E., Lytra, V., and Ilankuberan, A. (2015). 'Divine games and rituals: How Tamil Saiva/Hindu siblings learn faith practices through play.' *International Journal of Play*, *4*(1), 69–83.

Gregory, E., and Ruby, M. (2011). The 'insider/outsider' dilemma of ethnography. Working with young children and their families. *Journal of Early Childhood Research*, *9*(2), 162–74

Gumperz, J. J. (1964). Linguistic and social interaction in two communities. *American Anthropologist*, *66*, 137–53.

Hammersley, M. (2018). What is ethnography? Can it survive? Should it? *Ethnography in Education*, 13(1), 1–17.

Hammersley, M., and Atkinson, P. (1983). *Ethnography Principles in Practice*. London: Routledge.

Heath, S. B. (1983). *Ways with Words: Language, Life and Work in Communities and Classrooms*. Cambridge: Cambridge University Press.

Heller, M. (2009). Doing ethnography. In L. Wei and M. Moyer (eds.), *Blackwell Guide to Research Methods in Bilingualism and Multilingualism* (pp. 249–62). Malden, MA: Blackwell.

Heller, M. (2007). Bilingualism as ideology and practice. In M. Heller (ed.), *Bilingualism: A Social Approach* (pp. 1–22). New York: Palgrave Macmillan.

Hymes, D. (1996). *Ethnography, Linguistics, Narrative Inequality: Toward an Understanding of Voice*. London: Francis and Taylor.

Ilankuberan, A. (forthcoming 2021). British Tamil Teenagers Navigating Faith Literacies and Identities Through Religious Film. Unpublished PhD Thesis. Goldsmiths, University of London.

Kenner, C., Kwapong, A., Choudhury, H., and Ruby, M. (2016). Supporting children's learner identities through faith: Ghanaian Pentecostal and Bangladeshi Muslim communities in London. In V. Lytra, D. Volk, and E. Gregory (eds.), *Navigating Languages, Literacies and Identities: Religion in Young Lives* (pp. 213–26). New York: Routledge.

Long, S. (2016). Conclusion. In V. Lytra, D. Volk, and E. Gregory (eds.) *Navigating Languages, Literacies and Identities: Religion in Young Lives* (pp. 227–33). New York: Routledge.

LeBlanc, R. J. (2017). Literacy rituals in the community and the classroom. *Language Arts*, *95*(2), 77–86.

Lytra, V., Gregory, E., and Ilankuberan, A. (2016) Children's representations of the Temple in text and talk in a Tamil Hindu/Saiva faith community in London. In V. Lytra, D. Volk, and E. Gregory (eds.), *Navigating Languages, Literacies and Identities: Religion in Young Lives* (pp. 141–158). New York: Routledge.

Lytra, V., Gregory, E., and Ilankuberan, A. (2017). Researching children's literacy practices and identities in faith settings: Multimodal text-making and talk about text as resources for knowledge building. In M. Martin-Jones and D. Martin (eds.), *Researching Multilingualism: Critical and Ethnographic Perspectives* (pp. 215–28). Abingdon: Routledge.

Lytra, V., Volk, D., and Gregory, E. (2016). Introduction. In V. Lytra, D. Volk, and E. Gregory (eds.), *Navigating Languages, Literacies and Identities: Religion in Young Lives* (pp. 1–17). New York: Routledge.

Ochs, E., and Capps, L. (2002). Cultivating prayer. In C. Ford, B. Fox, and S. Thomspon (eds.), *The Language of Turn and Sequence* (pp. 35–55). Oxford: Oxford University Press.

Patiño-Santos, A. (2019). Reflexivity. In K. Tusting (ed.), *The Handbook of Linguistic Ethnography* (pp. 213–28). Abingdon: Routledge.

Rosowsky, A. (ed.). (2018). *Faith and Language Practices in Digital Spaces*. Bristol: Multilingual Matters.

Rosowsky, A. (2008). *Heavenly Readings: Liturgical Literacy in a Multilingual Context*. Clevedon: Multilingual Matters

Rogoff, B. (1990). *Apprenticeship in Thinking. Cognitive Development in Social Context*. Oxford: Oxford University Press.

Sarroub, L. (2005). *All American Yemeni Girls: Being Muslim in a Public School*. Philadelphia, PA: University of Pennsylvania Press.

Schieffelin, B. B., and Ochs, E. (1986). Language socialisation. *Annual Review of Anthropology*, *15*, 163–91.

Scribner, S., and Cole, M. (1981). Unpackaging literacy. In M. Farr Whiteman (ed.), *Writing: The Nature, Development and Teaching of Written Communication* (pp. 57–70). Hillsdale, NJ: Lawrence Erlbaum.

Souza, A. (2016). Language and religious identities. In S. Preece (ed.), *Routledge Handbook of Language and Identity* (pp. 195–209). New York: Routledge.

Souza, A., Barradas, O., and Woodham, M. (2016). Easter Celebrations at home: Acquiring symbolic knowledge and constructing identities. In V. Lytra, D. Volk, and E. Gregory (eds.), *Navigating Languages, Literacies and Identities: Religion in Young Lives* (pp. 39–55). New York: Routledge.

Street, B. V. (1984). *Literacy in Theory and Practice*. New York: Cambridge University Press.

Vygotsky, L. S. (1978). *Mind in Society: The Development of Higher Psychological Processes*. Cambridge, MA: Harvard University Press.

Wasser, J. D. and Bresler, L. (1996). Working in the Interpretive Zone: Conceptualising Collaboration in Qualitative Research. *Educational Researcher*, *25*(5), 5–15.

4 Narrative

Zayneb E. S. Al-Bundawi

4.1 Background, History, and Key Terms

We tell stories all the time. When you ask someone if they remember the first time they met their partners or how they come to know each other, how they felt when they had their first child, or how they survived the COVID-19 crisis, usually stories will emerge as answers to these questions. We live by stories: we tend to narrate them whenever we have the chance to do so. Narrating stories does not take place in a vacuum; it occurs when we communicate with others. The terms 'narrative' and 'story' may be used interchangeably, though Halverson, Goodall, and Corman (2011, p. 1) make a distinction between them seeing a narrative as formed by a group of stories and a narrative as 'not a single story, but a collection of stories, and a collection is systematic because the stories are components that relate to one another with coherent themes, forming a whole that is greater than the sum of its parts'. This idea is shared by Elleström (2019, p. 35) who views a story as 'the scaffolding core of a narrative ... represent[ing] events that are temporally interrelated in a meaningful way'. Stories can be narrated in different ways, so the same story may be interpreted differently depending on the context in which it occurs. Stories can also differ for several reasons, like who our audience is, the sociocultural position we occupy or the phase of life we are in. Metaphorically speaking, narratives are TV screens that we watch and the stories are the pixels forming these screens.

Labov and Waletzky (1967[1997]) investigate stories structurally, arguing that a typical story consists of the following components:

1. Abstract: The abstract summarises the story and it usually occurs at the beginning of the narrative. Abstracts give us the essence of the upcoming story and prepare the listener for what to expect next. Abstracts sometimes are presented by clauses like: '*Did I ever tell you about the day I fell from a boat?*' or '*Something funny happened the other day*' (De Fina and Georgakopoulou, 2012, p. 28).

2. Orientation: Orientation provides background information in relation to the 'when', 'where', and 'who' questions, (i.e. it provides information regarding the setting and characters involved in the story).

3. Complication: Complication is the main action of the story and according to De Fina and Georgakopoulou (2012, p. 29) it 'represent[s] the main body (skeleton) of a narrative, i.e. the basic events around which the story revolves.' Usually past-tense verb forms are used within this section.

4. Resolution: The resolution is the outcome of the events reported in the complication. Resolution often answers the question: 'What finally happened?' or 'How did it end?'

5. Coda: The coda is a statement that shows the closing of the story and offers a link to the present time. Due to the coda's linking function, narrators 'can refer to the present effects of the events told in the story, follow a character's evolution after the story has ended, or offer a moral lesson' (De Fina and Georgakopoulou, 2012, p. 29).

6. Evaluation: An evaluation is a statement 'that tell[s] the listener what to think about a person, place, thing, event, or, more globally, the entire experience described in a narrative' (Minami, 2015, p. 79). Evaluation answers the 'So what?' question or 'Why this story was narrated/told?'

Although this model has been criticised by a number of scholars (for example, Schegloff, 1997) for neglecting the interactional aspect of stories, it does have some advantages because it offers a description of a narrative and its constituents that helps us label a text as narrative and provides an important tool in the analysis of narrative as it assists 'to locate the narrator's beliefs and attitudes in a story' (De Fina, 2003, p. 48).

Going back to narratives and their functions, Deppermann (2013) argues that 'narratives provide particularly powerful resources for positioning' and De Fina and Georgakopoulou (2012) show how positioning analysis of narrative 'affords an analytical apparatus for linking local telling choices to larger identities'. Through narratives, people take positions toward their past selves or toward others. Bamberg's model of (narrative) positioning, as De Fina and Georgakopoulou (2012, p. 164) indicate, has been adopted in many studies that involve interviews and conversational stories because 'it affords an analytical apparatus for linking local telling choices to larger identities'. Bamberg's (1997) model is composed of three levels which are formulated into three questions as shown in Figure 4.1.

The first level is concerned with the story world and how the characters are positioned in relation to one another in that world. According to Bamberg (2009, pp. 139–40), the first level focuses on 'analyzing the *way* the referential world is constructed, with characters (self and others) emerging in time and space as protagonists and antagonists' [emphasis in original]. In other words, at this level, an attempt is made to explore how characters are construed within the story events; are they agents, targets, protagonists, or antagonists? The second level is concerned with the storytelling world and the interaction that takes place between narrators and their interlocutors, that is, how they position

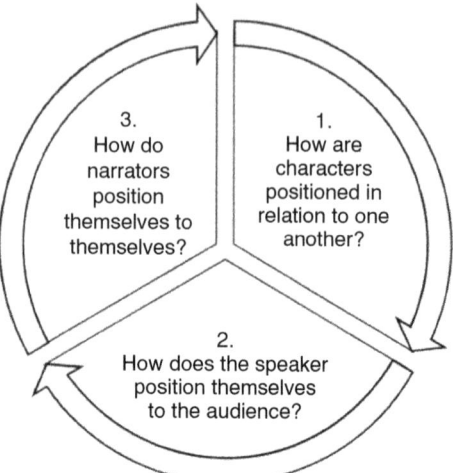

Figure 4.1 Questions about storytelling

themselves to them. The second level takes into consideration what the purpose of the narrative is in this setting and how it is co-constructed by both the narrator and the audience. The third level is concerned with the social/moral and how narrators define themselves, or in Bamberg's (1997, p. 337) words 'how do narrators position themselves to themselves?' (i.e. how narrators define themselves in relation to master/global narratives). This suggests that the third level works by connecting the first two levels, which are related to the narrated events in the here and now of the storytelling situation to speakers' ways of making sense of their identities within wider terms of understanding as provided by global macro discourses.

It is important to note that the first two levels of positioning are not separate from the third one but rather they are connected to each and by analysing them we will reach the construction of identity which is manifested clearly in the third level:

By positioning the characters at the content plane with regard to one another, the speaker positions him/herself with regard to the listener; and this process works simultaneously the other way around. The coordination between these two planes results in the establishment of a moral position for which the speaker can be held accountable. (Bamberg, 1997, p. 335)

Applying these three levels to a very well-known story like the Cinderella story would be of help to clarify what these three levels refer to. The plot of this story talks about a beautiful and kind-hearted young girl who lives happily with her father and mother. The mother dies and Cinderella's father remarries a wicked woman who has two wicked daughters. Cinderella's stepmother mistreats her and to Cinderella's agony her father dies and leaves her with her stepmother and the two wicked stepsisters who treat Cinderella as a servant and work on humiliating her by all available means. Cinderella's life changes when she attends a ball where she meets the charming prince who falls in love with her and after some twists they are meant for each other. The characters involved in this plot are many but some, like Cinderella, the prince, the stepmother, and stepsisters, are characters positioned as protagonists and antagonists, or main and secondary characters. The plot and the positioning of the characters within the story world come under level 1. The interaction that takes place within this story, that is, interactions between those characters and the way they position themselves to their interlocutors comes under level 2 of Bamberg's model. For example, a parent may tell the story of Cinderella to their child to highlight the importance of personal character and perseverance in the light of difficulty. Moving to level 3, the Cinderella story itself has become a master narrative, at least in Western communities, in which kindness and good deeds achieve victory over malice and wickedness. While narrating the Cinderella story, the context within which this story is narrated will assist on deciding on how the narrator positions themselves in relation to master narratives. If the story is told to a child with the aim of entertaining them, then the narrator will take on the role of an entertainer. But even choosing the Cinderella story over another children's story will be indicative of the way this person defines themselves. The Cinderella story encompasses the idea of hope, among many other ideas/ themes, so choosing it could indicate that the narrator is an optimist rather than a pessimist, for example.

De Fina (2013, p. 58) describes the third level as a 'middle ground' between micro and macro approaches of analysis; it is a middle ground because it 'allows for linking local talk and identities with socio cultural processes and relations that surround and have an impact on the local interaction in more or less direct ways'. The links between the local level of interaction and the global/ideological level can be made by taking into consideration patterns that occur in the data. The way in which an individual views an issue may be common among other members of the community and might indicate common positioning uses.

Master narratives, mentioned under the third level of positioning, are 'socially accepted associations among ways of using language, of thinking, valuing, acting, and interacting' (Gee, 1999, p. 17). In a similar vein, Bamberg (2005, p. 287) defines 'master narratives' as a term that refers to 'pre-existent socio-cultural forms of interpretation'. Both definitions emphasise the social aspect of the master narratives being accepted and circulated within a community. They achieve this level of being master/global by being circulated through means like official documents, the media, or daily conversations. Their circulation increases until they become invisible and acquire the status of being 'taken-for-granted as "Truth"' (McKenzie-Mohr and Lafrance, 2017, p. 191). The plural form of the word 'narrative' associated with the term 'master' suggests that there is not only one master narrative but usually a set of widespread narratives. Narrators are not always expected to comply with the master narratives circulated within a community because they can agree with, disagree with, or display neutrality toward them (Bamberg, 2004).

4.2   Key Topics, Questions, and Debates

Through narratives, people construct their identities and by analysing narratives we can have a clearer image of these identities. Narratives represent the ground upon which identities are constructed (De Fina, 2003; De Fina et al., 2006). Johnstone (1996: p. 56) argues that 'the purpose of narrating is precisely the creation of an autonomous, unique self in discourse.' In a similar vein, Bamberg (2004, pp. 358–9) indicates that 'by offering a narrative, the speaker lodges a claim for him/herself in terms of who he/she is'. Narratives offer the speakers the platform through which they can show their identities and are therefore important sites of identity work for religious believers, particularly in talking about their experience of the divine and the supernatural in their day-to-day life.

At the time of speaking/narrating, the construction of identity emerges and is negotiated with the speaker's interlocutors. The speaking context involved in this chapter is the interview setting so the negotiation of identities that takes place happens between the interviewee/narrator and the interviewer. The study of narrative shows then that there is, in a sense, no 'objective' narrative. The speaker and audience are always interacting to construct the narrative and this can occur in active interaction or implicitly as the speaker takes into account their actual and imagined audiences.

The role of listeners in the co-construction of narratives is emphasised by narrative analysts. Coates (2001, p. 82) argues that '[t]he terms "narrator" and "audience" set up a false picture of an active story-teller and a passive group of listeners, whereas the reality is that co-participants (the audience) are always co-authors in some sense'. Similarly, Lucius-Hoene and Deppermann (2000) state that the presentation of stories in interview settings is always done *with* the interviewer particularly in situations that involve stories requiring recalling memories. Thus, the listener/audience can be a narrative co-author in two ways: when the interviewer contributes to the storytelling by listening, paying attention, backchannelling and using nonverbal signs; and when the narrator pays attention to and responds to the listener/interviewer. On one hand, the narrator would have an idea about what the listeners prefer or what interests them. On the other, the narrator themselves would have an aim behind this narrative in relation to the specific audience which would have an influence on the design of the narrative (Lucius-Hoene and Deppermann, 2000).

The co-construction of narratives is potentially then a problematic area for religious language and teaching, particularly where there is an expectation that a text or teaching is divinely inspired or the word of God. While analysts may look at narratives told in or about religious and sacred texts from a narrative perspective, religious believers themselves may hold different beliefs about those texts and the parameters for retellings, interpretations, or translations of those stories. Narratives based on some religious texts might expand or extrapolate on different points with the texts or reimagine or retell the stories in different ways. Or believers might argue that the stories cannot be retold or reimagined because they are without error in their original telling and can only exist in one form.

Beliefs about master narratives are also important in analysis of religious narratives because believers might have very clear ideas of how right and wrong, good and evil interact in the world and the stories that they tell are often explicitly influenced by those beliefs. In particular, when those beliefs about right and wrong are derived from sacred texts which often have in them narratives about religious believers or divinely inspired characters or God, the development of narratives of day-to-day life can implicitly and explicitly draw on these stories to make sense of the actions and beliefs of particular people.

Religious believers often gather in communities as well, both in formal ritual settings and in informal settings. These communities of religious believers together often share particular ways of speaking about the world, drawing not only on their shared beliefs, but also on their own localised experiences of being believers in a particular place and time. Different religious communities will tell different stories of their experiences depending on their position in society and the extent to which their own belief system is accepted as a part of the broader social context or if they are subject to persecution or discrimination or marginalisation within the broader cultural context. Minority sects within religions can also have different stories that are told within their community that might contrast with the dominant stories told by the more powerful or influential.

Deciding on which master narratives are referred to by interlocutors and their links with the local level of interaction is not easy. De Fina (2013) therefore encourages adopting ethnography to investigate the nature and role of particular master narratives in particular communities. By carrying out ethnography, one can understand better the master narratives that are invoked by the local narratives. Despite this encouragement, Deppermann (2013, p. 84) warns that resorting to ethnography should not be interpreted as 'a call for resorting to cultural discourses "known" to be relevant by the researcher' but rather to those that are relevant to the participants. Master narratives are therefore so accepted and consumed by a community that they go unnoticed and this makes reaching them difficult without ethnographic support. The analyst must therefore be aware of the ways stories develop from and within these narratives and work to make sense of meanings of narratives on the different levels from which they emerge.

4.3   Case Study

On the plains of Karbala, a city in southern Iraq, in 680 AD, Hussein, the grandson of the Prophet Muhammad and the third Shi'i Imam for Twelver Shia, who believe in twelve imams, was killed in a fearful battle along with seventy-three people of his family and companions (see Ayoub, 1978). The martyrdom of Hussein at the hands of the ruling Caliph Yazid in the battle of Karbala is not a mere historical event for Shi'i Muslims but rather a milestone. Hussein and Yazid were rivals over leadership of the Muslim community. According to Aghaie (2005, p. 44) 'Yazid was portrayed as morally corrupt, religiously impious, and politically oppressive. Hussein, on the other hand, was represented as pious, just, and capable'. Hussein is remembered from that battle on and his memory is commemorated year after year. The commemoration takes place mainly in Muharram and Safar, the first two months of the Islamic calendar. This commemoration works, as Mirshahvalad (2019, p. 13) writes, as 'a centuries-long leitmotif that connects the Shi'as' past and present and operates as their identity source'. For Blomfield (2010), this commemoration works on bringing cohesion and solidarity within the Shi'i community. Rituals associated with this commemoration are practiced by Shi'i Muslims; one of those rituals is the holding of *majales*, 'lamentation assemblies where the stories of the martyrs of Kerbala are recited for the evocation of grief' (Takim, 2005, p. 195). People who attend and participate in these *majales* are reminded of what happened to Hussein in that fearful battle and in that way they find solace because whatever they encounter in life would not be as hard as the calamities Hussein had to endure. Also, by being exposed to such texts, the participants of those *majales* feel close to Hussein and to the Prophet's holy family.

Various texts are employed within the *majales'* religious discourse. Texts like the Quran, the story of the battle of Karbala, the sermons, the speeches given by people within these *majales*, and the laments are all linked up to Hussein, his martyrdom, suffering, and sacrifice. Dealing with these texts in separation from their context would create a great loss of meaning. In addition to this, separating these texts from their context would be difficult to achieve. Thus, undertaking and adopting an ethnographic approach was a plausible solution. Adopting such an approach will assist in studying how the aforementioned texts are incorporated into the lives of Shi'i Muslim women who live in diaspora.

How those texts are taken up, circulated, and employed in the everyday lives of the participants, and how they take up those texts and discuss them, how they address me and tell me narratives that have the Karbala story's flavour, how they represent themselves and make sense of their lives through telling stories related to Karbala and Hussein is the focus of this research. Specifically, I am looking at how religious texts embedded in rituals are incorporated into the lives of Shi'i women who live in the UK, that is, how this supposed 'Shi'i diasporic' identity is constructed and perhaps maintained in a non-Muslim community and what roles these texts play in these women's lives. I therefore spent the months of Muharram and Safar in two successive years, 2014 and 2015, participating in the *majales*, observing the rituals and conducting interviews with the women involved in the rituals held in an Islamic Centre in the city of Cardiff in Wales.

The ethnographic fieldwork adopted in collecting the data for this study includes a number of ethnographic methods: participant observation; audio-recording the sermons and rituals; and two types of interviews – focus groups and semi-structured interviews. All these methods are supplemented by extensive field notes. The interviews were conducted with a small group of women – those who were participating in the rituals and showed willingness to be interviewed. The interviews enabled me to explore with my participants the ways in which sacred texts informed their daily lives and provided examples of the use of sacred texts in identity work within the interviews themselves. Interviews are of use when open-ended questions require further follow- up questions and when it is difficult to get information regarding a certain topic in any other way.

Sixteen semi-structured interviews, along with many informal conversations, were conducted with the women who participated in the rituals. The interview context encouraged the participants to come up with narratives in answer to some of the questions posed by the interviewer/researcher, particularly when the questions themselves were in narrative mode; narratives emerge when the participants are defining who they are. Parallel narratives in particular have been employed – narratives which are personal accompanied by parallel religious narratives related to the Karbala story. Narratives will be analysed to show how the women of this study define themselves to the interviewer and to themselves (often in collaboration with the interviewer), through the narratives they tell and the way they tell them within the interview setting.

All the interviews were supported by ethnographic notes and observations. In the following, I show two narrative extracts derived from interviews with two participants: Amira and Walaa. Amira is a Computer Science PhD student from the city of Karbala in Iraq, while Walaa is a pharmacist, accompanying her husband who is a Mechanical Engineering PhD student, who also comes from Karbala. For both women, their stay in Cardiff is temporary and bound to their study or their spouses' study in university.

In the first extract, Amira is responding to a question about whether she considers not attending the *majales* held in Cardiff because she comes from the city of Karbala and she is well informed and acquainted with the story of the Karbala battle which is almost always repeated in each one of the *majales*.

Extract 1 Amira's Narrative

 1 **AMIRA:** we go through different situations
 2 for example concerning- the other day I went through a bad situation
 3 because I felt worried about my brother
 4 so whenever I hear the story [the battle of Karbala story]
 5 I say
 6 may Allah help her [Zayneb, Imam Hussein's sister]
 7 how she endured all this pain
 8 and how she managed (.)
 9 while for me he [her brother] just got ill
10 and stayed in bed
11 and I couldn't help it
12 **INTERVIEWER:** yeah
13 **AMIRA:** after this [incident] as if it's the first time
14 in which I hear the story of Lady Zayneb
15 there're certain incidents
16 you wouldn't feel the calamity of Lady Zayneb
17 unless you go through similar situations
18 **INTERVIEWER:** right
19 AMIRA: you'd really feel her suffering
20 **INTERVIEWER:** uhmm
21 **AMIRA:** whenever I hear her story
22 I feel her pain
23 and how she may Allah help her endured all these calamities
24 while for me I couldn't endure
25 that my brother stayed in bed
26 how about her and her brother's head was cut off (.)
27 in comparison with her mine is nothing

Two stories are combined in the extract above: one is personal while the other is religious. In the personal story, Amira's brother is ill and she is concerned about his well-being. Going through this experience makes Amira think and she compares her mitigated situation with that of Zayneb, Hussein's sister, which is so severe. The comparison results in a change in the way Amira looks at Zayneb and how she appreciates her courage. The religious story talks about Zayneb and the way she survived a very difficult situation and stayed strong. Zayneb witnessed the killing of her brother, Hussein, in the Karbala

Table 4.1 *Amira's matrix narrative*

Abstract	we go through different situations (line 1)
Orientation	for example the other day I went through a bad situation (2)
Complication	I felt worried about my brother (3)
	he just got ill (9)
	and stayed in bed (10)
	I couldn't help it (11)
Resolution	after this [incident] as if it's the first time (13)
	in which I hear the story of Lady Zayneb (14)
Evaluation/Coda	whenever I hear her story (21)
	I feel her pain (22)
	and how she endured all these calamities (23)

battle and she managed to survive it. Zayneb's situation is much harder than that of Amira.

The personal narrative can be labelled as the matrix narrative which talks about Amira and what she went through when her brother got ill. Following Labov and Waletzky's (1967/1997) model, this narrative can be analysed as shown in Table 4.1:

In this matrix narrative, no information is given to us about Amira's brother except that he was ill and because of this illness he had to stay in bed. Amira uses the phrase 'my brother'; this brother's name is not mentioned at all in the narrative. The use of this phrase is significant because it shows the strong relationship that connects Amira to her brother and that she loves him. It is like the use of the same phrase in the embedded narrative when she talks about Zayneb, Hussein's sister. From a narrative perspective, the use of this phrase positions Amira as the main character and her brother as a secondary character to her in the narrative. Amira is construed as a weak person, someone who cannot endure the calamities of life when they touch upon one of her family members, her brother. Amira is a sensor because she 'felt' worried and 'went' through a bad situation.

The religious/embedded narrative talks about Zayneb and her brother Hussein. This narrative can be analysed as shown in Table 4.2:

The religious/embedded narrative violates the rules of linear narration and it is told in reverse order. This way of narration indicates the sense of familiarity with this religious story. It is so well known for Shi'i Muslims that it is told in reverse, minimum details are given, and the characters names are not all given, yet it is still understood by both interlocutors. Hussein's name is not given, just as in the previous matrix narrative. From a level 1 perspective, this positions Zayneb as the main character in the story and shows the strong relationship that links her to her brother Hussein. She is the one who not only witnessed the

Table 4.2 *Amira's embedded narrative*

Evaluation/Coda	whenever I hear the story [the battle of Karbala story] (4)
	I say (5)
	God help her (6)
Resolution	she endured all this pain (7)
	she managed (8)
	she endured all these calamities (23)
Complication	her brother's head was cut off (26)

brutal killing of her brother but she endured and stayed strong. Zayneb is construed as a strong person, someone who endured calamities. Zayneb is an active person, someone who 'endures' pain and difficulties and this is evident in the repetition of the resolution and the verb 'endured', juxtaposed with the tragic and cruel act of beheading reported as the sole complicating action in this narrative. Zayneb was exposed to a very hard situation – her brother was killed – but she endured pain and managed.

From a level 2 perspective, Amira, in this embedded narrative, is construed as a sympathetic person, someone who would feel sympathy towards others. Amira is also a sensor here because she 'heard' the story and 'felt' Zayneb's pain. Zayneb is a strong woman but Amira had not appreciated how strong she was, likely because she had not gone through the same situation. Amira might have respected Zayneb before for purely religious reasons; she is a Shi'i so she might have had an intuitive appreciation for her. Amira is comparing her situation with that of Zayneb. They are both women who have brothers who were in bad situations. The fact that Amira chose Zayneb in particular to compare herself with is significant from a level 3 perspective. Amira takes Zayneb as a role model from whom she learns patience. Also, being passive here might suggest that Amira wants to present herself as a kind sister who is attached to her brother. Family relationships, in terms of the sister–brother relationship, are found in both the matrix narrative and the embedded narrative.

The parallelism and the interweaving of the personal and religious stories, as in the aforementioned extract, shows how *majales* texts (Zayneb's story in this extract) are used as exemplars for the participants and become interwoven into their own personal lives. Through this extract, Amira is juxtaposing the everyday world and the religious world that is advocated in the *majales* and it also shows how Amira uses the *majales* and the Husseini stories told there to reflect on her own life and to emulate what she hears in them. Participating, listening, and remembering the Karbala story has brought out change in the participants' lives, a change that came from reflecting and learning.

In another narrative extract, Walaa responds to a question that asks if Walaa, as a woman, feels more sympathy towards the men or the women in the Karbala battle:

Extract 2   Walaa's Narrative

1   **INTERVIEWER:** you as a woman do you sympathise more with the women or with
    the men characters
2   **WALAA:** you mean in Al-Taff epic [another name of the Karbala battle]
3   **INTERVIEWER:** yes I mean
4   I'm sure now-
5   I think
6   you'd say
7   that you sympathise with Imam Hussein
8   because he (.) he (.) we can say
9   he is the key person (.) in Al-Taff battle
10 but you as a woman do you sympathise more with men or with women
11 when you hear their story
12 **WALAA:** every session has a different discussion
13 which means
14 I can't see or hear a lamenter laments Hussein (.)
15 and imagine Hussein
16 how he fought
17 and how he fell on the battle ground
18 and not to feel sad (.)
19 at the same time I can't help not to feel sad
20 when I hear
21 that Zayneb was mistreated
22 how they burnt down her tents
23 how she took responsibility of the children
24 and she is the one
25 who wasn't seen [by strange men before] (.)
26 for four years in Kufa no one has seen her (.)
27 when she used to go to visit her grandfather's tomb
28 her father would turn the lantern off (.)
29 this means no one has seen her
30 then she is taken captive from one country to another walking distances bare-footed,
    hungry, thirsty, wearing her abaya [full-length outer black garment] with no veil
31 so no (.) no one understands a woman but a woman like her (.)
32 no one would feel a woman's suffering but a woman like her

Walaa's extract contains three stories interwoven together. The extract contains two parallel matrix narratives: one is related to Hussein and the other to his sister, Zayneb, at the time of the Karbala battle which took place in 680 AD. Hussein fought what was known to the interlocutors as the Karbala battle, and he was killed in that battle (lines 16–17). Zayneb, at that battle, was mistreated, her tents were burnt down, and she had to take care of children (lines 21–3). Both interlocutors are familiar with the Karbala story, so they both are aware that the 'tents' here refer to the tents used by Hussein and his family and companions in their camp; and that the 'children' were Hussein's children and the children of his other family members and companions who accompanied him in this battle. Zayneb, by the end of this battle and after Hussein's death, was taken captive by Hussein's enemies (line 30).

Walaa embeds another narrative about Zayneb in this second narrative (lines 24–8). The embedded narrative is also about Zayneb but at an earlier time. Walaa narrates how Zayneb lived and behaved when she was with her father in Kufa, a city in southern Iraq when her father was the ruling Caliph there (from 657-661AD). In Kufa under her father's rule, Zayneb lived in seclusion and away from the eyes of strange men. Her father was so protective that when she wished to visit her grandfather's (the Prophet Muhammad's) grave, her father would take her at night and he would turn the lantern off so that no one would see her (lines 24–8).

The three stories are all told in a linear sequence. Although there might be some missing divisions, there are no violations to the linear sequence of the divisions suggested by Labov and Waletzky's (1967[1997]). The extract relies on shared knowledge possessed by the interviewer and the interviewee. Walaa is aware that the interviewer is a Shi'i, so she is comfortable omitting certain details. She does not refer to the Karbala battle explicitly; 'the battle ground' (line 17), 'the tents' (line 22), and 'the children' (line 23) are all mentioned with no further explanation relying on the interviewer's knowledge of the Karbala battle's story. Walaa is familiar with Shi'i literature and by her omissions she presupposes that the interviewer has the same knowledge. By relying on this shared knowledge, Walaa is building rapport with the interviewer which positions her as a fellow Shi'i.

From a level 3 perspective, Walaa comes up with three stories – two are related to the Karbala battle while the third is related to a time prior to that battle, She

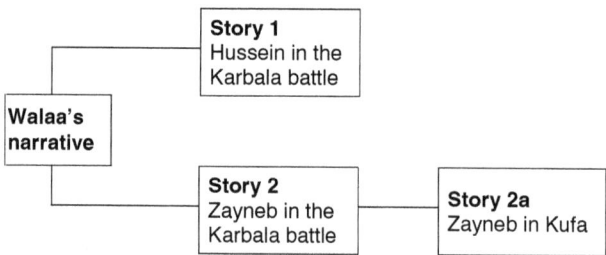

Figure 4.2 Walaa's Narrative

narrates these without giving full details relying, as mentioned, on her interlocutor's knowledge. At the same time, by narrating in this way, Walaa defines herself as a knowledgeable woman; someone who is acquainted and familiar with the Shi'i literature. Being familiar also assists Walaa in defining herself as a pious woman who is keen on attending *majales* and thus exposed to the Karbala narratives.

In sum, the stories that people tell about their own lives can embed sacred texts and stories, and understanding narratives in religious interaction requires attention to the functions of both the participant's experience and their attempt to understand it in terms of a larger story. This shows how storytelling and master narrative are crucial for making sense of life in religious communities and developing pious identities.

4.4   Future Directions

From a language and religion perspective, narratives about sacred texts like those analysed in this chapter are particularly good sites for further research because they involve a number of texts, the Quran, the sermons, the speeches and the laments; each one of these texts has its role and importance within the rituals. These rituals are particularly important when considering groups like Shi'i Muslims or Shia, who form a minority within the Islamic world and in the diaspora, thus they have a status of 'double minority' (Scharbrodt, 2011). Double minority groups, like Shi'i Muslims in the UK or Orthodox Jewish communities in the USA, are generally underrepresented and underexplored. Analysis of discourse around rituals like those commemorating the Karbala battle sheds light on community rituals, practices, and values that might be difficult to access in other contexts. The interaction between narratives from religious or sacred texts and their retelling in community contexts has the potential to reveal how hermeneutic activity can be part of day-to-day life.

Code-switching within religious communities and practices presents a rich area of study in relation to narrative: looking at the significance of this switching, its function and the reasons behind it can be elaborated to have a clearer image of minority and/or diasporic communities. In the case of this study, the use of Arabic and the occurrence of code-switching (which has different manifestations in the context under study) offers important insights about how multiple codes enable speakers to address different audiences and how each code is associated with different values, histories, etc. Studying how and when code-switching occurs in narratives, and in this case, switching between Arabic and English, has the potential to further illustrate how children in diasporic contexts are incorporated into the rituals and familiarised with the practices.

Code-switching is also an important site for narrative when it occurs between dialects; for example, in order to bring the audience to tears, the reciter of laments and poems in the *majales* changes the tone of his voice. Many preachers and people who deliver sermons follow this strategy. From my observations, the audience (since the majority of them are Iraqis) are much moved when the reciter uses the Iraqi dialect in his laments even if he is not an Iraqi. This same idea was expressed by Deeb (2005), whose study of *majales* and *masirat* (processions) in modern Lebanon made a distinction between 'traditional' Ashura and what she calls an 'authenticated' Ashura: she states that reciters tend to use the Iraqi dialect in their laments because the Iraqi dialect is, as one of her informants says, 'the dialect of compassion and longing' (Deeb, 2005, p. 254). All of my participants chose to speak Arabic and the Iraqi dialect, in particular. This choice was justified by stating that the discussion of matters related to the Husseini *majales* and religion would be more appropriate in a language that would help them express themselves fully. They are all fluent speakers of English, but they were worried that they might run out of words or expressions in the middle of discussing a particular issue. However, choosing Arabic over English and the Iraqi dialect over Standard Arabic (SA) did not prevent the participants from code-switching. At some points, they shifted from the use of Arabic into English and from Iraqi dialect to SA. Further study of the dynamics of this, particularly in religious narratives, is likely to further illustrate how language, religious identity, and narrative intersect.

Collaboration among researchers between religion scholars and language scholars is also important, particularly in considering religious narratives where sacred texts are involved. The Quran was revealed to the Prophet Muhammed in Arabic and thus Arabic has acquired the status of being a sacred language for Muslims. Exact translations of the Quran are hard to find and the translations available are closely related to the interpretation of the Quran rather than the language of it, which is highly refined and poetic. Poetic language is also found in the laments read in the *majales*; these laments get harder to translate if the colloquial language or dialects are used in them. Sacred texts, language/dialect, context, and translation all need to be taken into consideration when working with religious communities and gatherings. What was of great help when I worked with my participants is the fact that I am an Iraqi Shi'i Muslim woman. Being Iraqi helped in understanding the dialect, being Shi'i helped in understanding the rituals, and being a woman helped in understanding the viewpoints of the participants. In other words, being an 'insider' helped to a certain extent. For other researchers who are 'outsiders' and would like to study a community similar to the one mentioned in this study, it would be highly recommended to take these points into consideration.

The aspects of narrative and particularly solidarity, community-building, and liminality, are all rich aspects of interest to social sciences scholars. The *majales* held in diaspora offer the participants the opportunity to be united with fellow Shi'is, even if they are total strangers. *Majales* assist in establishing solidarity and community building in diasporic spaces. By sharing mourning and commemoration rituals with other women, the women of the current study work on creating ties of solidarity with each other and with other Shi'i Muslims who practise the same rituals; that is, they help in creating an 'imagined [Shi'i] community' (Anderson, 1983). They are also creating ties of solidarity with the Prophet and his family through which they can express their loyalty to the Holy Family. Further research into these narratives in Shi'i communities would certainly help researchers better understand interaction between sacred texts and local contexts. Moreover, the same research methods and approaches could be applied to other diasporic, minority communities, looking, for example, at the role of stories and code-switching between Hebrew, Yiddish, and local languages in Jewish communities.

Gatherings and communities of practice of religious communities are rich sites where narrative analysis can reveal important aspects of religious identity particularly among members of diasporic religious communities. They can be liminal spaces in which identities are protected to some degree and maintained sometimes. Hybrid identity work is created; identities that do not belong fully to either of the two places yet have features of both produced at the same time. In this study, the participants were keen on practising the same rituals that they have used to practise in Iraq, but they were ready to modify them to suit their new environment. The Islamic Centre in Cardiff has worked as a liminal space where the participants can meet up and practise their rituals away from the outside, foreign surroundings and is, in some sense, a refuge point which reminds them of home and origins and at the same time helps to maintain their identities as Shi'i Muslims. In the same way, other sites of religious community expression and solidarity – in Muslim, Jewish, Christian, or Buddhist communities – in other contexts could be important sites for further work by religious language scholars interested in the role of narrative in building and developing community and individual identity in diasporic contexts.

The analysis of a sample of the Shi'i Muslim women's narratives in this study shed light on the practices of those women in a diasporic community, and suggests that research into narrative in religious language requires an in-depth understanding of the religious communities in which those narratives are occurring. This analysis and similar analyses might assist in bridging community relations because they show a different picture of Islam and potentially other religious communities that are misunderstood in contexts where they are the minorities. Shi'i Islam, like other minority religions, are ill represented in the media where the focus can be on controversial practices. Analyses of the role of language and ritual could then help in, the study of minority religions and their different branches in the West, with a particular focus on migrants and migration studies and underrepresented communities. By combining studies of narrative in ritual with a focus on community identity, fuller pictures of these communities will emerge.

4.5   References

Aghaie, K. S. (2005). The origins of the Sunnite-Shi'ite divide and the emergence of the Ta'ziyeh tradition. *The Drama Review, 49*(4), 42–7.

Anderson, B. (1983). *Imagined Communities: Reflections on the Origin and Spread of Nationalism*. London: Verso.

Ayoub, M. (1978). *Redemptive Suffering in Islam: A Study of the Devotional Aspects of Āshurā in Twelver Shi'ism*. The Hauge: Mouton Publishers.

Bamberg, M. (1997). Positioning between Structure and Performance. *Journal of Narrative and Life History, 7*(1–4), 335–42.

Bamberg, M. (2004). Considering counter narratives. In M. Bamberg and M. Andrews (eds.), *Considering Counter-Narratives: Narrating, resisting, making sense* (pp. 351–71). Amsterdam and Philadelphia: John Benjamins Publishing Company.

Bamberg, M. (2005). Encyclopedia entries on 'Agency', 'Master Narratives', and 'Positioning'. In D. Herman, M. Jahn, and M. L. Ryan (eds.), *The Routledge Encyclopedia of Narrative Theory*. London: Routledge.

Bamberg, M. (2009). Identity and Narration. In P. Hühn, J. Pier, W. Schmid and J. Schönert (eds.), *Handbook of Narratology* (pp. 132–43). Berlin: Walter de Gruyter.

Blomfield, B. (2010). From ritual to redemption: Worldview of Shi'a Muslim women in Southern California. In Z. R. Kassam (ed.), *Women and Islam* (pp. 303–24). Santa Barbra: Praeger.

Coates, J. (2001). 'My mind is with you': Story sequences in the talk of male friends. *Narrative Inquiry, 11*(1), 81–101.

Deeb, L. (2005). From mourning to activism: Sayyedeh Zaynab, Lebanese Shi'i women, and the transformation of Ashura. In K. S. Aghaie (ed.), *The Women of Karbala: Ritual Performance and Symbolic Discourses in Modern Shiᶜi Islam* (pp. 241–66). Austin: University of Texas Press.

De Fina, A. (2003). *Identity in Narrative: A Study of Immigrant Discourse*. Amsterdam and Philadelphia: John Benjamins Publishing Company.

De Fina, A. (2013). Positioning level 3: Connecting local identity displays to macro social processes. *Narrative Inquiry, 23*(1), 40–61.

De Fina, A., Schiffrin, D., and Bamberg, M. (2006). *Discourse and Identity*. Cambridge: Cambridge University Press.

De Fina, A., and Georgakopoulou, A. (2012). *Analyzing Narrative: Discourse and Sociolinguistic Perspectives*. Cambridge: Cambridge University Press.

Deppermann, A. (2013). How to get a grip on identities – in-interaction: (What) does 'Positioning' offer more than 'Membership Categorization'? Evidence from a mock story. *Narrative Inquiry, 23*(1), 62–88.

Elleström, L. (2019). *Transmedial Narration: Narratives and Stories in Different Media*. New York: Palgrave Macmillan.

Gee, J. P. (1999). *An Introduction to Discourse Analysis: Theory and Method*. London: Routledge.

Halverson, J. R., Goodall, H. L., and Corman, S. R. (2011). *Master Narratives of Islamist Extremism*. New York: Palgrave Macmillan.

Johnstone, B. (1996). *The Linguistic Individual*. Oxford: Oxford University Press.

Labov, W., and Waletzky, J. (1997[1967]). Narrative analysis: Oral versions of personal experience. In J. Helm (ed.), *Essays on the Verbal and Visual Arts*, (pp. 12–44). Seattle and London: University of Washington Press.

Laceulle, H. 2018. *Aging and Self-Realization: Cultural Narratives about Later Life*. Bielefeld: Transcript Verlag.

Lucius-Hoene, G., and Deppermann, A. (2000. Narrative identity empiricized: A dialogical and positioning approach to autobiographical research interviews. *Narrative Inquiry*, *10*(1), 199–222.

McKenzie-Mohr, S., and Lafrance, M. (2017). Narrative resistance in social work research and practice: Counter-storying in the pursuit of social justice. *Qualitative Social Work*, *16*(2), 189–205.

Minami, M. (2015). Narrative, cognition, and socialization. In A. De Fina and A. Georgakopoulou (eds.), *The Handbook of Narrative Analysis* (pp. 76–96). Chichester: Wiley.

Mirshahvalad, M. (2019). Ashura in Italy: The Reshaping of Shi'a Rituals. *Religions*, *10*(3), 200.

Scharbrodt, O. (2011). Shaping the public image of Islam: The Shiis of Ireland as 'moderate' Muslims. *Journal of Muslim Minority Affairs*, *31*(4), 518–33.

Schegloff, E. (1997). Narrative analysis 30 years later. In M. Bamberg (ed.), Oral versions of personal experience: Three decades of narrative analysis. *Journal of Narrative and Life History*, *7*(1–4), 97–106.

Takim, L. (2005). Charismatic appeal or communitas? Visitation to the shrines of the Imams. In P. J. Stewart and A. Stratheen (eds.), *Contesting Rituals: Islam and Practices of Identity-Making* (pp. 181–203). Durham: Carolina Academic Press.

5   Multimodality

Sarah Turner

5.1   Background, History, and Key Terms

While language may be the first thing that comes to mind when we think of 'discourse', religious or otherwise, it is not the only tool that we have at our disposal to communicate our messages. Take, for example, a Christian church service. Language clearly plays a very important role in the communication taking place in such an event, but there are other ways that particular meanings and messages are communicated, too: the music of the hymns; visual symbols and iconography such as candles, the cross, or images of Christ; the physical actions of standing, kneeling, or taking the sacrament; or even the use of clothing in the liturgical vestments that may be used. Like language, each of these practices is *communicative*, being used to convey particular meanings, and like language, these meanings are understood by members of the communities in which they are found. As discourse analysts, we can consider each of these practices in much the same way as we do language, analysing each one for what it brings to the communication going on in a particular event. Such an analysis is known as *multimodal discourse analysis*.

Multimodal discourse analysis (see Kress, 2009; Kress & Van Leeuwen, 2001, for a broad overview) works on the principle that we have many tools, or 'modes', at our disposal to communicate our messages, and each has its own particular affordances and constraints; things that it allows us to do well, and things that it does not allow us to do so easily. Preaching a sermon, for example, is probably most reliably achieved through spoken or signed language, and not through the modes of image or dance! In undertaking a multimodal discourse analysis, we analyse the role of these different modes and what they can bring to the message. We do not normally consider the modes to be working in isolation, however; a multimodal analysis of the aforementioned hypothetical Christian church service would not only focus on, for example, the role of music (although this would be a very interesting analysis to do in its own right). Instead, a multimodal discourse analysis focuses on how several different modes work together to convey meaning in a particular way, and what each contributes to the overall message.

Multimodal discourse analysis has been applied to a very wide range of communicative events, and a brief look at these also gives an insight into the range of different modes that can be analysed. For example, Bourne and Jewitt (2003) used a multimodal analysis of gesture, gaze, movement, and posture in a secondary school English-literature classroom to explore how teachers developed strategies to help their students connect with the texts they were studying in a deeper way. Online interaction, too, is notoriously multimodal (Sindoni, 2014), with internet users drawing on a range of communicative resources such as writing, speech, video, music, and images in the form of emoji, photos, and memes to convey meaning. Website designers are particularly sensitive to the way particular choices in terms of colour, images, and layout affect the way in which meaning is communicated. Moran and Lee's (2013) research into cosmetic surgery websites demonstrated how such multimodal choices encouraged cosmetic procedures, through pathologising normal, 'unmodified' bodies, normalising modification, and presenting cosmetic surgery as an easy option. Offline, even the use of physical space, for example, in the context of museum exhibitions, can be analysed from a multimodal perspective, as demonstrated in Meng's (2004) analysis of *From Colony to Nation*, an exhibition in Singapore detailing Singapore's history. Meng analyses the layout of the exhibition, along with the objects and photographs presented in it and the language of the displays, showing how these modes are brought together to construct a particular ideology and promote a particular view of historical events.

Meaning making, then, is achieved through more than just language. Multimodal discourse analysis can shed light on how communicative modes other than spoken or written language, when used in conjunction with these, can serve a range of communicative functions and facilitate communication. For religious discourse, this is especially interesting when we consider the range of modes at play in religious communication and practice. I introduce three here: images, music and sound, and movement and ritual. The chapter will then take as its focus one specific movement-based communicative mode: that of gesture.

5.1.1   Images

Religious practice has a key visual component, with most religions throughout history comprising some form of visual imagery (Moore, 1977). This may be due in part to the fact that images have the power to present a familiar, recognisable view of a figure or concept where written sources may not provide one (Morgan, 1999). Images of Christ, for example, portray Him in a way that is instantly recognisable, despite the fact that His appearance is never described in the New Testament (Morgan, 1999, p. 1). Such recognisable images may also serve as symbols through which believers may construct and articulate their beliefs in community with others, and may also form part of devotional practice (Morgan,

1999, 2005). Images have the power to stimulate an emotional response, to focus devotion, and to fix and immortalise transient religious experience into a form that can be revisited (Moore, 1977). In some religious traditions, visual images and artefacts become a means through which worshippers can communicate directly with the Divine. Take, for example, the Hindu *darshan*: 'the ritual act of seeing and being seen by the deity, an encounter that occurs within the gaze of a statue or image in the temple or at a shrine' (Morgan, 2005, p. 48). Such images may be seen as symbolic devices, acting as a focus for devotion and meditation, or may be seen as constituting the very deity the image depicts (Morgan, 2005), but the importance of the visual is clear.

The choice and layout of artefacts and statues can also convey key concepts from a religious tradition's worldview. In Buddhist temple art, for example, large statues of gate or threshold guardians (*dvarapala*), often armed and threatening, guard the entrances to sacred areas. In the Buddhist tradition, these figures represent physical desire and fear, the two temptations holding us back from nirvana. Interestingly, analogous figures are found in other religious traditions; the cherubim who guard the Tree of Life in the Garden of Eden in the Old Testament (Genesis 3:22–24), and the 'Spirit Bringers' (*ethkaynaáshi*) found in Navaho sand paintings, who open the way into sacred areas (Campbell, 2002, p. 49).

5.1.2   Music and Sound

There is a close relationship between music and religion, with music finding a place in almost every religious tradition. As Ellingson (2005, p. 6248) notes,

Navajo priests are 'singers'; the primary carriers of Sinhala traditional religion are drummers and dancers; and the shamans of northern Eurasia and Inner Asia use music as their principal medium of contact with the spirit world. Through the centuries, priests, monks, and other specialists have sung the Christian masses, Buddhist pujas, Islamic calls to prayer, Hindu sacrifices, and other ceremonies that form the basis of organised religious observances in the world's major religions.

Music may serve an organisational function in religious practice, in particular used to demarcate time. For example, the use of music may signify the beginning or end of a particular practice, or highlight a particular element of it. The tempo of music may be manipulated to create perceived compression or expansion of time, while a building in intensity may precede the climax of ritual practice. A return to a previous musical motif may symbolise a return to a previous moment, idea, or concept (Ellingson, 2005). This quality of music, characterised by repetition and return, has been considered a metaphor for a cyclical understanding of birth, life, and death, allowing music itself to symbolically demonstrate the ideas of transcendence, resurrection, and rebirth held in esteem by many of the world's religions (Engelhardt & Bohlman, 2016, p. 24).

5.1.3   Movement and Ritual

There is a vast body of literature devoted to the study of ritual, in which 'it becomes quickly evidence that there is no clear and widely shared explanation of what constitutes ritual or how to understand it' (Bell, 1997, p. ix). Following Zuesse (2005, p. 7834), however, we can define ritual for our purposes as 'those conscious and voluntary, repetitive and stylised symbolic bodily actions that are centered on cosmic structures and/or sacred presences' – the body becoming a 'vehicle for religious experience'. At their heart, rituals can be considered examples of multimodal communicative events, encompassing a range of communicative modes including image, music and sound, and physical movement such as dance, gesture, or the adoption of particular postures.

Ritual behaviours, like the individual modes that constitute them, are communicative. Take, for example, the ritual of baptism found in Christian practice, in which one 'descends into a pool of water and emerges from the other side spiritually cleaned, committed, and "made new"' (Bell, 1997, p. 36). The physical act of baptism constitutes a symbolic 'washing clean' from sin, and a metaphorical renewal, but it also signifies to those in attendance that such a shift has taken place, and that the individual who has been baptised has now taken their place among the children of God. The Baptism service followed by the Church of England may include the words 'Today God has touched you with his love and given you a place among his people', making this new role explicit. Posture can similarly communicate meaning, such as the deferential postures required by Islamic formal prayer, the act of bowing to the shrine in Buddhist *puja*, or the act of kneeling to receive the sacrament in the Christian Eucharist. In these ways, adherents both enact and demonstrate their submission to their object of worship.

The final movement-based communicative mode to be introduced here is gesture, which will constitute the focus of the rest of the chapter. Gesture itself is a familiar concept which arguably needs no definition, but for the purposes of clarity, it is worth identifying what constitutes a 'gesture' when it is being used as a communicative mode, and what does not. Here, we can turn to Kendon, who defines gesture as a 'visible action when it is used as an utterance or as a part of an utterance' (Kendon, 2004, p. 7), later elaborating to categorise gestures as 'actions that have the features of manifest deliberate expressiveness' (Kendon, 2004, p. 15). McNeill (2016, pp. 4–5) proposes a caveat to Kendon's definition, that one cannot assign *deliberate* status to a gesture; it is not the goal of a speaker to gesture per se, but to communicate, in which gesture may play a role, but from these definitions we can establish a clear working definition of gesture. Gestures are visible bodily actions which are *communicative*; they convey some meaning, either by themselves, or in conjunction with another communicative mode (normally speech). Other bodily movements that may take place during conversation, such as scratching an itch, smoothing one's hair, or adjusting one's clothing are rarely considered communicative and are not therefore the subjects of gesture analysis (Kendon, 2004, p. 8). Gesture can be considered a *mode*, and can therefore be analysed as part of a multimodal discourse analysis in conjunction with other communicative modes.

Because we use gestures for a range of communicative purposes, there are a number of corresponding types of gesture. Different gesture scholars vary somewhat on the terminology they assign to these gesture types, as reviewed and summarised by McNeill (1992, p. 76). However, the different gesture classification schemes proposed over the years are all 'basically the same', sharing a common ancestor in a particular classification devised by Efron in 1941 (McNeill, 1992, p. 75). The scheme I outline here was developed by McNeill and is particularly well-suited to those starting out in gesture analysis as it does not rely on fine subdistinctions between the different gesture types. However, as we will discuss later, it is up to the analyst to develop a methodological framework that most accurately suits their needs.

The first distinction to be made is between *representational* and *beat* gestures. Representational gestures can be 'defined as gestures that depict action, motion, or shape, or that indicate location or trajectory' (Kita, Alibali & Chu, 2017, p. 245). *Beat* gestures, on the other hand, are those which are synchronised with the rhythm of the speech, and do not appear to relate to the content of what is being said (McNeill, 1992, 2016). They may, however, serve a pragmatic function through highlighting and emphasising particular parts of the message (McNeill, 2016, p. 8).

Representational gestures can be further divided into three subtypes: iconic, deictic, and metaphoric (McNeill, 1992). An *iconic* gesture is one which relates closely to the meaning of the speech it accompanies; an account of pulling back a bowstring, for example, may be accompanied by a gesture miming such an action. *Deictic* gestures are 'pointing' gestures, used to 'point' to things; often abstract concepts having been metaphorically given physical locations. If you were to say 'Now *that's* what I'm talking about!' accompanied by a finger pointing gesture on *that*, you would be performing a deictic gesture.

Like iconic gestures, *metaphoric* gestures are also 'pictorial'. However, instead of representing a literal action that corresponds to what is being talked about (drawing back the bowstring in a discussion of shooting a bow, for example), metaphoric gestures present concretised representations of an abstract concept. At this point, it would be useful to take a step back and introduce a key text in the field of metaphor research. In 1980, Lakoff and Johnson wrote their seminal text *Metaphors we Live By*, in which they introduced their *conceptual metaphor theory* (Lakoff & Johnson, 1980). Metaphor had long been considered a creative rhetorical embellishment, a way of orna-menting and embellishing language. Lakoff and Johnson, however, argued that metaphor represented a fundamental part of human language and cognition. Indeed, they argued, we can engage with and express abstract concepts because we are able to relate them, through metaphor, to more physical, familiar, tangible experiences. Time is often talked about in terms of money; we can *spend*, *save*, or *waste* it, or even *invest* it in pursuits in the hopes of reaping the rewards later on. Ideas are often talked about as if they were physical objects (an instance of a widespread phenomenon of figurative thought known as *reification*) – often edible objects, at that. You may need to take some time to *digest* a concept, for example, you may even find it *difficult to swallow* until you *chew on it* a little more. Perhaps it was just *half-baked* in the first place! Metaphorical expressions such as these are often found in language. The metaphor may not seem particularly obvious when we talk about *giving* someone an idea, or *getting something across* to someone – but these meta-phorical phrases may be physically enacted in gesture through physically 'offering' an idea to a listener. This would be an example of a metaphoric gesture.

5.2   Key Topics, Questions, and Debates

5.2.1   Gesture, Language, and Thought

McNeill (1992, p. 11) uses a musical metaphor in his account of gesture, stating that gesture 'orchestrates' speech. Gestures may not always occur, but when they do, they are used to elaborate on what is being said, and even at times 'exhibit images that cannot always be expressed in speech' (McNeill, 1992, p. 11). Historically, speech has been considered to take a prime position in communication, with gesture seen as an 'add-on', relegated to the realms of embellishing and emphasising what is being said (McNeill, 2016). However, empirical evidence leads us to conclude that language and gesture cannot be separated; indeed, gesture and speech are united, both being instrumental in conveying a speaker's intended meaning (McNeill, 2016, p. 3).

However, not only do gestures provide meaning in themselves, but the use of gestures has also been shown to aid a speaker in communicating linguistically. According to Kita's (2000) 'Information Packaging Hypothesis', the use of gestures helps speakers to organise their messages into 'packages' suitable for sharing verbally. It does this by engaging *spatio-motoric* thinking, that is, cognition relating to movement and spatial awareness. This provides an alter-native method of organising information that is not available when engaging solely in *analytic* thinking (the default mode engaged in speaking). When these two 'modes' of thinking (i.e. spatio-motoric and analytic), coordinate and converge, the speaker acquires more ways of organising their thoughts in ways that are suitable for linguistic expression.

Another key affordance of gesture is its ability to *schematise* information, 'deleting or stripping away some elements of a representation, and maintaining others' (Kita et al., 2017, p. 257). This allows speakers to focus on particular parts of a concept or object, frees up cognitive resources for other tasks due to its 'lightweight' nature, all while allowing for change, development, and elaboration of the message.

Experimental studies have provided evidence for these theories, through demonstrating that people produce more gestures if the message to be conveyed is not easily stated linguistically. From a psycholinguistic perspective, gesture can be considered the physical, observable manifestations of mentally simulated actions (Hostetter & Alibali, 2008); we gesture because we are simulating a particular action in our minds. According to this model, a gesture occurs when the activation of the premotor cortex caused by this simulation spreads to the motor cortex, a point known as the 'gesture threshold' (Hostetter & Alibali, 2008). We see evidence for this in experimental studies that demonstrate that when describing the size and shape of an object, gestures are likely to be used more frequently (Kita et al., 2017), as speakers mentally simulate physically handling the object. The same applies to more abstract concepts, too. Speakers 'explore' in gesture when they struggle to put their ideas into words, providing evidence for the idea that gesture provides access to different parts of the conceptual system (Kita et al., 2017) and helps people to conceptualise their messages more fully.

Gesture, therefore, represents a link between what we say and what we think. It helps us to formulate our messages and may even express further meaning over and above what we express linguistically. It is reasonable to suggest, therefore, that the analysis of gesture can provide insight into how individuals think about and conceptualise particular topics and concepts.

5.2.2   *Metaphor, Gesture, and Religious Discourse*

We have already seen above that gestures can express abstract concepts, and that 'metaphoric' gestures constitute a part of McNeill's (1992) classification system. However, as Cienki (2008) notes, much of the original work on metaphoric gestures focused on gestures demonstrating the conduit metaphor. This metaphor refers to how ideas are often spoken about as if they are objects that can be transferred from one person to another in communication, giving rise to phrases such as 'it's hard getting these ideas across' (McNeill, 1992, p. 147) or 'I didn't get much out of the lecture'. However, conduit gestures are not the only form of metaphoric gesture. The use of gesture has been analysed to shed light on the way speakers metaphorically conceptualise such abstract concepts as the passage of time (Calbris, 2008), mathematics (Núñez, 2008), numbers (Winter, Perlman & Matlock, 2013), and grammar (Mittelberg, 2008).

Gesture can also provide insights into how the speaker is conceptualising what they are discussing. Müller (2009) notes that even highly conventional-ised metaphors can be accompanied by gestures that seem to enact the literal meanings of these gestures. In other words, gesture can shed light on the extent to which a metaphor, expressed linguistically, is being processed as a metaphor in the mind – how much the 'metaphoricity' of a particular expression has been activated (Müller, 2008, p. 221). Such an insight has clear implications for metaphor research in helping to uncover the extent to which metaphors are activated in thought, thus telling us something about the nature of metaphor and how it functions in the mind – but unless we are also metaphor researchers, this might not be so interesting to us as religious discourse analysts. What we can take away from Müller's message, however, is that gesture may also tell the analyst something about the very way speakers are conceptualising and framing the topics they are talking about, as McNeill (1992) proposes.

Such an insight is particularly interesting when analysing religious dis-course. Metaphor, as Dorst (Metaphor chapter) notes, is frequently used to conceptualise and express abstract concepts, as it is the mechanism by which we can talk about the abstract more easily by relating it to the concrete and the familiar. Metaphor is often seen as a way of talking about internal, emotional phenomena, especially when these are considered highly significant for the speaker, and our analysis of such metaphors can yield useful insights into an individual's lived experiences of these phenomena; see, for example, analyses of metaphors used in accounts of end-of-life care (Semino et al., 2017), cancer (Gibbs & Franks, 2002), pregnancy loss (Littlemore & Turner, 2019), and anorexia (Skårderud, 2007). Metaphor can thus be considered an important phenomenon in discourse which deals, as religious discourse so often does, with the abstract, the poetic, and the ineffable.

Religious belief is an internal, cognitive phenomenon, but it draws on deep-seated social constructs and may potentially involve a belief in an external entity (which may, perhaps paradoxically, also live *internally* in the believer). Within religious discourse, we are likely to see a convergence of the concrete and the abstract, the literal and the metaphorical; what is a metaphor for one individual may be highly literal for another, or even considered pure fantasy, depending on their belief system. This potential complexity is also reflected religious experience. An individual's religious belief may be predicated on internal experiences of what they consider to be 'divine', which are often spoken of in highly metaphorical terms, even though the experiences them-selves may be literal for the person experiencing them. Metaphor, in this respect, is not a static phenomenon, but rather a dynamic quality which grows up out of the discourse in which it is found, and can mean different things to different conversational participants (Jensen, 2017). Gesture, as we saw above, can add another layer, potentially providing an insight into the way an individual conceptualises what they are talking about, over and above the linguistic content of their message.

Gesture has been shown to connect internal experiences of belief with external reality, for example, in Makboon's (2013) looking at dharma orientation lectures of the I-Kuan-Tao cult in Thailand. Makboon showed how different gesture types were used to convey abstract religious concepts such as the 'soul' and 'nirvana'. As she explains, the participant, Natakrit, believes himself to have been chosen by the gods to help break sentient beings out of the continuous cycle of death and reincarnation, thus freeing them from suffering and helping them to achieve nirvana. Through metaphoric gestures, Makboon argues, Natakrit demonstrates his conviction that such concepts as the cycle of reincarnation are 'real'. His use of deictic gestures, too, demonstrates a belief that locations such as 'heaven' are tangible, physical locations that can be referred to through pointing. It is through the use of metaphoric gestures that Natakrit is able to give physical reality to these abstract concepts. For Makboon, such gestures demonstrates Natakrit's conviction in what he is saying.

Evola (2010a) has also explored how two religious believers communicated about abstract religious concepts, such as God, heaven, good, and evil. He grounds his analysis in a number of pervasive metaphors in religious thought: good is up/bad is down; the idea of 'moral accounting' which gives rise to such ideas as Christ 'paying the debt' of sin; and metaphors for God as being a strict father or nurturing parent. He explores how two Christian interview respondents draw on these concepts in ways that related to their own personal experiences of the world, and how their gestures and elicited drawings contribute to their communication of these messages. Evola (2010b) also compares the gestures used by a Christian and a Satanist, demonstrating how the two employ very different gestural systems to indicate their different relationships with the idea of God. He argues that multimodal analysis – comprising speech, gesture, and drawings – can be used as a powerful tool to 'paint a more complete picture' of an individual's religious beliefs and attitudes (Evola, 2010a, p. 57).

5.3   Case Study

The study from which these findings are taken was designed as a small pilot study for a larger work. In it, I wanted to investigate the role of gesture in conversations about religious belief (or lack thereof), and explore areas of systematicity in the use of particular gesture types.

In this study, ten people participated in 5–10 minute interviews, although these were designed to have as little researcher input as possible. They were given the following information in advance:

During the session, we will ask you talk about:
- *Your religious or spiritual beliefs (or lack thereof)*
- *How you perceive the concept of 'God'/what 'God' means to you*
- *The process through which you developed these convictions*
  You'll be encouraged to talk about these things but you will not be interrupted, questioned, or asked to justify or defend your answers at any point.
  You may like to spend a little time thinking about what you might like to say in advance, but please do not prepare a speech or bring in notes!

The sessions took place in a quiet location, and were video-recorded. Participants were also asked to fill in a brief questionnaire in which they selected the religion with which they identified, if any, and also assigned a numerical value to the strength of their conviction, and the importance of their believes in their day-to-day lives. The interviews were transcribed and the video recordings of the interviews were annotated for gesture.

As Mittelberg (2008, p. 119) notes, there is as yet no unified, agreed-upon methodology for gesture coding and analysis. With this in mind, it falls to the analyst to develop an analytical framework that best serves their research purposes. However, in coding gestures, the following pieces of information are usually necessary:

1. Hands. This includes handedness (i.e. left or right), the shape of the hand, the orientation of the hand, and the location of the hand in the gesture space;
2. Motion. What trajectory is the hand tracing, and in what direction? Where in the gestural space is the motion taking place? (McNeill, 1992, p. 81; Mittelberg, 2008, p. 121)

From these pieces of information, as McNeill (1992) notes, the analyst can then identify the potential meaning of the gesture, and what it may represent. In this project, I focussed on *representational* gestures (be they iconic, deictic, or metaphoric).

For this chapter, I will look at just two participants, exploring the way they use gesture to talk about the way they see God and their relationship with Him. It should be noted that different faith traditions may conceptualise God as being female or agender and may also capitalise the pronoun used to refer to God. In keeping with the Christian beliefs of the two participants under discussion here, I follow the convention of referring to God as Him here. I hope to demonstrate that the participants use gesture in different ways, and that these gestures can be said to reflect their different conceptualisations of God. However, some common themes in their use of gesture also emerged, which were noted across the whole dataset.

The two participants under discussion here are Robert and Esther (both pseudonyms). Both are Christians, both self-define as having very strong levels of conviction in their religious beliefs, and both say their faith plays a very important role in their day-to-day lives. Robert is a member of the Church of England, while Esther is a member of a Charismatic/Evangelical church. I focus on specific extracts from their transcripts, and for our purposes here I consider the following elements of gesture:

- Hand height in gestural space
- General hand shape: whether the hands are open or closed
- Any movement in gestural space, and its directionality

Robert

We look first at the following extract from Robert's transcript.

Logically I would justify my faith by saying that I believe life has a purpose, and in order for life to have a purpose I think there has to be something greater than humanity which gives life its purpose. And ... that's my identification of God, so, erm, not in an anthropomorphic way but as what is greater than humans ... There is an internal logic to Christianity ... It's about understanding human life, a religion that has incarnation at the heart of it: God becoming human.

How do I perceive God? Well that's part of the challenge of Christianity as well ... the idea of the trinity, that you have three persons in God, and you know, there is a tradition of imaging God the Creator which goes back a very, very long way, and is surprisingly monochrome.

For me, trying to work out what faith is about is the strong element of reason followed by the possibility of a revelation in a way.

1. Logically I would justify my faith by saying that I believe life has a purpose.

Robert uses a low, lap-level gesture to talk about his logical justification ('I would justify my faith') (see Figure 5.1). His hands are palm-up in front of him, as if he were holding a physical object. This is quite a conventional 'reification' metaphoric gesture; he is presenting his beliefs, an abstract concept, as a physical object that can be held. He then raises this gesture to talk about his more abstract beliefs as he begins 'I believe'. This first section of the extract demonstrates a potential link between gesture height and the level of abstraction of what is being discussed.

The next part of the sentence ('in order for life to have a purpose I think there has to be something greater than humanity which gives life its purpose') sets up another pattern found in the data, in which it seemed that an open-handed gesture correlated with a more abstract topic under discussion. Here, Robert is

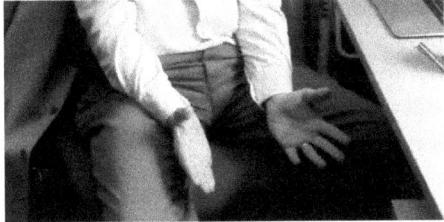

Figure 5.1 Justify my faith

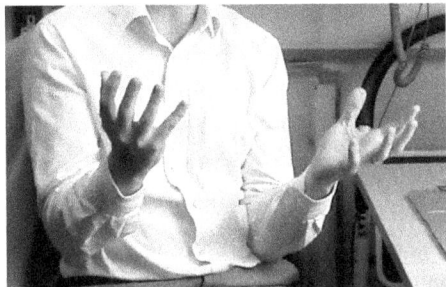

Figure 5.2 My identification of God…not in an anthropomorphic way

gesturing with his right hand only; his left hand is resting in his lap. Humanity, being more concrete and tangible, is accompanied by a closed fist, whereas the abstract 'something greater' is represented by an open hand. When he talks about 'giving life its purpose', this open hand also metaphorically enacts the 'giving' as Robert moves his hand forward, as if offering the listener an object.

2. That's my identification of God, so, erm, not in an anthropomorphic way but as what is greater than humans …

Here, Robert is using both hands to gesture once more (see Figure 5.2). His 'identification of God' is accompanied by an open-handed gesture, palms up, at chest level – similarly to the gesture he used to talk about his beliefs in the first section. This enables him to set up an interesting gestural comparison between his identification of God, and humanity; that God is 'what is greater' than humanity. As he says the words 'as what is greater than humans', he begins by bringing both his hands together, fists closed, before opening out the gesture to be more expansive and open-handed, analogous to the gesture he uses when talking about his identification of God. In doing this, he sets up a gestural opposition between humanity (closed fists, small, and contained) and God (expansive, wider, and less contained).

3. There is a tradition of imaging God the Creator which goes back a very, very long way and is surprisingly monochrome.

Here, again, the gestures seem to relate to the abstract or concrete nature of what is being said. With this section, Robert begins by using just his right hand to gesture, resting his left hand in his lap. On the word 'tradition', he uses a closed fist to represent a conception of tradition as being more concrete and less abstract. As he begins to talk about 'imaging', however, Robert uses both hands, opening them out and moving them away from his body, perhaps indicating that he sees the imaging as more abstract. From this space, 'God the creator', is accompanied by a large, expansive gesture, with his open hands, palms up, moving in a circular motion away from his body as he seems to metaphorically 'feel his way' around this far more abstract concept.

4. For me, trying to work out what faith is about is the strong element of reason followed by the possibility of a revelation in a way.

The final extract from Robert's transcript introduces another gestural theme which we touched upon earlier; that of more abstract concepts being lower down in the gestural space. The action of 'working out what faith is about', with its strong links to logic and reason, is accompanied by a gesture that is quite literally 'grounded'. His left hand comes to rest flat on the desk beside him, raising to hover above the surface when he mentions the more abstract 'possibility of revelation'. What is particularly interesting here is that Robert is also looking at his hand. Directing the gaze at something has strong interactive implications, in which the speaker is encouraging their listener to direct their attention to the same topic (Müller, 2008). This seems to mirror Robert's attitudes towards his faith – that it is most important that it has strong foundations in logic and reason, and he wishes the listener to attend to this point accordingly.

5.3.1   Esther

In the extract from Esther's transcript, she is describing the Pentecost festival, and the changes it brought to the idea of a relationship with God within the Christian tradition. We will see that Esther's gestures seem to mirror this shift in the way God's relationship with His people is being conceptualised. As she explains in her account, she considers this to be a crucial moment in the history of her faith tradition, and a key factor in her religious beliefs. Interestingly, this was made clear through her gestures just before she began this part of the transcript. When Esther started her interview, she was holding a flask in her left hand. At the moment where she says *if you like, the **times***, she puts this flask down, freeing up both hands for her gestures and possibly signalling the importance of what she is about to say.

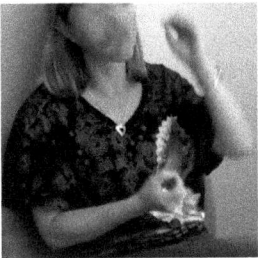

Figure 5.3 Really interacting with His people

5. It's really symbolic in terms of the big narrative of the Bible because it was a way of showing that at this point erm in terms of the, the if you like the times or the periods in which God was, er, really interacting with His people, that it was just no longer God up on a mountaintop talking to one person, it was no longer Jesus in one person being here interacting with disciples, but now it was God interacting directly with each person really individually.

Here, for Esther, the Pentecost festival represents a time when God was *'really interacting with His people'*. This phrase is accompanied by a two-handed gesture (see Figure 5.3). Her right hand is closed, palm-up, around the level of her waist. Her left hand is the same in hand shape but is at the level of her face. As later becomes apparent, the raised left hand represents God, while the right hand represents humanity. It is interesting to note that both hands are closed. Through this, Esther seems to be conceptualising the idea of God as a concrete entity, as real and tangible to her as the humans with which He interacts. This contrasts with her comparison of how God previously interacted with humans, as we will see next:

6. It was no longer God up on a mountaintop talking to one person.

The gesture accompanying 'God up' is quite different to the previous gesture, where God was 'really interacting with His people'. Here, Esther opens her left hand and raises it above the level of her head, palm facing out to her left. This could indicate a far more abstract view of God, and the increased height of the gesture further indicates a certain distancing from what is being said (and, indeed, the people with whom He interacts). As she explains that He was 'up on a mountaintop talking to one person', she uses both hands to create a depiction of a 'mountain' shape, touching her fingertips together at the level of her face. Her use of this 'mountain' shape here may demonstrate that it is of particular salience to the point that she is making; perhaps she wishes to underline the distance between God and His people before Pentecost, and the journeys those who sought to communicate with God needed to take.

7. But now it was God interacting directly with each person really individually.

As Esther talks about 'God interacting directly with each person' here, her accompanying gestures provide an interesting contrast to her previous 'interaction' gestures. Her hands return to their original configuration, with her left hand (representing God) up at the level of her head, and her right hand (humanity) at the level of her waist. At first, the hands are slightly more open. However, here the gesture is dynamic. Both hands move towards each other; humanity, represented by the right hand, is raised as God, represented by the left hand, is lowered, to meet in a middle space. By this, Esther seems to be indicating that God is not the only actor in His communication with His people, and humanity is not a passive recipient of His message. This seems to cohere with the more personal, more individual relationship with God that she considers the occasion of Pentecost to afford. We can see, too, that the hands close as the gesture develops towards the end of the sentence, again demonstrating a more concrete, less abstract conception of the relationship.

As noted previously, gestures also serve pragmatic functions, highlighting key areas of the message and directing the hearer's attention to elements that the speaker deems important. For Robert, his marked gaze at his hand when talking about how his faith should be logical can be taken as an indication that for him, it is logic and rationality that are key components of his faith. For Esther, her use of the 'mountain' gesture draws attention to what she is saying, highlighting it as a key piece of information that should be attended to. Even though she is discussing something that no longer happens – in her narrative God *no longer* speaks to one of His people on a mountain top – her gesture use indicates that it is still a very important point. She highlights it as a way of drawing a comparison between the former methods God used to communicate, and the very personal, individual relationship that she believes the faithful can have with him through Pentecost.

Although we have only briefly touched on two participants, two commonalities have emerged; that of the closed/open-hand gestures, and the height of the gestures used. However, across the ten participants in the study, some further commonalities emerged, which are elaborated upon further in Turner (in preparation). These commonalities can be described in terms of conceptual metaphors, each of which are then enacted through gesture. I include a short description of each here.

VALUES AND BELIEFS ARE PHYSICAL LOCATIONS

Several of the participants in the study produced gestures that indicated that values and beliefs were being construed as physical locations – often a 'ground' or a 'foundation' given that these were produced by flat-handed, palm-down gestures occurring low in the gestural space. We saw this occurring in Robert's transcript, when he talked about a faith grounded in logic and reason with his hand flat on the table. Another participant, having spoken of his beliefs, concluded with the phrase 'I suppose that's where I'd sort of be now', with both hands held flat, palm-down, hovering just above his lap. Such a metaphorical conceptualisation of belief also allowed participants to produce gestures that implied movement towards particular belief systems, while not necessarily wholeheartedly adopting them. As one participant spoke of 'edging towards' a belief, she used a similar flat-handed, palm-down gesture at lap level, but moved one hand out to the side, as if 'feeling her way'. Such gestures may indicate the way people's beliefs are held; as being firm, solid, immovable, or as being concepts to be approached, explored, engaged with dynamically.

CONCRETE, 'HUMAN' IS DOWN, ABSTRACT IS UP

There are a number of linguistic metaphors in English that relate to the idea of more concrete, tangible concepts being 'down' while more abstract concepts are 'up'; one can be *down to earth* and *grounded*, or one can *have one's head in the clouds* or perhaps even be *away with the fairies* (Lakoff & Johnson, 1980). Gesture height seemed to correlate with the conceptual metaphor motivating such linguistic metaphors, with higher gestures indicating more abstract concepts and representations. We saw examples of this metaphor at work in the gestures of Esther and Robert, but another participant in the study gave an interesting example of this in his discussion of God. He said, 'in the concept of God, God seems rather more austere and separate than, you know, benevolent but not, not you know like a mate in that sense'. Throughout this utterance, he was producing a very conventional 'reification' gesture. Both hands were in front of him, palms turned to face each other, as if he were holding a physical object. However, the height of this gesture changed with the different ideas of God he was addressing. From a starting point at around lap level, the gesture rose on 'austere and separate', then fell again on 'benevolent ... not like a mate.' Again, for this participant, a more 'austere' and 'separate' God appears also more abstract.

VAGUENESS IS WIDTH/OPENNESS, CONCRETE IS CLOSEDNESS

As we have seen, there seemed to be a correlation between the openness of the hand and the extent to which the participant was describing something that they considered to be vaguer or more concrete. Again, this correlation was also noted in other participants in the research study. One participant identified herself as 'not at all' religious, but 'very' spiritual, saying, 'I don't label myself as having a certain religion as such ... just a belief in the self or the power of the mind.' She, too, used conventional reification gestures when talking about particular concepts, but again, the closeness or openness of her hands seemed to relate to her attitudes towards the ideas she was discussing. For example, she spoke about how her beliefs were 'more based around physics, than erm, religion, I suppose'. Her conventional reification gestures here were far more closed and contained for 'physics' than for 'religion', as if 'physics' was a

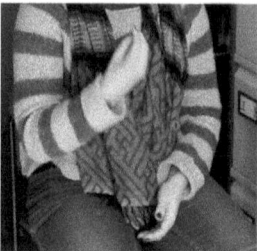

Figure 5.4 The [self]…Chi which is [like the centre core] energy state

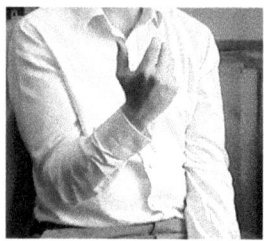

Figure 5.5 There is an [internal logic to Christianity]

smaller, more manageable object for her to hold than religion. Later, she spoke of her belief in 'the self', and in Chi, which she defined as the 'centre core energy state' (see Figure 5.4). In speaking of these concepts, she uses a single closed-hand gesture, perhaps demonstrating her view of these concepts as more tangible. Interestingly, Robert used a very similar gesture when talking about the 'internal logic to Christianity', as shown in Figure 5.5.

DISAGREEMENT IS DISTANCE, AGREEMENT IS CLOSENESS

Participants' gestures were closer to their bodies when they spoke about things they agreed or aligned with, and further away when they did not. In some cases, this even led to metaphoric gestures that mimed 'pushing' concepts away (see Figure 5.6). Such a gesture may provide insight into the strength of conviction a speaker holds about what they are saying.

Conversely, the closed gestures used by the participant when talking about the self and Chi, shown in Figure 5.4, were held close to the body. Physical distance in gesture, therefore, can metaphorically indicate the extent to which the speaker aligns themselves with the concepts under discussion.

Figure 5.6 It just felt like participating in something that is [nothing to do with me]

5.4   Future Directions

Multimodal analysis may shed new light on the ways in which speakers are conceptualising the topics they are addressing in their verbal communication, perhaps also allowing the analyst new insights which may be overlooked in a monomodal linguistic analysis alone. In the two participants introduced here, some commonalities emerged in the way they used gesture to communicate about the concepts under discussion, particularly in terms of whether these were being considered as more or less abstract. This was particularly interesting in the case of Esther's transcript, where the idea of God and His interaction with His people seemed to become more concrete and more tangible following the Pentecost event, as reflected in her use of gesture. In this way, gestures can serve to communicate what these concepts mean for the speaker and how they are being framed.

Deictic and beat gesture analysis might also yield interesting insights into how individuals are structuring their messages and drawing attention to specific parts of them (McNeill, 1992). However, it is also important to take into account the overall gesture profile of an individual, as speakers have their own idiosyncratic ways of using gesture. McNeill observes that this is especially noticeable in the context of metaphoric gestures; speakers may develop their own particular images for abstract concepts, which are then reflected in gesture. Despite this, however, these images share a core of meaning (McNeill, 1992, p. 163). For gesture analysis, therefore, it seems likely that a close analysis of individuals' gesture profiles in comparison with others could help the analyst to identify areas where differences in gesture represent differences in conceptualisation, or differences in gesture use overall.

Gesture analysis can be applied to a range of data and could be insightful in a wider range of contexts. Future research could usefully focus on religious discourse across a range of communicative functions. For example, a gesture analysis of preached sermons could provide interesting insights into how gesture contributes to explanation of abstract theological concepts, or to persuasion if the communication is intended to evangelise. An analysis of gesture in the context of religious ritual could also explore the extent to which gesture communicates alone, or alongside other communicative modes apart from speech (e.g. through sound, image, or scent). In any event, gesture analysis has the power to shed light on a speaker's intended meanings, attitudes, and conceptions. The analysis of gesture, through its ability to provide insight into cognitive processes, could lead to an increased understanding of a speaker's point, and the emotional/evaluative content of their message. Such research may therefore have the ability to facilitate communication between members of different religious communities, promoting tolerance and understanding between those of different faiths.

Multimodal analysis, of course, encompasses far more than just gesture. To conclude, therefore, it is worth returning to some of the communicative modes introduced previously, and reflecting on how multimodal analysis may profitably be applied to religious discourse in future. From a visual perspective, a multimodal analysis could provide new insights into the way image and text come together to convey meaning within the context of sacred texts. Other fruitful avenues of enquiry may involve an analysis into religious imagery and iconography, exploring how these are used to both construct and convey particular religious understandings. For researchers interested in comparative religious studies, such an analysis of images and symbols may even serve to identify common ground between different religions, as demonstrated by Campbell's (2002) example of the Buddhist *dvarapala* and their Judeo-Christian and Navaho counterparts discussed in Section 5.1. Spatially, an analysis of religious architecture could demonstrate the ways in which particular layout choices communicate particular perspectives, similar to Meng's (2004) museum exhibition analysis.

A multimodal analysis of religious ritual practice could provide interesting insights into how spiritual belief is conveyed, not only linguistically but through a conjunction of other modes such as movement, gesture, posture, sound, and image. Music, too, may be analysed as a metaphorical vehicle for the conveyance of meaning in the context of religious practice, in conjunction with other modes.

For those interested in addressing religious communication from a more functional perspective, communicative events such as sermons, testimonies, or proselytising could prove fruitful sources of data. An analysis of such events could demonstrate how a range of different modes are brought together to help to fulfil the overall purpose of that communication, be that information, didactic, or persuasive. Multimodal discourse analysis, therefore, can build upon findings from discourse analysis through exploring the multimodal elements of such events, thus providing deeper insights into their forms and functions.

5.5   References

Bell, C. M. (1997). *Ritual: Perspectives and Dimensions*. Cary, IN: Oxford University Press.

Bourne, J., & Jewitt, C. (2003). Orchestrating debate: A multimodal analysis of classroom interaction. *Reading*, *37*(2), 64–72.

Calbris, G. (2008). From left to right: Coverbal gestures and their symbolic use of space. *Metaphor and Gesture*, *2*, 27–53.

Campbell, J. (2002). *The Inner Reaches of Outer Space: Metaphor as Myth and as Religion*. Novato, CA: New World Library.

Cienki, Alan. (2008). Why study metaphor and gesture? In Alan Cienki & C. Müller (eds.), *Metaphor and Gesture* (Vol. 3, pp. 5–25). Amsterdam; Philadelphia: John Benjamins Publishing.

Ellingson, T. (2005). Music: Music and Religion. In L. Jones (ed.), *Encyclopedia of Religion* (pp. 6248–56). 2nd ed., Vol. 9. Detroit: Macmillan Reference USA.

Engelhardt, J., & Bohlman, P. (2016). *Resounding Transcendence: Transitions in Music, Religion, and Ritual*. Oxford: Oxford University Press.

Evola, V. (2010a). A Multimodal Analysis of Individuals' Beliefs and Metaphors in Words, Gestures and Drawings. In F. Parrill, V. Tobin, & M. Turner (eds.), *Meaning, Form, and Body* (pp. 41–60). Stanford, CA: CSLI Publications.

Evola, V. (2010b). Metaphors, Religious Systems and Multimodal Cognitive Semiotics. Discourse, Gesture and Artwork of Street Preachers and a Satanist (Metafore, sistemi religiosi e semiotica cognitiva multimodale. Discorsi, gestualità e disegni di predicatori di strada cristiani e di un satanista). *Sistemi Intelligenti*, *XXII*, 23–48. https://doi.org/10.1422/31947.

Gibbs, R. W., & Franks, H. (2002). Embodied metaphor in women's narratives about their experiences with cancer. *Health Communication*, *14*(2), 139–65.

Hostetter, A. B., & Alibali, M. W. (2008). Visible embodiment: Gestures as simulated action. *Psychonomic Bulletin & Review*, *15*(3), 495–514.

Jensen, T. W. (2017). Doing Metaphor: An Ecological Perspective on Metaphoricity in Discourse. In B. Hampe (ed.), *Metaphor: Embodied Cognition and Discourse* (pp. 257–76). Cambridge: Cambridge University Press.

Kendon, A. (2004). *Gesture: Visible Action as Utterance*. Cambridge: Cambridge University Press.

Kita, S. (2000). How representational gestures help speaking. In D. McNeill (ed.), *Language and Gesture* (pp. 162–85). Cambridge: Cambridge University Press.

Kita, S., Alibali, M. W., & Chu, M. (2017). How do gestures influence thinking and speaking? The gesture-for-conceptualization hypothesis. *Psychological Review*, *124*(3), 245.

Kress, G. (2009). *Multimodality: A Social Semiotic Approach to Contemporary Communication*. London: Routledge.

Kress, G., & Van Leeuwen, T. (2001). *Multimodal Discourse: The Modes and Media of Contemporary Communication*. London: Arnold.

Lakoff, G., & Johnson, M. (1980). *Metaphors We Live By*. Chicago, IL: University of Chicago Press.

Littlemore, J., & Turner, S. (2019). Metaphors in communication about pregnancy loss. *Metaphor and the Social World*, *10*(1), 45–75.

Makboon, B. (2013). The 'Chosen One': Depicting religious belief through gestures. *Journal Multimodal Communication, 2*(2), 171–194.

McNeill, D. (1992). *Hand and Mind: What Gestures Reveal about Thought.* Chicago, IL: University of Chicago Press.

McNeill, D. (2016). *Why We Gesture: The Surprising Role of Hand Movements in Communication.* Cambridge: Cambridge University Press.

Meng, A. P. K. (2004). Making history in from colony to nation: A multimodal analysis of a museum exhibition in Singapore. In K. O'Halloran (ed.), *Multimodal Discourse Analysis: Systemic Functional Perspectives* (pp. 28–54). London: Continuum.

Mittelberg, I. (2008). Peircean semiotics meets conceptual metaphor: Iconic modes in gestural representations of grammar. In A Cienki & C. Müller (eds.), *Metaphor and Gesture* (pp. 115–54). Amsterdam; Philadelphia: John Benjamins.

Moore, A. C. (1977). *Iconography of Religions: An Introduction.* London: SCM Press Ltd.

Moran, C., & Lee, C. (2013). Selling genital cosmetic surgery to healthy women: A multimodal discourse analysis of Australian surgical websites. *Critical Discourse Studies, 10*(4), 373–391.

Morgan, D. (1999). *Visual Piety: A History and Theory of Popular Religious Images.* Berkeley and Los Angeles, CA: University of California Press.

Morgan, D. (2005). *The Sacred Gaze: Religious Visual Culture in Theory and Practice.* Berkeley and Los Angeles, CA: University of California Press.

Müller, C. (2008). What gestures reveal about the nature of metaphor. In Alan Cienki & C. Müller (eds.), *Metaphor and Gesture* (pp. 219–45). Amsterdam; Philadelphia: John Benjamins.

Müller, C. (2009). *Metaphors Dead and Alive, Sleeping and Waking: A Dynamic View.* Chicago, IL: University of Chicago Press.

Núñez, R. (2008). A fresh look at the foundations of mathematics: Gesture and the psychological reality of conceptual metaphor. *Metaphor and Gesture*, 93–114.

Semino, E., Demjén, Z., Hardie, A., Payne, S., & Rayson, P. (2017). *Metaphor, Cancer and the End of Life: A Corpus-Based Study.* New York: Routledge.

Sindoni, M. G. (2014). *Spoken and Written Discourse in Online Interactions: A Multimodal Approach.* New York; London: Routledge.

Skårderud, F. (2007). Eating one's words, Part I: 'Concretised metaphors' and reflective function in anorexia nervosa—An interview study. *European Eating Disorders Review: The Professional Journal of the Eating Disorders Association, 15*(3), 163–74.

Winter, B., Perlman, M., & Matlock, T. (2013). Using space to talk and gesture about numbers: Evidence from the TV News Archive. *Gesture, 13*(3), 377–408.

Zuesse, E. M. (2005). Ritual. In L. Jones (ed.), *Encyclopedia of Religion* (pp. 7833–48). 2nd ed., Vol. 11. Detroit, MI: Macmillan Reference USA.

6   Rhetoric

Beau Pihlaja

6.1   Background, History, and Key Terms

Rhetoric traditionally studies persuasion. Although public, political speech was historically the focus of rhetorical studies, researchers have also used rhetorical analysis to reveal persuasive dynamics in writing, teaching writing, analysing literature, and evaluating and producing technical or professional communication – all with an increasing focus on everyday language practices. Researchers have also historically studied relatively stable 'rhetorical situations' into which people speak, circumstances that create a need or *exigency* for a timely, *kairotic* (or fitting) written or spoken response. One of the challenges for using and studying rhetoric is that you 'can start rhetorical investigation anywhere, and you can get everywhere from there' (Segal, 2008, p. 2). Consequently, histories of rhetoric are contested spaces, debated and challenged both within the discipline and as applied to study religious language (e.g. Schüssler Fiorenza, 1999).

Rhetoric as a Western practice and scholarly discipline is typically traced to the work of Plato and his successor Aristotle. Plato's view was decidedly negative, seeing rhetoric as a tool to deceive audiences. However, although Aristotle still subordinated rhetoric to philosophical speculations as a topic and practice of the learned free person, he approached the topic far more positively. Aristotle's systemisation of practices and theory in *On Rhetoric*, as well as his definition of rhetoric as 'the available means of persuasion', serves as the field's foundation, impacting educational practices in the ancient and modern world. Rhetoric has also always been intimately linked to the accumulation and assertion of power and authority and its key concepts intersect and build on one another to make meaning both in the service of, and against the exercise of, political and social power.

Rhetoric centres several relationships in its analyses, relationships organised towards *persuasion*, attempts to get others to align their actions and thoughts with one's own. Classically, rhetorical encounters are organised by a 'triangle' that includes a *rhetor* making an *argument* in a specific *situation*, all to persuade an audience. Arguments can be complex and made in formal contexts such as courts or in conversation as in Plato's dialogues. Rhetoric focuses on how the persuasive appeal of *logos* (or 'word', 'rationality') or logical argument central to an exchange, the premises, and the syllogistic constructs are used to make a case. Rhetoric can also be used to track the role of a rhetor's *ethos* ('nature', 'disposition') or credibility which is crucial to an argument's situational effectiveness. Rhetoric's final major mode of appeal is the concept of *pathos* ('suffering'). Rhetoric highlights how an audience is persuaded not only by the logical structure of an argument, nor simply the credibility of the one making the argument, but also by emotional appeals that 'move' them to accept an argument.

Emotional appeals are often cast negatively, denigrated as manipulative and subordinate to logic or a very clinical conception of 'credibility'. But as feminist scholars especially have argued, even a purported 'lack' of emotion – the attempt to position emotional appeals as hyper-localised, perhaps frenzied and irrational compared to the calm, cool dispassionate rationality of logic (the former often associated with women and the latter with men) – is itself a rhetorical appeal (Schüssler Fiorenza, 1999). Thus, a perceived minimisation of emotional appeal is its own kind of *pathos* which is integrally linked to prior relationships of power and domination.

Rhetors are always and everywhere embodied, the product of material relationships and histories that render their arguments specific, contextual, even coherent. Intersectionality (Crenshaw, 1989) describes how different social, political, and legal forces and institutions intersect in individual persons' and groups' lives to both erase their uniqueness and uniquely intensify their marginalisation and oppression. These material realities are particularly relevant in the study of religious discourse and rhetorical analyses can help researchers map the expansive way *rhetorical situations* shape how rhetors speak, write, or otherwise act to persuade. These situations, often precipitated by a particular event or set of conditions, provide a reason or impetus – the *exigence* – for rhetorical intervention. *Audience* is therefore also key for rhetoric and presupposes that an argument or rhetor's ability to persuade is significantly dependent on an audience's 'persuadability'. Unlike laws of physical motion, where objects set in motion continue until interrupted, logical arguments, speakers' credibility, and what emotions will sway an audience depend on the specific makeup of the audience in a specific situation and even a specific location. Indeed, rhetoric is a process of *invention* whereby rhetors seek out arguments crafted to persuade particular individuals and groups.

Rhetoric has historically tried to track and trace 'forms' and types of arguments. Classical rhetoric organised arguments into basic forms: judicial, deliberative, and epideictic. Judicial or forensic rhetoric involves arguments exploring whether a wrong has been committed as in a courtroom trial. Deliberative rhetoric involves arguments about what to do under certain circumstances, as in a legislature where representatives argue about whether or how to best craft a law. Epideictic rhetoric refers to speech in which one might praise a person or group as in a eulogy or, conversely, heap scorn and blame on a person or group as in a 'jeremiad', a religious screed against a nation's purported sins.

In global Christian circles especially, an expansive sub-genre of education and practice ('apologetics') circulates around making and learning to make defensive arguments (apologia) for beliefs and actions in various situations. Apologetics is not limited to Western Christian practice, however. Every religion has some form of outreach practice intended to either persuade others to join it or at the very least 'bear witness' to the faith's essential truths and practices. Islamic dawah has also developed both in dialogue with, and counter to, ongoing proselytising efforts of Christians. In the new era of social-media driven circulation of ideas and arguments, new forms of apologia proliferate; for example, atheists make increasingly visible arguments against a belief in any deity (see, especially, S. Pihlaja, 2018). Consequently, apologetics are an important rhetorical form for those studying religious language use.

The dynamics on which rhetoric focuses, its key terms and attempts to categorise arguments' various forms, can be and certainly are addressed by other theoretical/methodological approaches to studying religious discourse, all no doubt with their own key terms and areas of emphasis. However, rhetoric at its most useful aims to track these dynamics *together*, with a special emphasis on arguments' contexts and audiences' role in co-creating the conditions for persuasion's success, or lack thereof, akin perhaps to the linguistic concept of intersubjectivity. Rhetoric's historical concern with the *enthymeme*, a form of rhetorical argument that leaves a premise unstated to be understood or supplied by the audience, makes it valuable for parsing discursive silences in exchanges between speakers and those they seek to persuade.

In its earliest Sophistic form, its later systemisation under Aristotle, Quintilian, Cicero, and even on into its modern resurgence, rhetoric is fundamentally a probabilistic exercise. Aristotle distinguished between 'inartistic proofs' and 'artistic proofs'. 'Inartistic proofs' were simply appeals to external arguments, laws, witness claims, or religious beliefs. 'Artistic proofs', however, were those that needed to be 'invented' by a rhetor, developed systematically for a specific situation and audience. In practice, rhetorical studies are inherently interdisciplinary and rhetors and scholars of rhetoric will likely have to call upon a wide variety of tools, frameworks, and models by which to make or analyse arguments. They may call upon historical studies in the service of putting the current moment in context. They might use the latest understanding of human psychology and cognition as they refine their persuasive techniques or analyse why a particular argument works. They might study economic principles in thinking through the material conditions under which arguments might be more open to acceptance.

The rise of the 'New Rhetoric' facilitated a shift back to thinking about audience's constituting role in argumentation (Perelman & Olbrechts-Tyteca, 1969). A preoccupation with rhetorical 'situations' sought to establish context's crucial role in both determining arguments and shaping them (Bitzer, 1968). Attempts to re-integrate a nuanced, systematic logical process with rhetorical argumentation proved influential as well in the twentieth century (Toulmin, 2003). At the same time, Burke's (1969) idiosyncratic but generative work emphasised rhetoric's value for engaging language as a symbol system and language use as a fundamentally dramatic exercise. Recently, rhetoric's development in the USA especially has taken up the question of how the material, embodied, and physical world impacts and shapes arguments, for example, in terms of the rhetorical situation itself (B. Pihlaja, 2018) or in the translational rhetorical work that must happen in and between groups (Gonzales, 2018). This has also led to a concern with how rhetoric is theorised and taught in a multicultural, diverse, ever-shifting, often asymmetrical power-relations. Cultural rhetorics has also pushed back on the Western scientific domination of all other conceptions of the world via language in the service of colonising power (Haas, 2007; Powell, 2002).

Attempts to study specifically the rhetoric of *religion* have also been somewhat divergent and fragmented. In one sense, rhetoric was a tool used *within* religions to think about their organisation, perpetuation, and theorisation of themselves. However, the study of the rhetoric of religions from something like an 'outside' or scholarly perspective has been fraught. As we will discuss, religions, especially their conservative expressions, tend to side with Plato in their suspicion about the implications of human language as a seat for finding, revealing, or perpetuating Truth. Studying 'the rhetoric of religion' is difficult not only because religious adherents and their would-be scholarly observers are often mutually suspicious of one another. As Brian Jackson (2015) has argued, just defining what might constitute 'a religion' to discuss the 'rhetoric of' can prove difficult. Even if one assumes the existence of the divine, or transcendent, or supernatural, this is fundamentally a 'rhetorical, not an ontological, decision' (Jackson, 2015, p. 24). Assuming divinity or a transcendental reality is of course not proof that the supernatural exists and/or acts in the world or even a claim about whether one really believes such claims in speaking about them. It is only to say that 'religious rhetoric' should be somewhat constrained, referring to rhetoric that 'superimposes over rhetorical situations the existences and activities of forces beyond the natural world' (Jackson, 2015, p. 22). Whether or not one follows Jackson's distinctions or definitions, he illustrates the challenge of teasing out a difference between rhetoric of religion versus rhetoric about religion.

Regardless, the connection between rhetoric and religion has been something of a mutual constant even in the modern era. Kenneth Burke, previously cited, traced connections between a study of rhetoric and religion in his *The Rhetoric of Religion: Studies in Logology* (1970). Burke sees in the structure and use of language something like the 'analogy of being' (anologia entis) in many Christian conceptions of the universe that grounds human relations in the revelation of divine relations. As DePalma and Ringer summarise, 'For Burke, the study of religious rhetoric is valuable because it provides a means by which to comprehend the functions of explaining human motives' (DePalma & Ringer, 2015, p. 263). This is particularly useful in analyses of texts where motivations may be intentionally or unintentionally obscured.

6.2   Key Topics, Questions, and Debates

Rhetoric, like many of the forms of analyses outlined in this book, is about studying and practicing language use in context, with a particular focus on how we are persuaded or dissuaded from taking action in our increasingly complex and interconnected world. The scientific or scholarly study of rhetoric is challenging because of this complexity and can cause some to dismiss using rhetoric to study religious language. As a necessarily fluid and interdisciplinary field, rhetoric has been organised partially around two key topics which themselves have their own separate but intersecting, ongoing questions and internal debates all having special application to analysing religious discourse: the relationship of language to reality and ethics in rhetorical arguments and research.

For Plato and many after him, the sophists and their progeny were disconnecting language from Truth. Plato believed the highest realities were ultimately stable and irrefutable, and consequently argued they ought to be used to organise everything from our individual pursuits to the political organisation of a city or state under the auspices of the philosopher-king. Additionally, the sophist practice of being paid to teach the wealthy how to make arguments was troubling from a sociopolitical perspective – sophists could use rhetoric to make the worse argument 'seem the better'. Indeed, Plato's discomfort with this use of rhetoric remains with us today as rhetoric is just as likely to be a term of dismissal as in 'mere words' – at best simply a matter of style or worse a tool of deception – with no philosophical connection to reality or Truth (Jarratt, 1998, p. xvi). Although Aristotle's perspective on rhetoric was not as negative as Plato's, Susan Jarratt (1998, p. xvi) emphasises that rhetoric is subordinate to the deeper philosophical 'search for universals' in his larger philosophical project. In the end, the 'proof' that rhetoric could provide in its appeals was not ironclad. The proofs were 'artistic' meaning contingent, probabilistic, made via the invention process of developing an argument, attention to style, the three modes of appeal (*logos, ethos, pathos*), etc. 'Inartistic proofs', by contrast, were simply appeals to law, witness claims, or legal contracts/oaths.

Ultimately, the probabilistic nature of rhetoric can be troubling for religious adherents who often believe their use of words implicitly and explicitly lays claim to 'reality' or describes a reality independent of humans' perspectives. Consequently, much Western Christian religious writing and thought has tended to side conceptually with Plato over and against the sophistic rhetorical tradition, believing that—whatever else it does—language should not be uncoupled either from a stable Truth or at the very least the *pursuit* of a stable Truth, a key issue for theologians and church leaders wrestling with the paradox implicit in any scholarly endeavour: what does it mean to use words to speak of a Truth, or the Divine, or Reality that *transcends* the words, arguments, and images themselves?

Because rhetoric has always challenged and been challenged by the complicated relationship language has to reality, these questions are intimately connected to how we ought to organise our individual and collective lives. Rhetoric has always been concerned with what the right way is to use language to persuade, evaluate language use, or study language use in fair and just ways. Given religions' inherent concern with what it means to be good or holy or correct in one's beliefs in practice (orthodoxy/orthopraxis), rhetoric's disciplinary commitment to making credible and ethical arguments, establishing how and why a speaker is considered credible to one or another audience, is also of particular interest.

Rhetorical analysis, especially in the USA, had for some time been moving away from a narrow focus on the speech of 'great' (white) men in political context, or even the extent to which women and groups marginalised from the centres of western power have either participated in and or shaped that public, political speech from within or without (Fredlund, 2016). Instead, an intensification of focus on what historically had been identified as the 'rhetorical situation' and its relationship to 'genre' emerged. Miller's (1984) definition of genre as typified 'rhetorical actions based on recurrent situations' helped push beyond scholars' tendency to think primarily in terms of taxonomies or classifications of types of rhetorical forms, to insist that the context constitutes genres of rhetorical intervention. This tracks too with the turn in linguistics towards incorporating the social context in linguistic analysis.

The proliferation of digital media has only intensified and compounded the nature of these situations and our understanding of them, often better described as a bewildering array of rhetorical *ecologies* (Edbauer-Rice, 2005) that are either forced to interact even as previously discrete often largely segregated social contexts 'collapse' in to one another or, counterintuitively, where individuals and communities find themselves increasingly isolated from one another in the 'filter bubble' that mediating texts and technologies create, resulting in a polarised society. Edbauer-Rice's interest in the 'network' as a metaphor for thinking through the links between a social context and 'publics' variously defined signals a growing interest in rhetorical studies with the embedded, *material* conditions in which rhetoric happens or is deployed in a given 'situation'.

Recently, Scott Barnett and Casey Boyle (2017) have built on this interest in the material, beginning with the premise: 'Things are rhetorical ... Things provoke thought, incite feeling, circulate affects, and arouse in us a sense of wonder' (p. 1). This new focus is part of a larger move in the humanities to be concerned with the physical, inanimate world we inhabit. For example, scholars of rhetoric had historically discussed the nature of *kairos*, a complex, amorphous sense that the 'time is right' or the occasion propitious to intervene rhetorically in terms of the social or political conditions in which a rhetor might find themselves. Thomas Rickert (2013) sought to expand our conception of *kairos* to include physical space, the interaction between caves, cities, and islands and recognise them as integral to creating the circulation and development of human language use and rendering it rhetorically effective or ineffective. These debates about the ways we might establish and analyse rhetoric and rhetorical situations have drawn scholars back to questions of political structure and engagement, a matter of 'ultimate concern' for rhetoric since at least Plato. However, Indigenous scholars and scholars of cultural rhetorics in the wake of the 'material turn' in particular have made the point repeatedly that Indigenous cultures recognised the interdependence of human language use and the material world long before and independent of Western rhetorical scholarship which took it up as a matter of interest much later (Haas, 2007; Powell, 2002).

This focus on the material in rhetorical study has special bearing on any attempt to analyse religious language use from a rhetorical perspective. Religions are often organised around, coordinated with, even sometimes opposed to the physical, material world (Hutchings & McKenzie, 2016). Much religious language is directed towards properly situating humanity's relationship to not only one another but our relationships in a shared world. Of course, religions frequently assert that the divine is invisible, that prophets must not be iconised, or that material desire is suffering's origin. At the same time, the material world remains a mediating force in any religious practice, organising adherents' language use. Bread and wine, the positioning of the body relative to the east, the centring function of beads and icons all connect the ineffability of the divine or the spiritual to the here and now, shaping all of life and therefore necessarily the use of language in these contexts.

Beyond the organising function of the material for liturgical or devotional language practice, the turn to the material reveals the connection between religious practice and public policy around technical environmental concerns. Indigenous peoples have frequently invoked their cosmology in rejecting governments' energy policies and practices, for example, while resisting attempts in the USA to run an oil pipeline on and near Indigenous land

(Campbell, 2017), though ultimately the militarised action of the police violently cleared them from the site. Even in religious communities historically suspicious of and resistant to environmental advocacy and intervention as among US, predominantly white evangelicals, language and the material interact in attempts to persuade intra-group members to reconsider their prior stances (Baake, 2019; Hayhoe, 2019).

Flowing in and out of this question of how we relate to the world in an ethical, just, moral, or 'right' way is the question of how do we engage, deal, or cohabitate with others who are *different*? Whether that difference is one of language, ethnicity, political affiliation, or religious practice, humans struggle to cope with difference as a practical matter and it shows in our difficulties speaking to and about one another in ways that do not devolve into denigration and attack. Rhetoricians of course have their own proposals for engaging with difference, for example Burke's concept of *identification* and the creation of connections across that difference. Another proposal for engaging difference is Krista Ratcliffe's notion of 'rhetorical listening'. Ratcliffe (2005) defines this as a 'trope for interpretive invention' (p. 17) and it involves four 'moves':
1. Promoting an *understanding* of self and others
2. Proceeding within an *accountability* logic
3. Locating identifications across *commonalities* and *differences*
4. Analysing claims as well as the *cultural logics* within which these claims function

Ratcliffe notes that these moves are interrelated, recursive, and may not be symmetric in every situation. However, because rhetorical output and the study of that output commonly thinks of it as an outward focused, externally directed activity with a zero-sum, win–loss frame, beginning conceptually with an emphasis on an *understanding* of one's self and others may slow our attempt to rhetorically establish or constitute ourselves in the most self-serving way and lay the groundwork for later identifying with one another across commonalities and differences. Coupling a logic of accountability to this process of understanding and identification along with an acknowledgement of the culture within which our logic operates is an important refinement of our understanding of credibility and ethical practice.

As a method and ethical matter, rhetorical listening provides us with the means to 'lay' our defensive rhetorical responses 'alongside' that to which we are responding, to 'sit' patiently with one another and cultivate understanding of ourselves and one another in that moment, to proceed as if accountable to one another, doing our best to locate identifications (Burke) both along lines of commonality and difference, and finally commit to understanding our logic in that moment (whatever it may be) as a cultural product and therefore relative (as in related) to other logics that must be taken into account when engaging rhetorically across difference. Indeed, if we are 'in this together' by virtue of our shared physical proximity, positioning ourselves as accountable to one another may lay the groundwork for more peaceful and just rhetorical encounters and situations.

6.3   Case Study

On 14 June 2018, the then head of the Department of Justice (DOJ), Attorney General (AG) of the United States, Jeff Sessions gave a speech to a group of US law enforcement officers. Sessions took the opportunity to defend his department's 'zero tolerance policy' towards prosecuting every person who crossed the southern US border without documentation at any place other than an established port of entry. As part of this intensification of longstanding policy, the department also chose to separate children who crossed with adults – often their parents or family members – during their detention, a practice that had been limited under previous administrations.

This so-called 'family separation' policy became a flashpoint in the Trump Administration's first year in office, sparking legal challenges and protests at the border and throughout the USA. Knock-on effects of the policy continued well into Trump's first term with oversight investigations revealing the administration apparently had no clear plan at the outset for tracking or managing separated children and enabling reunification, had separated more children from their guardians than initially reported, and had potentially adopted out separated children to American families, often through religious welfare organisations connected to the administration's major players. Pushback came from American religious leaders, both progressive and conservative, who denounced the separation policy as especially objectionable on moral grounds, contrary to the teachings of Christ explicitly or by implication. Indeed, given the title of the speech on the Department of Justice website, it was precisely the critique from religious leaders that prompted Sessions to make his speech in June of 2018.

The title of the speech as prepared for delivery, 'Attorney General Sessions Addresses Recent Criticisms of Zero Tolerance by Church Leaders', emphasised its purpose (refer to the full text Sessions, 2018). In the speech, Sessions made several arguments in defence of his department's insistence on prosecution and family separation. Of special interest here was his aside addressed specifically to 'our church friends':

Let me take an aside to discuss concerns raised by our church friends about separating families. Many of the criticisms raised in recent days are not fair or logical and some are contrary to law.

First- illegal entry into the United States is a crime – as it should be. Persons who violate the law of our nation are subject to prosecution. I would cite you to the Apostle Paul and his clear and wise command in Romans 13, to obey the laws of the government because God has ordained them for the purpose of order.

Orderly and lawful processes are good in themselves and protect the weak and lawful.

Please note, Church friends, that if the adults go to one of our many ports of entry to claim asylum, they are not prosecuted, and the family stays intact pending the legal process.

While the bulk of Sessions's speech rehearses several arguments regarding the history of immigration as it has been treated as a political, legislative, and legal matter, this aside and the speech's title may strike those unfamiliar with the scripture and its role, reception, and use particularly in American protestant Christianity as confusing and odd. Anyone with even a passing knowledge of America's vaunted tradition of the 'separation of church and state' may also find the use of a particular faith's scriptural text by the highest-ranking law enforcement official of a purportedly secular government perplexing at best, unnerving at worst.

Rhetorical analysis can trace the internal logic of Sessions argument as represented in the text of the speech. Throughout the speech, Sessions argues that crossing the border at any place but a port of entry is illegal, it breaks the law. As he notes 'Under the laws of this country, illegal entry is a misdemeanour. Re-entry after having been deported is a felony'. The logic of the argument up to this point is relatively simple and can be paraphrased: This is the law, breaking the law should result in prosecution, our zero-tolerance policy is an attempt to enforce the law. This simple syllogism sets up Sessions's attempt to address the widespread moral and emotional outrage of reporting that summer in the wake of the policy of both the trauma children had experienced by separation and the reporting about the conditions under which children were being detained.

Sessions cites 'the Apostle Paul' and the 'clear and wise command in Romans 13, to obey the laws of the government because God has ordained them for the purpose of order'. The passage, explicitly verses 1 through 4, found in Paul's letter to the Romans states:

[1]Let every person be subject to the governing authorities; for there is no authority except from God, and those authorities that exist have been instituted by God. [2] Therefore whoever resists authority resists what God has appointed, and those who resist will incur judgment. [3] For rulers are not a terror to good conduct, but to bad. Do you wish to have no fear of the authority? Then do what is good, and you will receive its approval; [4] for it is God's servant for your good. But if you do what is wrong, you should be afraid, for the authority does not bear the sword in vain! It is the servant of God to execute wrath on the wrongdoer. (NRSV)

Sessions invokes Paul's words as evidence specifically against objections to policy he supports on Christian moral or ethical grounds by tying 'the law' and 'legality' – not to the practice of shared democratic, representative governance resulting from free, fair, and open elections – but to the purported divine ordination of the 'laws of the government'. He also provides a gloss on Romans verses 3–4 when he asserts 'God has ordained them for the purpose of order'. Sessions continues: 'Orderly and lawful processes are good in themselves' and that they 'protect the weak and lawful'.

Sessions's invocation of a Christian text might seem out of place to audiences who assume that the personal religious beliefs of agents of the state should remain distinct and in no way determinative for how those agents execute their oaths of office. Indeed, it is this invocation which may stand out, creating confusion or concern for a large part of the US populace. The reference is posited to establish Sessions's credibility in making this argument – especially against policy criticism from specifically Christian representatives or institutions. It is a response grounded in a particular approach to thinking about and using individual scriptural passages, especially in American Protestantism generally and in evangelical contexts specifically where 'scripture' is also the 'word of God'. Sessions in this speech is calling upon the divine credibility assumed in Romans 13 as part of his defence of the Administration's policy.

The critique of the family separation policy in 2018 was driven in no small part by a natural empathy for border crossers triggered by the visceral reporting and visual imagery appearing in reports from the border, children crying as their parents are questioned by Customs and Border Patrol officers, audio of separated and detained children crying for their parents, and pictures of children sleeping on mats on the ground behind chain link barriers – images which became themselves the site of heated argument about their reflection of reality. In light of this, Sessions's speech may seem to *lack* emotion – he frames his argument as the dispassionate application of logical reason: Laws are good. Laws should be enforced. We are simply enforcing the law. However, a lack of emotion can be deployed in contrast to opponents or critics displays of emotion as a way to connect with one's audience should they see themselves as superior for being calm and collected in their reasoning while also supporting the implication that an argument has not been unduly swayed by one's emotions.

In the immediate act of giving the speech, Sessions's audience is a gathering of law enforcement officers. In invoking Romans 13 in this way, Sessions has implicitly positioned his immediate audience, again, agents representing and invested with the authority of the government, as 'servants of God' who, should they act harshly in the eyes of critics, are simply 'executing [God's] wrath on the wrongdoer' (Romans 13:4). To what extent individuals in the room willingly accepted that elevation of their status or saw their work in that way regardless of their personal religious beliefs, it is impossible to say from the text of the speech. But it is a significant element of Sessions's rhetorical appeal here. By juxtaposing this text in this way, Sessions, via enthymeme – an argument with an unstated premise – rhetorically elevates the work of security state officials to that of divine agents.

Sessions's credibility in quoting Romans 13 in defence of a particular policy is narrowly determined by which audiences will find it compelling. First, the audience must accept that using a particular scripture is at all a meaningful piece of evidence in favour of any argument for government policy, much less this one. Without a shared belief that Romans 13 has anything to do with US immigration policy, never mind its particular form and application as put forth by AG Sessions on behalf of the law enforcement community, it is not clear that audience members who were and are American citizens but are Muslim, Jewish, Buddhist, or atheists for that matter, would find this compelling.

The logic that undocumented border crossing is a crime warranting both detention and separation from accompanying minors is operating again implicitly but no less forcefully at the heart of Sessions's speech. Because there is disagreement culturally in the USA and globally about whether it is appropriate to detain undocumented border crossers, punishment for misdemeanours rarely involves more than a citation and a fine with enormous latitude given for the police in the USA at least to decide whether to cite violators or not. Were state security officers and officials who set policy to decide, say, that amputation or corporal punishment were fitting for minor crimes, it is not clear in Sessions's syllogistic logic for the divine sanction of (his) governing authority what would mitigate it or why others should accept it.

Of course, those who invoke a singular divine entity as the ground for all beings' existence likely do not acknowledge, or necessarily welcome, competing claims about the nature of things from disparate or competing 'cultural logics', especially any that threaten or reject their belief in their divinity's authority to determine the nature of things. It is significant that the mediating concept between the divine authority Paul invokes in Romans 13 and Sessions's defence of the family separation policy is 'order'. Indeed, the logical connection slips a bit rhetorically when Sessions declares that 'Orderly and lawful processes are good in themselves'. A logical (and theological) circularity that has plagued Christians and many monotheistic religions rears its head: Is the Good what God declares? Or does God declare things because they are Good?

All of this sets aside the question of whether it is reasonable to identify the 'authorities' of Romans 13 with the representative governmental processes and their representatives in the USA. This point is very much contested and debated, as Sessions's politically partisan review of America's recent history of immigration policy and practice in other parts of the speech suggests. It is nothing like 'settled law' with broadly agreed-upon punishments for its violation or justifications for why 'authorities' are only to be obeyed when they are firm and uncompromising (as Sessions seems to insist) but not when acting more leniently or humanely. Indeed, Sessions appears to understand this problem when elsewhere in the speech he tries to call upon his various audiences' shared humanity when casting the policy as a deterrent against child endangerment.

The forceful response to this speech in particular gives evidence that even conservative religious audiences balked at the claim that child separation was at all reasonable or just. Members of Sessions's own Christian denomination, the United Methodist Church, called for formal discipline to be brought against him. The complaint called for him to be chastised in part for 'Dissemination of doctrines contrary to the standards of doctrine of the United Methodist Church' and cites his use of Romans 13 as contradicting 'Disciplinary commitments to supporting freedom of conscience and resistance to unjust laws' (*A complaint regarding Jeff Sessions*, 2018). Later revelations of the administrative sloppiness with which the policy appears to have been carried out all for a relatively minor crime (a misdemeanour, as Sessions concedes) did very little to sway audiences not already convinced of the underlying logic.

This demonstrates that although rhetorical analysis may help us map and analyse various relationships in and among specific uses of religious language to persuade various audiences for various purposes, it can run up against limits both in analysis and one's capacity to respond. The 'flattening' of the earth in a geo-political sense that occurred in the late twentieth century, along with its digital integration via the Internet and social media, at first seemed to be heralding a new global order that may open up delightful new improvements. But one should not, as a matter of analysis, reduce these complexities to the singular influence of rhetorical output – though rhetoric operates in and around them at every level. Nor should one necessarily expect to sway, stem, or otherwise reverse these shifts via rhetorical rebuttals if only the precise combination of *logos*, *pathos*, and *ethos* be identified for each individual audience in each specific context. Situations, rhetors, audiences, and arguments feed on each other, developing, reacting, fragmenting, and morphing. Edbauer-Rice's notion of the rhetorical 'ecology' and not simply 'situation' here is apt (Edbauer-Rice, 2005). The world is far more complicated than it has ever been before with far more mediums and contexts through which rhetorical messages flow and may disrupt than ever before.

6.4   Future Directions

Because of rhetoric's interdisciplinary nature, coupled as it can be with any number of approaches (many of them suggested in this volume), it can help forge new paths in examples of religious language use both large and small. As a frame for religious discourse analysis, rhetoric can aid any project concerned with interactions between rhetors and audiences. These interactions can include, of course, those among humans as in Paul's self-defence (apologia) before an audience in the court of King Agrippa who responds to the apostle's recounting of his conversion and subsequent ministry with the question 'Are you so quickly persuading me to become a Christian?' (Acts 26:28, NRSV). It can also include interaction between the divine and humans, as with the angel Gabriel's audience with Muhammad in the cave on Mount Hira (Qur'an 96.1–5).

Perhaps rhetoric can provide a starting place for analysing divine addresses where divinity is its own audience, for example, the mysterious 'us' that opens the Torah's account of humanity's creation, 'Let us make humans in our own image'.

However, rhetoric holds the most promise when it listens specifically to rhetors who come from the 'wrong places' (Ronald & Ritchie, 2006, p. 6) and who are illuminating a 'different way'. Furthermore, this approach is particularly revealing when it traces not only rhetors' and audiences' discursive relationships but the variety of material conditions shaping those situations or ecologies of interaction. As Ronald and Ritchie note, rhetorical theory's value lies in its 'asserting possibilities of a different ethos – one that is not tempered, distant, cool, or objective; one that lends specificity to material differences, from a different, gendered, othered perspective that insists on the inextricable links between experience and rhetoric, language and action' (Ronald & Ritchie, 2006, p. 9).

As a flexible organising approach to study, rhetoric allows scholars to pull together those questions most pressing in our time, for example, the nexus of race, gender, sexuality, and religious texts and practices both in the present or as historically practised and understood. For example, Christina V. Cedillo (2015) introduces 'rhetorical androgyny' expressed in depictions of Francis and Clare of Assisi through medieval texts and compared with Franco Zeffirelli's 1972 depiction in the film *Brother Sun, Sister Moon*. Cedillo's analysis shows how gender representation can be rhetorically deployed relative to a person's identified sex in hagiographical works. Cedillo marks the imbalance with which that rhetorical flexibility in depicting women's and men's gender fluidly applies to Clare of Assisi as a woman compared to Francis for whom "feminine" characteristics demonstrate a greater evidence of their sanctity. Cedillo nevertheless shows that this religious depiction of female androgyny in religious contexts opens up space for the relatively unconstrained expression of gender identity compared to the social limits often imposed on women in medieval and modern contexts.

Using a radically different form and subject matter, James Chase Sanchez's and Joel Fendelman's work in the 2018 documentary film *Man on Fire* explores the rhetoric around the sublimated racial history of Sanchez's east Texas hometown of Grand Saline. In 2014, Charles Moore, a local white minister in the Methodist church, set himself on fire in a parking lot, ending his life. The only explanation given for his self-immolation was a note Moore left on his car windshield protesting what he believed to be a history of racism in the town. Here the material intersections of the event allow Sanchez and Fendelman to explore the complex rhetorical power inherent in local spaces via traces of historical racism, self-harm as embodied protest, competing expressions of the same religious beliefs, and even silence.

With other approaches, rhetoric understands religious language as always situated, mediated, and re-mediated to audiences by texts, clergy in sermons, laity in private conversation, believers in competing religions, and even conflict with those who reject the religious altogether. Rhetoric's special concern with audiences' role in persuasive contexts has been increasingly challenged by globalisation and the proliferation, collision, and creation of very different audiences who either had rare or minimal contact historically or had not previously existed. Every audience is diverse but the seemingly infinite diversity of audiences in the modern world is a continued area of needed research. Coupled with this is the challenge of intensified fragmentation and the polarisation of audiences socially, politically, and culturally which is magnified by – though not necessarily caused by – increased contact via the Internet, social media, and the online economy. Researchers and students of religious language use may wish to use rhetoric as a tool to explore the rhetorical situations and ecologies that both establish and feed this fragmentation amidst the intensified 'context collapse' between religious believers of different kinds or no religious belief at all (S. Pihlaja, 2018). Edbauer-Rice's (2005) concept of rhetorical ecologies has special potential for further application in modern religious and inter-religious language use.

At the heart of the challenge created by this proliferation of audiences is the question of how to cope with, embrace, or reject differences in the exercise of material political power. Its material and political power long recognised (Biesecker & Lucaites, 2009), rhetoric can help us analyse how religious language is deployed rhetorically to support social, political, and cultural inclusion or exclusion (as in our case study). Rhetorical address of all kinds can expand the boundaries of who is welcomed into a community and it can restrain, limit, or exclude all whilst arguing how this too is a form of 'justice'. Indeed, the question of whether to include or exclude is a central theme of religious texts, practices, and strife. Rhetoric can help trace how religious language operates to both resist and maintain, create, or destroy sociopolitical/cultural power.

Research in this area ought to simultaneously note the material contexts and circumstances operating in and around rhetorical religious language use. Language, even religious language use, is powerful but it is enabled by very material factors, from money, guns, to walls. Building on modern research and debates in rhetoric about the role of the material in shaping rhetoric (Barnett & Boyle, 2017), as well as just engagement with difference (Sackey et al., 2019), religious language use can be studied for its role in appealing to and persuading audiences – especially among communities most resistant to change in those areas – to order our relationship to the material world with justice and humanity whether at national borders or in the climate generally (Hayhoe, 2019; Soerens & Yang, 2018).

Related to the modern challenge of audiences and increased contact across difference is the proliferation of rhetorical contact by a wider variety of rhetors on and via the Internet. While the hope for increased digital connectivity may have been that this increased exposure would necessarily result in increased tolerance and acceptance of difference, religious or otherwise, on a global scale, this has yet to prove true. Scholars of religious language may want to build on recent work in digital rhetorics to explore not only how technological infrastructures transmit religious discourse but how it is setting the conditions for the ways we experience our online world (Banks, 2011; Noble, 2018; Reyman, 2018). Scholars and practitioners of religious rhetorics may also find recent work studying the circulation of iconography in conjunction with its material context useful (Gries, 2015) as well as explorations of digital intersections with our embodied practices of engagement and translation in multiracial, multilingual contexts (Banks, 2011; Gonzales, 2018). And given rhetoric's intrinsic concern with *ethos*, what constitutes just and ethical language use, scholars may find explorations of how technology, rhetoric, and ethics intersect especially fruitful as they study religious language use (Colton & Holmes, 2018).

6.5   References

A complaint regarding Jefferson Sessions. (2018, July 18). http://s3.amazonaws.com/ Website_Properties/news-media/documents/A_Complaint_regarding_Jefferson_ Sessions.pdf.

Baake, K. (2019, May 17). Oil Is a Gift from God. Are We Squandering It? ChristianityToday.com. Accessed December 17, 2019. www.christianitytoday.com/ ct/2019/june/fossil-fuels-oil-stewardship-climate-change.html.

Banks, A. J. (2011). *Digital Griots: African American Rhetoric in a Multimedia Age.* Carbondale: Southern Illinois University Press.

Barnett, S., & Boyle, C. (eds.). (2017). *Rhetoric, through Everyday Things.* Birmingham: University of Alabama Press.

Bitzer, L. F. (1968). The rhetorical situation. *Philosophy and Rhetoric, 1*(1), 1–14.

Biesecker, B. A., & Lucaites, J. L. (2009). *Rhetoric, Materiality, & Politics.* Oxford: Peter Lang.

Burke, K. (1969). *A Rhetoric of Motives.* Berkeley: University of California Press.

Burke, K. (1970). *The Rhetoric of Religion: Studies in Logology.* Berkeley: University of California Press.

Campbell, P. B. (2017, May 15). "Those are our Eiffel Towers, our pyramids": Why Standing Rock is about much more than oil. *The Guardian.* www.theguardian

.com/science/2017/may/15/those-are-our-eiffel-towers-our-pyramids-why-standing-rock-is-about-much-more-than-oil.

Cedillo, C. (2015). Habitual gender: Rhetorical androgyny in Franciscan texts. *Journal of Feminist Studies in Religion 31*(1), 65–81.

Colton, J. S., & Holmes, S. (2018). *Rhetoric, Technology, and the Virtues*. Salt Lake City: Utah State University Press.

Crenshaw, K. (1989). Demarginalizing the intersection of race and sex: A black feminist critique of antidiscrimination doctrine, feminist theory and antiracist politics. *University of Chicago Legal Forum*, 139–67.

DePalma, M.-J., & Ringer, J. M. (2015). Charting prospects and possibilities for scholarship on religious rhetorics. In M.-J. DePalma & J. M. Ringer (eds.), *Mapping Christian Rhetorics: Connecting Conversations, Charting New Territories* (pp. 262–87). New York: Routledge.

Edbauer-Rice, J. (2005). Unframing models of public distribution: From rhetorical situation to rhetorical ecologies. *Rhetoric Society Quarterly, 35*(4), 5–24.

Fredlund, K. (2016). Forget the master's tools, we will build our own house: The woman's era as a rhetorical forum for the invention of African American woman-hood. *Peitho, 18*(2), 67–98.

Gonzales, L. (2018). *Sites of Translation: What Multilinguals Can Teach Us about Digital Writing and Rhetoric*. Grand Rapids: University of Michigan Press.

Gries, L. E. (2015). *Still Life with Rhetoric: A New Materialist Approach for Visual Rhetorics*. Salt Lake City: Utah State University Press.

Haas, A. M. (2007). Wampum as hypertext: An American Indian intellectual tradition of multimedia theory and practice. *Studies in American Indian Literatures, 19*(4), 77–100.

Hayhoe, K. (2019, October 31). I'm a Climate Scientist Who Believes in God. Hear Me Out. *The New York Times*. www.nytimes.com/2019/10/31/opinion/sunday/climate-change-evangelical-christian.html.

Hutchings, T., & McKenzie, J. (2016). *Materiality and the Study of Religion: The Stuff of the Sacred*. Abingdon: Taylor & Francis.

Jackson, B. (2015). Defining religious rhetoric: Scope and consequence. In M.-J. DePalma & J. M. Ringer (eds.), *Mapping Christian Rhetorics: Connecting Conversations, Charting New Territories* (pp. 17–30). New York: Routledge.

Jarratt, S. (1998). *Rereading the sophists: Classical rhetoric refigured*. Carbondale: Southern Illinois University Press.

Miller, C. R. (1984). Genre as Social Action. *Quarterly Journal of Speech, 70*, 151–167.

Noble, S. U. (2018). *Algorithms of Oppression: How Search Engines Reinforce Racism*. New York: New York University Press.

Perelman, C., & Olbrechts-Tyteca, L. (1969). *The New Rhetoric: A Treatise on Argumentation* (J. Wilkinson & P. Weaver, trans.). Notre Dame, IN: University of Notre Dame Press.

Pihlaja, B. (2018). Activity theory, actor-network theory, and culture in the twenty-first century. In R. Rice & K. St. Amant (eds.), *Thinking Globally, Composing Locally: Rethinking Online Writing in the Age of the Global Internet* (pp. 182–203). Salt Lake City: Utah State University Press.

Pihlaja, S. (2018). *Religious Talk Online*. Cambridge: Cambridge University Press.

Powell, M. (2002). Rhetorics of survivance: How American Indians use writing. *College Composition and Communication 53*(3), 396.

Ratcliffe, K. (2005). *Rhetorical Listening: Identification, Gender, Whiteness.* Carbondale: Southern Illinois University Press.

Reyman, J. (2018). The rhetorical agency of algorithms. In A. Hess & A. Davisson (eds.), *Theorizing Digital Rhetoric* (pp. 112–25). New York: Routledge.

Rickert, T. (2013). *Ambient Rhetoric: The Attunements of Rhetorical Being.* Pittsburgh: University of Pittsburgh Press.

Ronald, K., & Ritchie, J. (2006). Introduction. In K. Ronald & J. Ritchie (eds.), *Teaching Rhetorica: Theory, Pedagogy, practice* (pp. 1–12). Portsmouth: Boynton/ Cook Publishers.

Sackey, D. J., Boyle, C., Xiong, M. N., Ríos, G. R., Arola, K. L., & Barnett, S. (2019). Perspectives on cultural and posthumanist rhetorics. *Rhetoric Review, 38*(4), 375–401.

Sanchez, J. C. (Producer), & Fendelman, J. (Director). (2018). Man on Fire. New Day Films.

Schüssler Fiorenza, E. (1999). *Rhetoric and Ethic: The Politics of Biblical Studies.* Grand Rapids: Fortress Press.

Segal, J. Z. (2008). *Health and the Rhetoric of Medicine.* Carbondale: Southern Illinois University Press.

Sessions, Jeff. (2018). Attorney General Sessions Addresses Recent Criticisms of Zero Tolerance By Church Leaders. The United States Department of Justice. www .justice.gov/opa/speech/attorney-general-sessions-addresses-recent-criticisms-zero-tolerance-church-leaders

Soerens, M., & Yang, J. (2018). *Welcoming the Stranger: Justice, Compassion & Truth in the Immigration Debate.* Downers Grove: InterVarsity Press Books.

Toulmin, S. E. (2003). *The Uses of Argument: Updated Edition.* Cambridge: Cambridge University Press.

7   Translation

Philip Wilson

7.1   Background, History, and Key Terms

The Hebrew scriptures record how God is said to have punished the citizens of Babel for their pride in attempting to build a tower to reach heaven; from now on they would no longer be able to understand each other (Genesis 11:1–9). Barnstone (1993) comments, 'With the fall of Babel, God dispersed the word, gave us tongues and the solitude of difference, and also the impossible but pleasurable duty to repair our separation' (p. 3). Translating religious language is one way of effecting this repair. It is a controversial activity, because it deals with matters that are of ultimate importance for believers. Particular translations will command loyalty from particular faith groups, and translation decisions may both reflect and influence faith positions, such as Luther's use of 'faith alone' for 'faith' in his German rendering of Romans 3:28, which mirrors Lutheran theology (see Luther's 2002 defence of his translation).

   In this chapter, I link the translation of religious discourse to the modern discipline of translation studies, which is defined by Venuti (2012, p. 13) 'as the formulation of concepts designed to illuminate and to improve the practice of translation'. Scholars in translation studies describe target texts, construct theories about translation, and ask how translators can approach their task. Translation studies exists because translation is not straightforward, is not a scientific process of finding equivalents by which anybody with a knowledge of two languages and access to a good dictionary can magisterially render a source into a target text. Barnstone (1993, p. 39), in contrast, describes how the translator's 'every word choice invokes a decision of conscience, painful or happy'. (Overviews of sacred text translation include: Hare 2014, a survey of the conceptual issues at stake in translating scripture; Israel 2014, a theorisation of the translation of the sacred in terms of colonial constructions and postcolonial perspectives; Long 2005, a collection of essays by various authors that examine the wider picture of translating the sacred and offer case studies from different world religions; and Long 2013, an investigation of the motives of sacred text translation alongside its specificity.)

There are, certainly, a vast number of relevant primary and secondary texts from the world's religions that might be considered in a study of translating religious discourse and texts. The aim of this chapter is to put forward principles which can be generally applied to the translation of religious discourse, particularly sacred texts. I use English as the target language in examples, but translation studies, of course, takes place worldwide and scholars resist any tendency to see translation only from a western or anglophone perspective. By 'translation', I mean 'interlingual translation' rather than 'intralingual translation' (within a language) or 'intersemiotic translation' (from verbal to nonverbal signs), following the classification of Jakobson (2012), who defines interlingual translation as follows: 'Interlingual translation or *translation proper* is an interpretation of verbal signs by means of some other language' (p. 127). The 1611 Authorized King James Version of the Bible (henceforth King James Bible) (2008) is thus an interlingual translation, an instance of translation proper. It functions as a representation of the Hebrew and Hellenistic Greek scriptures for anglophone readers.

Downes (2012, p. 3) argues that 'our languages are the means by which religious thinking is made manifest and disseminated'. Given that there are more languages than can be possibly mastered by any one user, translation has been linked with religion since the invention of writing. To give two examples from the Hebrew scriptures: certain of the Proverbs are translations from Egyptian (Barton, 2019), while Barnstone (1993) describes the Book of Job as a disguised rendering of a Babylonian myth, arguing that translation is frequently a historical process for creating originals. Translated religious texts are indeed often (but not always) treated as originals by their users (Long, 2005) and in the postmodern globalised world the translation of the sacred increases in importance. The Christian Bible, for example, remains the world's most translated text, with the 2019 Digital Bible Library containing 1,408 full translations in 1,004 languages. Sacred texts, it is generally held, should be available to all people, regardless of which languages they speak.

There are at least two and potentially three stages in the process of translation: first, the source text must be read for translation (which is a different practice from reading for information or for pleasure); second, the target text must be written; third, the target text may be theorised (by critics, by the translator in paratextual material, by translation scholars, by readers). If we follow Boase-Beier's (1998) recommendation that the training of translators should consist in 'showing them how language works' (p. 41), then the translator of religious discourse needs to focus on how religious language works, which will involve investigation into how religious language differs from other kinds of language use. Stiver (1996), for example, argues that religious language 'may appropriately convey meaning by and not despite its imprecision . . . its immersion in communities of tradition . . . its heavy reliance on metaphor ... and its largely narrative shape' (p. 13). To render a Japanese Zen anecdote into English, for example, is a different kind of undertaking from translating a Japanese technical manual. The fact that they are written in the same source language is of limited relevance. Scholars frequently distinguish between literary and non-literary translation (cf. Barnstone, 1993), and the translation of religious language has more in common with the former, with what Boase-Beier and Marian de Vooght (2019) argue about the translation of poetry:

It is about recognising someone else's story, understanding the way the teller has chosen to tell it, and passing it on to others. Of course, to do this it is necessary to know the original language. But, more than this, you have to discover what the poet was doing with the original language: how it was transformed, how it was shaped, how it was made to fit or undermine its content. (p. 17)

Such translation is not about getting it right in any positivist way. The Japanese technical manual needs to have its facts correct in English translation, so that I can operate a product safely and successfully, but the Zen anecdote demands a more holistic approach from its translator, so that someone else's story can be passed on to me.

Religious discourse is translated for many reasons: to convert; to strengthen community; to promote scholarship and research; to respond to literariness; to facilitate the learning of a source language; for political reasons (such as to enable a colonising power to understand the colonised). The translation of sacred scripture has led to fierce debates among scholars and believers, even to persecution and murder. William Tyndale's execution in 1536 for heresy, for example, was the official response to his English edition of the Christian Bible, of which only the Vulgate Latin version was then authorised for general use by the Catholic Church. Tyndale's fate is a reminder that translating religious discourse is always about more than linguistic transfer. As Shackle (2005) argues, 'For while the spiritual may be the common property of humankind to translate as it will, scriptures have faith communities that look on any transla- tion both eagerly for the evidence of the spirit and critically for evidence of a proper fidelity' (p. 28). A sacred text is more than just a document; it plays a role in the lives of individuals and communities and both supports and determines how people live.

Polizzotti (2018) formulates the debate by reference to the clash between the Bible translator Jerome (c.342–420), who was concerned to produce a readable Latin version, and the theologian Augustine of Hippo (354–430), who worried that such literary translation might in some way dethrone the source text: 'Jerome approached translation with a poet's ear; Augustine with a bureaucrat's eagle eye. Their opposing stances make them, quite literally, the patron saints of an all-too-human debate that rages to this day' (Polizzotti,

2018, p. 21). How we conceive of translation matters because translation practices 'result from theories, however preliminary and unformed those theories might be' (Boase-Beier, Fisher, and Furukawa, 2018).

In translating religious discourse, we encounter within a specific context all the major problems of translation, such as questions of equivalence and fidelity or the issue of how translations find a place in a literary polysystem. We note how translations can take on a life of their own, how the very choice of a text to translate can canonise that work: the many English translations of the Sanskrit *Bhagavadgītā* (Song of the Lord), for example, have given it a central place in the west's construction of Hinduism, divorcing it from its parent text the *Mahābhārata* (Great Story) (Israel, 2014). In short, we come across the sort of problems that have led to the formation of translation studies as a discreet discipline.

Translation can also give prestige to the target language, as with the King James Bible or translations of the Qur'an from Classical Arabic into Turkish after the twentieth-century language reforms of Mustafa Kemal Atatürk. There is also the issue of what is *not* translated. Many Buddhist scriptures remain inaccessible to anglophone readers because of the lack of translators, while Wulfila's fourth-century Gothic Bible deliberately omits the warlike Books of Kings for fear that they would set a bad example to the Goths.

Translation is a necessary task in a multi-lingual world and stands in need of investigation if it is to be understood and if it is to be done better in the future. The seventeenth-century French literary translator Nicolas Perrot d'Ablancourt recorded that there had only ever been two criticisms made of his work: the texts that he chose to translate and the way that he translated them (d'Ablancourt, 2002, p. 157). Here are the two central issues that arise in any discussion of translation: which texts should be chosen for translation, and which strategies, among the many available, should be chosen? These issues therefore arise also for those who translate the sacred and they are examined in the next section.

7.2   Key Topics, Questions, and Debate

To read about the translation of religious discourse is to encounter frequent assertions that the sacred cannot be translated at all. The subtitle of Long's 2005 anthology of articles on translation and religion is the punning 'Holy Untranslatable?' and Shackle's chapter in that volume ends with the statement that he is a 'firm believer in the ultimate untranslatability of the holy' (Shackle, 2005, p. 32). The feeling is strong in many religious traditions that language is unable to cope with invisible realities, that we can never satisfactorily translate our primary vision of the sacred into words. Augustine, for example, writes in his *Confessions* (2008): 'But in these words what have I said, my God, my life, my holy sweetness? What has anyone achieved in words when he speaks about you?' (p. 5). The difficulty presented here is translating from the language of thought into natural language, of trying to find words for what is experienced as ineffable.

Translating from one language to another then presents another level of abstraction. Once words are somehow found and written down to express the sacred, interlingual translations can be and are written, as a visit to any library will show (see Wilson 2019). The question now arises of whether religious discourse *should* be translated. If not, believers and scholars would have to learn source languages in order to read sacred texts, as happens in many faiths. We have a question of authority, not of linguistics. By refusing to allow vernacular translations of Jerome's Latin Bible, for example, the medieval Catholic Church was able to maintain power in the hands of its clergy. Consequently, sixteenth-century Protestant reformers made Bible translation a priority, allowing all believers access to the scriptures, and indirectly instigating further reform.

Some languages have been viewed as inherently sacred, so that to translate them is to desecrate what is holy. Bennett (2018) identifies nine sacred languages: Avestan (Zoroastrianism); Church Slavonic (Russian Orthodox Christianity); Classical Arabic (Islam); Coptic (Coptic Orthodox Christianity); Ge'ez (Ethiopian Orthodox Christianity); Hebrew (Judaism); Latin (Catholic Christianity); Pali (Theravada Buddhism); Sanskrit (Hinduism). Bennett (2018) argues that translation is threatening to those who hold a language to be sacred because for them it destroys the *transcendent* nature of that language when it is replaced by another. The source language is itself seen as partaking in ineffability. Muslims, for example, view the Qur'an as a 'linguistic miracle' that will always elude the understanding of mortals and cannot as such be translated (Abdul-Raof, 2005).

Questions of translation become questions of power, about who has the right to authorise a translation and who can stipulate the translator and the method of translation. Religious leaders may even decide who can and cannot read in translation. Such issues are political. The translation of Zoroastrian scriptures from Avestan into living languages, for example, has been for Parsi reformers a way for 'the true monotheism and ethical message of Zoroaster to shine through, and ... cancel out the power of the priesthood and their ritualistic obfuscations' (Bennett, 2018, p. 176). Avestan translation has been contested, showing how languages stand in for '[a] whole constellation of historical, aesthetic, theological, and political concerns and anxieties' (Bennett, 2018, p. 175). We are never just dealing with words on the page.

Even when believers see their language as sacred, then, translation may and does still take place, particularly when religions seek to make converts and maintain particular ways of living. A complete ban on translation could be self-defeating. Even within Islam, where the Qur'an is only understood to be in its true form in Arabic, Muslims have produced translations. The Prophet Mohammed sent a Greek translation of a Qur'an verse to the Byzantine emperor Heraclius (Hare, 2014) and translations of the Qur'an are readily available in many languages, *accompanying* rather than replacing the Classical Arabic source text (which is used in formal worship) for those who cannot read it. Latin has now lost its privileged status in Catholicism. Downes (2012), with reference to the Christian Bible, argues that 'translation is presupposed by the very idea of scripture. As an array of languages, scripture *is* dissemination in translation' (p.128). The Hebrew scriptures include Aramaic verses in Daniel and Ezra, for example, while the Christian gospels record sayings of Jesus in Hellenistic Greek, many of which are described by scholars as renderings from Aramaic sources. Translations of these scriptures are in turn used as proxies for the source texts in an ongoing process.

Granted that scriptures are in fact translated, it can be asked if there is any guarantee that what we are reading is authentic, that we are not dealing with a counterfeit, given that the words of the source text authors have been replaced by those of the translator(s). Downes (2012) records how he was told on proposing his book on religious language that the project would not be possible 'without going back to the texts of the great religions in their original languages ... translations are said to be inadequate' (p. 122). We find this distrust of translation in popular sayings such as 'to translate is to betray' or 'poetry is what is lost in translation' (often falsely attributed to Robert Frost). In order to see why such beliefs about translation are ill founded, we can revisit Jakobson's (2012) definition of interlingual translation as the 'interpretation of verbal signs' (p. 127). The aspect of interpretation is easily forgotten. A translator is always faced with a number of choices, at the level of both word and sentence, and any choices that are made will in turn determine later choices. If we take 'equivalence' to mean that one text must be exactly the same as another, then translation is *necessarily* inadequate (Barnstone, 1993). What translators as interpreters *can* give us through interpretation, however, is 'related difference' (Barnstone, 1993).

'Related difference' can be best understood by an example from the New Testament. Text (1) is from Luke 6:20, a saying of Jesus that reverses the usual way in which societies view the poor. I have transliterated and glossed the Hellenistic Greek (taken from Aland et al., 1968). (Glossing is a translation-studies tool that allows readers without knowledge of a source language to work out what is going on in a source text.)

1.   Μακάριοι οἱ πτωχοί, ὅτι ὑμετέρα ἐστὶν ἡ βασιλεία τοῦ θεοῦ.
       Makarioi hoi ptōchai, hoti humetera estin hē basileia tou theou.
       happy the poor because yours is the kingdom of-the God

Texts (2) and (3) below are taken from the King James Bible (2008) and King's 2004 *The New Testament* respectively and can be described as interlingual translations of Luke's Greek. Both function as representations, as texts that replace other texts and that can be used in related ways.

2.   Blessed *be ye* poor: for yours is the kingdom of God.
3.   Congratulations to the poor – for yours is the Kingdom of Heaven.

The verbal signs of the first-century Hellenistic Greek source text have been interpreted into seventeenth-century English in Example 2 and into twenty-first-century English in Example 3. To translate religious discourse in any age is to engage in exegesis: what does it mean to see the poor in this way? In Example 2, the King James translators italicise the English words that they have added and that have no counterparts in the source text. They choose the word 'Blessed' to translate 'Makarioi', to imply that God is at work in doing the blessing. This implicature is confirmed in the second half of the beatitude. Their translation also preserves the source text's parallelism, a typical feature of ancient Middle Eastern verse (Barton, 2019). King's translation in Example 3 avoids 'blessed', perhaps because that adjective has by now become too well established in the lexical space surrounding the Sermon on the Mount, due to the influence of earlier translations like the King James Bible, and has as such lost any power to shock; he offers a translation choice that makes the reader stop to ask why on earth the poor should be congratulated. His rendering wrenches language out of the ordinary and changes the way that the world is seen by the reader, following the practice of Jesus. The parallelism of the source text is again maintained.

If we are fully to account for the translation processes going on here, we need to use not only linguistic but also cultural tools to describe both text and context (cf. Long, 2005). The King James Bible carries prestige, as noted previously. It was authorised for use in Anglican worship by James I and is viewed by many as a masterpiece of English style. Smith (2008) in the Bible's Preface speaks of how translation 'openeth the window to let in the light' by enabling direct access to the word of God, (i.e. providing a text that could be used by the 'unlearned' in worship and private devotion)' (p. lvii). King's (2004) translation is a recent work in a crowded field by a Catholic scholar who states that his aim is 'to allow the reader to experience what it was like to hear or read the particular document for the first time' (p. 10). We can see, then, that each version aims to function in parallel ways to those in which the original scriptures could be used. The stress is on practice, on potential similarity of use.

Our conception of translation depends on our conception of language (Downes, 2012). If we see language as a code, then we shall be tempted to think that we can change one text into another with no difficulty, as discussed. The etymology of the word 'translation' (carrying across) both suggests and supports this view. A bishop can be translated from one diocese to another without mishap, and the relic of a saint can be safely translated from one shrine to another, but when a text is translated into another language, there is an inevitable change: 'an understanding of translation is only as good as the linguistic and pragmatic theory in which it is embedded' (Downes, 2012, p. 124). When we translate, the task is to find what Downes (2012), following relevance theory, calls 'optimal relevance'; he describes what must have happened when words of Jesus were translated from Aramaic in the process that would lead to the Gospels:

> The thoughts have to be made manifest in Greek so that a monolingual Greek-speaking Jew of the diaspora, or a gentile audience, seeking to comprehend the translator through processing for optimal relevance will construct similar thoughts to those communicated by Jesus in Aramaic; at least sufficiently so that the lineage of related mental representations can be said to continue. (p. 125)

Both Example 2 and Example 3, despite being written some 400 years apart, are part of a continuing 'lineage of related mental representations' that links them through similarity to an earlier source.

We can take the argument further by seeing 'equivalence' as something that is not discovered but constructed. Hermans examines the quasi-miraculous translation of the *Book of Mormon* by Joseph Smith in 1823. Smith's English is held to have replaced a text (now lost) written in an unknown script of divine origin. Hermans (2007) concludes that 'equivalence is *declared*' (p. 24) by the Mormon community. The declaration of equivalence is made not on linguistic grounds or on account of any inherent related features that texts share, but by an authority, just as the different language versions of the Belgian Constitution are declared equivalent in Belgian law (Hermans, 2007). In other circumstances, such as Muslim worship and devotion, translations are declared to be non-equivalent, but play their part alongside an original, and are deliberately signalled *as* translations, versions, interpretations, glosses, cribs. Texts that have been rewritten in new languages are part of what Wittgenstein (PI 241) calls 'forms of life' and must be investigated as such (see Wilson, 2016).

7.3   Case Study

Case studies are central to the practice of translation studies. As Saldanha and O'Brien (2013) argue, they make us recognise that a translation does not come out of nowhere but is a product of complex mechanism. In this section, I will examine my translation of the second of two anonymous magical sayings, the so-called Merseburg Charms (German: *Merseburger Zaubersprüche*) written in Old High German in a tenth-century monastic manuscript. They are the only surviving German texts that directly invoke pre-Christian gods and are considered to be the product of a long oral tradition.

The source text from my own work (Wilson, 2015) is given as Example 4. I have glossed the Old High German. My translation is given as Example 5.

4.   Phol ende Uuodan uuorun zi holza.
      Phol and Uuodan went to wood
      du uuart demo Balderes uolon sin uuoz birenkit.
      there was to-the Balder's foal his foot wrenched
      thu biguol en Sinthgunt, Sunna era suister;
      thus charmed it Sinthgunt Sunna her sister
      thu biguol en Friia, uolla era suister;
      thus charmed it Friia Uolla her sister
      thu biguol en Uuodan, so he uuola conda:
      thus charmed it Uuodan so he well could
      sose benrenki, sose bluotrenki, sose lidirenki:
      so leg-sprain so blood-sprain so limb-sprain
      ben zi bena, bluot zi bluoda,
      bone to bone blood to blood
      lid zi geliden, sose gelimida sin.
      limb to limb thus limed be

5.   Phol and Wodan rode into the wood.
      and the foal of Balder sprained its foot.
      There Sinthgunt charmed it and Sunna, her sister;
      there Freia charmed it and Volla, her sister;
      there Wodan charmed it as he well could:
      as bone-sprain, so blood-sprain, so limb-sprain:
      bone to bone, blood to blood,
      limb to limb, that they may be limed.

The spell is apotropaic because it is designed to reverse the bad luck of a horse spraining its leg. The spell is based on the belief that the god Balder's horse was healed when his father recited a charm and that something similar can happen to the reciter of this text. It does not just transmit information about the gods but activates those gods. Words, as Wittgenstein (PI 546) remarks, are deeds. The source text can therefore be described as religious in its invocation of a supernatural reality. It belongs to an Indo-European tradition of spells that first depict a situation involving superhuman forces and then address those forces with a view to them changing our world. The resurgence of the Germanic gods in neopaganism also gives the spell a link to contemporary religious forms of life.

It is worth considering whether the spell should be translated at all. Translating poetry may be seen as a waste of time, following the dictum falsely attributed to Frost (see previous). The magic of the poem may very well be intrinsically wedded to the source language, so that it can be efficacious even if spoken by somebody with no knowledge of Old High German. Bennett (2018) describes how many religious believers hold that we do not need to understand a prayer for it to be efficacious. To translate the spell, however, is a way of responding to its literariness and an acknowledgement of the other Indo-European languages that must have been involved in the transmission of its cognitive scenario, thus furthering the multilingual lineage. An English translation opens a window onto a pagan world and allows anglophone readers access to a poem that has considerable power in its own right even if they do not believe in its gods (just as Pindar can be appreciated by those who do not acknowledge the Greek pantheon). Poems have effects on readers, and translators can strive to recreate these poetic effects in the target language in an act of 'creative transposition' (Jakobson, 2012), that is, a recognition that they may have to do different things in the target language if they want to allow readers the possibility of reacting to a poem as a poem rather than as a crib.

The spell contains seven proper nouns. It might be thought that to translate names is a simple matter of transference. (I do not expect my name to be different in a German document.) However, even with names there is no equivalence that can be read off as if from a table. The Germanic god whom the source text calls 'Uuodan' is usually designated in English as 'Odin' (and named as such in the popular graphic and filmic Marvel Universe). He is also referred to as 'Woden' in English, while 'Wotan' would be relevant to devotees of Richard Wagner's *Ring* cycle. There are in fact hundreds of names for this god. The choice of 'Wodan' in the target text brings readers to the source text by showing them (in a bilingual edition) that they are reading a recreation of an Old High German text. And this one choice in its turn rules out others, something that is true not only of the words that translators select but also of the strategies.

The translation maintains the stylistic features of the spell that make it an incantation, such as the use of repetition; the caesura, which divides each line antiphonally; the use of compound nouns to designate the three types of sprain. Old High German tends to use alliteration rather than rhyme as a binding technique, but here as well as alliteration I use rhyme (wood/foot, could/ blood, sprain/limed) as well as maintaining the terminal repetition in lines 3 and 4 in order to heighten the incantatory effect. There is also a movement in both source and target texts from the initial description of a scene to the invocation with which the piece ends, a movement that is typical of Indo-European spells. I have also imitated the parallelism in the last three lines that is, I infer, designed to activate divine action through word-play, and is therefore not ornamental but essential.

The translation is necessarily an interpretation, a recreation, because languages never map onto each other perfectly. As Jakobson (2012) argues, languages differ 'in what they *must* convey and not what they *may* convey'

(p. 129). French can translate 'the chair', for example, but must use feminine gender in *la chaise*, which is not the case in English. Thus, (4) has *zi holza* in line 1, but to translate this item as 'to wood' is not a grammatical possibility for the twenty-first-century writer of English, where an article must be used, and I have translated it as 'to the wood', although 'to a wood' would also have been possible.

In translating poetry where form is an essential part of the source text, how to represent the source-text form in the target language is a key challenge. Other strategies are available. It could be published as a gloss, as in example (4). There is a distinguished history of interlinear glosses in the delivery of religious texts – in Aramaic targums, for example, where Hebrew is glossed by Aramaic; or in the Northumbrian Lindisfarne Gospels, where Latin is glossed by Old English – with Benjamin (2012) claiming that the 'interlinear version of the Holy Scriptures is the prototype or ideal of all translation' (p. 83). However, glosses cannot stand alone as translations (Barnstone, 1993). A plain prose translation could be written, which would employ correct grammar without being set out as a poem or attempting to recreate poetic effects, whilst utilising the stylistic potential of prose. Many bilingual poetry anthologies use this strategy. Yet if a translation is a representation, then it is reasonable for readers to expect that a text-type in language A should be represented by the same text-type in language B. Even if perfect equivalence is impossible, even if equivalence can only be declared, a source and a target text can stand in a relation of similarity to each other, as argued here. In Wittgensteinian terms, translators can find strategies to play the same language games in the target text that they discern in the source text, as I have argued elsewhere (Wilson, 2016).

The published translation faces the original German, which means that readers can compare source and target. The anthology contains an introduction and notes. Such paratextual material by translators becomes part of the reading of the target text, just as readers of the King James Bible have the opportunity to read Smith's Preface, which discusses many issues, including: the function of translation in general; the translators' strategy in basing their work on previous English versions; the need to tread a middle way between religious extremes (see Barnstone, 1993).

Published translations can make it appear that source texts are stable and fixed, whereas the situation is often more fluid, especially with older works, which frequently exhibit manuscript variation. The Book of Jeremiah, for example, 'existed in two forms, a longer and a shorter one and with the chapters in different orders' (Barton, 2019, p. 441), so that any Bible translator has to decide from which to work. Translation is an activity where many agents are involved: authors, editors, scholars, translators, readers. In translating the spell, for example, I have had to rely on work done by Germanists, who discovered the text, published it, contextualised it, and drew attention to its literary merit through their critical labours.

The translation case study examines translation products in order to try to show the deliberated choices that translators must have made, which leads here to the conclusion that we should see translation 'not as an exact science that could strive for or even achieve equivalence, but rather as a creative, imaginative and political act' that reflects 'a range of local agendas, expectations, and priorities' (Ricci, 2014, p. 544). To look at the translation of the religious text forces us to re-evaluate language, communication, and religion itself. Other versions of the Merseburg spell are possible in English, just as there are a wide variety of translations of major religious texts. Translations go out of fashion, become outdated in their language, adapt to new developments in scholarship and creativity, result from the market demands of publishers, and reflect or propagate the views of different groups. Benjamin (2012) speaks of translation as how texts survive: 'For its continuing life, which could not be so called if it were not the transformation and renewal of a living thing, the original is changed' (p. 77). Many religious texts have a life in translation that is denied to them as source texts, such as the early Mesopotamian myths of the Babylonian and Assyrian gods, which are now widely available in English although very few people can today read Akkadian, which was only deciphered in the nineteenth century after becoming extinct.

Barton (2019), in an overview of modern Bible versions, identifies three main approaches taken by translators: the revising of earlier versions; the writing of new versions in contemporary idiom; the writing of imitative versions. Here I have chosen the third option when approaching this text (i.e. writing an English version that imitates the poetics of the German). Other situations call for other strategies. To some extent this decision was forced on me by current practices in poetry translation. A translation for an Old High German textbook might call for a gloss, however. Another possibility would be to give more than one translation alongside the source text, perhaps in conjunction with an internet site, to show that all translational representations are provisional.

7.4   Future Directions

As Hare (2014) asserts, 'many of the challenges that earlier translators [of religious texts] faced will remain for future translators' (p. 541). Sacred text translation, in particular, is an ongoing endeavour as religions continue to develop and adapt to new contexts, and as languages themselves continue to evolve and emerge in those contexts. More than 400 Bible translation projects are currently being undertaken into languages where no translation yet exists, for example, whilst the 84,000 Project aims to translate the entire Buddhist

Tibetan canon into English, thus providing a resource for believers and scholars.

What will necessarily change are the contexts of translation. The humanities, where translation is both practised and theorised, are undergoing an interdisciplinary turn 'that is having an impact on how we can think about cultural forms of life and the social order' (Downes, 2012, p. 1), and such a turn will have influences on practice and theory. Translation studies is interdisciplinary by its nature and will continue to look to other disciplines (such as philosophy or linguistics) in order to describe practice and to construct theory, while translators, who are living in a world where things are becoming more interconnected (Bennett, 2018, p. 205), will engage with new theories in order to improve practice.

One area and agent of change is the internet, where the translation of religious discourse flourishes (see *Media*, this volume). Users have access to many versions of major texts and there are numerous translation tools available. Given the massive number of untranslated religious works online, amateur translation is bound to grow within an increasing number of languages, in line with recent developments in crowd translation (as evidenced in game relocation). Such a development would go against the tendency for religious texts to be translated by experts such as linguists or theologians (see Bennett, 2018), but there is no reason why experts cannot work in a supervisory capacity as well as doing their own work.

Dialogue is at the heart of translation. Translation agents – scholars, translators, editors, publishers, etc. – from different traditions need to speak to each other. Boundaries must be broken not just between disciplines but between religions if we are to become aware of different but related ways of translating the sacred and of conceptualising that translation. An example of how this can be undertaken is the translation dialogue set up by Robinson (2016) in the context of Daoism between Chinese thinkers such as Laozi and Western thinkers such as Pierre Bourdieu. I am inevitably writing within the Western tradition of translation studies and must recall how it is only too easy for me to impose Western paradigms onto texts and practices from non-Western cultures, how even the very dichotomy Western/non-Western is open to question. The way that the vernacular Bible has been accepted as a proxy for a set of Hebrew and Hellenistic Greek texts may have helped to form a particularly Western view of looking at texts – like viewing translation as a process of finding equivalents – and it is important for Western scholars to look at other practices, such as the insistence in Islam that Qur'an translation is not possible (even though interpretations can be written to be used alongside the scriptures) or the Asian tradition of writing translations alongside lengthy commentary.

There will doubtless be increasing use of commentary by all translators: to justify decisions that have been taken; to allow readers to view the target text in relation to the history of the source text and its translation (or non-translation); to show how interpretation is at the heart of all translation in terms of the translation choices made. Paratexts can also make it clear to readers that the translation of religious discourse – on account of the size and difficulty of many key works – is frequently a joint effort. To give two examples: the second-century-BCE Greek Septuagint is supposed to have been translated from the Hebrew scriptures by seventy (or seventy-two) scholars, while the King James Bible was the result of six committees revising earlier work in English, such as Tyndale's. Paratextual material can also allow translators and editors to discuss matters of theology and exegesis, which again can help readers to reconstruct and to understand the translation decisions that have been made. Paratextual material is more and more likely to be found online as internet access becomes more common and as the tools of information technology develop. Translation studies will doubtless continue to establish itself as a discipline and will begin to influence other fields rather than drawing from them. An example of good practice is a recent special issue of *Religion* (Frenz and Israel, 2019), which examines the conceptual importance of translation for the comparative study of religion.

As more texts are translated, experimental translation is also likely to flourish. Radical English versions of the New Testament are now available, for example: graphic novels, relocations, poetic translations, editions including non-canonical texts (like Gnostic gospels). Such experimental translation is possible precisely because non-experimental renderings exist, to which readers can turn if they wish. An American reader of the sixties was unlikely to think that a setting of the life of Jesus in twentieth-century Georgia is a source text, given that the story of Jesus is so well known in the USA; inferring this fact allowed Clarence Jordan (1968) the freedom to show the reader the radical message of the New Testament as well as to critique contemporary American churches and the endemic racism in US society.

Radical change will also come about with respect to those who do the translating. The translation of religious discourse has been dominated by men, as is to be expected given that the world's religious hierarchies are male and that sacred translation has a long-standing relationship with religious authority. However, changes in political structures mean that women are emerging as translators in all traditions. Theoretical avenues are also being opened to translation scholars by new areas of enquiry in the humanities, such as the role that translation has played in colonisation or in the construction of gender, and the translation of religious discourse can be brought into these debates.

Translation as a practice is itself the subject of religious discourse, given that many religious traditions have stressed the importance and the dignity of the translator. The Buddha is reputed to have spoken of the significance of dialect variation in the spreading of his teaching, and Christianity has its patron saint of translation, the Bible translator Jerome. Translation theorists often use the language of religion in order to describe the task of the translator, following the example of Benjamin (2012), who in his discussion of the translator's task adopts the terminology of the Kabbalah, an esoteric Jewish tradition that sees the holiness of texts as lying in their potential for transformation. Wright (2016) describes literary translation in ways that stress the immaterial: it is a 'spiritual endeavour' (p. 7), a 'meditative practice' with a 'spiritual dimension' (p. 18), a 'metaphysical enterprise' that 'gives us an insight into the nature of language and thought' (p. 19).

I conclude with an example of how the translation of religious discourse can go wrong – clearly a serious issue when it comes to texts by which people live their lives – and of how it can go right, with reference to English translations of the second/third century Sanskrit *Yoga Sūtra* by Patañjali. According to Raveh (2008), the *Yoga Sūtra* has frequently appeared in versions that 'have suppressed or even defused the world-renunciation directives of this ancient philosophical text in their eagerness to project more moderate, palatable images of yoga to their anticipated audience in the west' (p. 179). Ranganathan (2008) analogously remarks that many translators disastrously impose 'contrary systems of philosophy from the history of Indian thought' upon the work (pp. 2–3). His own translation solution is to offer the Sanskrit source text by individual *sūtra* [verse], followed by: a transliteration and gloss of the Sanskrit words; his English translation of the verse; and a philosophical commentary on the content. One thing that immediately strikes the reader is how there can be no question here of one-to-one equivalence at the level of word, verse, or text. The opening word of the first *sūtra* of the source text, for example, is *atha*, which Ranganathan glosses as '(auspicious particle) now, certainly, therefore', and which he translates as 'Thus' (Ranganathan, 2008, p. 71). He comments that the use of *atha* is a typical way of beginning an Indian philosophical *sūtra*; it is a choice by the source text author that shows readers that they are dealing with a philosophical and not an esoteric text. The target text is radical in presentation and also scholarly because it is based on a reading and exegesis of Indian philosophy, as is made clear in the paratext.

Translation is always more than a linguistic phenomenon, as I have argued throughout this chapter. Ranganathan's *Patañjali* shows readers differing aspects of the source text and indicates how these can be recreated in translation. *Sūtra*-s 13, 33, and 48 are even given alternative translations that are 'equally acceptable' (Ranganathan, 2008, p. 87). It is a model of how translation can be done in the twenty-first century to keep religious discourse alive. The translation of religious discourse will always be about how far we can recreate the universal within a local setting, while respecting both the original and the new. Different translators will offer different solutions, some of which will succeed and some of which will not. There is an analogy here with the phenomenon of religion itself. Prophets and sages hear a transcendental word and try to express it within a particular idiom, which then begins to spread through other forms of translation. Translation may be one of the best metaphors for religion that we have.

Acknowledgements

Many thanks to the following for their support and advice: Jean Boase-Beier, Bill Downes, Valerie Henitiuk, Shyam Ranganathan, Ross Wilson; and to Arc Publications for permission to cite from *The Bright Rose: Early German Verse 800–1280* by Philip Wilson, translation copyright © 2015.

7.5   References

Abdul-Raof, H. (2005). Cultural aspects in Qur'an translation. In L. Long (ed.), *Translation and Religion: Holy Untranslatable?* (pp. 62–72). Clevedon: Multilingual Matters.

d'Ablancourt, N. P. [1654] (2002). To Monsieur Conrart. Tr. by D. G. Ross. In D. Robinson (ed.), *Western Translation Theory from Herodotus to Nietzsche* (pp. 157–9). Manchester: St. Jerome.

Aland, K., Black, M., Martini, C., Metzger, B., & Wirkgen, A. (eds.). (1968). *The Greek New Testament*. London: United Bible Societies.

Augustine. [400] (2008). *Confessions*. Tr. by H. Chadwick. Oxford: Oxford University Press.

Barnstone, W. (1993). *The Poetics of Translation*. New Haven and London: Yale University Press.

Barton, J. (2019). *A History of the Bible*. London: Allen Lane.

Benjamin, W. [1923] (2012). The translator's task. Tr. by S. Rendall. In L. Venuti (ed.) *The Translation Studies Reader* (pp. 75–83). 3rd ed. London and New York: Routledge.

Bennett, B. P. (2018). *Sacred Languages of the World*. Chichester: Wiley.

The Bible: Authorized King James Version [1611] (2008). Oxford: Oxford University Press.

Boase-Beier, J. (1998). Can you train literary translators? In P. Bush & K. Malmkjær (eds.) *Rimbaud's Rainbow* (pp. 33–41). Amsterdam: John Benjamins.

Boase-Beier, J., Fisher, L., & Furukawa, H. (eds.). (2018). *The Palgrave Handbook of Literary Translation*. London: Palgrave Macmillan.

Boase-Beier, J., & de Vooght, M. (eds.). (2019). *Poetry of the Holocaust*. Todmorden: Arc.

Downes, W. (2012). *Language and Religion*. Cambridge: Cambridge University Press.

Frenz, M., & H. Israel (eds.). (2019). Translation and religion: Crafting regimes of identity. Special Issue of *Religion*, *29*(3).

Hare, T. (2014). Translation and the Sacred: Translating Scripture. In S. Bermann & C. Porter (eds.), *A Companion to Translation Studies* (pp. 531–42). Chichester: Wiley Blackwell.

Hermans, T. (2007). *The Conference of the Tongues*. Manchester: St Jerome.

Israel, H. (2014). Translating the Sacred. In S. Bermann & C. Porter (eds.) *A Companion to Translation Studies* (pp. 557–69). Chichester: Wiley-Blackwell.

Jakobson, R. [1959] (2012). On linguistic aspects of translation. In L. Venuti (ed.) *The Translation Studies Reader* (pp. 126–31). 3rd ed. London and New York: Routledge.

Jordan, C. (Tr.). (1968). *The Cotton Patch Version of Luke-Acts*. New York: Association Press.

King, N. (Tr.). (2004). *The New Testament*. Stowmarket: Kevin Mayhew.

Long, L. (ed.). (2005). *Translation and Religion: Holy Untranslatable?* Clevedon: Multilingual Matters.

Long, L. (2013). The translation of sacred texts. In C. Millán & F. Bartrina (eds.), *The Routledge Handbook of Translation Studies* (pp. 464–74). London and New York: Routledge.

Luther, M. [1530] (2002). Circular letter on translation. In D. Robinson (ed.), *Western Translation Theory from Herodotus to Nietzsche* (pp. 84–9). Manchester: St. Jerome.

Polizzotti, M. (2018). *Sympathy for the Traitor*. Cambridge, MA: MIT Press.

Ranganathan, S. (Tr.). (2008). *Patañjali's Yoga Sūtra*. London: Penguin.

Raveh, D. (2008). Lost in translation: Shifts of self and identity in the English versions of Patañjali's *Yogasūtra*. In P. Nikolaou & M.-V. Kyritsi (eds.), *Translating Selves* (pp. 169–82). London: Continuum.

Ricci, R. (2014). Story, sentence, single word: Javanese and Malay Islamic literature. In S. Bermann & C. Porter (eds.), *A Companion to Translation Studies* (pp. 543–55). Chichester: Wiley-Blackwell.

Robinson, D. (2016). *The Dao of Translation*. London and New York: Routledge.

Saldanha, G., and S. O'Brien (2013). *Research Methodologies in Translation Studies*. Manchester: St. Jerome.

Shackle, C. (2005). From gentlemen's outfitters to hyperbazaar: A personal approach to translating the sacred. In L. Long (ed.), *Translation and Religion: Holy Untranslatable?* (pp. 19–32). Clevedon: Multilingual Matters.

Smith, M. [1611] (2009). The Translators to the Reader. In *The Bible, Authorized King James Version with Apocrypha* (pp. liii–lxix). Oxford: Oxford University Press.

Stiver, D. (1996). *The Philosophy of Religious Language*. Oxford: Blackwell.

Venuti, L. (ed.). (2012). *The Translation Studies Reader*. 3rd ed. London and New York: Routledge.

Wilson, P. (Tr.). (2015). *The Bright Rose: Early German Verse 800-1280*. Todmorden: Arc.

Wilson, P. (2016). *Translation after Wittgenstein*. London: Routledge.

Wilson, P. (2019). Demanding the impossible. In D. Large, M. Akashi, W. Józwikowska & E. Rose (eds.), *Untranslatablity: Interdisciplinary Perspectives* (pp. 99–113). London: Routledge.

Wittgenstein, L. [1953] (2009). *Philosophical Investigations*. Tr. by G. E. M. Anscombe, P. M. S. Hacker and J. Schulte. Chichester: Wiley-Blackwell.

Wright, C. (2016). *Literary Translation*. London: Routledge.

8   Institutions

Kate Power

8.1   Background, History, and Key Terms

For many people, the phrase "institutional religion" connotes something negative: in short, oppressive, overbearing, authoritarian clerics attempting to limit individual freedom and constrain individual behaviour. "I'm not *religious*; I'm *spiritual*" has become a popular refrain, as fewer and fewer people of faith in places like the United Kingdom, Canada, and Australia are choosing to express that faith through engagement with religious institutions. Yet, religion remains one of the basic social institutions, alongside economics, education, the family, and the state. Within each of these broad social structures, we find both informal and formal institutions. Informal institutions include the traditions, norms, and values that constitute particular cultures, while formal institutions might best be described as organizations shaped by rules, laws, norms, and differing degrees of power and influence. Both types of institution impact our lives in many ways, and the implications of (formal and/or informal) institutional change can be both far-reaching and significant.

One prominent, internationally recognized definition of "religious institutions" centers on "[c]hurches, temples, mosques and other places of worship and institutions that exist to support and manage the practice of a specific set of religious beliefs" (UNESCO Institute of Statistics, 2020). More specifically, this list might be extended to include schools, camps, retreat centers, networks for religious education, and religious charities. This broad definition accounts for a range of religious traditions including Buddhism, Christianity, Hinduism, Islam, and Judaism, as well as other traditional (e.g. Ásatrú, the Bahá'í Faith, Sikhism, Taoism, Zoroastrianism) and new religious movements (e.g. Temple of the Jedi Order, Scientology). It also potentially encapsulates interfaith organizations and many further types of institution, including museums, publishing houses, relief organizations, religious orders, research centers, and sporting and youth groups associated with specific religions.

Religious institutions are key sites for the production and consumption of religious discourse, and the texts produced by and within these institutions perform both formal and informal functions. These texts can also serve sacred and/or secular – liturgical, ceremonial, didactic, governmental, socio-cultural, and other – purposes. Drawing on Benson's (2000) insightful critique of the "often *anti*-religious stance embodied in secular*ism*" (p. 520, emphasis original), I use the term "secular" here to refer to texts and purposes that are "non-sectarian or focused on this world," although not necessarily "religion-free" (p. 520). Sacred texts such as the Vedas (Hinduism) or Guru Granth Sahib (Sikhism) not only provide religious instruction, but also promote a connection with divine reality. Other forms of religious discourse include doctrines, laws, and liturgical texts. Doctrines such as the Four Noble Truths (Buddhism) or the Doctrine and Covenants of the Church of Jesus Christ of Latter-Day Saints circumscribe a religion's "true" beliefs, and may be used to defend against misinterpretation. Similarly, laws such as the Halakah (Judaism), *fatāwā* (Islam), or Wiccan Rede prescribe a religion's legal or moral system, while liturgical texts such as the Yasna (Zoroastrianism) or Book of Common Prayer (Anglicanism) shape the devotional practices of religious adherents. Each of these text types expresses religious authority, insofar as each encodes beliefs and/or behaviors for religious adherents to follow. In many cases, they also convey the authority of religious institutions – and, for this reason, religious texts have become key sites of struggle for religious power.

Power is a basic component of all social relationships, and scholars have shed a great deal of ink attempting to define and describe it. While reviewing that literature falls outside the scope of the present chapter, Bourdieu's (1979) notion of "symbolic power" is worth mentioning here. Bourdieu defines symbolic power as both "power to construct reality" (p. 79) and "power to constitute the given by stating it, to show forth and gain credence, to confirm or transform the world view and, through it, action on the world, and hence the world itself" (p. 82). This type of power is clearly discursive in nature: for discourse not only reflects reality, but also has considerable power to speak it into being.

For Bourdieu (1991), "religious authority" is one realization of symbolic power, and symbolic power, in turn, is subject to competition as diverse agents "struggle for the monopoly over the legitimate exercise of religious power over the laity and over the administration of the goods of salvation" (p. 22). The history of the canonization of Christianity's New Testament scriptures provides a particularly salient example. A wide range of scriptures were in circulation throughout the Roman Empire at the same time as – and were quoted by early church leaders alongside – the now-canonical Gospels. However, these texts were not included in the New Testament canon, which was formalized through a series of Church councils, over the course of several hundred years. As Ehrman (2003) observes,

The group that emerged as victorious and declared itself orthodox determined the shape of Christianity for posterity – determining its internal structure, writing its creeds, and compiling its revered texts into a sacred canon of Scripture. Had things turned out otherwise, not just the Christian Church but all of history would have been quite different. (p. 159)

Similar struggles for the power to prescribe orthodoxy and/or orthopraxy are also seen in other religious traditions.

The previous example highlights an important distinction between "religious power" and the "power of a religion." The former entails using religious beliefs and/or meanings to influence people, whereas the latter involves the exercise of power (whether religious or not) by religious institutions and their members (ter Borg, 2018, p. 196). My main concern in this chapter is with "religious power" and the processes by which it is acquired. However, the intersection of religious and political power can also be seen outside religious institutions. For example, the place of religion in secular politics has been explored from numerous angles, including the affinity of different religions with democratic principles and governments, and the impact of religious affiliation on political participation. Also of interest to scholars are the contributions made by religious individuals and institutions to civil society (and to democratizing processes in particular), as well as questions about the rightful place of religion in the public sphere and the legitimacy of religious arguments in public debate.

The distinction between political power and religious power may be difficult to differentiate at times, particularly when politicians draw on religious rhetoric or when religious leaders speak out on political matters. The use of religious rhetoric in secular politics has attracted considerable scholarly attention in recent decades, with studies analyzing both overt mentions of God, faith, prayer, and religious themes, and more subtle forms of "multivocal communication" (Albertson, 2015, p. 5), wherein "religious code" (Calfano and Djupe, 2008, p. 329) is used to attract religious insiders while evading outsiders' notice (and possible disapprobation). In referring to the "wonder-working power" of the American people, for example, former US President George Bush alluded to, but did not explicitly reference, an evangelical/Pentecostal hymn – thus signaling a "shared religious affiliation" with select members of his audience (Albertson, 2015, p. 6). Yet, while explicit religious mentions are commonplace in the USA, the same is not true in all locations. Indeed, the reverse might be said of Canada. When Stephen Harper closed his 2006 Prime Ministerial victory speech with the phrase "God bless Canada," for example, leading newspapers portrayed him as both "crass" and "unCanadian" (as noted in Sibley, 2008).

While the use of religious rhetoric in major public elections has been a popular field of study for several years, elections conducted outside conventional political systems have hitherto eluded the gaze of critical discourse analysts. Yet, the election of a spiritual leader is an important event for many people and the central themes of public politics – namely, power, influence, and authority – are arguably no less salient within ecclesiastical leadership competitions than in secular public elections.

Many religious communities rely on democratic processes when choosing their leaders. These processes differ from each another, as well as from the election of secular officials, with respect to their traditions, rituals, and terminology. What they share, however, and what sets them apart from secular public elections is their selection of a spiritual (rather than merely a political, economic, or cultural) leader. Democratic processes within religious institutions can be particularly important for those marginalized by church hierarchies and traditions (most notably women and LGBTQ individuals); but they are also key moments for those wishing to uphold or return to past practices. For example, given the considerable religious power held by Bishops, episcopal elections within the Anglican Communion represent critical moments of consolidation or change, which can influence profoundly the spiritual and personal lives of church members. However, these are by no means the only occasions on which religious and political power converge. Democractic processes are used in many religions for diverse purposes – and, in each case, represent an important nexus between religious and political power.

8.2   Key Topics, Questions, and Debates

The two key topics addressed by this chapter are, first, that religious power is established, maintained, and contested within religious institutions through democratic processes (among other means); and, second, that these processes can be analyzed discursively by examining texts produced at key moments within the lives of religious institutions.

Critical Discourse Analysis (CDA) is an approach to analyzing language use that focuses on power, which makes it particularly appropriate to studying religious power and its realization within the democratic processes of religious institutions. While there are several versions of CDA, each with its own emphasis, some common threads run throughout all of these approaches (Wodak and Meyer, 2009). First, CDA recognizes language use as a social practice that not only reflects but also contributes to establishing and maintaining power asymmetries. Second, CDA scholars often analyze language use within institutions, particularly politics and the media, where power asymmetries have a material impact on people's lives. Third, CDA considers language use in context, although what constitutes an appropriate 'context' for discourse analysis is often debated. Finally, CDA sits within a broader "critical" paradigm. Like 'context,' 'critical' is both a polysemous and a contested term: often read as shorthand for 'left-wing,' it more properly means being both skeptical and self-reflective (Wodak, 2007).

CDA is both a well-established and a widely used analytical approach, but it is not without its critics (for a review of which, see Breeze, 2011). Chief among the charges levelled at CDA is that its political motivation gives rise to unsystematic, biased, and circular analyses. Further critiques center on CDA's insufficiently close analysis of the linguistic features used in specific texts, on the one hand, and inappropriate (too much or too little) attention to the contexts within which those texts are produced and consumed. Still other critics have argued for a more constructive approach to discourse analysis. Martin (1999), for example, advocates for the analysis of "discourse that inspires, encourages, heartens" (p. 52), and this call for new forms of Positive Discourse Analysis (PDA) has been taken up across numerous theoretical and empirical studies. It has also reinvigorated debate about the meaning and nature of 'critique.'

One approach to CDA – known as the Discourse-Historical Approach (DHA) – addresses and transcends most of these critiques, while retaining CDA's characteristic interest in and concern to redress power imbalances. It does so by combining theoretically informed social critique with detailed linguistic analysis and a systematic approach to the consideration of context (Wodak, 2001). Three key questions emerge from the use of this approach, however.

First, the DHA seeks to analyze texts in their social and political context, which raises the question: What counts as context? Diverse context "levels" (Wodak, 2001, p. 67) potentially influence the way in which texts are understood. These include "the mental representation of the participants about the relevant properties of the social situation in which participants interact, and produce and comprehend text or talk" (van Dijk, 2005, p. 75), but also:

1. the immediate, language or text internal co-text;
2. the intertextual and interdiscursive relationship between utterances, texts, genres and discourses;
3. the extralinguistic social/sociological variables and institutional frames of a specific 'context of situation' (middle range theories); [and]
4. the broader sociopolitical and historical contexts, which the discursive practices are embedded in and related to (Wodak, 2001, p. 67).

Second, interdisciplinarity is a defining characteristic of the DHA, but this raises the question: What kind of interdisciplinary work is needed to understand religious power? The DHA argues that critical discourse analysts should draw as needed on theoretical frameworks from outside linguistics, such as history, politics, sociology, and psychology (Wodak, 2001) – but that they should seek to avoid dilettantism by building interdisciplinary research teams whose members agree on topics, definitions, terminology, and perspectives. Of course, where a discourse analyst already has expertise in a relevant field, the need for team-building lessens.

The third key question that emerges from using the DHA to study religious power in institutions concerns its focus on analyzing *topoi* (singular *topos*): What are topoi, and how are they identified? Topoi are "content-related warrants" used to arrive at particular claims or stances (Wodak, 2001, p. 74), but the DHA has often been critiqued for failing to provide detailed reconstructions of those warrants. In response, Kotwal and Power (2015) model how this can be done in three stages: identifying the claim or stance in a given text; locating the arguments upon which that claim is made or stance taken; and formulating a conditional or causal proposition showing how those arguments legitimate the claim or stance in question.

A final key question of relevance to this chapter concerns how religious institutions respond to cultural changes, and particularly those changes that intersect with and challenge traditional discursive constructions of religious power. For example, when Canada legalized same-sex marriages in 2005, several religious groups participated in the public debate causing different denominations, as well as both intra- and interfaith coalitions, to line up on either side. The dividing line between these groups involved their respective understandings of Scripture and, more fundamentally, of divine revelation. Where the latter is viewed chiefly in terms of "a personal-dialogical encounter between God and humanity" (Fehige, 2013, p. 41), the perceived authority of Scripture tends to decrease, allowing more heterogeneous interpretations to emerge, including those favourable to same-sex marriage. By contrast, where revelation is understood "primarily as epiphany (God appears in something else) or as an instruction of statements (God dictates sentential truths)," Scripture tends to be viewed as authoritative and to be read as a "handbook of sexual ethics," in which homosexual relations are traditionally prohibited (Fehige, 2013, p. 41).

8.3   Case Study

In 2013, the Right Reverend Michael Ingham retired from his position as Bishop of New Westminster, within the Anglican Church of Canada, after nearly twenty years. During his tenure, Ingham had been a highly controversial figure, approving the blessing of same-sex relationships some three years before they were legalized in Canada ("Angry Anglicans," 2008). His retirement generated considerable excitement over whether his successor would shepherd forward or shut down the changes he had introduced. Thus, the 2013 New Westminster episcopal election provides an interesting case study to investigate many of the key issues in contemporary religious institutions, including both the ways in which these institutions respond to social change, and how religious elections resemble and differ from secular public elections.

The worldwide Anglican Communion selects many of its leaders through democratic processes. In 1989, for example, Barbara Harris was elected Bishop Suffragan of Massachusetts, becoming the first female bishop in the Episcopal Church of the United States. Then, in 2013, Pat Storey was elected as the first female bishop in the Church of Ireland and her election was followed closely by that of Libby Lane in 2014, as the first female bishop in the Church of England. Each of these elections overturned centuries of tradition, furthering gender equality within international Anglicanism (for more detail, see Power, 2015). The process for electing Anglican bishops is somewhat idiosyncratic, depending on the Canons of each Diocese, but in New Westminster a majority vote was required among each order of delegates (clerical and lay), with the vote conducted by secret ballot. The Revd. Canon Melissa Skelton was the clear frontrunner from the first round of voting and her ultimate election as Bishop of New Westminster fulfilled the hopes of many that Bishop Ingham's liberal legacy would continue. However, it took three rounds of voting for Skelton to secure the requisite majority.

Through analysis of official campaign materials, using features that both resemble and differ from secular political discourse, analysis shows how candidates position themselves in relation to the role of "bishop" and how their self-presentations display sensitivity to the intertextual, situational, and wider (sociopolitical, historical, ecclesiastical) contexts. I will begin by looking specifically at the context of episcopal campaigning, before considering in turn the campaign materials prepared by Skelton and her fellow candidates.

8.3.1   Episcopal Campaigning

A first overarching observation about the 2013 New Westminster episcopal election is that it differs significantly from secular public elections in being a decidedly in-house affair, which received minimal attention and commentary from the mainstream media. The major local newspaper ran a single article in the lead-up to this election, briefly introducing the candidates, speculating as to the likely winner, and including a link to the Diocesan website, where candidates' campaign materials were posted. Otherwise, however, the election proceeded outside the public eye, such that – notwithstanding the internal heterogeneity of the Anglican Church – the candidates' campaign materials must be viewed as having been narrowcast.

Second, this election both resembles and differs from secular public elections insofar as both the candidates and the position issues were pre-framed by the Diocese of New Westminster. The Diocese selected eight candidates: an equal number of males and females, but only one theological conservative alongside seven liberal contenders. This part of the election process might be compared to candidate preselection in Canadian secular elections, were it not for the obvious difference that all eight candidates were endorsed by a single party (i.e. the Diocese). Also, contrary to stereotypical views that religious institutions are inherently sexist, the slate of candidates showcased more gender diversity than was common in Canadian secular elections at the time, in which women represented less than one third of candidates (Everitt, 2015). However, the 2013 New Westminster episcopal election appeared to suffer from a "supply-side" shortage of conservative candidates, following the highly public and acrimonious decade-long feud within the Diocese, prompted by Ingham's blessing of same-sex marriages (2002–12), which saw several conservative parishes disaffiliate from the Anglican Church of Canada.

The Diocese provided each candidate with a Profile outlining the key characteristics of and issues faced by the Diocese (as determined by the Diocesan Office), inviting them to respond to these issues in their campaign materials. The following issues were listed under the heading "Challenges and Opportunities for the Diocese":

> reconnecting with one another and diocesan leadership; healing, renewing, and growing communities; Strategic Plan 2018 and the Anglican Communion's Five Marks of Mission as adopted by the Diocese; ministry to youth, young families and seniors; and attending to diversity and our multiethnic context.
> [. . .] Our challenges – and our opportunities – lie in our response to our surrounding demographics. We know that some of our parishes are small, that some of our buildings are in need of repair and upgrading and that many of our people are ready to respond through ministry to the world around them.

A further section entitled "Dissenting Congregations" was devoted to the Diocesan dispute over same-sex marriages, which was framed chiefly in terms of its impact on the Diocese (rather than outlining details of the dispute). Here, the Diocese was said to be "still feeling the effects" of the dispute, including "financial, spiritual and emotional" costs that remained "a matter of continuing concern to the Diocesan officers" and which called for "[f]urther reconciliation" (A Profile of the Anglican Diocese of New Westminster, 2013, pp. 21–22). Thus, in order to be seen to be speaking on topic, candidates needed to address the above concerns in their campaign materials; as in a secular public election, however, they were free to lend greater or lesser weight to individual issues, as they saw fit.

Third, unlike in a secular political election, the Diocese exerted considerable control over the shape and content of candidates' campaign materials, largely standardizing them and thus limiting opportunity for individualization. For example, the Search/Nominations Committee required candidates to submit a full curriculum vitae, a written statement comprising answers to two questions, and a video message presenting their views on Anglican ethos, sacramental life, and their understanding of the role of Bishop within this Diocese.

Candidates were given further confidential guidelines about how to prepare their materials, and – with the exception of one candidate living and working in New Zealand – were required to use the videography services of the Diocesan Communications Officer. Furthermore, unlike in a secular public election and much more like an advertized job description, the Diocesan Profile enumerated several qualities sought in a new Bishop. This list included attributes such as a "prayer life and spirituality [that] are integrated into everything she or he does," "a clear understanding of Aboriginal context," "strong leadership capabilities," and "courage and vision" (A Profile of the Anglican Diocese of New Westminster, 2013, p. 27). Also included were activities such as "set[ting] the theological direction of the Diocese," "us[ing] all his/her gifts to inspire and unite our Diocesan community," "communicat[ing] the experience of Anglican spirituality to those who are seeking and yearning to experience God," and "respect[ing] diverse views" (p. 27). These descriptors constructed the Diocese's view of an ideal Bishop, in relation to which candidates were invited to position themselves. However, the actual import of these attributes and activities for the election outcome is unclear, because – as in a secular political election – the electoral process did not require Synod delegates to vote based on Diocesan selection criteria.

Finally, the Diocese of New Westminster managed the distribution of candidates' materials, posting them on the Electoral Synod and Diocesan websites, and distributing them to churches throughout the Diocese, where they were typically displayed on foyer noticeboards. Importantly, unlike in contemporary secular public elections, no further digital or social media were involved. Moreover, the cost of producing and distributing candidates' materials was negligible and covered entirely by the Diocese, removing both the dynamics of and the controversies around fundraising that are common in secular public elections. As with its limited media coverage, this part of the election points to restricted participation in democratic processes within religious institutions. In this case, only two people per parish were able to vote for the spiritual leader of the Diocese: one clergy and one lay person.

8.3.2   The Winner: The Revd. Canon Melissa M. Skelton

The Revd. Canon Melissa Skelton secured a majority vote from both clerical and lay delegates in the final round of the New Westminster episcopal election. These results show her to be both a popular candidate and a successful communicator within the context of this election, so it is worth focusing in some detail on her campaign materials before considering those of her less successful fellow candidates.

Mainstream media representations of Skelton following her election win highlighted her gender (woman), nationality (American), and professional background (business executive) (Bailey, 2014). Yet, Skelton's own self-categorization in her campaign materials focuses on her previous religious job descriptions (*Canon for Congregational Development and Leadership; Director of the new Diocesan School for Leadership*) and personal qualities (*I am essentially a relational being*). She also assigns to herself attributes that both she and the Diocesan profile link to the role of Bishop, namely: an appreciation for diversity (*a love of being with and serving across a diversity of individuals and groups*); spirituality (*I do my best to be faithful in prayer and worship*); and leadership capabilities (*natural and engaging leadership style*).

Skelton makes effective use of "topoi" (Wodak, 2001, p. 74) drawn from church tradition to warrant her eligibility for the role of Bishop, particularly the view that the validity of a divine "call" is ultimately confirmed by others. For example, Skelton demonstrably responds to both the ecclesiastical nature of this election and the explicit prompts issued by the Search/Nominations Committee by foregrounding her *call to the Episcopacy*. In doing so, she strategically signals her spiritual capital as the recipient of a divine calling. Yet, she avoids explicit boasting – which could undermine her bid for the episcopacy (pride traditionally being regarded as a sin) – using both hedging to downgrade (*I believe myself to be called* ...) and reported speech to avoid (*those I work with* ... *have confirmed that they see gifts for the episcopacy in me*) direct self-praise. In this way, Skelton downplays her own agency in seeking out the role of Bishop, just as successful women have been found to do in analogous contexts (Wagner and Wodak, 2006).

Skelton was also adept at managing position issues. For example, she mentions the *difficult twenty years* experienced by the Diocese leading up to this election and she outlines some paths to achieving *a sense of healing and reality of unity in the Diocese* in future. However, she presupposes and thus backgrounds details of the church's conflict over same-sex marriage, and she did not explicitly state her own stance on this matter until after the election. Instead, Skelton indirectly signals her (affirming) stance, using the "religious code" (Calfano and Djupe, 2008, p. 329) of 'diversity' (*a love of* ... *diverse styles of life*) to position herself as a theological liberal. She displays similar sensitivity to local social, historical, and political issues by claiming to *relish the challenges and joys of the Cascadian context*, mentioning in particular the *'spiritual but not religious' character of the region, its multifaith and multicultural character, and its Aboriginal/First Nations context* (Todd, 2017), without indicating which she perceives as *challenges* and which as *joys*. This avoidance of "politically risky topics" mirrors the strategic indirectness often found in secular politics (Obeng, 1997, p. 49), showing Skelton to be both highly aware of and skillful at tailoring her communication to her audience.

Skelton's campaign materials imply both her own affiliation with and her orientation to a theologically and socially liberal Anglican audience. One key indication of Skelton's liberalism – and her perception of Electoral Synod delegates as sharing that affiliation – is the lack of explicit (or, indeed, implicit) biblical references in her campaign materials. Given the centrality and authority assigned to scripture by traditional Christianity, Skelton's complete omission of biblical references positions her (and her sense of her audience) on the "liberal, progressive" side (Weber and Thornton, 2012, p. 400) of modern religion's chief dividing line. Moreover, Skelton's direct quotation of Michael Ramsey – former Archbishop of Canterbury and prominent advocate for the decriminalization of homosexuality – further exemplifies appealing indirectly to liberal voters without explicitly categorizing herself as a liberal candidate.

8.3.3   The Runners-Up

Of the seven runners-up in this election, only one was known to be theologically conservative (Rev. John Oakes, Postdoctoral Fellow, Harvard Divinity School). One was living and ministering in New Zealand (the Rev. John Hebenton, Vicar, Anglican Parish of Gate Pa), and another in Toronto (the Rev. Dawn Davis, Incumbent, Trinity Church, Toronto). The remainder were ministers within the diocese (the Rev. Ellen Clark-King, Cathedral Vicar, Christ Church Cathedral; the Rev. Lynne McNaughton, Vicar, St. Clement's Church, North Vancouver; the Rev. Richard Leggett, Rector, St. Faith's Anglican Church; the Venerable John Stephens, Priest-in-Charge, St. John's Anglican Church).

Like Skelton, several of these runners-up explicitly categorize themselves in terms of their previous religious job descriptions (e.g. *as Archdeacon of Burrard*) and personal qualities (e.g. *a deeply joyful and hopeful person of faith*). Further direct self-categorizations include candidates' denominational affiliation (e.g. *we as Anglicans*), skills and gender (e.g. *I am an excellent teacher who loves her work*), sexuality and family relationships (e.g. a male candidate: *I job shared with my wife*). Indirect self-categorizations are also made. For example, conservative candidate John Oakes demonstrably oriented to "evangelicalism," by which I mean "biblicism" (e.g. *we believe in the vital importance of scripture*); "crucicentrism" (e.g. *our new bishop will only be able to be a "faithful steward" of God's "holy word and sacraments" by ... nurturing a Christ-centred vision of ministry and mission*); "conversionism" (e.g. *I am passionate about mission and evangelism*); and "activism" (e.g. *active engagement in social justice issues*) (Bebbington, 1989, pp. 2–3). However, he did not use that label to categorize himself – perhaps because of its negative connotations – preferring instead to call himself *a cradle Anglican*.

The runners-up also assign to themselves various predicates through which they simultaneously construct the role of "bishop" and position themselves in relation to it. These attributes and activities include: leadership and relational skills (e.g. *good facilitation skills, pastorally sensitive*); managerial experience (*leading a team that served five bishops*); a particular perspective on biblical knowledge and interpretation (e.g. *a more mature understanding of the Scriptures*); theological priorities (e.g. *I value ecumenical cooperation and interfaith dialogue*); academic credentials (e.g. *I've worked and studied at four different seminaries*) and affiliations (e.g. my colleagues at Vancouver School of Theology); character traits (e.g. *a "Teflon" skin*); and personal spirituality (e.g. *a healthy, grounded spiritual life*). Two candidates stand out as unique in this respect, however. The first (Ellen Clark-King) re-narrated the Biblical metaphor of *the good steward* using feminine pronouns, thus radically re-construing (and opening up to herself) a role that, until recently, was reserved solely for men. By contrast, the second (John Stephens) was the only candidate to explicitly categorize himself as *not able to offer all* of the Diocesan selection criteria.

The campaign materials produced for this election display a noticeable consistency in their use of the "topos" (Wodak, 2001, p. 74) of "calling" to warrant candidates' eligibility for the role of Bishop. In brief, this *topos* might be articulated as follows: *If God has genuinely called someone to a position of church leadership, they should be accepted as eligible for that role; but, if someone is not so called, they should not be admitted to the position.* The consistency with which this *topos* is invoked by the runners-up in this election follows from the Search/Nominations Committee inviting candidates to explain "why they felt called to the Office of Bishop." This is an important question given the "tension between calling and career" within the church, particularly as one progresses up the ranks of church leadership (Christopherson, 1994, p. 224); it is also a question that probes for theological understanding and, as such, generates both similarities and differences in response.

Like Skelton, several runners-up display the conventional Christian understanding that – in order to be accepted as valid – an individual's sense of "calling" to ministry must be corroborated by others (e.g. *I offer myself as a candidate because ... a significant number of friends and colleagues have asked me to; ... a felt personal call, which I have, needs also to be a call of the church*). Most runners-up also signal that claiming to be "called" by God is a delicate and potentially face-threatening act, fittingly accompanied by mitigating strategies such as hedging (e.g. *I believe myself to be called; my sense of a call*), genericization (e.g. *we're all called*), and humblebragging (e.g. *I have been surprised by the intensity of my sense of being called to this ministry*). However, some runners-up depart from this script. For example, Dawn Davis makes no claim to be "called" to the episcopacy, notwithstanding the Search/ Nominations Committee's prompts; she does, however, discuss God's collective call on the church (e.g. *we are being called back to the basics of our faith*). Unexpectedly (and perhaps provocatively), John Hebenton states that he does not *feel called* to the episcopacy in New Westminster, but that he *will trust the work of the Holy Spirit through [the Diocesan] process, and if [he is] chosen, will understand that [he has been] called.*

The runners-up also incorporate an eclectic variety of other voices within their campaign materials. These range from American comedian Robin Williams (*There's a funny t-shirt out there that has on the back of it the top ten reasons for being an Anglican according to Robin Williams*) to a fifth-century prayer (*God is carrying out the plan of salvation*). Moreover, the runners-up put these voices to diverse uses. For example, five candidates display their fulfilment of this Diocesan selection criterion by citing contemporary theologians: "We seek a Bishop who is well read in current theological thinking and can set the theological direction of the Diocese." Like Skelton, several candidates further align themselves with the Diocese of New Westminster, as well as with the wider Anglican Communion, by citing the Diocesan Profile, the Five Marks of Mission (themselves cited in the Profile) (The General Synod of the Anglican Church of Canada, 2019), and the Book of Common Prayer and/or Canadian Book of Alternate Services (both used regularly throughout the Anglican Church of Canada).

Similarly, several candidates position themselves as continuous with historical Christianity by citing Celtic Christianity (*that thin space that Celtic understanding of where heaven and earth come together*), sixteenth- and eighteenth-century theologians (*this goes back to the roots of our church . . . Richard Hooker ah and . . . Wesley*), and a seventeenth-century prayer (*thanksgiving . . . for the hope of glory*). Four runners-up also cite the Bible, three of whom mention specific verses. In some of these cases, biblical metaphors are recruited to explain candidates' understandings of the episcopacy (*the biblical image which speaks to me most clearly of the work of a bishop is that of the good steward*) and the Eucharist (*it's forming us into the body of Christ*). In others, specific verses are used to warrant candidates' enumeration of the credentials needed by church leaders (*1 Timothy 3:1–7*) and their conceptualizations of "the Anglican ethos" (*we strive to honour Christ's twofold commandment to love God and love our neighbours as ourselves*), as well as a perceived need for redemption on the part of all creation (*Romans 8:22*). Various words and phrases common in contemporary Christian vernacular, some of which originate in the Bible, are also used by several runners-up (e.g. *God's grace; the good news of Jesus Christ*).

Finally, one runner-up (John Hebenton) stands out for his use of self-quotation – specifically, for quoting at length his Master's thesis, which describes *the Anglican liturgical tradition*, and for including within his campaign materials hyperlinks to both his blog and an online collection of his sermons. As the sole international candidate, this runner-up would understandably have been motivated to bridge the geographic and cultural divide between himself and Canadian Anglicans – although, he also uses several te reo Māori expressions, which potentially distance him from New Westminster voters. However, these expressions serve to identify the candidate with the Māori people and, thus, support his construal of ministering in New Zealand as being analogous to working with Canadian First Nations (*I have to admit I do not know the context of the First Nation people of Canada. However I bring the experience of working closely with Maori and Polynesians*).

In sum, while the runners-up in this election displayed some of the same linguistic patterns found in Skelton's winning campaign materials – most notably, although not without exception, balancing the *topos* of 'calling' with avoidance of boasting – they differed from her in several important respects. Perhaps most notable among these differences was the runner-up candidates' use of intertextuality, allowing voices other than their own to speak through their campaign materials. In academic writing, authors "select sources which they consider to be persuasive within the context of their own discipline and study" (Charles, 2006, p. 494). I suggest that the same holds true in religious institutions: whom and/or what a (would-be) religious leader cites signals whom and/or what s/he considers authoritative, and thus persuasive; but those views may well not be shared by others within the same institution.

8.4   Future Directions

Wodak (2009) observes that "'doing politics' is highly context dependent, influenced by national traditions and political systems, by the habitus of politicians, the modes of performance, the many embodied personality features, organizational structures, and antagonistic political interests" (p. 26). I suggest that the same is also true of democratic processes within religious institutions. The New Westminster episcopal election was "situated in, shaped by and constructive of circumstances that [were] more than and different to language" (Anthonissen, 2003, p. 297). However, discourse analysis can shed considerable light on the establishment, maintenance, and contestation of religious power within religious institutions.

Future analysis might examine the countless moments within religious institutions in which religious decisions are made – and religious power is claimed and assigned – outside the public eye. This exploration might address how relationships of power are negotiated between clergy at different levels within hierarchical religious organizations, as well as between clerical and lay members of religious institutions. Relatedly, examining abuses of power within religious institutions, some of which may not come to light until years or even decades have passed, is important. For example, the tragic prevalence of sexual abuse within the Catholic Church (and other religious institutions) is just one area in which religious warrants have been used to legitimize and mask the exploitation of vulnerable people. Religious institutions' responses to such abuse have already attracted attention from critical discourse analysts, but further work could draw on Positive Discourse Analysis to examine and promote more responsible and restorative engagement by religious institutions. As documented by Australia's Royal Commission into Institutional Responses to Child Sexual Abuse (Commonwealth of Australia, 2017), for example, religious institutions' governance, leadership, and culture are all critical areas in which the sexual abuse of children can be prevented – and each of these areas is shaped, at least in part, by discourse.

Therefore, the discursive dimensions of religious institutions' governance and organizational practices should also be explored. For instance, discourse analysis could enhance our understanding of how religious leaders and volunteers are recruited and managed. The adoption by religious institutions of business and bureaucratic discourses is also worth exploring, as is the discursive positioning of religious institutions during times of social change. Key questions here include how religious institutions situate themselves in relation to public discourse, how changing attitudes about religion (and religious institutions) affect their discourse, and how religious institutions endure in times of change.

The relationships between diverse religious institutions and the State – including both their disparate claims on and approaches to exercising power, and their historical, economic, and sociopolitical interconnectedness – also invite consideration via CDA. During the COVID-19 pandemic of 2020, for example, religious communities in Canada and the USA displayed contrasting responses to public health orders concerning "social distancing." Both countries have enacted legislation to protect religious freedom (i.e. the Canadian Charter of Rights and Freedoms, and the First Amendment of the US Constitution). It was chiefly in the USA, however, that conservative Christian and Hasidic communities used religious warrants to resist government restrictions on public gatherings designed to prevent the spread of COVID-19. "Religious freedom" arguments have also been invoked repeatedly in the USA to oppose public health care legislation, whereas Canadian religious groups have not only cooperated with public health recommendations but also tend to view freely available public health care as both a human right and a religious obligation (Klassen, 2011). The relationship between religious institutions and the State also plays out in discourses produced by the latter. While the use of religious rhetoric by US politicians has received extensive scholarly attention, this is less true of both political leaders from other countries, particularly throughout the Majority World, and politically motivated social movements, such as the Arab Spring.

The self-presentation of religious leaders and the types of argument used by religious institutions with their own "internal" audiences also merit attention, including inter alia how religious institutions respond to contemporary social and political issues and how those responses balance spiritual and other priorities. Future research could examine the extent to which greater public awareness of and respect for diversity (cultural, linguistic, racial, and/or sexual) has affected how religious institutions interact with their own members, and the impact of these changes on their discursive practices. Many Christian churches in Australia, for example, have adopted the increasingly common public practice of offering an "Acknowledgement of Country" at the start of meetings and events, as a way of showing respect for Aboriginal and Torres Strait Islander people as the First Australians, Traditional Owners, and ongoing custodians of the land. This emerging discursive practice is not uncontentious, however, with some religious leaders viewing any engagement with Aboriginal and Torres Strait Islander culture as syncretistic.

Media coverage of religious institutions is a further opportunity for discourse analytic research, including the effects of new media and the Internet on religious institutions' ability to retain and assert religious power. For example, media representations of religion – and some religions, in particular, most notably Islam – often focus on violence and injustice, neglecting the peaceful and benevolent work toward social justice in which many religious institutions participate and show leadership. Using Positive Discourse Analysis to explore the discursive practices and power of religious institutions in such contexts would make for a very valuable contribution to scholarly understanding. By situating religious discourse within both its institutional and wider sociopolitical contexts, discourse analytic work could demonstrate both the relevance of close linguistic analysis to Religious Studies inquiries, and the rich arena of religion as a research site for discourse analysis.

8.5   References

Albertson, B. L. (2015). Dog-whistle politics: Multivocal communication and religious appeals. *Political Behaviour, 37*, 3–26.

Angry Anglicans. (2008). *The Economist*, 386 (8573).

Anthonissen, C. (2003). Interaction between visual and verbal communication: changing patterns in the printed media. In G. Weiss & R. Wodak (eds.), *Critical Discourse Analysis: Theory and Interdisciplinarity* (pp. 297–311). New York: Palgrave Macmillan.

Bailey, I. (2014). Q&A Rev. Melissa Skelton: A bishop with business sense. *The Globe and Mail*, January 2, 2014. www.theglobeandmail.com/news/british-columbia/a-bishop-with-business-sense/article16182397/

Bebbington, D. W. (1989). *Evangelicalism in Modern Britain: A History from the 1730s to the 1980s*. London: Routledge.

Benson, I. (2000). Notes towards a (re)definition of the "secular". *University of British Columbia Law Review, 33*(3), 519–549.

Bourdieu, P. (1979). Symbolic power. *Critique of Anthropology, 4*(13–14), 77–85.

Bourdieu, P. (1991). Genesis and structure of the religious field. *Comparative Social Research, 13*, 1–44.

Breeze, R. (2011). Critical Discourse Analysis and its critics. *Pragmatics, 21*(4), 493–525.

Calfano, B. R., & Djupe, P. A. (2008). God talk: Religious cues and electoral support. *Political Research Quarterly, 62*(2), 329–339.

Charles, M. (2006). The construction of stance in reporting clauses: A cross-disciplinary study of theses. *Applied Linguistics, 27*(3), 492–518.

Christopherson, R. W. (1994). Calling and career in Christian ministry. *Review of Religious Research, 35*(3), 219–237.

Commonwealth of Australia. (2017). *Royal Commission into Institutional Responses to Child Sexual Abuse.* www.childabuseroyalcommission.gov.au.

Ehrman, B. D. (2003). *Lost Christianities: The Battles for Scripture and the Faith We Never Knew.* Cary, NC: Oxford University Press.

Everitt, J. (2015). Gender and sexual diversity in provincial election campaigns. *Canadian Political Science Review, 9*(1), 177–192.

Fehige, Y. (2013). Sexual diversity and divine creation: A tightrope walk between Christianity and science. *Zygon: Journal of Religion and Science, 48*(1), 35–59. doi:10.1111/j.1467-9744.2012.01314.x

Klassen, P. E. (2011). *Spirits of Protestantism: Medicine, healing, and liberal Christianity.* Berkeley and Los Angeles: University of California Press.

Kotwal, A., & Power, K. (2015). Eating words: A discourse historical analysis of the public debate over India's 21013 National Food Security Act. *On the Horizon, 23*(3), 174–189.

Martin, J. R. (1999). Grace: The logogenesis of freedom. *Discourse Studies, 1*(1), 29–56. doi:10.1177/1461445699001001003

Obeng, S. G. (1997). Language and politics: Indirectness in political discourse. *Discourse & Society, 8*(1), 49–83.

Power, K. (2015). Religion, power and public self-representation. In A. Jule (ed.), *Shifting Visions: Gender and Discourses* (pp. 49–68). Newcastle upon Tyne: Cambridge Scholars Publishing.

A Profile of the Anglican Diocese of New Westminster. (2013). Vancouver. www.vancouver.anglican.ca/Portals/0/Downloads/DiocesanProfilePublicationforwe b10-10-2013.pdf.

Sibley, R. (2008, September 27). One Nation under God. *Ottawa Citizen.*

ter Borg, M. B. (2018). *Religion and power.* In P. B. Clarke (ed.), *The Oxford Handbook of the Sociology of Religion* (pp. 194–209). Oxford: Oxford University Press.

The General Synod of the Anglican Church of Canada. (2019). Five Marks of Mission. www.anglican.ca/ask/faq/marks-of-mission/.

Todd, D. (2017, March 26). B.C. breaks records when it comes to religion and the lack thereof. *Vancouver Sun.* https://vancouversun.com/news/staff-blogs/b-c-breaks-records-when-it-comes-to-religion-and-the-lack-thereof.

UNESCO Institute of Statistics. (2020). Religious Institutions. http://uis.unesco.org/en/glossary-term/religious-institutions.

van Dijk, T. A. (2005). Contextual knowledge management in discourse production: A CDA perspective. In R. Wodak & P. Chilton (eds.), *A New Agenda in (Critical) Discourse Analysis: Theory, Methodology and Interdisciplinarity* (pp. 71–100). Amsterdam & Philadelphia: John Benjamins.

Wagner, I., & Wodak, R. (2006). Performing success: Identifying strategies of self-presentation in women's biographical narratives. *Discourse and Society, 17*(3), 385–411.

Weber, C., & Thornton, M. (2012). Courting Christians: How political candidates prime religious considerations in campaign ads. *The Journal of Politics*, *74*(2), 400–13. doi:10.1017/s0022381611001617

Wodak, R. (2001). The discourse-historical approach. In R. Wodak & M. Meyer (eds.), *Methods of Critical Discourse Analysis* (pp. 63–94). London: SAGE.

Wodak, R. (2007). What Is Critical Discourse Analysis? Conversation with Gavin Kendall. *Forum Qualitative Sozialforschung/Forum: Qualitative Social Research*, 8 (2). www.qualitative-research.net/index.php/fqs/article/view/255/561.

Wodak, R. (2009). *The Discourse of Politics in Action: Politics as Usual*. Basingstoke: Palgrave Macmillan.

Wodak, R., & Meyer, M. (eds.). (2009). *Methods of Critical Discourse Analysis*. 2nd ed. London: SAGE.

9   Media

Stephen Pihlaja

9.1   Background, History, and Key Terms

Religion in the contemporary world is impossible to discuss without some mention of media. Technological advancement has played an important role in the development and transmission of systems of belief over time, allowing for practices, doctrines, and sacred texts to survive. For researchers interested in investigating the religious discourse in technologically mediated contexts, a range of complex issues can present themselves, including how and to what extent the mediating technologies, be they books, phones, or televisions, change the ways in which people communicate about religious belief and practice and how the use of those technologies helps develop new ways of thinking about and engaging with and in religious belief and practice.

In the contemporary world, media can include any form of technologically mediated communication. This can include books, television shows, online newspapers, and mobile messaging apps. Media discourse can include any discourse in which the communication between people is facilitated by technology. The study of media discourse might include a focus on particular technologies in a general way and the ways in which the affordances, or the possibilities for communicating, that the technologies provide give rise to particular genres of communication, like the television preacher. This genre of religious discourse is specifically linked to the affordance of one-to-many broadcast technology, across time and geographic distance. At the same time, discourse on technologies – such as the Internet – can't necessarily be grouped into a single genre, given the various ways technologies develop and come to be used. Various different routes for analysis are therefore available. In considering religious discourse, researchers might find it difficult to discuss, for example, religion online without making some further distinctions about what about discourse on the Internet they're specifically interested in.

Within Applied Linguistics, the study of media has been particularly the focus of Critical Discourse Analysis and the work Norman Fairclough (1989, 1995). Through this lens, the study of media discourse focuses on the ways in which ideologies are produced and sustained in media discourse and how these ideologies serve the powerful through favouring their voices and marginalising the voices of the less powerful. Within religious discourse analysis, van Noppen's (2006) *Critical Theolinguistics* has taken principles from Critical Discourse Analysis and applied them specifically to religion in political discourse, for example, in looking at the messaging of George W. Bush and showing how religious language was present, but concealed in his discourse (van Noppen, 2012). Critical studies of religious media discourse are particularly useful in showing how religious language is used within social and political systems to build and maintain support and how media is important in spreading those messages.

Since the 1990s, the media has grown to include online interaction, originally described as Computer Mediated Communication and investigated as a new field for discourse analysis (Herring, 2004). The novelty of online interaction, and in particular the anonymity, asynchronicity, and physical distant of users, means new ways of interacting with potentially new outcomes of belief and practice also became the object of analysis, observed well in Hutchings' (2017) history of online churches. The concept of 'church' was mapped onto online environments, with clear connections between offline practices being developed in online spaces and the affordances of the technology shaping how individuals interacted with one another. These analogies between online and offline practices are often also present in discussion of online communication, with electronic messaging being understood conceptually and represented visually as 'mail' or online forums being described and understood as 'boards' which on which users 'post'.

With the development of computers for personal and mass communication, scholars made a distinction between 'old' and 'new' media, separating mass media in the form of mediums like newspapers, radio, and television from the discourse that was emerging online, noting in particular the breaking down of the traditional roles of media producers and consumers. Although old media required capital and infrastructure to communicate, often in a few-to-many model, Internet connections allowed for communication back and forth between media producers and consumers, and at least in theory, gave the ability of mass communication to individuals with relatively little capital and influence. Researching and writing about, for example, the influence of television preachers seen by millions of people as old media differed substantially from blog posts written by a pastor for their congregation, which might be only seen by a handful of people who might also interact with him personally.

The split between old and new media is now, however, tenuous. Researchers have long considered whether a meaningful distinction between these two categories can be made (Manovich, 2001). Moreover, with the development and spread of mobile technologies, technologically mediated communication has increasingly converged. Traditional 'old' media like television news shows are now regularly viewed online and every major newspaper has a significant online presence, with many readers often not engaging at all with the physical edition of that same newspaper. Religious believers now read their sacred texts on their phones, with apps providing them with personalised devotional readings or alerting them to the call to prayer or guiding them through mediation practices. Seeing a clear delineation between a person's online and offline religious practices has become increasingly difficult and there is little reason to believe that in the short to medium term, the integration of technology in the day-to-day interaction of religious believers is likely to become less pronounced.

Because of this integration, a key concern for the study of language, media, and religion is the interdependent relationship of technological, cultural, and societal development. Hjarvard (2013) usefully describes this as 'mediatisation' and argues that shifts in communication over new technologies change how the messages themselves come to be produced and consumed in contemporary social processes, not only how messages are sent and received. If YouTube videos which are short and contain positive messaging tend to perform better than long-form textual exposition, users may be more inclined to produce content which fits this pattern. Conversely, if videos which are controversial and engage in arguments with other users tend to gain more interest, users might be more prone to produce controversial messages which provoke backlash. In both cases, the content of the messages that is being sent through the medium is affected by what the platform and the audiences on that platform value. The consideration of the role of media in changing how people interact is particularly important in the analysis of religious discourse in the contemporary world where the prevalence of mediated communication in physical spaces has increased. Worshippers in physical churches will have access on their phones to a variety of different translations of the Biblical text during a sermon. Young Muslims looking for guidance about what elements of their job might be considered haram or unacceptable can look on YouTube for a variety of different commentaries from different Imams from a range of perspectives.

For researchers in religious discourse, the different approaches to media discourse from this historical perspective are still important for informing how research is addressed. The interplay of old and new media itself can be the focus of research, as in Bruce's (2017) work looking at the representation of Muslims and Catholics in tabloid press. This study highlighted how the discourse of tabloid news was received and developed in comments sections of particular stories. New contexts for interaction can therefore reflect both the stable ways of talking about religious practices and beliefs in generic ways and emergent practices that are made possible by those new technologies. The analysis of this discourse then requires both an historical perspective and a depth of knowledge to understand and describe ways of communicating about religious belief and practices at the same time as tracking developments to understand how religious discourse is developing in these new contexts.

9.2   Key Topics, Questions, and Debates

Historically, the focus on media as particular genres like television preaching or radio programmes was possible (Bhatia, 2002), but the interaction of different media types in online spaces may make the same sort of categorisation difficult. The television preacher is a clear example of how the technology affected not only how a message could travel, but the content of the message, with a focus on media values in a way that a local pastor preaching to a limited, physically present audience didn't. How media shapes religious discourse, both in what messages are sent and how those messages are sent, is therefore key issue for researchers. The focus of the research might be the platform itself (such as YouTube interaction) or the use of media to spread teaching (such as sermons presented on a variety of social media sites) or particular groups' (Scientologists, for example) use of media. Each different research focus will give rise to different ways of approaching the media and determine whether particular tools may be useful. The extent to which analysis of multimodality, for example, is necessary will differ depending on the content being analysed and the researcher's aims.

When looking at religious discourse on media, deciding what should count as religious discourse and how to approach a particular kind of interaction is a difficult issue. In studies of religious language, historically, there has been a focus on discourse that is explicitly of a religious character – sermons, prayers, hymns (Chilton and Kopytowska, 2018). Researchers can, of course, focus on these same forms of discourse in mediated contexts – prayer in online forums, or in television programmes. But as Critical Theolinguistics (van Noppen, 2006) has shown, religious language can and regularly does appear in contexts that are not explicitly of religious character. For researchers interested in considering religious discourse in technologically mediated contexts, a key issue continues to be what should and shouldn't be included in these investigations and to what extent should analysis of religious language, however that is conceived of in the study, be the focus of any analysis.

Mediatisation highlights how technologically mediated communication is not simply a change in the medium through which a message is sent, but also affects the content of the message as it is distributed. The extent to which media then affects religious belief is a more contentious topic, particularly when researchers include the insider view of religious practitioners themselves (the *emic* view in anthropological and ethnographic literature) on their own religious practices and communities. Although researchers may present evidence that religious belief and practice are changed by technology, religious believers may be more reticent to describe their use of technology in this way or to see it as having brought changes to the fundamental elements of their faith. For example, discussion of Islam on YouTube may include extensive focus on the position of Muslims in relation to Christianity and the position of Jesus Christ within Islamic theology specifically because the English-language Internet with users based primarily in countries with Christian histories means that all religions are understood in analogy to Christianity.

Researchers then must, as they will need to do in any analysis of religious language, balance their observations and analyses of the religious language with the perceptions of language use within the relevant communities. The need for situated discourse analysis is not, of course, limited to studies of religious communities and religious language, and has long been a theme in analysis of discourse, including Interactional Sociolinguistics with its roots in Linguistic Anthropology and the methods of Hymes and Gumperz (1972), developing forms of data analysis that include both analysis of interaction and interviews of speakers about their communication. This kind of discourse analysis that foregrounds social and cultural production is also a feature of Linguistic Ethnography (Creese, 2008; Rampton et al., 2004). Following a recursive methodology in the same way as ethnography from an anthropological perspective, linguistic ethnographers are open to research questions and methods developing as their investigation progresses (see Lytra, *Ethnography*, this volume). Linguistic Ethnography investigates the relationship between how communication practices are viewed from outside and inside a community by positioning the researcher as a participant-observer and recognising the importance of taking into account the researcher's own assumptions and biases (Tusting and Maybin, 2007).

For researchers investigating religious language in technologically media contexts, considering the texts themselves and the response to them within religious communities is essential to understanding how discourse *works* within those communities. Researchers must therefore focus analysis on the empirical evidence for shifts in belief and practice in mediated contexts, but also the extent to which those shifts are felt and perceived by the religious believers themselves. The inclusion of the perspective of the religious believer on understanding and interpreting religious discourse is a key issue to consider in doing research on religious communities. The balance of insider and outsider (or *etic*) views of discourse is a challenge for any researcher, including the extent to which the researcher's own beliefs and practices influence their analysis of religious discourse data. The presence of digital media in the day-to-day lives of religious practitioners and researchers may make the distinction between outsider and insider perspectives even more difficult to separate, as everyone's discourse is often mediated through technology as a regular part of contemporary life.

9.3   Case Study

Social media sites allow religious believers to interact with members of their own religious community and grow their influence as religious leaders, while at the same time reaching out to new users and potentially engaging in Evangelical outreach. To see how different users employ social media to present their beliefs, looking at how they position themselves in what they say to people from their own faith and other faiths can be a fruitful area of study. To illustrate this, I will focus on two users: Joshua Feuerstein and Ali Dawah, two users I have written about extensively (Pihlaja, 2018, 2021).

Both Feuerstein and Ali Dawah represent particularly interesting figures on social media for the ways in which they mix elements of traditional media presentation of their respective faiths in online spaces. In the simplest terms, Feuerstein sounds like a television evangelist, but rather than presenting himself as standing on a stage in a suit with a live audience, he speaks directly to his viewers through a mobile phone recorded in portrait mode. Ali Dawah similarly draws on traditional genres of presenting Islamic teaching, with Ask the Sheikh episodes and videos of him debating Christians, but recorded for and presented on YouTube and Instagram, the latter often in short snippets meant to be viewed in passing as users scroll through their feed. In both cases, understanding their discourse and discourse practices requires a contextual understanding that includes the social media platform and the history of evangelists that they exist within. To do this, two methods can be employed.

First, placing religious media discourse presented by individuals in online spaces requires understanding the social context of the text production, something that is a key part of Critical Discourse Analysis' (Fairclough, 1995) understanding of the three dimensions of text production and consumption: any text exists within a social context with producers and consumers which makes the text itself meaningful. In situations of mass communication, newsworthiness might be more obvious and require less specialist knowledge because text producers are responding to current events that are known by a broad selection of viewers and readers. For users on social media, where interaction among users can play a particularly important role, being able to understand what might have prompted the production of a particular video and the issue to which a user might be responding is important. Both Feuerstein and Ali Dawah's content can be the direct result of the postings or activity of other users. To capture this element of the text production, using ethnographic methods (Androutsopoulos, 2008), particularly longitudinal observation, can help put particular videos and interactions in a meaningful context. This is particularly important on social media where users might post and then delete content, while still referring to the deleted content in their future posts, and also for understanding the religious communities and potential antagonists to whom users are responding.

Second, after having a means of understanding and describing the context, discourse analytic tools appropriate to the research questions of the researcher can be used to describe and analyse different elements of the discourse. For example, in my own work attempting to describe the differences in topics covered by Christians, atheists, and Muslims in their different social media postings, large corpus analysis of keywords (Baker, 2006) in comments has been useful in seeing how different topics are more or less important in different users' social media presence. However, looking at disagreements in biblical interpretation in one series of exchanges among Christians on YouTube, analysis of the dynamic use of metaphor (Cameron et al., 2009) was more useful in tracing how disagreements among the users arose.

In the case studies of Feuerstein and Ali Dawah, thinking about how the users position themselves as religious figures in relation to their audience and other users can be useful in answering questions about why they present themselves the way that they do and why they discuss their particular topics. For this analysis, I will use Narrative Positioning to look specifically how the users tell stories to position themselves and their users in relation. The interaction in and around a story can be analysed on a variety of levels and Bamberg (1997) describes positioning occurring on three levels:

1. the interaction of characters within individual stories or narratives (Level 1),
2. the interaction of storyteller and audiences (Level 2), and
3. a storyteller's identity in relation to the larger social environment (Level 3).

In Bamberg's model, stories are told in particular contexts for particular reasons and they reflect in their telling and reception the ideologies of those involved in the interaction around the stories. By examining these different levels of positioning, the researcher can come to describe what the user is doing in their production of the media text, not simply as an artefact itself, but one that is meant to explain how they view their audiences and what they might be attempting to accomplish in the presentation of particular stories at particular times. The analysis can then also shed light on the social conditions in which the stories are told, allowing some reflection on the position of the media producer.

For this analysis, I'll look at two stories, one told by Ali Dawah and one told by Joshua Feuerstein. The first video, taken from Joshua Feuerstein's Facebook page, follows Feuerstein's typical format of video production – recorded in portrait mode on a mobile phone with Feuerstein looking directly at the camera and his face dominating the screen. Viewed on a mobile phone, the audience is addressed with a face-to-face intimacy, as if Feuerstein is speaking directly to everyone. His messages often have a very personal tone, as though Feuerstein is speaking directly to each person. Like many of Feuerstein's videos, it is only a few minutes long and appears to have been rehearsed, with the story having a structure and Feuerstein using few fillers and pauses and very little editing of the video.

In the video, Feuerstein tells a well-known story of hiker Aaron Rowston overcoming a terrible disaster wherein he was trapped in crevice of a mountain after falling and had to cut off his own arm to free himself. Feuerstein uses this story to draw an analogy to individuals overcoming their own person difficulties. He says:

Extract 1: Cutting away

You may have already heard his story
his name is Aaron Rowston
he was a mountain climber who
was made famous in the movie *127 Hours*
while he was climbing alone
he found himself in a predicament
a situation where
his arm gets trapped between the mountain and a rock and
he's not able to move
127 hours he hangs there
suspended between life and death until he finally makes a very painful
but important decision
he takes a swiss army knife
he cuts through the flesh
he cuts through the bone
and he cuts his arm off
was able to somehow escape to freedom
you know it wasn't much later that he was in in a press conference
and and a news reporter asked him
at what point did you make that decision to
to cut off your arm
I mean that seems like a crazy thing to do
I that that had to hurt
and he said yes
but I made a decision when I realised
that I could either die with an arm
or I could live
without one
so I ask you
is there a relationship or a friendship
or maybe you're just tied to the memories of your past
maybe there's something in your life
that you need to cut away from today
maybe there's something that's holding you back
maybe there's something that has you handcuffed
that you're not able to grab ahold of your destiny
and your future
I know what that's like
I know what it's like to be in a relationship
that was killing me

I know what it was like to be stuck in a relationship where
the other person kept hurting me hurting me hurting me
but I was so afraid to leave because I didn't know what was out there
I didn't know
if I could get anybody else
so I challenge you today
as tough of a decision as it might be
as much pain as you think that it might cause
I promise you
it's worth it in the end

The story of Aaron Rowston is presented as being well known and one that viewers are likely to recognise from its popularisation in the film *127 Hours*. In the story, there is only one character, Rowston, who becomes stuck during a climbing accident and is forced to cut off his own arm to escape. Feuerstein relates the story to several metaphorical situations where in the viewer, referred to as 'you', is mapped on to Aaron, with things in their life that they might need to 'cut away', things that they are 'handcuffed to' in their lives, particularly negative relationships (see chapters in this volume on *Cognition* and *Metaphor* for more on potential ways researchers might focus on these particular elements of discourse). The story itself is very basic and Feuerstein doesn't give many specifics about the kinds of situations to which he's referring – the 'relationships' he refers to could apply to friendships, romantic relationships, etc. Instead, he speaks generally about being 'hurt' by others and the 'pain' that might be caused in ending a relationship.

The story, however, has a further purpose when considering Bamberg's second level of positioning: the relationship of the story with the teller and the hearer. In this level, Feuerstein positions himself as an advocate and encourager of the viewer, an ongoing, consistent positioning of himself across many of his videos. This relationship is an intimate one because even though the videos are one-to-many broadcasts, Feuerstein speaks to the viewer as though they are engaged in a personal interaction. Feuerstein's representation of himself is made possible by the technology; although it may have analogous relationships with offline interaction or previous mediated communication methods, Feuerstein's positioning of himself and the audience is uniquely the product of the technology and the platform that allows for him to have access to users in intimate spaces where they view his videos on the phone.

The video also draws on an established positioning of pastor and congregation. Feuerstein is an authority figure, someone who can 'challenge' the audience to act, even actions that might cause them pain because he can assure them that the pain will be 'worth it in the end'. This authoritative position can require difficult actions of the viewer, but assures that they will be taken care of, even though no clear description is given of what that care might be. There is little evidence in Feuerstein's videos, nor in the comments, that users are engaging with Feuerstein in a personal way or that he is providing genuine personal, pastoral care. Feuerstein's pastoral position does not involve offering pastoral support to his viewers.

This story also shows how identifying discourse as 'religious' can be difficult when looking at particular stretches of text or talk. In this video, there is no mention of God or the Bible, and no explicit reference to anything that could identify Feuerstein as a Christian. Instead, the metaphorical references to 'cutting away' can be understood both in terms of embodied metaphor; that is, metaphorical language that most human beings would be able to understand from their lived experience. At the same time, the story can be heard in terms of religious metaphors taken from the Bible, notable Matthew 5:30 were Jesus refers to cutting off a hand that causes one to sin. The viewer is encouraged to think of the experience of Aaron Rowston metaphorically as it relates to relationships in their lives, rather than explicitly in terms of Jesus' teaching about sin. This allows Feuerstein to speak to a broad audience of Christians and non-Christians, those who aware of the biblical teaching and those who are not, by using metaphorical language.

The video is posted on Facebook, where popularity is measured by the number of views the video has and how many times it has been shared across the platform: Feuerstein goes on to encourage users repeatedly to share video. However, claiming that the platform influences how the message is produced misrepresents the relationship between the video and the platform. The video is itself a product of Facebook; it exists in the way that it does because Feuerstein has produced the video specifically for the platform. This can be seen in the physical properties of the video; for example, in the fact that Feuerstein shoots the video in a portrait rather than a landscape orientation. The video is meant to be viewed through the Facebook app rather than on a computer screen or a television, or through another app like YouTube, which wouldn't, at the time, present the video to the viewer in a full screen portrait orientation.

More important, however, for analysts of religious discourse is the ways the content of the video, the message that Feuerstein shares, is influenced by Facebook as a platform for sharing content. If a key metric of success on Facebook is the extent to which a video is viewed and shared by others, then producing content that is broadly accessible for a large audience and which users are willing to share with their own friends on Facebook likely has an effect on how Feuerstein addresses issues in his videos and considers topics and content for production. Facebook is not only then a platform for presenting the religious messages, but one that values certain messages over others. Feuerstein's success is predicated on his ability to produce content that his users share.

The second video, made by Ali Dawah, was published on YouTube and makes reference to a previous video that Ali has made and subsequently deleted, where he apparently responded very angrily to a video of a young women in a hijab dancing on the street in a way that he and others perceived as inappropriate for a Muslim woman. The video of the dancing was widely viewed and Ali Dawah's first video (which he extracts at certain points in the subsequent video he posted), includes him angrily denouncing the woman and her dancing. However, after the video, he contacted the woman and took down his initial response. In this second video, he and Musa, his friend who sits with him during the video and offers occasional thoughts on Ali's position, describe their initial reaction and why they felt the way that they did. Ali then includes extracts of a recording he made in which he interviewed the young woman from the video and where she expresses remorse. Ali Dawah responds positively to the woman's showing of remorse and assures her that Allah has forgiven her, and encourages his viewers to not judge her and to stop sharing the video online.

Extract 2 occurs at the beginning of the video where Ali Dawah and Musa discuss both the video and their response to it. The extract touches on their decision to take down their initial response video having reconsidered it. Unlike the story told by Feuerstein, this one includes recalling events that happened to the teller and to some of the viewers of the video as well. Ali Dawah says:

Extract 2: A Very Inappropriate Dance

> As you guys know
> there's a video that's gone viral
> where there's a sister
> who's doing a very inappropriate dance
> with another
> uh
> man
> in public
> and this is gone viral
> um
> and so we decided to do a video
> last night which we did
> and we was really upset to be honest
> and I'm sure
> a lot of you guys were upset
> because
> it's sad to see that
> you know
> it's
> it's just that

we have that
thing for our religion
and we understand a lot of us hate
seeing certain things
done by
practicing looking individuals

Compared to the story told by Feuerstein, this one includes both events that are ongoing and present circumstances which are a part of the story's development. The telling of the story provides insight into how Ali Dawah views himself as a leader within the Muslim community. The basics of the story involve 'a sister' and another man 'doing a very inappropriate dance ... in public'. They are recorded and the video upsets many people because it reflects poorly on Muslims. The story is particularly interesting in a study of discourse on and about media, because the video that Ali Dawah and Musa make is, in a sense, a part of the story itself insomuch as they are characters in the story: the Muslims who are upset with the 'practice-looking' woman for the dance. Their own response and the video they make is a part of the discussion.

The telling of the story and using it as an occasion to make their own response video also positions Ali Dawah and Musa as leaders in their community and the audience as needing guidance in how to respond to the video. Ali Dawah does not play any part of the video within his own video, but this recursion is common in YouTube discourse and even without editing the video into his own response, Ali is able to position the video within the narrative about its reception. The telling of the story now included as characters the viewers and those who responded angrily to the video. Ali Dawah and Musa then become participants in the unfolding narrative about the video and position themselves in both Levels 1 and 2 of the story. The video and its reception is an ongoing story wherein the response to the video is a part of the moral reasoning about the video itself. The event is ongoing and the video that Ali Dawah makes at one point is neither the beginning nor end of the story. To analyse the video, the media text, requires analysis of a developing story, one that will likely continue to develop in new directions.

The video shows how viewers of content on social media can be implicated in that content. Action possibilities for the viewer include active responses like commenting on a video or sharing it or making a response video where they can recontextualise the message for their own purposes. This participation has the possibility to have real effects on religious belief and practice because it rewards certain actions. If active engagement with religious media texts (either through affirmation in liking videos, or clearly voicing your own opinion about the video) is rewarded through increased visibility on the site and providing social capital to create more views, shares, comments, etc., engaging content is value above any other kind of content. And because the platforms reward engagement, the creators encourage viewers to engage actively with the videos, making them participants in the production of moral reasoning about any of the issues they address in their videos. The creators who can create the most engaging content (i.e. the content with which users are most likely to interact) are the most likely to increase their visibility and authority.

In the video, the position of the characters in the story, both the woman who was filmed and the viewers in their responses, are positioned in terms of their religious identity, an identity that should both affect how they act in the ongoing story of the video as participants who have a role in sharing and talking about the video, and as individuals are hearing the story and considering its implications for what is right belief and practice. Ali Dawah goes on to say:

Extract 3: Us Muslims

> Sadly as
> us Muslims
> we
> when we see such videos
> we
> take it too far
> we start insulting individuals
> swearing
> insulting
> calling them all kinds of names
> and it's
> taking our boundaries
> you know
> we should hate the sin
> rather than the sinner
> yes
> the action is wrong
> it's very very wrong
> it's really bad
> but
> it does not give us a right to start
> naming the individual
> believe me
> behind this I'm sure
> you need to understand that

The video also provides a good example of the ways in which 'religious discourse' can be difficult to delineate. The discussion about the inappropriate dance involves religion explicitly. Belief and practice are at the heart of his stated frustration about the video. At the same time, the story is also one of Internet bullying and what should and shouldn't be shared in online spaces. Religious belief and practice are not extricable from the discussion of day-to-day life and the moral reasoning in the interaction between Ali Dawah and Musa, and eventually with the woman herself is both structured in religious terms and the ethics and norms of interaction.

The use of 'we' throughout the extract to refer to 'us Muslims' also creates an important blending of the characters in the story about the response to the video and the viewer of the video being watched at the moment. By referring to the actions as being done by 'us Muslims', Ali both includes others in his negative reaction and includes himself in the other negative responses made by others who are attacking the woman. All the negative responses to the video are categorised together as 'going too far' with some exemplar actions including 'insulting', 'swearing', and 'calling all kind of names', but also suggests that the responses are motivated by wanting to do something which they should do: 'hate the sin'. Ali also reiterates that the action is 'very very wrong' and 'very bad', but that these bad actions do not justify the bad action of some responses.

The positioning of the viewer, Ali Dawah, and the negative responders together highlights how contemporary social media consumption often conflates characters in stories, and the teller and the audience, in the same social world even when users do not physically occupy the same places. The lack of distinction between those acting in the video, those acting online, and the video viewers shows how a passive position is not possible when viewing the video. Ali's positioning demands that everyone be involved in the moral reasoning he is engaged in. The viewer is not meant to simply watch the video, but take a position in relation to what Ali argues. This implication is, as I note, a regular part of social media discourse as 'engagement' is so important, but it is a key part of religious discourse as well, that often includes calls to action and sees everyone as needing to act in light of a moral or spiritual reality that is being presented by the religious speaker. In the third level of positioning, the speaker, audience, and characters in the story are all under the same responsibility to act in a way that is acceptable in Islam, particularly if the viewer is also a Muslim.

The implications of this unity of all people is that religious discourse online contexts can very rarely be treated as *only* interaction between people on a particular site and that there is always a need for the analysts to consider the extent to which the discourse is being performed with an audience in mind. Of course, linguists have known for a very long time that all social life should be considered a kind of performance, but the nature of online interaction makes that audience very present in the interaction between people and also offers the possibility that the audience could become a part of the conversation. Ali's discourse makes clear that he sees the viewer as having a responsibility in relation to the video and the subsequent drama, even if that responsibility is to simply avoid particular kinds of material that is being shared and therefore not contributing to its further spread.

In the case of social media interaction then, the technological affordances position the user as always both producer and consumer. To be an audience member is also to be implicated in any drama that arises because the viewer is always able to interact with and contribute in the spreading of information. Moreover, the position of the producers and consumers is always framed by the site in which they interact, either through the specific affordance of the site and what it allows/disallows and encourage/discourages, or through the implicit monetisation of the interaction on the site, even if that is simply watching the video. To watch the video, to visit the site, is to create value for the platform where the content is being presented. Analysts must take this into account in their analyst when attempting to understand why certain behaviours emerge and are encouraged and others not. Platforms and sites that are owned and operated as business are never neutral and interaction on them is always influenced by these different elements of site and platform design.

For users like Feuerstein and Ali Dawah, the pressures of needing to create engaging content are often explicit – both encourage users to share their content, to like it, and to comment on it. This occurs within the context of specific religious belief and practice, and both users are also encouraging what they see as pious behaviour among their audiences. The action of engaging with the content becomes conflated with being pious. This is of course not new for religious leaders – the televangelist asking for money to support their ministry is also blending support for the leader with religious piety. What is perhaps more novel is how social media further conflates the capital interests of the platform with the religious piety of the users through an implicit relationship between actions which are seen as pious and furthering the capital interests of the platform. Feuerstein's imperative to 'Share if you care' shows how a religious motivation for an action can and is co-opted for the capital advantage of a religious social media company. Facebook only desires the 'sharing'. If the motivation of 'caring' can be exploited to that end, then it is useful for the platform. Analysing the discourse and understanding why users are saying what they are, requires attention to not only the words and the context, but also the implicit capital and political actors behind that interaction.

9.4   Future Directions

The analysis I have presented suggests a convergence between what happens on the screen in media 'content' and the world of the viewers. Although meaningful distinctions can still be drawn between the worlds of the viewer and the content producer in the instances discussed here – for example, most of the viewers of Ali Dawah's videos are not regularly interacting with him in offline spaces – the distinction between those spaces, particularly in the sense that one is 'real life' and the other is not, is particularly problematic in the videos we discussed in this chapter. The 'real' life of the young woman in the video is materially affected by the angry response she receives online. Moreover, her experience of what should and should not be acceptable as Muslim becomes a central part of this experience, with real effects on her mental and spiritual health, as she reports it to Ali Dawah. Attempts to analyse the interaction as simply a media event or as media content, or to analyse the video alone as a media text without taking into account the responses of others, are unlikely to provide a full picture of the event.

The role of media broadcasting and one-to-many presentations of belief and practices are likely to continue to be important in a world where users have access to content from different voices in different local contexts. In the beginning of the internet age, we have seen the ways in which media can provide a vehicle for dominant expressions of religious belief to further consolidate their influence. At the same time, small religious communities and religious leaders who may have been marginalised in the past have also managed to amplify their own voices. The tension between the local and global, and the processes by which ideas, beliefs, and practices travel between these different scales and spheres like all kinds of discourse (Androutsopoulos, 2010) will likely continue to be important elements in tracking and tracing the development of religious belief .

The future of studies of religious discourse in media is, as any discussion of the future of media communication, dependent on the development of technology. Predicting what technologies will emerge in the short to medium term and how religious believers will adapt these technologies is impossible to predict. There has thus far been little wholesale rejection of technology by prominent religious traditions in the West, and the trend has been to adapt to and engage with technologies as they have developed rather than to reject them. If current trends persist, religious believers *will* continue to use technology to communicate about their beliefs and practices and that use of new technology will reflect previous practices. This may, of course, change, particularly as technology continues to develop its ability to make moral judgements based on information it is provided and potentially in the future, the ability of technology to develop its own heuristics for making moral judgements. Depending on how technologies develop and evolve, the possibility for conflict between particularly believers and particular technologies, or indeed between believers using these technologies, is certainly possible.

The role of artificial intelligence in the development of religion in mediated contexts will therefore continue to be an important area of research, particularly as the possibility of machine learning to provide users with content that is specifically catered to them and their needs. Trammell (2015), for example, shows how daily devotional apps consider the personal preferences of individuals to produce content for users, in the same way that other consumer products do. Research into the effects of this personalisation in the development of religious belief over time will necessarily include both analysis of the technology itself and reports from users on how they are affected by these technologies. To the extent that all interaction on social media is itself a commodity that companies seek to acquire, how religious believers adapt to, are manipulated by, and exploit these affordances will certainly affect how religious belief and practice develops in technologically mediated contexts.

The proliferation of information about different religions, for people who have extensive access to a variety of different information sources, is juxtaposed with the ways in which technologies feed users into 'filter bubbles' (Pariser, 2011), where platforms present users information which supports their own worldviews while suppressing information with which they might disagree. The extent to which media continues to grow more polarised will have important effects on how religious belief and practice develops over time, and whether religious discourse, like political discourse, grows more insular, or whether the affordance of acceptability to other points of view leads to development within religious traditions. These two futures are, of course, not exclusive and it is more likely that we will see developments in both directions, with discourse analysts needing to pay attention to the myriad effects of mediatisation.

For any religion which has developed past local contexts, technology will have undoubtedly played a role in its spread and will continue to play a role in how it develops going forward. The analysis of media texts and the processes of mediatisation must therefore be central to any study of religious discourse, at least in understanding the contexts of interaction. As mobile technologies continue to proliferate and become increasingly integrated into the social world, the processes by which they change, manipulate, and adapt to individuals must be at the forefront of religious discourse analysis. The extent to which analysis can consider the different contexts and influences on any individual interaction will predict the extent to which the analysis can provide robust, indepth findings about those interactions.

9.5   References

Androutsopoulos, J. (2008). Potentials and limitations of discourse-centred online ethnography. *Language@Internet*, 5. www.languageatinternet.org/articles/2008/1610.
Androutsopoulos, J. (2010). *Localizing the Global on the Participatory Web: The Handbook of Language and Globalization* (pp. 201–31). Chicester: Wiley-Blackwell.
Baker, P. (2006). *Using Corpora in Discourse Analysis*. London: Bloomsbury.

Bamberg, M. (1997). Positioning between structure and performance. *Journal of Narrative and Life History*, *7*(1–4), 335–42.

Bhatia, V. (2002). Applied genre analysis: A multi-perspective model. *Ibérica: Revista de la Asociación Europea de Lenguas para fines específicos (AELFE)*, 4, 3–19.

Bruce, T. (2017). New technologies, continuing ideologies: Online reader comments as a support for media perspectives of minority religions. *Discourse, Context & Media*.

Cameron, L., Maslen, R., Todd, Zazie, Maule, J., Stratton, P., & Stanley, N. (2009). The discourse dynamics approach to metaphor and metaphor-led discourse analysis. *Metaphor and Symbol*, *24*(2), 63–89.

Chilton, P, & Kopytowska, M. (2018). *Religion, Language, and the Human Mind*. Oxford: Oxford University Press.

Creese, A. (2008). Linguistic ethnography. *Encyclopedia of Language and Education*, *2*, 229–41.

Fairclough, N. (1989). *Language and Power*. London: Longman.

Fairclough, N. (1995). *Critical Discourse Analysis: The Critical Study of Language*. London: Pearson.

Gumperz, J., & Hymes, D. (1972). *Directions in Sociolinguistics: The Ethnography of Communication*. New York: Wiley-Blackwell.

Herring, S. (2004). Computer-mediated discourse analysis: An approach to researching online behavior. In S. A. Barab, R. Kling, & J. H. Gray (eds.), *Designing for Virtual Communities in the Service of Learning* (pp. 338–76). Cambridge: Cambridge University Press.

Hjarvard, S. (2013). *The Mediatization of Culture and Society*. London: Routledge.

Hutchings, T. (2017). *Creating Church Online: Ritual, Community and New Media*. London: Routledge

Manovich, L (2001). Post-media aesthetics. In Marsha Kinder & Tara McPherson (eds.), *Transmedia Frictions: The Digital, the Arts, and the Humanities* (pp. 34–44). Oakland: University of California Press.

Pariser, E. (2011). *The Filter Bubble: What the Internet Is Hiding from You*. New York: Penguin UK.

Pihlaja, S. (2018). *Religious Talk Online: The Evangelical Discourse of Muslims, Christians, and Atheists*. Cambridge: Cambridge University Press.

Pihlaja, S. (2021). *Talk about Faith: How Debate and Conversation Shape Belief*. Cambridge: Cambridge University Press.

Rampton, B., Tusting, K., Maybin, J., Barwell, R., Creese, A., & Lytra, V. (2004). UK Linguistic Ethnography: A Discussion Paper. Linguistic Ethnography Forum website: www.ling-ethnog.org.uk.

Trammell, J. (2015). Jesus? There's an App for That! Tablet Media in the "New" Electronic Church. In Mark Ward (ed.), *The Electronic Church in the Digital Age: Cultural Impacts of Evangelical Mass Media* (pp. 219–37). Westport, CT: Praeger.

Tusting, K., & Maybin, J. (2007). Linguistic ethnography and interdisciplinarity: Opening the discussion. *Journal of Sociolinguistics*, *11*(5), 575–83.

van Noppen, J. P. (2006). From theolinguistics to critical theolinguistics: The case for communicative probity. *ARC, The Journal of the Faculty of Religious Studies, McGill University*, *34*, 47–65.

van Noppen, J. P. (2012). God in George W. Bush's Rhetoric. www.o-re-la.org/index.php/analyses/item/175-god-in-george-w-bush%E2%80%99s-rhetoric.

10   Community

Andrey Rosowsky

10.1   Background, History and Key Terms

Ritual, or liturgical, languages can play an important role in the development and maintenance of faith community identity in minority settings. Recent sociolinguistic theory such as 'translanguaging (García & Wei, 2014), 'flexible bilingualism' (Blackledge & Creese, 2010) and metrolingualism (Otsuji & Pennycook, 2010), has problematicised language practices in a context of superdiversity. However, more established theory on language including maintenance and shift (Fishman, 1991) and, importantly, language performance (Bauman, 1975), still provide useful frames for understanding language in religious communities. Devotional practice can be carried out in a range of languages and this contributes to complex and fluid linguistic repertoires, particularly of young people. On the one hand, devotional practice can lead to greater stability for the sacred language in terms of language shift. On the other hand, the community (usually spoken) languages within which it is situated experience attrition. Furthermore, the use of community prestigious languages (such as Urdu, Persian, and H-Punjabi) in devotional practices such as poetry and song and which itself is a significant discursive means of shaping belief for its practitioners, leads to a modest revival in the maintenance – or (re) discovery – of heritage languages and devotional literature. Adding to this linguistic complexity is the growing use of English for devotional purposes, leading to an even greater variety of discursive interactions, modes, and genres through which young people negotiate their religious and linguistic identities.

The linguistic or discursive nature of a religious community is complex and varied. However, in terms of preferred language for ritual purposes, two main models appear to present themselves. On the one hand, there are religious communities exhibiting complete vernacularisation, where the principal and sometimes only language of the religious domain is either the majority language of that territory or any one (or combination of) minority community language(s). Such is the case, for instance, with the diverse Christian, predominantly Protestant, religious communities around the world. If any 'special language' is invoked, this is likely to be a particular register of the majority language rather than a different variety altogether (Keane, 1997). For example, in Anglican English-speaking congregations, a particular religious register of Standard English arguably prevails in sermons, hymns, and in other domain-specific genres. This register's linguistic proximity to Standard English might vary slightly from one context to another but no one experiences it as an incomprehensible or alien variety. It remains a recognisable-to-all register with certain linguistic features, particularly in the lexicon, denoting its special role in the religious domain. In this sense, it is a language register no different in status to registers such as legal English, business English or, indeed, academic English. This is equally the case even in multilingual congregations where more than one language may be utilised. In some West African evangelical churches, two or more languages are used, often in parallel using interpreters or sometime sequentially, to accommodate the linguistic needs of different sections of the community. These languages, even though in the religious domain they may also constitute recognisable religious registers of those languages, are still the varieties used by those communities more generally for interpersonal communication in the same way as in the monolingual contexts previously described (Amfo and Omoniyi, 2019).

On the other hand, and constituting the second main model of ritual language practice, many religious communities are characterised by having access to a special liturgical language which plays an essential role in ritual, religious education, and ceremony. This language is invariably archaic, often wedded to a sacred text at the heart of the religion's origins and often quite linguistically distinct and different from the language of interpersonal communication within the same community. Such is the case with many Orthodox Christian communities where the language used for ceremony, ritual, and artful recitation is often an ancient and linguistically distant relative of the community's principal language for interpersonal communication. Different varieties of Church Slavonic, for example, serve the liturgical needs of the various national Orthodox congregations. However, and possibly constituting a third model in itself, many religious communities exhibit even greater linguistic distance with a liturgical language (Bennett, 2018, uses the term 'sacred' languages for these languages) which is not related linguistically at all to the language of interpersonal communication within the community. Such is the case in most of the non-Arabic speaking Muslim world where the liturgical language is a variety of Classical Arabic. In the Arabic-speaking world itself, the relationship between the liturgical language and the community vernaculars is more akin to that prevailing in the Orthodox Christian churches as just described.

Given these three models, the acquisition and performance of what some have called 'liturgical' (Rosowsky, 2008), others have called 'religious classicals' (Fishman, 1989), and still others (Bennett, 2018) have called 'sacred', languages have often been a neglected, and at times, misrepresented and misunderstood language practice in some of the sociolinguistic literature. In respect of religious communities, therefore, in circumstances of both monolingualism and multilingualism, liturgical languages play an important role in the community's linguistic repertoire - the range of language varieties and language resources accessible by an individual, passively or actively.

The presence, therefore, of a special liturgical language in a community's linguistic repertoire contrasts starkly with any common language of interpersonal communication with the notable exception perhaps of the Catholic Church fighting a limited rearguard action with Latin-speaking clerics in the Vatican. For world religions including some forms of Christianity, Islam, and, to some extent, Buddhism and Hinduism, multilingualism with a liturgical language is characteristic. Moreover, for religions with a significant ethnic dimension, such as Judaism and Sikhism, there are different trajectories. In general, outside of the ultra-orthodox Haredi communities, a growing minority within the Jewish community worldwide (Staetsky and Boyd, 2015), the Jewish diaspora has tended to adopt the local, majority language. Historically, the development of Ladino and Yiddish stands testament to the community's ability to adopt and adapt to local languages whilst retaining a significant element of separate linguistic development (i.e. Yiddish is linguistically a variety of German and Ladino a variety of Spanish). However, despite these variations, the linguistic feature that often unites the many dispersed communities of one faith is its liturgical language.

A liturgical or sacred language is usually understood as a language, or variety of a language, reserved for ritual or recitational purposes and usually associated with a text that is considered seminal and sacred by the adherents of that faith. As such, it functions as one part of a diglossia with the community's vernacular and standard language(s). In terms of practice, knowledge of a liturgical language is necessary for the performance of certain rites but, as importantly, carries significant symbolic value in the formation of religious identity. Religious communities with a liturgical language often collectively invest heavily in the acquisition of liturgical literacy, ensuring each generation is equipped with enough knowledge of the language to perform necessary rituals, however minimal that knowledge might end up being (Safran, 2008).

From a historical perspective, many world religions and their communities have had a discrete liturgical language to sit alongside either their vernacular or standard varieties, although much of the Christian world in recent centuries, particularly the Protestant world, has rejected discrete liturgical languages in favour of ritual in the vernacular. Pre-Reformation Christendom and many contemporary Eastern rite churches manifest a wide range of discrete liturgical languages, sometimes linguistically related to the vernaculars but often constituting different languages altogether. Latin, Ecclesiastical Greek, Ethiopian Ge'ez, Egyptian Coptic, and Syriac are just a few examples of these special languages. Outside of the Christian world, Classical Arabic, in its Qur'anic variety, is the sole liturgical language of the Muslim world where the overwhelming majority of adherents are non-Arabic speakers. Before the re-vernacularisation of Hebrew in Israel, Biblical Hebrew was mainly present in the Jewish community as a discrete liturgical language, although it also had a restricted scholarly function. Depending on one's view of Israeli Hebrew (Zuckermann, 2003), this situation continues today despite re-vernacularisation with the spoken and even the standard Modern Hebrew contrasting starkly with its ancient and liturgical forbear. Chinese-speaking Buddhist novices still learn to recite in ancient Pali, a language no longer spoken by anyone, and the many varieties of the Sikhs' Guru Granth Sahib means much of its recitation is the liturgical variety rather than the pedagogical, which has to take place in local vernaculars.

The linguistic distance between a spoken or standard language and liturgical or sacred language has generally been driven by temporal and spatial distance. Firstly, such linguistic disparity is a normal consequence of gradual and natural linguistic evolution. The conservative nature of the language of sacred texts inevitably leads to them lagging behind the natural evolution of the vernacular. This is the case in all Arabic-speaking territories where the current range of spoken Arabics all exhibit significant distance (to varying extents admittedly) from the language of the sacred texts of Islam. Modern Standard Arabic (MSA), which acts as a formal lingua franca across the Arabic speaking world, differs less but still significantly from the classical language of the sacred texts (Versteegh, 2001). Communities therefore become accustomed to this diglossia, which, reinforced by clear demarcation in certain religious domains, remains one of the most common and rigorous diglossias to be found anywhere in the world.

Secondly, linguistic distance occurs spatially, particularly as religions and their texts migrate into new territories where different languages, unrelated to the liturgical language, are spoken, such as Islam in different eras moving into, for example, China, southern Europe or East Africa. Whether this happens through conquest or proselytisation, the linguistic outcome is usually the same. The Latin of early Christianity spread into a non-Latin-speaking world but was maintained as the language of liturgy of the Catholic Church until as late as the Second Vatican Council in 1962–5. The Muslim territories of Southeast Asia, largely peacefully converted by Arab traders and scholars a thousand years ago, maintain a carefully demarcated diglossia between local languages and the liturgical language of Islam.

Furthermore, this dual origin for discrete liturgical languages exists both indigenously and in circumstances of migration. In many parts of the world, religious communities have had this diglossia for millennia or centuries. Other parts of the globe, particularly in Western countries, have only recently experienced such diglossia (though pre-Reformation Western Europe knew a clear diglossia between Latin and local vernaculars). These have arisen as a result of new and recent pathways of migration, from East to West and from South to North. These fledging communities were initially prompted by post-colonial processes due to the breakdown of the major European empires and more latterly by migratory movements arising from what some call globalisation (Robertson, 1992), others call North–South economic tension (Thérien, 1999) and also from the general late twentieth and early twenty-first centuries' haphazard movement of peoples caused by war, famine, and economic breakdown – all of which can be traced back to the former two causes for migration. This in turn has led to further complex relationships among languages as minority languages have shifted to majority ones and the liturgical language has either assumed a new diglossia with the majority language or becomes part of a triglossia (usually transitional) with both minority and majority languages.

The consideration of liturgical languages as important elements of individuals' and communities' linguistic repertoires has been carried out by a relatively small number of language scholars. Fishman (1989) included what he called 'religious classicals' in his account of minority languages arguing that they have a highly symbolic function in terms of religious and religio-linguistic identity. He gives further examples of liturgical languages such as Lutheran German (used by the Amish) and Church Slavonic. In cases where only a vestigial or minimal knowledge of the liturgical language is retained or acquired, there is a need to recognise this symbolic function and acknowledge the intimate link between language and ethnic or religious identity even where the language is either not used or used in what some might consider a restricted way. Safran likewise recognises the role played by the acquisition of what he has called 'sacerdotal' languages in the formation of identity using the example of Biblical Hebrew which he asserts 'has been considered a sine qua non for believers and is studied, albeit often to a minimal extent, by almost all to whom Jewish identity remains important' (Safran, 2008, p. 186).

Finally, within the field of language shift, many (e.g. Ferguson, 1982; Fishman, 1989) have remarked upon the resilience of liturgical languages in the face of dominant majority-language contexts. This is in stark contrast to the fate of spoken and standard minority vernaculars more commonly, which follow the usual trajectory of shift to the majority within a few generations. A community's linguistic repertoire – often one of the key determining features of 'community' – where it contains a liturgical language can often therefore retain an element of diglossia in the domain of ritual whilst in the domain of interpersonal communication any such diglossia has long disappeared. The linguistic profiles of many Western Jewish communities are perhaps portents of what could potentially occur within more recent Muslim, Hindu, and Sikh communities present in the West. Among Reform and Progressive Jewish communities, and some orthodox ones too, the original vernacular of Yiddish shifted many generations ago and the diglossia that remains is that of the community's first language (the majority language of whichever country they are citizens) and the liturgical language, Biblical Hebrew. There is already evidence that in the UK at least, community vernaculars are shifting to English. The resilience of the liturgical language however, at least in the Muslim community, means a similar diglossia to that present in most of the Jewish community is likely to emerge.

10.2   Key Topics, Questions, and Debates

Within sociolinguistics, linguistic repertoire has been a key concept since it was first used in the works of Gumperz and Hymes (1972). Linguistic repertoire has been used to denote the parameters of speech communities, another sociolinguistics concept with a relatively long history. In recent times, both these concepts have been considered problematic by conditions of rapid change in patterns of human mobility and modes of communication (including electronic ones). The move from relatively 'fixed' and stable speech communities to more fluid and unpredictable patterns of group language use has led some (Blommaert and Backus, 2013; Busch, 2012) to question the usefulness of 'speech community' and 'linguistic repertoire', as previously articulated, as accurate metaphors for current linguistic realities. Much of this recent work has arisen from an analysis of new forms of human groupings (networks and other clusterings) prompted by this rapid change. Among many transnational groupings, the inclusion of a liturgical language has also tended to complexify original and settled patterns of language repertoire.

For example, liturgical language acquisition has taken place through a mediating language for centuries, even millennia. South Asian Muslims in their heartlands have been, and are still, inducted into the Classical Arabic of the Qur'an through local languages such as Urdu and Bengali. In Southeast Asia, the liturgical language has been taught in many places via Bahasa Malay. In transnational contexts such as in diaspora and in less stable patterns of migratory settlement, the community languages often shift to the majority language. This leaves the acquisition of the liturgical language to be mediated through hitherto novel and culturally distant languages such as English and French. In the UK at least, Jewish children learn the language of the Torah through English, Sikh children learn the language(s) of the Guru Granth Sahib through English, and Muslim children are now acquiring their liturgical language through English. The learning of Xish (the minority language) via Yish (the majority language) (Fishman, 1991) is a common occurrence in the pedagogy of minority languages. What adds to the complexity is the transitional condition of the shift to the majority language which is nearly always uneven and can lead to a range of language resources being deployed in places of worship in the service of liturgical language acquisition.

In many of the diaspora religious communities, the minority language long associated with the community's faith can give way to the majority language. In these cases, the liturgical language has to be taught through the new majority language, and this is, historically, quite often the language of the community's former occupier/coloniser. Largely, a pragmatic view is taken and despite vestigial rearguard actions taken by language activists to retain the minority language, the reality of a critical mass of young people urgently needing to acquire the basics of liturgical language tends to win over any argument around minority language maintenance. An associated development is that generational shift to the majority language eventually reaches the new teachers of the liturgical language and classroom strategies and teaching resources in the majority language gradually develop.

The association of the previous minority language with the faith, however, in some cases, has led to a degree of co-sanctification arising for that language (Fishman, 2006). A removal of this language from the religious domain is often seen as a loss to not only the linguistic heritage but also the religious heritage of the community. In South Asian Islam, Urdu and Persian (Farsi) are often considered in this category whereby the function of religious poetry, although not revered to the same extent as the language of the liturgical language (in this case Classical Arabic), can still draw upon a degree of sanctity in religious domains. The usurping majority language, by contrast, is often compared unfavourably in this respect. However, even a cursory historical view would indicate that Urdu and Persian, erstwhile and contemporary majority languages in their heartlands, may have also been compared unfavourably once upon a time when measured against the sanctity of the language of the sacred texts.

In some religious communities, the status of the liturgical language is such that any attempt to secularise or vernacularise it is seen as anathema. In a counterexample to how minority-spoken languages gradually shift to the majority language, Haredi communities have retained Yiddish as their preferred language of interpersonal communication for it serves as an effective means of keeping Hebrew sacred and therefore acts as a strong driver in the maintenance of this minority language both in Israel and elsewhere in the world. Unsurprisingly, Yiddish in secular contexts has suffered the same shift to the majority language as other minority languages.

Therefore, when a liturgical language exists as part of a community's repertoire, the resources of that community are likely more regularly directed to its maintenance and transmission to subsequent generations in a manner not matched by the community's attention to its spoken vernaculars. Ferguson (1982, p. 101) reminds us that 'in voluntary migration . . . religious affiliation' will tend to be language conservative to the greatest extent for the language of sacred texts'. Fishman (1989. p. 229) likewise writes that the religious classical remains a 'robust feature ... of ethnocultural membership throughout the world and is 'more resistant to change'. This persistence of the liturgical language appears to be strongly linked to personal and collective identity. Safran identifies its acquisition as a key variable in notions of religious identity, 'some familiarity with Hebrew has been considered a sins qua non for believers and is studied, albeit often to minimal extent, by almost all to whom Jewish identity remains important' (Safran, 2008, p. 186).

Linked to the place of liturgical languages within linguistic repertoires is its role in language shift and language maintenance. In standard accounts of the shift of minority languages to the majority languages in diaspora conditions and other transnational contexts, community-spoken vernaculars are often replaced by the majority language within three to four generations. A number of scholars have remarked upon the greater staying power of the liturgical language in similar conditions. Religious communities tend to invest considerable time and resources into the maintenance of their liturgical languages, often in stark contrast to the support provided for spoken and even literary community languages. Thus classes are organised, teachers are employed, and syllabuses are adopted which have as their aim the eventual acquisition of liturgical literacy for the new generation.

Such places of learning have sometimes had a bad press both from academic and more public sources. The accusation of 'learning by rote' is perhaps the most regular but uncontroversial accusation levelled at faith-based supplementary schools (Cherti and Bradley, 2011) – the principal institution by which new generations acquire their liturgical language. More seriously, such schools, particularly in recent times, have been seen as bastions of pre-modern thinking and indoctrination. In the UK, Jewish cheders and day schools, particularly those in the ultra-orthodox community, have attracted adverse media attention (Abrams, 2015). In addition, similar disapprobation has been visited upon mosque schools which have been regularly associated with extremism and, given the increased scrutiny and creeping securitisation surrounding Muslim communities in general since the events of 2001, it has been almost inevitable that they would become an educational setting of interest for politicians, policymakers, media agencies, and researchers alike. As Seddon comments,

[The stigmatisation of young Muslims] materialised ... through the suspicion of madrassahs (Islamic schools), which were perceived as places where extremism could be infused into young people, and therefore key sites which the Government planned to intervene in by closing the ones deemed extreme and proscribing a standard curriculum for the rest. This is reminiscent of Britain's colonial era in India, when the British authorities established their own madrassahs to ensure Muslims were being educated 'the correct' way (Seddon, 2004, p. 24).

Many minority language communities place high value on the preservation of their cultural and linguistic heritage, religious or not. The growth of the supplementary school (an inverse parallel to the growth of international schools elsewhere in the world) in many Western contexts has been identified as an important factor in the success or otherwise of intergenerational cultural transmission. The faith-based supplementary school, despite probably being the most widespread and numerous of schools, has often been looked at with suspicion in the Western world, and puzzled at because of its pre-modern nature in the face of growing secularisation. Christian Sunday Schools are no longer a regular feature in many Western societies though they were as recently as fifty years ago. It is in the faith-based supplementary schools of modern diaspora where liturgical language is mainly acquired. Methods for such acquisition largely remain wedded to pedagogies that have been superseded in mainstream education – though the recent emphasis on learning to read through enhanced phonics in the UK and in other English-speaking countries is not a million miles away from these more traditional methods. A primer designed to teach children how to decode the Hebrew alphabet is not much different to one designed to do the same for Sikh children preparing to decode the Guru Granth Sahib. Superficial differences conceal what is pretty much a standard sequence of learning and uttering consonant and vowel sound–letter correspondences, syllables, simple words, and verses from the sacred texts themselves. More recently, evidence has shown how some faith-based supplementary schools have adopted pedagogical strategies from mainstream education, particularly in student–teacher relationships, teaching materials, and the use of technology (Rosowsky, 2019).

Part of the suspicion of faith-based supplementary schooling often links to a prevailing sociopolitical discourse scornful of multiculturalism and multilingualism. In the UK, successive political leaders have accused minority religious communities of deliberately isolating themselves socially and linguistically. In the USA, the English Only movement is likewise targeted at minority communities (Lawton, 2013). In respect of the latter, the anachronistic complaint that the majority language is not being used in such communities reveals deeply held notions of a preferred monolingualism by political leaders for their citizens. The complex multilingual linguistic repertoires of religious communities are marginalised with little attempt to understand the value religious adherents place on these languages. Such linguistic marginalisation is naturally assimilated as individual and collective marginalisation.

10.3   Case Study

Given the current size of the UK Muslim community and its demographic profile (majority are below the age of thirty), mosque school education is probably the most widespread form of supplementary education in the UK today. It is probably also the most systematic and uniform in its aims and purpose of all supplementary schools. Above all, its purpose is facilitating the acquisition of the community's liturgical language, a variety of Classical Arabic dating to the seventh century CE, sometimes known as Qur'anic Arabic. This variety is so named to distinguish it from the much broader variety of Classical Arabic which has been used in Islamic scholarship and which has developed over a much longer duration. The language of the Qur'an derives in the main from a variety of Arabic known in a certain region of Arabia at a particular moment in the seventh century CE. According to Muslim belief, the language of the Qur'an has never changed from that moment and has been considered by Muslims worldwide as sacred for over 1,400 years.

For the past twenty years, I have been researching the language practices of Muslim religious communities in the north of England. These practices have centred primarily on the acquisition and performance of the communities' liturgical language but have also included the performance of other devotional language genres such as poetry and song. At the onset of this research, liturgical language practice was examined through the lens of literacy and it was not hard to find opinion that considered the variety of reading that took place in these contexts to be a deficit model of reading which foregrounded reading accuracy over referential meaning (Smith, 1994). The children who attended the mosque school in order to be inducted into reading the liturgical language would also sometimes transfer this mode of reading to the mainstream classroom, unconsciously slipping into a reading even in English that also foregrounded reading accuracy over comprehension (Rosowsky, 2001). However, what was missing in such superficial observations was the value the communities placed on the acquisition of liturgical language. This appeared to be an importance far more tangible than that which was given to the maintenance of the community's spoken languages (Pahari, Pothwari – varieties of Punjabi) or even its literary language, Urdu. The investment of time, money, and resources in the establishment of mosque schools for this purpose was (and is) considerable. An ethnographic study carried out at the beginning of the twenty-first century was able to flesh out in more detail the complex and rich role played by the liturgical language within the community (Rosowsky, 2008).

However, the interplay between the liturgical language and the rest of the community's linguistic repertoire, which included a sacred language (Bennett, 2018), co-sanctified H (or High)-languages (Ferguson, 1959; Fishman, 2006), vernacular spoken L (or Low)-languages, and majority standard and local varieties, turned into a recurring theme for the next two decades. This manifested itself in several ways.

Firstly, the interplay of language involved in the teaching of the liturgical language was fluid in the sense that different languages at different moments were the mediating language within the community. That these languages were themselves subject to language shift meant that a major development over this period was the transformation of the pedagogical language(s) to the majority language. Pahari, Pothwari, Pashto, and Urdu were noticeable in these mosque schools at the end of the twentieth century either as the first language of the children attending or at least as the 'language of intimacy' (Fishman, 1965) found in their families which they shared, albeit sometimes only partially. English, though, was gradually becoming the preferred language for interpersonal communication among this younger generation and when this was consolidated through mainstream school, this led to communication issues in the mosque schools between teachers, often recruited from overseas and not speaking fluent English, and their young students. A gradual linguistic migration of the majority language into the hitherto ethnolinguistic domains of the mosque schools (and in other community domains) has now led to the current circumstances where teachers are more likely to be UK-born and first-language English speakers who are more than able to communicate effectively with their students. An added factor to this rapprochement is that these new generation teachers themselves experienced both the earlier mosque school language practices and the mainstream equivalents and so have been able to adapt and transform many of the communicative and pedagogical practices of the current generation of mosque schools (Rosowsky, 2019).

One thing you're missing is that we've been through the schooling system. That's unique. We relate with the kids. They can't get away with being what we've been through. We see what they see. We've done what they are doing. So they no longer, we don't need a magnifying glass. We have it on them already. 'Don't tell me about Facebook. I know more than you do'. 'How dare you. Twitter? How come you don't follow that?' '*Stazi*, you're on Twitter?!' I know more games they do. That kind of stuff is different. Which was not there in the past. (Ali, Mosque School teacher, interview transcript extract from 2016)

The other main way the liturgical language interplayed with the community's now-changing linguistic repertoire was in the field of devotional poetry and song, particularly as it impacted upon young people. A crucial observation regarding the acquisition of liturgical language has been its performance nature. Whilst more orthodox models of reading have emphasised meaning over form, in the performance genre of the verbal arts, the opposite is often true. As Bauman (1975, 2000) shows, the performance genre in language can be far more about the quality of the exterior expression than it is about the centrality of meaning, which itself is often neglected in order to stress the outward qualities of the performance. The children and the teachers in the mosque school and in their acquisition and subsequent liturgical language practices (prayer, recitation) unerringly value the accuracy and formality of the performance.

In other devotional language practices within the community, similar emphases have been identified. Reciting or singing in a language (liturgical or a co-sanctified literary language) where meaning is often inaccessible, a similar emphasis on outward form is evident. Many young Muslims spend time and resources in the learning and performing of devotional poetry and song. I use the phrase 'poetry and song' as a way of conveying the intermediate mode of performance that much devotional practice consists of. The notion of 'music' is a complex one in the Islamic world with various positions taken on its validity within religious contexts. In general, and in most traditional religious contexts, it is not admitted and even where, to the ear of an outsider, devotional performances may sound 'musical', there is usually a semantic distinction made between 'music' and the sound of devotional performance. Faruqi and Faruqi (1986) present a hierarchy of sound in Islamic contexts that privileges the recitation of liturgical language and co-sanctified genres such as religious poetry over performances that veer towards the musical in a narrow sense. This manifests itself universally in the Muslim world. In religious contexts, in the Arabic speaking world, the verb 'aghani' ('to sing') is generally used for secular singing. The Arabic verb 'inshad' (literally, 'to intone') is used for religious performance hence the derived words 'nasheed' (an Islamic 'song') and 'munshid' (an Islamic 'singer'). Similarly, children in UK mosque schools will often be heard using the English verb 'read' when describing the act of performing devotional poetry and song.

Yeah, Ahmed Hussain, he came to my school and started reading. He did a performance in my school. In assembly. In front of the whole school. Before he read it, he said to everybody, if you know this nasheed, you can *read* with me [italics added]. (Naeem, 11. Extract from interview transcript, 2015)

Yeah. You know when you have a behaviour problem. I had that and then I had two teachers who mentored me and when we were sitting down they made me laugh and we had a chat. They told me to read and then I read an Arabic. Only to those two because I felt positive about it. I told them about the university event and that I *read* over there [italics added]. (Junaid, 12. Extract from interview transcript, 2015)

(NB *Naat* is an Urdu word for a poem devoted usually to the Prophet.)

In both of these examples, the verb 'read' is used for what others might understand as 'sing'. The same verb is used for prayer and even for uttering the Islamic call to prayer.

These multilingual devotional performances, which elsewhere I consider part of 'ultralingual' practice (language performance where referential meaning is absent or partial for both performer and audience, see Rosowsky, 2021), together with their regular acquisition and performance of the liturgical language in ritual, constitute, therefore, a major part of these young people's linguistic repertoires and an essential element within their religious identities, both as individuals and as a collective. Knowledge of devotional poetry is often praised and recognised by their peers and individuals are often feted for their performances.

I'm confident with Arabic ... These two are confident with it ... They're really good at Arabic *naats*. (Akhter, 13. Extract from interview transcript, 2015)

In school, someone ages ago, I didn't go to the school, I saw this on YouTube, 'Pine Valley's Got Talent', this boy he sang like X-factor, and he won, reading, like, *naats*. He's at university now. (Rafiq, 12. Extract from interview transcript, 2015)

However, as with the interplay between the liturgical language and other languages and varieties, a similar linguistic tension is present when considering these non-liturgical devotional performances. This, too, contributes to the complex and fluid dynamic of the linguistic repertoires in the community, particularly among the younger generation. The poetry and 'songs' performed can be in Classical Arabic (which very few of the performers understand), Urdu (which might be better understood by some but by no means all), H- or literary Punjabi (again which only some might understand) and, increasingly, English. The presence of the latter in devotional performance is a growing aspect of such performance within the community and in similar communities throughout the UK (generally those that follow a Sufi-sympathetic orientation such as the Barelvi movement which still dominates most Pakistani-heritage mosques and their integrated mosque schools). The gradual shift of the community-spoken languages to English is no doubt partially responsible for the increase in English-language devotional performance. However, the broader lingual-religious phenomenon of the English language fast becoming a lingua franca for the worldwide Muslim community is also playing a large role here. The presence of English, though, has an in-built tension, particularly for the older generations who often consider it an inappropriate vehicle for devotional practice in Islam.

Our parents are not really understanding that there is such a thing as *naat/nasheed* in English. All their lives they've heard *naat* in Urdu. They've never thought someone could be praising the Prophet in English also. (Haroon, 25, performer of devotional poetry. Extract from interview transcript, 2011)

You get the feelings, special feelings, through the words that you can't get in English. Maybe in 50 years or so there will be a poet who writes *naat* in English ... that when people read it they will feel that love coming out of the words ... but you can't get in English at the moment what you get in Urdu or Arabic. (Shahid, 23, performer of devotional poetry. Extract from interview transcript, 2011)

This highly complex and rich repertoire, together with the spoken varieties of the community (Pahari, Pothwari, as well as a variety of Northern English, Standard English), bridge the different elements of religious, cultural, and ethnic identity across the community. The different trajectories of each language and variety (or merely cluster of language resources) means there is no sense of a fixed or stable speech community in the older sense. The fluidity of these language practices varies from one individual to another and for every individual at different moments in their lives.

10.4   Future Directions

In the language practices described previously, technology is important in the acquisition and continuing performance of liturgical language practices and non-liturgical language practices. The ubiquity of mobile technology has resulted in changed practices in many religious domains. Spolsky (2018) relates how his daily Hebrew prayer practice has been transformed by the availability and accessibility of mobile devices which facilitate observance of his regular scriptural practices. Pandharipande (2018) reports on how online ritual in Hinduism has given renewed vigour to Sanskrit practices which have been receding in the face of other vernaculars, including the English language. The use of electronic technologies is also now a regular part of some acquisition practices with software, data projectors, and iPads mediating the liturgical languages of various faiths. One observed result of this has been the move from the communal experience to the individual one. Traditional liturgical language practices have centred on communal rituals and ceremonies. The move to an online religion experience has often resulted in a more private experience. From the online worlds of Second Life churches to the online portals available for Hindu Satsang and Puja, there have been various online strategies for mediating the liturgical language. As much of the liturgical language experience of the everyday worshipper could have been as much a communal and aural experience as an individual literacy-oriented one, the move online has often required a necessity to partake more actively as an individual. The increasing range of technologically enhanced means of communication, therefore, where rituals and teaching can be accessed from any part of the world at any time of the day (the asynchronous nature of online activity) is leading inevitably to a greater individual experience of faith (see Campbell, 2013). The well-established use of online mediation of prayers, fatwas and other decision-making functions can shape an individual's beliefs and practices independent of any offline traditional collectives.

Where access to the liturgical language in its original form (particularly its script) is challenging, transcription and/or transliteration of the liturgical language has become more commonplace. This development matters with some liturgical languages but not with others. Where the script is understood as also having a divine origin or at least a very close divine association (as in Islam or in Judaism), the acquisition of the liturgical language includes the mastery of the script. Where this is not the case, transliteration can take place. In Hinduism and Buddhism where language can be more fluid and responsive to local needs,

Sanskrit or Pali litanies can be recited using a range of scripts. The move online results in different strategies for representing the liturgical language on screen, often using the different modes of communication available to electronic technologies (sound, still and moving image, transitions, layout). Liturgical language practice online will likely be developed further. For example, in respect of liturgical language acquisition there are already many online courses, programmes, and resources that allow for such acquisition without attending traditional institutions. Perhaps, most obviously, is the now-ubiquitous use of the mobile phone to access, download, and store liturgical language resources. This is allowing for liturgical language practice to be supported in an ever-increasing range of contexts and situations.

The prevailing securitisation agenda in respect of religious schools and the ways in which the teaching of liturgical languages is often misunderstood will likely continue at least into the near future. The age-old critique of liturgical language acquisition and performance will still take place. From Paul the Apostle's accusation of 'vain repetitions', through Calvin's reprise of the same notion to contemporary think-tank reports focusing on 'learning by rote' (Cherti and Bradley, 2011), the performance of liturgical language will remain misunderstood and misrepresented in many circles. There are signs, however, of more positive and sympathetic treatments coming from religious education scholars who are researching the urban religious diaspora of Europe. Gent and Berglund (2018) focus on mosque schools in London and Stockholm respectively to show how there could be more rapprochement between pedagogies in faith-based supplementary schools and mainstream schooling, showing how, for example, skills of memorisation, long-since neglected in much Western pedagogy, can transfer usefully across to school settings.

Finally, the centrality of liturgical languages to those communities which have them must be reasserted. As mentioned previously, the precariousness of minority spoken languages in circumstances of diaspora is not usually matched by a similar precariousness with liturgical languages. Otsuje and Pennycook's (2010) observation of the persistence of the old within the fluid and mobile conditions of language change and shift is relevant here as there is nothing perhaps older within the community than its liturgical language. Different religions have different positions (and some religions have had different positions at different moments in their history) regarding their liturgy with some rejecting the idea that a particular language represents the heart of their faith practices. For those communities where a liturgical language is central, doctrinal, and theological foundations for such a position remain strong. The shift from Latin in Western Europe to local languages for purposes of worship and ritual was promoted by the doctrinal and theological debate of the Reformation. Any change in the status of the liturgical language for those communities which retain them would require an equally non-linguistic cause for any change.

10.5   References

Abrams, F. (2015). Why are Orthodox Jewish religious schools unregulated? *The Guardian*, August 11, 2015.

Amfo, N. A., & Omoniyi, T. (2019). Sociolinguistic domain analysis, linguistic practices and performance in religious worship. In A. Rosowsky (ed.), *Aspects of Performance in Faith Settings: Heavenly Acts* (pp. 76–89). Newcastle: Cambridge Scholars.

Bauman, R. (1975). Verbal art as performance. *American Anthropologist*, 77, 290–311.

Bauman, R. (2000). Language, identity and performance. *Pragmatics*, *10*(1), 1–5.

Bennett, B. (2018). *Sacred Languages of the World: An Introduction*. New York: Wiley.

Berglund, J., & Gent, B. (2018). Memorization and focus: Important transferables between supplementary Islamic education and mainstream schooling. *Journal of Religious Education*, *66*(2), 125–38.

Blommaert, J., & Backus, A. (2013). Superdiverse repertoires and the individual. *Tilburg Papers in Culture Studies*, 24. Doi:10.1007/978-94-6209-266-2_2.

Busch, B. (2012). The linguistic repertoire revisited. *Applied Linguistics*, *33*(5), 503–23.

Campbell, H. (ed.). (2013). *Digital Religion: Understanding Religious Practice in New Media Worlds*. Abingdon: Routledge.

Cherti, M., & Bradley, L. (2011). *Inside Madrassas: Understanding and engaging with British-Muslim Faith Supplementary Schools*. London: Institute for Public Policy Research.

Creese, A., & Blackledge, A. (2011). Separate and flexible bilingualism in complementary schools: Multiple language practices in interrelationship. *Journal of Pragmatics*, *43*(5), 1196–208.

Faruqi, I. R., & Faruqi, L. L. (1986). *The Cultural Atlas of Islam*. New York: Macmillan.

Ferguson, C. A. (1959). Diglossia. *Word*, 15, 325–40.

Ferguson, C. A. (1982). Religious factors in language spread. In R. L. Cooper (ed.), *Language Spread: Studies in Diffusion and Social Change* (pp. 95–106). Bloomington: Indiana University Press.

Fishman, J. A. (1965). Who speaks what language to whom and when? *La Linguistique*, *1*(2), 67–88.

Fishman, J. A. (1989). *Language and Identity in Minority Sociolinguistic Perspective*. Clevedon: Multilingual Matters.

Fishman, J. A. (1991). *Reversing Language Shift: Theoretical and Empirical Foundations of Assistance to Threatened Languages*. Clevedon: Multilingual Matters.

Fishman, J. A. (2006). A decalogue of basic theoretical perspectives for a sociology of language and religion. In T. Omoniyi & J. A. Fishman (eds.), *Explorations in the Sociology of Language and Religion* (pp. 13–25). Amsterdam: John Benjamins.

Garcia, O., & Li, W. (2014). *Translanguaging: Language, Bilingualism and Education*. London, UK: Palgrave Macmillan.

Gumperz, J. J., & Hymes, D. (eds.). (1972). *Directions in sociolinguistics: The survey of communication*. New York: Holt, Rinehart and Winston.

Keane, W. (1997). Religious Language. *Annual Review of Anthropology*, 26, 47–71.

Lawton, R. (2013). Speak English or go home: The anti-immigrant discourse of the American 'English Only' movement. *Critical Approaches to Discourse Analysis across Disciplines*, *7*(1), 100–22.

Otsuji, E., & Pennycook, A. (2010). Metrolingualism: Fixity, fluidity and language in flux. *International Journal of Multilingualism, 7*(3), 240–54.

Pandharipande, R. V. (2018). Digital religion and Hinduism in the United States. *World Englishes, 37*(3), 497–502.

Robertson, R. (1992). *Globalization: Social Theory and Global Culture.* London: SAGE.

Rosowsky, A. (2001). Decoding as a cultural practice and its effects on the reading process of bilingual pupils. *Language and Education, 15*(1), 56–70.

Rosowsky, A. (2008). *Heavenly Readings: Liturgical Literacy in a Multilingual Context.* Clevedon: Multilingual Matters.

Rosowsky, A. (2019). Sacred language acquisition in superdiverse contexts. *Linguistics and Education,* 53.

Rosowsky, A. (2021). *The Performance of Multilingual and 'Ultralingual' Devotional Practices by Young British Muslims.* Bristol: Multilingual Matters.

Safran, W. (2008). Language, ethnicity and religion: A complex and persistent linkage. *Nations and Nationalism, 14*(1), 171–90.

Seddon, M. S. (2004). Muslim communities in Britain: A historiography. In M. S. Seddon, D. Hussain, & N. Malik (eds.), *British Muslims between Assimilation and Segregation: Historical, Legal and Social Realities* (pp. 1–42). Markfield: The Islamic Foundation.

Smith, F. (1994). *Understanding Reading.* Hillsdale: Lawrence Erlbaum.

Spolsky, B. (2018). Afterword. In A. Rosowsky (ed.), *Faith and Language Practices in Digital Spaces* (pp. 237–241). Bristol: Multilingual Matters.

Staetsky, L. D., & Boyd, J. (2015). *Strictly Orthodox Rising: What the Demography of British Jews Tells Us about the Future of the Community.* London: Institute for Jewish Policy Research.

Thérien, J-P. (1999). Beyond the North-South divide: The two tales of world poverty. *Third World Quarterly, 20*(4), 723–42.

Versteegh, K. (2001). *The Arabic Language.* Edinburgh: Edinburgh University Press.

Zuckermann, G. (2003). Language contact and globalisation: The camouflaged, influence of English on the world's languages – with special attention to Israeli (sic) and Mandarin. *Cambridge Review of International Affairs, 16*(2), 287–307.

11 Education

Xin Gao and Juliet Thondhlana

11.1 Background, History, and Key Terms

The link between faith and education has long been established with diverse faith-based organisations being involved in various aspects of education including establishing and constructing schools, providing school materials, providing funding for school fees and teachers' salaries, and providing teacher training. Religion and education have been entwined from time immemorial with places of worship such as Jewish synagogues and temples, Islamic mosques, and Christian churches having traditionally also been sites of teaching and learning. Much of the teaching and learning focused on religious texts, (e.g. Qu'ran for Muslims, Torah for Hebrews, the Bible for Christians) and other forms of knowledge, for example, literature, philosophy, law, and ethics or morality. As religions spread, language (e.g. Arabic, Hebrew, Latin, Greek, Sanskrit, English) became a critical component of religious teachings for effective preaching and learning about and practising the religions. Religious institutions gave birth to some educational institutions as we know them today and religious or faith groups continue to provide education and run some educational institutions at all levels of education from nurseries to universities. In Islam, the word for university, Jami'a, was derived from the word for mosque (Jami). As nations have emerged and grown and some even become more secularised, the relationship between religion and education has persisted. Today religion and education can be viewed as either religious education or religion in education.

Religious education consists of learning or studying religious texts and doctrines for children of believers, adult believers, and new converts. Such learning takes place primarily within religious institutions (Christian Sunday school, Islamic Dawah school, Jewish Yeshiva school) and even private homes of believers, and has proselytising as its core. Such education teaches not only the principles of a particular religion but also how these can be applied to everyday life and as a basis for contributing to society. The schools are normally structured and follow a particular curriculum which may or may not lead to a qualification.

Religion in education is taught as part of a national curriculum and is not for proselytising. In some contexts, it may focus on a particular faith dominant in that country, such as Christianity in Christian countries, Islam in some Arabic countries (e.g. Malaysia, Saudi Arabia), Hindi and Sikh (e.g. India). However, as secularism has spread and strengthened in some contexts, nations have opened up to diverse religions, and embraced religious diversity in their curricula and introduced what they call Religious Studies or Religious Education (e.g. UK) with public or state schools adopting a more general multifaith approach where students learn about religions of the world. Other contexts are more stringent (e.g. America) and have banned the teaching of religion by public schools altogether only allowing teaching about religion which focuses on the historical, literary, and cultural value of particular religions.

English education has long contained a very strong moral dimension and had a very strong missionary agenda in the wider promotion of Christianity (Pennycook and Makoni, 2005) (in the same way the learning of Arabic has been central within the Islamic context), which also included improving the livelihoods of believers. In colonial contexts, however, this agenda was seen as having been highjacked by colonial regimes to effect control by making English an official language to be used in all formal contexts. English came to be one of the key requirements for further education and employment with missionaries widely suspected by some of colluding with colonial governments to advance colonial hegemony particularly as converted locals were recorded to have begun to look down upon their religious practices as primitive and demonic (Maxwell, 2006).

The implicit link between the teaching and learning of English as a Foreign Language (EFL) and the Christian religion has long been recognised (Wong et al., 2013). Later, when English Christian missionaries set out to preach the gospel around the world, the English language became a tool for the spreading and practise of Christianity and referred to as a missionary tool (Varghese and Johnston, 2007). Although in some contexts missionaries also endeavoured to learn, speak, and write in local languages, a common strategy or approach for 'reaching out' to 'non-believers' more widely was to offer English classes to them so that there would be a common language between the preacher and the preached. Language learning in missionary contexts therefore required learning special registers and expressions to meet situational Christian needs, which in turn was critical for spiritual growth and sustenance. These included not only specific religious interactions but access to desired livelihoods offered by a missionary education (Atkinson, 1972).

Christian churches continue to be fertile ground for the learning and practising of English. In her study of Christianity and language teaching and learning in the Chinese context, Ding (2013) found that her respondents' Christian faith was strongly linked to their second-language learning in diverse ways including opening opportunities for them to travel to China where they needed to learn Chinese and being motivated to learn Chinese so as to preach to Chinese people; and motivating some local Chinese people to learn English to enable them to read the English Bible, listen to sermons, and engage in Christian conversations in predominantly English-speaking churches established by foreign missionaries. In this case, English continues to be used as a tool for teaching and learning Christianity.

However, people studying English in Christian contexts may also use the connection to the church to develop their own social status through enhancing their English-language proficiency and related academic careers. Writing on the rise and spread of the Christian faith in China and its impact on English education, Yang (2005) observes while the primary reason for attending church may be to learn about Christianity, many see Christianity as providing the opportunity into an international space that offers them access to improve themselves academically and professionally. She argues that the interaction of spirituality, academic study, and aspirations is a subject of growing interest. In the related context of migration and student mobility, churches have been found to readily provide English language lessons partly as a charitable act but with an inevitable hidden agenda of introducing participants to Christian practice and love.

The demand for language within migrant populations globally continues to increase given its importance for accessing the host labour market, and for education and communication between parents, educational institutions, and communities (Madziva et al., 2016; Thondhlana and Madziva, 2017). More recent research on the link between Christianity and second language learning is showing how the church is stepping up by providing more structured and targeted English as second language training. Durham and Kim (2019) observe that with the limited available adult ESL programmes – the few existing programmes such as church-based and community programmes – are in demand and there is a critical need to support them to meet the need. For example, most of the teachers of these programmes are volunteers and may not have the required training to be effective. Chen and Yang (2017) found effective teaching requires that tutors take into consideration learners' cultural backgrounds in deciding appropriate teaching strategies, something volunteers may not be equipped to do.

The value of the programmes is highlighted in Chao and Kuntz's (2013) study of a church-based ESL programme established in a US city. The study also reports how such programmes may also cause identity tensions in relation to participants' own beliefs, as such the programmes may be seen as tools used by the church to proselyte. According to Chao and Kuntz (2013, p. 472) while the programmes may serve as "a linguistic, cultural, and community broker" to facilitate English learning and socialisation, the tensions may lead to some learners withdrawing. Whatever the motives may be, research is increasingly evidencing the 'integration of faith and learning', arguing faith to be a significant and effective tool for enhancing teaching, learning motivation and success (Lessard-Clouston, 2013).

Education, when religion is involved, is never therefore only about learning a skill, it is also tied to larger issues of spiritual formation and identity. In this regard there is also a clear link across religious education, colonialism, and capitalism. Religious institutions may use education to teach religious values and improve congregants' livelihoods while people in turn may exploit religion to gain social status as well as use it as an oppressive tool typical of colonial regimes.

11.2   Key Topics, Questions, and Debates

A growing body of literature links faith and language teaching and learning, but little work has yet been done on the influence of a teacher's values, faith, and spiritual identity on their teaching. For many religious teachers, teaching can be understood as a calling – teaching is driven by faith commitments, is headed in a certain direction, and is carried out in worshipful activity that exalts the glory of God rather than the glory of the self (Van Dyk, 2000). At the same time, Christian faith and the teaching profession pose a dilemma. In exploring these issues in-depth, Varghese and Johnson (2007), conducted a qualitative study by interviewing English teaching trainees at evangelical Christian colleges in America. Their study raised the notion that 'moral dilemmas' are key factors commonly facing the participants in the context of English language teaching, that is, how to maintain their 'requirement of witness' while respecting the interests of the profession of ELT (Varghese and Johnson, 2007, p. 25).

This can be seen explicitly in descriptions of teaching in applied theology. Snow (2001) encourages Christians to view language teaching as a way of serving God and argues that Christian English teachers can show the love of God by impressing such concepts as 'teaching as witness', 'teaching as ministry', and 'teaching as service'. In the language classroom, Smith's (2000) theoretical rather than empirical work suggests that teachers' Christian faith influences their teaching design and pedagogy, which is thus translated into classroom activities, and inevitably affects the discussion and interaction between teacher and students. The process of teaching, if not the content, seems to be characterised to some extent by the Christian faith and values held by the teachers.

Studies have attempted to account for religious behaviour using the existing 'capital' framework (Iannaccone, 1990) while others (Bourdieu, 2011; Rey, 2004) have proposed a new theory of 'religious' or 'spiritual' capital arguing that it is impossible to fully capture the distinctiveness of the resources that religion generates using human, social, or cultural capital. Bourdieu describes these resources as 'the legitimation of the social order, the sanction of wealth and power and the sense of meaning that religion brings to people's lives' (Bourdieu, 1987 cited in Rey, 2004, p. 337). Approaching religious phenomena in terms of spiritual capital may offer significant advantages; for example, it brings new understanding of religion as a cultural resource in the contemporary world; it links it to a long tradition of using 'capital' as a metaphor (connotations of exchange and circulation) for mobilising resources (Guest, 2007).

Bourdieu's conceptualisation has however been criticised for its narrow organisational focus which treats religion as an institution and not as a disposition. This is demonstrated by the treatment of the Roman Catholic church as a tool of 'oppression and exploitation' with respect to the dominant position of the priesthood. This approach excludes the possibility of seeing ordinary people as social actors who are able to manipulate religious symbols for their own benefit and therefore this view of religious capital is not immediately applicable to the complexities of the contemporary religious landscape and bounded communities such as denominations or congregations (Rey, 2004).

Building on Bourdieu's (1986) concept of cultural capital, Verter (2003) proposes a multidimensional theory which he coins 'spiritual capital'. His model recognises the deregulated religious marketplace and the changing nature of religion as a cultural resource in the contemporary globalised world. Conceptualised as a form of cultural capital, spiritual capital also exists in three forms: the embodied state (the individual's position, disposition, knowledge, abilities, tastes, and credentials in the field of religion), the objectified state (material and symbolic commodities related to religion and spirituality, like sacred texts, theologies, and ideologies) and the institutionalised state (organisational structures like churches or seminaries with power over spiritual goods, both material and immaterial). Drawing insights from these foundational conceptualisations, the Middlebrooks and Noghiu (2007) model of spiritual capital has been found helpful because it emphasises measurable changes at the individual level of analysis. It therefore presents a definition that includes descriptions of individual dispositions including:

(a) belief in something larger than self,
(b) a sense of interconnectedness,
(c) ethical and moral salience,
(d) a call or drive to serve, and
(e) the capability to transfer the latter conceptualizations into individual and organizational behaviours, and ultimately added value.

(Middlebrooks and Noghiu, 2007, p. 10)

A study based on the World Values Survey has shown that while the poor lack in financial capital, they are remarkably rich in religiosity (Norris and Inglehart 2004). The term spiritual capital has therefore more recently been used to articulate the idea that religion can affect pro-development transformation; that is, if this wealth of religiosity could be leveraged as economically beneficial spiritual capital, this could provide a new paradigm for development policy and practice (Shah and Shah, 2010). The devastation caused by, for example, the global economic crisis that began in 2008 which has led to a growing mistrust of political and economic institutions, has led theorists and public policy to pay attention to the concept of spiritual capital looking at how it interacts with other forms of capital in diverse human situations. Berger and Redding (2010) have noted a growing academic and social-policy interest in the concept of spiritual capital and revealed the close interaction between spiritual capital and the economy arguing that the spiritual realm affects the economy. As with other forms of capital (e.g. human/economic, social, cultural), the 'capital' in spiritual capital suggests resources that are fungible (spiritual in this case) in that they are accrued in one domain (religious) and consumed in other non-religious domains such as governance and the economy (Shah and Shah, 2010).

Recent research on social capital views religion as a significant factor in the formation of social networks and trust. This view is strengthened by the growing recognition in economics and other social sciences that religion has profound economic, political, and social consequences. In his influential 2000 study of the concept of social capital Putnam found that religion was arguably the most important source of social capital in the United States of America, contributing to more than half of the social capital in the country. It is argued that the greater the stock of spiritual capital, the greater the positive correlation with economic capital. This is evidenced by the close link of the notion of spiritual capital to current debates about trust, corruption, governance, sustainability, and entrepreneurship.

11.3   Case Study

How spiritual capital is 'operationalised' is a key question for religious discourse and education. To raise questions about the nature of spiritual capital, the tools that the spiritual capital generates, and its effect on their teaching practices, this case study is taken from ongoing ethnographic study of the role of Christian faith in English-language teaching and learning. As exploratory research, a purely qualitative approach was deemed appropriate in getting in-depth appreciation of the topic in question. Interview – a well-tested method for harnessing participants' in-depth thoughts, reflections, and opinions – was selected as the data collection technique because it was imperative to present the teachers' beliefs and experiences using their own words and to understand them through the teachers' eyes. Additionally, teachers' thinking, perceptions, and beliefs are tacit and not directly observable. They can only be studied through getting teachers' oral or written response to related questions. Therefore, the teachers' reflection of their faith and beliefs and how they manifest themselves through their teaching practice are regarded as the most appropriate source of information for this study.

The nature of the research required the sample in the study to be purposively selected: three Christian English language teachers from the same higher education institution in the UK were invited to take part. The participants grew up in Christian families, trained to be English language teachers, and had rich experience teaching English in various countries including China, Thailand, Lebanon, Southern Africa, and the UK for about fifteen to thirty years. Data were collected in two phases: individual semi-structured interviews with the teacher participants followed by a focus-group discussion with participants. Both phases are critical in initially getting individual perspectives, which then led to a second-stage in-depth exploration of key topics which emerged from these separate conversations.

The three study participants were Christian tutors of English to international students, at a UK university.

- *Sophia*, in her late thirties and has two language teacher qualifications and a Master's degree in TESOL. She became an English language teacher not 'intentionally', but because she liked English literature and being an English language teacher was a 'cherished' career in her home country. Despite growing up in a Christian family, she converted to Islam for three years while she was with her ex-husband, who is a Muslim, and then reverted to Christianity because she felt that 'this is the religion [for her]' in a recent year. She attends two different churches alternately but is not a registered member of either church. Apart from listening to the sermons, she also admits lack of active involvement within the church community.
- *Alice*, in her early fifties is currently doing her Master's degree in TESOL Sponsored by a Christian foundation, she and her husband had taught English for more than eleven years in remote parts of China, where usually they couldn't afford to have a native English teacher, in order to 'help to people to become successful in what is considered not a very prestigious place to be' as 'a way of serving God in that community'. Earlier, she worked for the British Council in a big city in Thailand for two years but she left because she felt that 'anybody could do that, it was not the same kind of service that we [she] felt were providing in China' and returned to China. She regularly goes to one church and participates in fortnightly home-group bible studies with fellow churchgoers, a small choir, and some events for women.

• *Maggie*, in her fifties, has a doctorate in Applied Linguistics. She taught English for Academic Purposes in Southern Africa before moving to the United Kingdom where she also taught English for Academic Purposes and TESOL. She was born in a Christian family and sees Christianity as a lifestyle and culture for her having been socialised in Christian practice. Maggie describes herself as a 'devote and practising Christian'. She goes to church every Sunday and attends various church activities during the week. She is also a church leader in her local church where she teaches the Bible and how to live a Christian lifestyle to children and teenagers.

The extracts which follow are from recorded interviews which involved three topics: (a) personal faith, (b) faith and the teaching profession, and (c) personal faith, teaching, and students' learning experience. During the refining stage of the interview schedule, another experienced Christian English language teacher gave a personal account of his thoughts and experiences in relation to the nature of the research questions, which served as a pilot phase for the instrument prior to using it in the research. In the second phase, further insight was sought concerning key points highlighted in the initial interviews. Throughout the conversations, the researcher encouraged the participants to tell their story so as to reveal the history of personal and professional experience. In the analysis and interpretation of the data, the exploratory nature of the investigation necessitated the use of an inductive approach in the analysis stage. Therefore, it was deemed fitting to use an explorative approach to allow the data to speak for themselves as well as to inform both coding and concept creation.

11.3.1   Factors that Guide Teachers and the Role of Faith

While it is beyond the scope of this chapter to explore the expected attributes of a good teacher, we draw from the related literature to understand our participants' behaviour more broadly. The English language teachers we interviewed reported faith to be a key driver of their particular teacher behaviours. Sophia said:

[It]'s . . . a compass that directs me . . . it helps me to be more reflective . . . when I finish with class, I tend [to] . . . think about things and say, did I do it right, could I have done it better? . . . I'm more conscientious because of my beliefs and my faith. It drives me to . . . constantly check myself and my teaching.

Among second language teacher education (SLTE) concepts, reflection is considered to be a key characteristic of effective teaching (Beauchamp, 2015) and the trait or personality of being 'conscientious' is considered to be critical for quality teaching (Arif et al., 2012). The literature notes that these would ordinarily be built into their teacher training curricula. While she does not specifically refer to her training, Sophia's use of '*more* reflective' and '*more* conscientious' (our emphasis) suggests that her deep trust in God's leading heightens and intensifies these behaviours which any effective teacher (Christian or not) would be expected to possess. Being a Christian or her 'belief in something larger than self' causes her to be 'more reflective' on her performance, continually searching for areas where she can improve the service she provides and make a real difference to the learning of her students.

Having a 'servanthood' attitude towards work was seen as important by Alice and Maggie:

God has a purpose for me as a teacher that I'm serving Him and through serving Him I hope that people see something of Christ in me.
I am guided by the Bible where it says 'Whatever you do [whatever your task may be], work from the soul [that is, put in your very best effort], as [something done] for the Lord and not for men' (Colossians 3:23) (MAGGIE)

As Maggie explained, doing her job to the best of her ability is a form of witness to the people around as well as an encouragement while setting an example for future teachers. Again here we would expect any good teacher to possess this quality. However, there seems to be a higher calling for Maggie in that her desire to give one's best through service to others is derived from the concept that the service is given for God's glory, a form of witness for God, which makes her internalised motives distinct from the ordinary teacher and the urge to do things for self. As Sophia and Alice explained:

[W]hen I came to mark projects ... I prayed 'Lord, help me to mark this carefully ... so that I'm not jeopardising that student, because of my own bias or weaknesses'. (SOPHIA)

[W]hat helped me to make ... decisions[s] was my Christian faith and not simply moral principles. (ALICE)

[Y]ou always try and consider how your decision is going to impact on other people ... your source of strength is different (ALICE)

In this regard, their views, which subsequently led to the decision-making, were a result of a complex process involving prayer, reading the Bible, or the Word of God given the emphasis of God's leading. As noted by Alice, 'your source of strength is different'.

In another demonstration of a life of servitude to God, 'a call or drive to serve', at the focus group interview one of the participants, Alice, also noted engaging in overt spiritual activities, which distinguished her teaching journey from that of the others. For example, sponsored by a Christian Foundation, Alice and her husband taught English for eleven years in remote parts of China that couldn't afford to have a native English teacher, despite many challenges they encountered. Decisions to persevere in difficult situations were informed by her Christian values. Alice highlighted their willingness to 'help people to become successful in what is considered not a very prestigious place to be' as 'a way of serving God in that community'. She reported previous involvement with "English corner" in China, where people can talk and practise English informally, and Globe Café, an outreach for international students who might be interested in knowing more about Christianity.

Maggie, an African teaching English in a UK context has faced challenges of her own to gain acceptance by students who come to the United Kingdom expecting to be taught by a native speaker. Asked how she coped, she said,

Before I start each day I pray that the Lord help me in everything including what I teach and how I teach. Although I am a highly qualified English language teacher it's not enough. I pray for wisdom in dealing with any negativity in my classroom; I pray for a sweet spirit so that I am likeable to my students and so that they see the good of Christ in me. It's important that my students not only see but also feel in their hearts that I have their interests at heart and want them to succeed in their studies. Only God can do that for me. I know that I speak in a different accent to my native English colleagues, but my learners must never feel disadvantaged and God makes that possible. It always works and I receive very positive evaluations from students which focus on how I am not only knowledgeable but kind-hearted, approachable, and patient. (Maggie)

Here we are made to see how the participant is able to transfer her spiritual capital into behaviours and 'added value'. The participant's emphasis on the notion of 'faith' was anchored on James 2 verses 14–16 where it is stated that 'faith without works is dead'. Christian values are perceived to be resources they draw upon when faced with difficult situations. Moreover, there was agreement with the other two participants that 'living out your faith in the way that you work' is not easily observable because of the 'subtle' and 'almost intangible' manner by which it is expressed. Actions are prompted by motives; however, although actions can be observed, motives, by contrast, cannot be seen.

11.3.2   On Their Journey to Become Good Teachers

Discussion with our participants also points to the development of other dispositions – including resilience, perseverance, inner strength, contentment – amongst Christians, which can be attributed to their belief in God who they argue oversees their lives. On an occasion where Alice's class was observed by new young teachers in a Chinese province, she recalled:

[I] think they were amazed at how well we knew the students . . . they hadn't thought that it was important to get to know everyone in the class. . . . our approach was we go in the classroom not to teach the knowledge but to teach the students and respond to their needs and difficulties rather than the material driving our teaching, it's the students that drive our teaching . . . there are techniques that may be new to them in the teaching, but also it was our attitude towards the students. (Alice)

This narrative demonstrates that, what tutors do not merely impart knowledge and skills to these young teachers but try to know the students and exercise sensitivity in meeting their other needs. This requires forming personal relationships with students to understand and address their needs and distinct learning difficulties appropriately. Both Maggie and Sophia emphasise responding not only to students' needs but to human needs in general, which is a key objective in their teaching. As Alice noted:

I see a student not just as somebody who needs English, but I see that person as a whole person. . . . I think it's about not judging and about seeing each individual as someone in need really and each individual is in need of something . . . as a Christian . . . my students are very important to me and I want to help them as best I can to achieve their full potential. (ALICE)

This may raise the question of whether their behaviour resembles what is ordinarily seen as good teaching (see, e.g. Korthagen, 2004; Palmer, 1990). As expressed by the teachers themselves, this is a common endeavour practised by effective teachers, Christian or non-Christian. They recognised that teachers coming from a non-Christian background could be effective and gifted in their role as teachers (Sophia). The main difference, however, is the motivation prompting the teachers to pursue a harmonious relationship with their students. As Sophia and Alice reflectively pointed out during the group discussion of the subject:

What is this extra thing that we're bringing in? . . . it's hard to just make a generalisation about it . . . I could be a good teacher maybe with or without Christianity [if] I'm gifted in that area. But from a personal perspective, what makes me better at my job, is being a Christian – for me . . . it's just that subtle extra ingredient. (SOPHIA)

Yes. It's the internal knowledge, isn't it? And the awareness of your motivation for doing things. And the strength with which you do things is in God's strength, and you draw on that. (ALICE)

Our study is consistent in showing that what sets our participants apart from non-religious teachers is their faith which they emphasised to have influenced them to behave and operate in specific ways. To this end, participants repeatedly cited biblical verses to validate their actions and practices. Key verses which came up prominently were the principle exemplified by Jesus in the Bible who, through his miracles, clearly demonstrated how to respond to people's needs: 'when the people are hungry, he fed them fish and bread, because they were hungry. So you need to . . . target the [needs of the] person' (Sophia). Thus, for our participants, relationship with students was emphasised as the true way of serving God, who in turn has power to bless them and allow them to prosper in their lives, in general.

Similarly, participants' professional visions and spiritual capital are nurtured through teaching. As Alice explained, doing her job to the best of her ability is a form of witness to the people around as well as an encouragement while setting an example for future teachers.

[W]e always tried to be fair . . . we always tried to be very professional in our work and show commitment to it. That was very important to us, not just that we were committed to what we were doing, but that students could see that we were committed . . . we want to engender that in them . . . so that they would be committed in their future positions as teachers. (ALICE)

However, our participants were aptly aware that missionary teachers, like novice and inexperienced teachers, may be lacking in terms of their skills and capacity to teach, despite their enthusiasm (Alice). They realised that faith alone was not sufficient to make one an effective teacher and there was a convergence of views, agreeing that the right training plus experience play a crucial role in teachers' effectiveness. In this way, we can see a complex interaction between the spiritual and the natural traits that drive teaching orientation within a faith context. As one of our participants summed up: 'I think as a Christian it impacts on all of my life . . . every aspect of my life. It underpins all my values; it underpins all my choices and my views. . . . It is . . . central' (Alice). This derives from a Bible verse found in Philippians 4:13: 'I can do all things through Christ who strengthens me.' There is a sense of agency on the part of the believer here in terms of making the decision to train to be a teacher and then to believe God for being able to use the training in a productive way.

11.3.3   Faith and Professional Action

As noted earlier, our participants strongly asserted their Christian identity and the desire to be able to live according to their Christian faith and to share their faith as compelled by the desire to tell others about the 'good news' found in the Bible. This obviously raises questions of indoctrination of learners, particularly, as some of the literature has noted what is seen as the inextricable intertwining of faith and professional work (e.g. Varghese and Johnston, 2007). Our participants are conscious, however, that they should draw from their faith in such a way that they are neither crossing the boundaries of their remit, nor of their role, nor violating any rules.

As a Christian, ultimately, we do want to spread the word of God. We do want people to know about Christ and to accept him, but at the same time, I think it's also very tricky to do that, because as a professional, you're expected not to bring in personal, whether beliefs or personal choices. (SOPHIA)

I have a responsibility as a Christian, we are told to tell the good news but I think there is a time and a place to do that and it's an abuse of that position as a teacher to use the time when I should be teaching to do that. (ALICE)

They did not talk about God directly in class, partially because there was a sense of realism that one's belief cannot be imposed on others.

I am neutral towards them, because obviously I have students from all walks of life, different religious backgrounds. Some of them do not even believe in God . . . . It is my job to treat them all the same, and especially from a Christian perspective. I have to accept people for who they are. I'm not here to judge them, so therefore I'm neutral. (SOPHIA)

Sophia explained the necessity to treat students equally no matter who they are, where they are from and what their beliefs are. 'I would never choose to discuss "There's only one God" or I would never try and use religious issues to discuss in class' (ALICE).

When teaching materials contain elements of Christianity, Sophia also explained that she treats it like any other teaching material (despite her personal interest in the subject), considers the students, and teaches in accordance with the course objectives. Similarly,

I think it comes back to the whole thing of respecting differences. In the classroom I don't shout about the fact that I'm a Christian . . . that everyone else should agree with me that Christianity is important to everyone. I think it's about respecting other people's faith but also perhaps making it clear that I'm a Christian and this is my view but I respect your view. (ALICE)

Both Alice and Sophia stressed the importance of showing sensitivity and 'respecting differences' especially in the context they are in. What is clearly expressed in the previous passages is that they endeavour to exercise professional neutrality, neither being judgemental as teachers, nor taking advantage of their authority, nor abusing their position to promote their Christian faith. Yet, given their expressed strong Christian standing in the context of interviewing, it is debatable so easy to know where to draw a line between teaching and sharing the Christian gospel.

However, for these teachers, they believe that they can do preaching through their behaviour – through reflecting the life of Christ – not by talking about God,

I do not need to explicitly mention God in my class. For me Christianity is a lifestyle and as such it is naturally expressed in my behaviour, in my attitude towards work, how I speak to others, accepting other people and caring for their needs and putting them first before my own, my morality and so on (MAGGIE)

Maggie, who strongly sees 'Christianity' as being entwined with day-to-day behaviour, highlights that it is not just about explicitly proclaiming

Christ but demonstrating his love through one's behaviour and practice. It is using the strength and ability of God to do the things that make humans flourish.

Although the participants expressed that they maintain a professional distance from their beliefs in the classroom, it is evident however, that it is difficult to remain neutral as an educator irrespective of one's background. As highlighted by the participants, their faith is likened to 'a personal compass' for Christian living 'influencing all aspects of life'. Therefore, separating the tutors' Christian beliefs from how they approach life is not just difficult but, in fact, impossible. They hold the belief that teaching is purposeful and direction driven and that to teach is to restore the wholeness of persons in our students: their faith embodies more than just moral values. It holds that completeness does not reside in the virtues of man but in the virtues of God, the source of all virtues.

Although the participants are conscious that their teaching-related actions and decisions are manifestations of how they live out their faith, their motives remain an internal disposition that cannot be observed, let alone assessed. Outward displays of kindness, concern, humility, fairness, respect, responsibility, and moral strength, amongst others, are characteristics that effective Christian and non-Christian teachers may both exhibit; the only difference lies with the motive, something only discernible by the God whom Christians serve. However, the participants understand that such expressions of faith have to be cautiously made so as not to turn into indoctrination. Since education is a moral act and consequently not value-free (West-Burnham and Coates, 2005) educational institutions' systems are underpinned by particular philosophies which teachers are expected to promote irrespective of their own beliefs and values. For example, a faith-based school or a Montessori school will expect their teachers to promote the school's values. These are considerations that teachers make which need to be balanced with their own value systems, as our participants appear to be doing.

11.4   Future Directions

The relationship between faith and development broadly, and faith and education more specifically, has been a subject of much interest over time, particularly within the faith world, but has received little attention in the academic world. More recently, academic interest has begun to grow, especially given the current global economic challenges, with studies beginning to explore the role of faith or religion in development. In the field of education, and in particular, language education, much still needs to be done for the field to leverage the positive impacts of faith. This section therefore suggests possible future directions for the field focusing largely on research.

Given the expected massive growth of activities in the field over the years and across faith groups that we know little about as academics, there is need for studies to be conducted on the diverse faith groups looking at, among other topics, educational aims and values, the underpinning philosophies and how these translate into school and classroom activities and the resultant impact on student success. A good starting point could be a broad-based systematic literature review or reviews that would cover both existing academic literature and the wealth of non-academic literature produced by diverse faith groups for their communities and others. On the latter, a simple Google search on faith or religion and education generates a wide range of documents showing a lot of activity in this field. There are, however, rather limited academic publications and it would be helpful to identify the topics that academics have found interesting to focus on. Such an exercise would help to further reveal and identify gaps and future directions for both academia and practitioners across faith groups.

In the context of the COVID-19 crises, for example, which has affected many aspects of human existence exhibiting diverse complexities and brought up a lot of uncertainty for the future of the world, there is a possibility that religion may play a more pronounced role in people's lives. There is a strong case for studies of the role of faith in education in terms of how faith groups respond to the challenges of, for example, educating children and sustaining the quality of education in the context of modern crises. Barnett's (1885) quote is pertinent in this regard:

When there was no education, Church schools led the way till the nation followed; now that there is bad education, it is for the Church schools again to lead. (Samuel Barnett, 1885, in Burn et al., 2001, p. v)

Further, given the role of faith in development in general as revealed by works emerging in economics and other fields, interdisciplinary studies are needed to help identify the extent to which faith can have wider impact.

In considering possible research approaches, collaborations could also be important: for example, within individual faiths bringing together academics and practitioners to give insiders a strong voice; involving diverse faith groups; involving cross-disciplinary teams; and bringing together insider and outsider researchers. Such collaborations would help to provide diverse lenses to fully explore this extensive field and offer insights into the function of religion within individuals' lives, particularly, the extent to which similarities can be seen across different beliefs and practices.

There is a general paucity of theorisation of the interaction of faith and education for the deployment of empirical studies. This is not surprising, given the limited research in the field. Spiritual capital, as shown in this chapter, can be useful in examining the specific experiences of language teachers who share a strong belief in biblical principles as underpinning their professional practice. However, this theory can be beneficial to an understanding of the dispositions that teachers of any faith bring to the classroom and the resultant behaviours that they exhibit and their effectiveness as teachers. The sample in this case study was very small and our findings are therefore limited to the three Christian teachers with whom we engaged. A larger study using this theory and engaging with teachers from a variety of different backgrounds is therefore necessary if conclusions about its viability are to be generalisable. More and diverse studies, for example, looking at fields other than language education and using other interdisciplinary lenses including grounded theory, would help generate possible new theories which would help in advancing the field.

Moreover, future studies may engage diverse populations within education, including students and management to gain broader insights into the relationship between faith and education. If religious capital is important in how teachers address teaching, then the same might be seen in how learners approach learning. In addition, given the growth of Christian population in postmodern context and the increase in English language learners (both Christian and non-Christian) seeking to learn English in the context of the church (Durham and Kim, 2019), there is a strong case for more studies of the role of the church in language education and the importance of the complementarity of teacher training and spirituality.

Finally, greater attention must be paid to the socialisation conditions which underline the relationship between faith and professional work (i.e. potentially associated with discomfort, conflicts, tensions, and dilemmas). For participants in this study, given that Christianity is acknowledged to be a significant aspect of their lives, their identities sometimes are hidden, or kept 'neutral' and not always translated into their words and actions. Sometimes faith teachers are silent – they are doing things but they are not talking about it, perhaps due to the fact that they are not given the forum to talk about it or, are worried about other people's reactions. Therefore, there is need to open up other sites to provide an enabling environment for teachers and other academics of faith as well as interested outsiders to write about and present their work on the topic at conferences and workshops. Also, in keeping with developments in other disciplines, more associations or religious discourse communities are needed to hear the voice of religious teachers as insiders and develop confidence in communicating the issues. In this connection, a central concern is that a sense of transparency with their religious identity is not only desired but put into action, whenever applicable. This may help open spaces for more and broader debates in the field which would help to test its benefits in educational practice.

11.5   References

Arif, M. I., Rashid, A., Tahira, S. S., & Akhter, M. (2012). Personality and teaching: an investigation into prospective teachers' personality. *International Journal of Humanities and Social Science*, 2(17), 161–171.

Atkinson, N. J. (1972). *Teaching Rhodesians: A History of Educational Policy in Rhodesia*. London: Longman.

Berger, P. L., & Redding, G. (2010). *The Hidden Form of Capital: Spiritual Influences in Societal Progress*. New York: Anthem Press.

Beauchamp, C. (2015). Reflection in teacher education: issues emerging from a review of current literature. *Reflective Practice*, 16(1), 123141.

Bourdieu, P. (2011). The forms of capital (1986). In I. Szeman & T. Kaposy (eds.), *Cultural Theory: An Anthology* (pp. 241–58). Chichester: John Wiley.

Burn, J., Marks, J., & Griffiths, B. (2001). *Faith in Education: The Role of the Churches in Education: A Response to the Dearing Report on Church Schools in the Third Millennium*. London: The Institute for the Study of Civil Society.

Chao, X., and Kuntz, A. (2013). Church-based ESL program as a figured world: Immigrant adult learners, language, identity, power. *Linguistics and Education*, 24 (4), 466–78.

Chen, D., and Yang, X. (2017). Improving active classroom participation of ESL students: Applying culturally responsive teaching strategies. *Theory and Practice in Language Studies*, 7(1), 79–86.

Ding, P. (2013). Cosmopolitanism, Christianity, and the contemporary Chinese context: Impacts on second language motivation. In M. S. Wong, C. Kristjánsson, & Z. Dörnyei (eds.), *Christian Faith and English Language Teaching and Learning: Research on Interrelationship of Religion and ELT* (pp. 189–205). New York: Routledge.

Durham, L., and Kim, S. (2019). Training dilemmas and recommendations with volunteer instructors in small, faith-based adult ESL programs. *TESOL Journal*, 10 (1), 1–11.

Guest, M. (2007). In search of spiritual capital: The spiritual as a cultural resource. In K. Flanagan & P. C. Jupp (eds.), *A Sociology of Spirituality* (pp. 181–200). Aldershot: Ashgate.

Iannaccone, L. R. (1990). Religious practice: A human capital approach. *Journal for the Scientific Study of Religion*, 29(3), 297–314.

Korthagen, F. A. (2004). In search of the essence of a good teacher: Towards a more holistic approach in teacher education. *Teaching and Teacher Education*, 20(1), 77–97.

Lessard-Clouston, M. (2013). Faith and learning integration in ESL/EFL instruction: A preliminary study in America and Indonesia. In M. S. Wong, C. Kristjánsson, & Z. Dörnyei (eds.), *Christian Faith and English Language Teaching and Learning: Research on the Interrelationship of Religion and ELT* (pp. 115–35). New York: Routledge.

Madziva, R., McGrath, S., & Thondhlana, J. (2016). Communicating employability: The role of communicative competence for Zimbabwean highly skilled migrants in the UK. *Journal of International Migration and Integration*, 17(1), 235–52.

Maxwell, D. (2006). Writing the history of African Christianity: Reflections of an editor. *Journal of Religion in Africa*, 36(3–4), 379–99.

Middlebrooks, A., and Noghiu, A. (2007). Reconceptualizing spiritual capital: A meso-model for organizational leadership. In S. Singh-Sengupta & D. Fields (eds.), *Integrating Spirituality and Organizational Leadership* (pp. 675–81). New Delhi: MacMillan.

Norris, P., & Inglehart, R. (2004). *Sacred and Secular: Religion and Politics Worldwide.* New York: Cambridge University Press.

Palmer, P. J. (1990). Good teaching: A matter of living the mystery. *Change: The Magazine of Higher Learning*, 22(1), 11–16.

Pennycook, A., and Makoni, S. (2005). The modern mission: The language effects of Christianity. *Journal of Language, Identity and Education*, 4(2), 137–55.

Rey, T. (2004). Marketing the goods of salvation: Bourdieu on religion. *Religion*, 34(4), 331–43.

Shah, R. S., & Shah, T. S. (2010). How Evangelicanism–Including Pentecostalism–Helps the Poor: The Role of Spiritual Capital. In P. L. Berger & G. Redding (eds.), *The Hidden Form of Capital: Spiritual Influences in Societal Progress* (pp. 61–90). London: Anthem Press.

Smith, D. (2000). Faith and method in foreign language pedagogy. *Journal of Christianity and Foreign Languages*, 1(1), 7–25.

Snow, D. B. (2001). *English teaching as Christian Mission: An Applied Theology.* Scottsdale, PA: Herald Press.

Thondhlana, J., and Madziva, R. (2017). English language as an integration tool: the case of Syrian refugees to the UK. In E. J. Erling (ed.), *English across the Fracture Lines: The Contribution and Relevance of English to Security, Safety and Stability in the World* (pp. 63–71). London: British Council.

Van Dyk, J. (2000). *Craft of Christian Teaching: A Classroom Journey.* Sioux Center, IA: Dordt College Press.

Varghese, M. M., and Johnson, B. (2007). Evangelical Christians and English language teaching. *TESOL Quarterly*, 41(1), 5–31.

Verter, B., (2003). Spiritual capital: Theorizing religion with Bourdieu against Bourdieu. *Sociological Theory*, 21(2), 50–174.

West-Burnham, J., & Coates, M. (2005). *Personalizing Learning: Transforming Education for Every Child.* London: Network Educational Press.

Wong, M. S. Kristjánsson, C., and Dörnyei, Z. (eds.). (2013). *Christian Faith and English Language Teaching and Learning: Research on Interrelationship of Religion and ELT.* New York: Routledge.

Yang, F. (2005). Lost in the market, saved a McDonald's: Conversion to Christianity in urban China. *Journal for the Scientific Study of Religion*, 44(4), 423–41.

12   Inter-religious Dialogue

Alain Wolf

12.1   Background, History, and Key Terms

The three Abrahamic faiths, Judaism, Christianity, and Islam, have at various times in their history engaged in dialogue, and to this very day, they co-exist, at times sharing in worship in the holiest places of our world. The prophet Muhammad on his travels is said to have stopped over in Bethlehem to say a prayer for his brother Jesus, and the Virgin Mary is more often mentioned in the Qur'an (thirty-four times), than she is in the New Testament (nineteen times) (Albera and Pénicaud, 2017, p. 28). Contact between the three Abrahamic faiths then, far from being the recent phenomenon that it appears to be, is as old as the faiths about which it is concerned. However, as Burrell (2004, p. 498) observes, if dialogue is hardly new, it is also enmeshed in a history of struggle. The crusades, for example, represented 'a delayed western reaction to Islam's spectacular spread' and later, western colonialism was a form of 'belated recovery' of the Holy Land, 'following the demise of the crusades' (Burrell, 2004, p. 498). Whatever view one has on the topic, it is undeniable that successful dialogue between the three Abrahamic faiths is still impeded by the way political strategies have sought to legitimise territorial ambitions through appeals to religion. And Burrell (2004, p. 48), again, asks: 'What hope have we of turning those same religious traditions into forces for reconciliation?'

The recent answer given by European lawmakers, prompted by concerns about security in the wake of several terrorist attacks, is to emphasise the language of secular citizenship as 'a factor for social cohesion [and] mutual understanding' (European Committee of Ministers, 2008). To set up the state as the highest authority has the effect of limiting the possibilities for any sort of dialogue between faiths and those of no faith because it centres the argument on secularism.

Indeed, here may be an appropriate place to offer a preliminary definition of inter-religious dialogue as the 'recognition of the possible truth in all religions' (Knitter, 1985, p. 208). And as Tillich (1963, p. 63) has usefully observed, any worthwhile discussion of inter-religious dialogue should start by addressing the question of the *telos* (end/fulfilment) of all things: the *telos* of Christianity is in the Kingdom of God whereas that of Buddhism is Nirvana. The realisation that both religions stand in opposition to earthly kingdoms enhances inter-religious understanding.

In any discussion of dialogue across religions, however, the diversities of the language used tumble together in an elaborate configuration of patterns, ranging from Huntington's (1993) exaggerated coinage of the 'Clash of Civilizations' to the naïve tendencies of the United Nations (2007) replacing negative terms with positive ones such as 'dialogue' and 'acceptance" to depict harmonious and peaceful co-existence, come what may. In the face of often-destructive struggles arising from the political use of religion, neither use of language, whether confrontational or aimed at creating peace, is likely to enhance the possibility for dialogue between faiths. This chapter sets the language of interfaith dialogue in the specific context of how different faiths are translated across cultures. 'Translation' here is defined loosely as the way sacred texts have been relocated across languages so that people who could not read Latin or Greek, for example, could still have access to the word of God in English. This concern with matters of translation has directed a further exploration of discourse, or the study of language beyond the level of the sentence (Wetherell, 2001; Yule and Brown, 1983) as opposed to the specifics of text translation, covered in more depth in Wilson's chapter (this volume).

'Implicit' and 'explicit' meaning and 'context' are key terms in this discussion of inter-religious dialogue. This is because much of what is communicated is not explicitly said. So one may perfectly understand the forms and the vocabulary of a given language, for example, the preposition 'on' and the words 'Tuesday' and 'morning' in the phrase 'on Tuesday morning', and yet one may still be unable to understand the full meaning of an utterance out of context. An example will serve to illustrate how powerless language as code is for successful recovery of meaning to take place. Let us imagine a meeting room in a Church building where Simon, a priest, asks Amos, his trainee, if he will attend the all-day retreat on Monday, and Amos says: 'I have an exam on Tuesday morning.' Now, Amos has expressed himself implicitly in that he has not said 'yes' or 'no', but Simon will have no problem disambiguating Amos's utterance on the basis of the non-linguistic context that if one has an examination on Tuesday, one is unlikely to be able to spend the day before on any other activity than revising. Let us now alter the non-linguistic context, and invite Amos to the retreat on Wednesday. He can say the same thing as before ('I've got an exam on Tuesday morning') and yet mean the opposite, namely that he can come along.

In order to understand the full meaning of an implicit utterance, we need to refer to the non-linguistic context; that is, understanding language as code is not enough. The study of these mechanisms by which speakers and hearers recover implicit meaning is known as Pragmatics (see Section 12.2.3 for more details). The chapter will also explore dialogism (Bakhtin, 1981), the concept that all living discourse, even the most seemingly monologic, is always oriented to others and is made up of language that has already been said; that any combination of words that we can think of 'carries within itself traces of preceding usage' (Todorov, 1984, p. 63). In other words, our identity is linguistically co-constructed and dialogically dependent on the language of others. Remarkably, definitions of dialogue are rarely provided by those who engage in inter-religious dialogue. Drawing on these two sub-branches of linguistics, pragmatics (see Wolf, 2012) and dialogism (Ducrot, 1984), I will use these concepts to present a case study using evidence from three documents relating to interfaith dialogue, and hope to demonstrate that dialogue across religions is limited without an authentic participation by interlocutors physically occupying the spaces where cultures overlap.

12.2   Key Topics, Questions, and Debates

The phrase 'language of inter-religious dialogue' is bound to mean different things to different people. This is primarily because the word 'language' can be understood in so many different ways: in the context of religion, we may be referring to the ancient languages in which the holy books such as the Torah, the New Testament, or the Qur'an have been written. We may also be talking about issues related to the translation of those ancient languages and to what extent this can enable the progress or constitute a hindrance to dialogue between faiths. I will therefore start by considering the role that translation has on our understanding of interreligious dialogue.

12.2.1   *The Languages of Sacred Texts: Translation and Incommensurability*

As I observed earlier, the translation of the Bible was an attempt to disseminate its content to the wider English-speaking public culminating in the *King James Bible*. By contrast, in Islam, the words of the Qur'an are said to be the actual utterances of God directly revealed to the prophet Muhammad in the seventh century AD so that any mediation by way of translation is discouraged. The Qur'an, because of the particular diction of Arabic is believed by most Muslim theologians to be *mu'jiz*, or 'inimitable' (Winter, 2001, p. 133) and untranslatable. Translations have been regarded as permissible as study aids (Winter, 2001) in parts of the Muslim world, where Arabic is not the native language. Similarly, in Judaism, the main public prayers can be said in the vernaculars 'in order that the people should understand the prayers that they address to God' (Weitzman, 2001, p. 70).

The translation of the Qur'an can be seen as a revealing exercise in what Winter (2001, p. 133) terms 'cultural relocation' with considerable implications for inter-religious dialogue. Some Christian translations of the Qur'an in the early Muslim centuries, for instance, were composed for the purpose of refutation (Winter 2001), with all the limitations that such activity would impose on future dialogue between Islam and Christianity. Cultural relocation is also part and parcel of Judaism which has brought the languages of Christian Europe into contact with Hebrew, for example, *messiah, sabbatical, jubilee* (Weitzman, 2001, p. 72).

The translation of religious texts leads on to the nature of religious translation in the context of inter-religious dialogue. The Muslim stance perceives translations to be distortions of source texts with any effort to translate the Qur'an being condemned as 'impious or even blasphemous' (Gaudé, 2010, p. 289). This is not an unusual idea in the field of religious translation. Many translators of the Bible were similarly accused of not being faithful to the word of God, starting with St. Jerome (395 AD), the translator of the Christian Bible into Latin. The issue of whether there can ever be a faithful translation of the source text is one, which is still a matter of debate. Put crudely, the argument hinges on the two related questions of faithfulness and intelligibility. Translators can aim to be faithful to the source text with the intention of producing a 'word for word', albeit at times unintelligible, translation. Alternatively, they can translate 'sense for sense' in a way that focuses on being intelligible to the target audience, at the risk of being unfaithful to the source text. The distinction can be traced as far back as St. Jerome (395 AD), who translated 'sense for sense'. He defended his translation in a statement, 'Indeed, I not only admit but freely proclaim that in translation from the Greek – except in the case of Sacred Scripture where the very order of words is a mystery – I render not word for word but sense for sense' (Jerome, 2004).

However, as St. Jerome himself found out, and I have previously argued (Robinson-Pant and Wolf, 2017), sense for sense translations are an 'ethical minefield'. They can be criticised for being unfaithful to the source text, having distorted it in some way or other, the distortions arising at times from ideological motives, or simply wanting to erase traces of foreignness for the benefit of the target culture. Venuti (1998), a well-known contemporary translation theorist, has elaborated on the distinction between sense for sense and literal translations. He distinguishes between domesticating translations which translate the source text in such a way as to make it intelligible to the cultural values of a dominant target audience, and 'foreignising' translations that leave noticeable traces of foreignness in the target text, thus possibly disturbing the receiving public by asking it to place itself in a foreign land.

Translation then is central to the analysis of dialogue across faiths. Translation may always, for some, be perceived as a form of ethnocentric betrayal. Neusner (1991), for example, has adopted such a position, seeing different religious traditions as closed systems which admit of no translation whatsoever. Neusner (cited in Ipgrave 2014, p. 49) describes the two traditions of Judaism and Christianity as 'completely different religions, not different versions of one religion'. This understanding of religious languages as incommensurable is also propounded by Hallett (2011, p. 1) inspired by Wittgenstein's (2009, p. 223) remark that 'if a lion could talk we could not understand him' as well as Clifford's (2005, p. 168) observation that there is no 'common core between religions . . . no underlying ethics to unite them'. Such radical incommensurability implies that the possibility of translation is 'ruled out *a priori*' (Hallett, 2011, p. 1), with no hope for a meaningful dialogue between individuals from different faith backgrounds.

The argument for incommensurability can go further in the sense that untranslatability is linked to hostility and the eventual disintegration of interreligious dialogue: 'Conversation between religions is pluralized or balkanized when they are seen as mutually untranslatable. Not only do they no longer share a common theme, such as salvation, but the shared universe of discourse forged to discuss that theme disintegrates' (Lindbeck, 1997, p. 427). Lindbeck admits that there may be ways of overcoming this, one of them being a form of religious bilingualism, that is, the mastering of many religious languages and the ability to communicate proficiently across them. But 'genuine bilingualism', remarks Lindbeck (1997, p. 427), 'is so rare and difficult as to leave basically intact the barrier to extramural communication posed by untranslatability in religious matters. Those for whom conversation is key to solving interreligious problems are likely to be disappointed.' Even those committed to incommensurability do acknowledge the existence of bilingual communication, even if they make the mistake of perceiving bilingualism as 'rare'. Going into the nature of bilingualism is beyond the scope of this chapter but suffice to say that far from being the peripheral phenomenon presented by Lindbeck, bilingualism is more widespread in the world than monolingualism. Not all bilinguals have balanced proficiency in both their languages, as Lindbeck presumably anticipates, but a theory of additive bilingualism (Lambert, 1975) would maintain that bilinguals can achieve cognitive flexibility and communicate in their languages in a great variety of ways. Section 12.2.2 explores the many ways in which translatability can be achieved across languages and religions.

12.2.2   *Translatability, Interstitial Theology, and Linguistic Hospitality*

An understanding of religions as 'fluid, cosmopolitan and non-absolute' (Ruparell, 2013, p. 117) is more likely to advance the cause of interreligious dialogue than debates about the incommensurability of divinity and the untranslatability of religious beliefs. The question of untranslatability, first, is one that is answered by highlighting the notion of hybridity in translation. Berman (1984), in his seminal work on translation, argues, for example, that the alleged untranslatability of poetry is dissolved into the phenomenon of translatability by means of borrowing and lexical neologism. Any translator is fundamentally confronted to a number of choices: (1) one can domesticate (*la francisation*): for example, the word 'pampa' can be translated as 'plaines pampasiennes'; (2) one can introduce borrowings (*l'emprunt*): that is, keep the word as 'pampa'; or (3) one can go halfway and 'naturalise' the borrowing (la *semi-francisation*): for example, 'porteño' becomes 'portègne'.

Hybridity then is the inevitable product of translation, that very spirit of freedom which creates real, palpable, alternatives of speaking, and ultimately, of being (Steiner, 1998). But, again, what precisely constitutes Steiner's (1998) 'alternative of being' in interreligious dialogue? There is a choice: either believers satisfy their own religious-centric needs, producing translations which erase the foreignness of the religious Other (see Ipgrave, 2014), or they subject themselves to what Berman calls *l'épreuve de l'étranger*, or 'the trial of the foreign', producing hybrid translations which consider the foreign religious Others in all their foreignness. Ipgrave's (2014) use of Bishop Kasper's phrase 'sacrament of otherness' can be understood this way. He is aware that the word 'sacrament' is Christian language, but he affirms a kind of hybridised use of it. The phrase 'sacrament of otherness' points to the very vitality of the Jewish people who defy all attempts to be reduced into mere bearers of Christian meaning. The word 'sacrament' has thus crossed into another religious culture and been hybridised whilst maintaining the irreducible nature of Judaism.

The word 'hybridity' is borrowed from Bhabha (2011), who defines the act of translating as an engagement with the foreign 'that reveals the interstitial; [...] becomes the unstable element of linkage, the indeterminate reality of the inbetween, that has to be engaged in creating conditions through which newness comes into the world' (p. 20). Such a conceptualisation of translation gives the translator a central role in enabling understanding between allegedly untranslatable, vague, and indeterminate contexts through finding the interstice, the open spaces, between languages. For it is this interstice, this open space, which enables languages to interact with one another very much like the interstice between the door and its frame allows it to function as a door. Ruparell (2013) rather astutely applies Bhabha's (2011) theorising and coins the phrase 'interstitial theology' to refer to a form of theology that 'seeks to hybridise elements of separate traditions' (Ruparell, 2013, p. 121). As he observes (Ruparell, 2013, p. 129) in relation to interfaith dialogue, 'a mutually shared area of reference [...] is built up in the interstice which separates them'. This kind of reciprocity, however, we only partly encounter in interreligious dialogue mainly because as hardened religious monolinguals, we rarely experience the pleasure of dwelling in somebody else's religious context. It is to this notion of context that we turn to now, seeking answers to two main questions: Does language use have socio-cognitive effects? How does context determine language?

12.2.3   Understanding Context

One branch of Linguistics which tries to answer questions about context is Discourse Analysis (DA, thereafter). DA has become widely used as a method of inquiry, if not systematically in the area of inter-religious dialogue (see Wijsen, 2013). Although DA includes distinctive, and some would argue (Levinson, 1983), incompatible approaches, its common concern is to give an account of how coherent and well-formed discourse is achieved (Wetherell, 2001; Yule and Brown, 1983). Another aim in what is known as *Critical Discourse Analysis* is to explain how language use may have an influence in sociocultural contexts, especially where ideologically motivated uses of language and power are concerned (see Fairclough, 1992). The theoretical basis of Critical Discourse Analysis owes much to the work of Foucault (1981) who establishes a close connection between powerful discourse and knowledge so that speakers cannot enter into the order of discourse if they do not meet certain requirements dictated to them by powerful institutions. This is because the production of powerful discourse is accompanied by a complex ritual of conditions, for example, appropriate gestures and behaviour and appropriate language use. Foucault's observations are relevant in the context of inter-religious dialogue. If discourse is reduced to predetermined conditions of meaning-making by those in power, there is little room for creative dialogue to take place. In Foucault's own words (1981, p. 55), it is not enough to decipher discourse strategies as if the world were transparent and readily interpretable, Il faut concevoir le discours comme une violence que nous faisons aux choses, en tout cas comme une pratique que nous leur imposons (Discourse must be perceived as a kind of violence we do to the contingent world, and in all cases, as a practice we impose upon it, [my translation]). As we shall see, DA invites practitioners of inter-religious dialogue to transcend established regularity or conventionalism by paying close attention to the external conditions which make any given discourse possible.

In the field of religious studies, contributions by scholars understandably reflect on the applicability of DA to theological concerns, and some more empirically oriented projects apply the methods of DA to analyse data of religious import. Wijsen's (2013) analysis of Islamic extremism in Tanzania and Indonesia is a good illustration of this approach. The study uses a model developed by Fairclough (1992) which focuses on three types of subject positions in society: 'the individual dimension or micro perspective, the institutional dimension or meso perspective, and the societal dimension or macro perspective' (Fairclough, 1992, p. 72). One of the examples Wijsen (2013) analyses is that of an interview of a participant whose house was rented to Noordin Mohammad Top, a famous terrorist from Malaysia, and is now visited by many tourists. The participant disagreed with Noordin's ideas, describing him as a 'disaster' (micro dimension). Nevertheless, she also perceived the situation as providing some 'blessings' as a new floor for the mosque could be paid for as a result of the tourists' donations (meso dimension). And Wijsen (2013, p. 75) concludes: 'This practice constitutes and is constituted by the commercialisation of religion in society (macro dimension)'.

The main problem with Wijsen's (2013) analysis, as he himself (2013) admits, is how one shows that 'language use has socio-cognitive effects' (p. 85). In other words, how does the language we use affect context, or vice-versa? In this respect, Wijsen (2013) gives the example of churches which use the language of business, consequently preaching a prosperity gospel. Discourse Analysis draws our attention to the non-linguistic macro-context in which discursive practices are conducted.

This is a major concern also addressed by the field of linguistic Pragmatics and three key concepts: (a) calculus of interpretation (explicit and implicit meaning), (b) dialogical co-construction, and (c) performativity.

(a)   Calculus of Interpretation   The first notion, which I have coined in earlier research as the *calculus of interpretation* (see Wolf, 2012), is the idea that meaning is achieved by speakers and hearers through a process of negoti-ation. In my example about Amos going to a religious event before his examination, we understood his implicit utterance 'My last exam is on Tuesday' from our assumptions about the static non-linguistic context (i.e. the meeting room in a Church, the fact that he is training for the priesthood, the system of setting examinations in the UK, what is involved in a religious retreat, etc.). There was also a dynamic context, that is, Simon successfully recovered meaning through a process of forming or cancelling psychological assumptions about Amos's utterances. If Amos had gone on to say in the first context, 'Oh, but that will give me a welcome break from revision', Simon's assumptions about individuals revising the day before an examination would have been cancelled and would have had to be replaced by another assumption to the effect that Amos, for example, was not very serious about his studies, or that he was so wonderfully clever as not to be affected by not revising the day before an examination. What is important for our discussion is that the *calculus of interpretation* is not different in kind when it comes to interactions across religions or across cultures. When speakers use a language other than their first, the forms they use (including vocabulary, word order, and intonation), can carry with them ambiguous meanings and inferences. Gumperz (1982), for example, who calls these forms 'contextualisation cues' studied a group of

Punjabi-speaking dinner ladies who, when they served customers in English, asked them if they wanted 'gravy' with a falling rather than a rising intonation. Similarly, an Italian friend of mine, often said 'goodbye' to me with a falling intonation. Gumperz (1982) found that the dinner ladies were perceived as being rude, and, likewise, I initially thought my friend was displeased with me. The important thing to note here is that, at the explicit level of what is said, we need awareness that speakers can use language forms incorrectly and generate inferences, unwittingly. In the case of my Italian friend, I needed to realise that his falling intonation was the result of what is done in his first language, and not that he meant to show displeasure. Incorrectly interpreting language forms can have a deleterious effect on relationships between individuals across languages, religions, and cultures. As Verschueren (2008, p. 29) puts it, 'Inferences [...] can never unthinkingly be connected with intentions.' The calculus of interpretation finds its most direct expression in Quash and Jenkins's (2009, p. 4) *Cambridge Interfaith Programme Academic Profile* where the focus is on clarifying the 'identity-bearing particularities' of the religious traditions from the outset.

However, communicative success may not always be achieved through the calculus of interpretation and the recognition of speakers' intentions. There are cases where misunderstandings are so deep that we need to attend to the 'socio-cultural presuppositions assumed by interactants' (Haugh, 2008, p. 224). In the case of what I have called a 'communicative cul-de-sac' (Robinson-Pant and Wolf, 2017), the notion of 'dialogical co-construction' is needed to negotiate the interaction further.

(b)   Dialogical co-construction The process of co-construction involves understanding oneself as consisting of different voices and identities. An example of this can be seen in Ducrot (1984) of a speaker saying to another: 'So I'm stupid, am I? Well, just you see!' The speaker of this 'I' does not express the opinion of himself as stupid. Rather, we interpret his utterance as an echo of a viewpoint expressed by an entity represented by 'you'. Language enables speakers to negotiate their identity through a process of integrating the opinions and viewpoints of others within their own discourse. Put in another way, we could say that our discourse contains within it the seeds of dialogue. Bakhtin (1981), in his illuminating theorising about utterance understanding, put forward the notion of 'dialogism' to refer to the relation between the discourse initiated by the 'I' and the discourse of others. Speakers then negotiate their identities by integrating the values, voices, and identities of others within their own discourse.

In inter-religious dialogue, the equivalent negotiation of voices and identities involves integrating two differing religious horizons within one person, and since we are not unitary selves, we depend on the other for the disclosure of truth. This idea is eloquently expressed by Burrell (2004, p. 54) who speaks about inter-religious friendships as not just an expression of complementarity but as 'a way of allowing the faith of others, with the access to the divine that it represents, to interact with our own faith commitment to draw attention to dimensions of our faith response which can effectively be blocked by the shadow-side of our tradition'. These different expressions of the same key concept of dialogical co-construction combine to form a coherent basis upon which inter-religious communication can effectively take place.

We have so far looked at interpretation in context using the concept of the calculus of interpretation and dialogical co-construction. The third concept I have used for an analysis of inter-religious dialogue (see Wolf, 2012) is drawn from 'Speech Act' Theory, namely that of performativity.

(c)   *Performativity*   It was the philosopher of language, Austin (1988), who made a useful distinction between acts that are only attempted (i.e. illocutionary acts), and acts that get performed (i.e. perlocutionary acts). This distinction is important because in using a language, we may perform an illocutionary act. For example, by saying 'Please forgive me!' I perform the illocutionary act of urging my friend to forgive me. This is quite a different thing from what we bring about by saying something (Austin, 1988), for example, 'I got him to forgive me', that is the perlocutionary force of an utterance.

For inter-religious dialogue, performativity means physically occupying the spaces where two religious traditions have a claim to a particular place (Wijsen, 2007). Meeting in those places is profoundly performative because it is a realisation of one's 'individual poverty' coupled with the need 'to transcend' oneself (Panikkar, 1979). The danger, as Krieger (1991) astutely observes, is that the place of encounter between cultures and religions may be seen as a field of battle. And, as we know, such places in the world do abound. The *Cave of the Patriarchs the Ibrahimi Mosque in Hebron* is the second most sacred site in the world for Jews. According to Genesis (23, 35, 49, 50) Abraham, Sarah, and their descendants are said to be buried there. The site is also the fourth holiest site in the world for Muslims for whom it is the sacred house of Abraham, a revered prophet of Islam. The sanctuary has been the site of conflict between Jews and Muslims in sharp contrast to Abraham's xenophilia. Currently, there is a form of cohabitation in the site heavily guarded by the Jewish military. Non-violence is thus a necessary condition of performativity because it 'grants humans a universal solidarity with the divine' (see Krieger, 1991, p. 157) whilst avoiding the dangers of self-interest and exclusivism.

12.3   Case Study

In the study of inter-religious documents that follows, I aim to illustrate how Pragmatics can help us to gain an understanding of that key relationship between discourse and its socio-cognitive effects in the non-linguistic context. I draw on an earlier study (Wolf, 2012) and address the practical processes of inter-religious interaction with reference to three key documents, which have all in their own fashion engaged with the conditions for inter-religious dialogue, namely:

1. The recommendation of the Committee of Ministers to member states on the dimension of religions and non-religious convictions within intercultural education adopted at the 1044th meeting of the Ministers' Deputies, 10 December 2008
2. The Way of Dialogue (Appendix 6 of the Lambeth Conference, 1988)
3. The Nostra Aetate declaration on the relation of the Church to Non-Christian Religions, The Second Vatican Council, Promulgated by His Holiness Pope Paul VI, 28 October 1965.

Two of the documents arguably come from 'mono-religious' traditions and the third from the secular field of European politics, thus making them unlikely candidates for an illustration of inter-religious interaction. The texts, however, were selected because they all attempt to address interreligious dialogue, and, in the case of the secular text, inter-religious dialogue in the context of national citizenship. It is in this sense that they serve as illustrations of how the notion of inter-religious dialogue is understood in three different traditions. Every effort, however, has been made not to enter into invidious comparisons between the documents since they so obviously originate from different contexts. *Nostra Aetate* has since been followed by other initiatives such as *Redemptoris Missio* (1990) and *Ecclesia in Europa* (2003) (see Thibon, 2010 for a historical overview of the development of inter-religious dialogue between Christianity and Islam). The analysis will focus on the ways they convey meaning based on the categories previously outlined and by commenting on the inconsistencies in the documents which potentially make the possibility for inter-religious dialogue problematic.

The first example relates to the *Nostra Aetate* ('In our Time') declaration promulgated in 1965 by His Holiness Pope Paul on the relationship of the Roman Catholic Church to Non-Christian Religions VI. This was the first recommendation of its kind and is generally recognised as the starting point of dialogue between Christianity and other religions (Thibon, 2010). The originality of the language used in the document and the progressive nature of its content is striking. The non-linguistic context is anchored in the present time of utterance (hence the title of the declaration):

1. When day by day mankind is being drawn closer together, and the ties between different peoples are becoming stronger, the Church examines more closely her relationship to non-Christian religions.

The use of the progressive aspect 'is being drawn' and 'are becoming' generate inferences of inchoate, or not fully developed, action. Dialogical co-construction starts off from a position of finding common aims between all faiths which, the document claims, are all ways of countering 'the restlessness of the human heart' by proposing 'teachings' and 'sacred rites'. What follows, however, is a comment which imposes a serious restriction on the possibility for dialogue:

2. The Catholic Church rejects nothing that is true and holy in these religions. She regards with sincere reverence those ways of conduct and of life, those precepts and teachings which, though differing in many aspects from the ones she holds and sets forth, nonetheless often reflect a ray of that Truth which enlightens all men. Indeed, she proclaims Christ, 'the way of truth, and the life' (John 14:6), in whom men may find the fullness of religious life, in whom God has reconciled all things to himself (2 Cor 5:18–19).

Ipgrave (2008) has noted the ambiguous nature of the conciliar call to affirmation in the first line of this paragraph. Although not explicitly stated, a clear implication is that there is unholy and untrue teaching in other religious traditions and that the Church rejects that teaching. Diametrically opposed to the notion of sincere reverence put forward by the Church is the abrupt shift to the Gospel of John (John 14:6), and its most exclusivist saying. Other religions are not rejected, however, so that the position espoused here is not that of outright exclusivism. Yet, nor are they totally accepted either. The convergence between the Christian message and other faiths is affirmed, but Christianity still is presented as moulding other faiths according to the truth of Jesus Christ. This form of religious inclusivism (see Hick, 1985) consists of acknowledging that salvation occurs in other traditions whilst wanting to attach the Christian label to them. Selective truths are incorporated into one's own position on one's own terms. This model of dialogue implies that one's religion is the model within which the others fit in: 'A field of tension emerges between a need to engage in dialogue with other faiths and that of safeguarding the theological truths of one's own' (Wolf, 2012, p. 16). In other words, the dialogical co-construction I referred to earlier of allowing the faith of others to interact with our own faith commitment is seriously jeopardised by the conciliar declaration.

Performative verbs with various illocutionary forces abound in *Nostra Aetate*. The use of the verbs, 'examines' and 'considers' indicates that the Church aims to perform particular kinds of illocutionary acts:

3. [. . .] The Church examines more closely her relationship to non-Christian religions. [. . .] She considers above all in this declaration what men have in common and what draws them in fellowship.

Language as form, as we saw earlier, is unable to determine the full meaning of an utterance such as (3) unless we combine the linguistic form with the specific context of the utterance. In this sense, Austin (1988) distinguishes between acts that are only attempted (illocutionary) and those that get performed (perlocutionary). When we perform illocutionary acts, we do not actually perform anything at all. Indeed, the declaration here does not elaborate on what the societal effects of its many affirmations may be in the sharing between faiths. Rather, it merely presents itself as asserting the recognised convention of universal humanity. And of course, the Church here presents itself as believing what is being asserting because that is what performing the illocutionary act of asserting means by convention. In other words, the gap between linguistic form and the non-linguistic context is not bridged.

The 1988 Lambeth Conference statement, *Jews, Christians and Muslims: The Way of Dialogue* is prominent in Anglican interfaith dialogue and its principles are the culmination of two Lambeth conferences, the decennial assembly of bishops of the Anglican Communion (see Ipgrave, 2008). The Lambeth text first defines its non-linguistic context of situation by imposing limitations on it. Consider the following:

4. Whilst dialogue with all faiths is highly desirable, we recognise a special relationship between Christianity, Judaism, and Islam.

The use of 'whilst' in this the first sentence suggests a plurality of voices in dialogue, voices which affirm the desirability of dialogue with all faiths, and voices which restrict it to the three Abrahamic faiths. There is, from the outset, the positioning of a hierarchy of faiths: those which have a special relationship with Christianity and those which do not. There is also a hierarchy of relationship articulated between Judaism and Islam. Whereas *The Way of Dialogue* clearly states that Christianity and Judaism share a common inheritance, the calculus of interpretation concerning Islam is made difficult on many levels because of a lack of expertise in crucial areas such as apostasy, for example:

5. There can be no genuine understanding [...] with Islam without quite detailed study by at least some experts.

The reason put forward by the document for this lack of expertise is that traditional Islamic thought has been untranslated. The recovery of meaning is thus impeded not only at the level of implied meaning, but at the linguistic level of what is said and not translated. From the perspective of dialogical co-construction, the call to affirmation of other faiths may be ambiguous, too, and the result of a concession:

6. If Christians wish their own faiths to be affirmed by others, they themselves must be open to the full force of the attraction of the partner in dialogue and be willing to affirm all they can affirm, especially when it resonates with the Gospel.

One of the interesting aspects of the Lambeth text, however, is the way that it conceptualises dialogue. From the very beginning of the document, the conditions for the possibility of dialogue are defined:

7. The essential condition of any true dialogue is a willingness to listen to the partner; to try to see them with their eyes and feel with their heart. [...] Understanding others means allowing them to define themselves in their terms rather than ours. [...] This means that in dialogue we may have to face some very different understandings of religion.

Ipgrave's (2008) interpretation of understanding here as an 'affective entry into the other' (p. 4) lays down not only the preconditions for genuine dialogical interaction but affirms other faiths, especially Judaism, with direct and undiluted enthusiasm. When it comes to the anticipated perlocutionary effects of dialogue, *The Way of Dialogue* is unambiguously clear: 'Both partner to the dialogue will be affected and changed by this process, for it is a mutual sharing.' Clear too are the challenges posed. Whilst the performative aspect of God's rule is inescapable in Christianity in so far as Christ is a historical figure and 'God's just rule has already broken into the affairs of this world', this cannot be accepted by Judaism. However, this major difference can be overcome, the Lambeth text argues, on the basis that both Jews and Christians share in the hope of the realisation of God's kingdom on earth and it is through Jesus Christ that Christians come to share this same hope: In my words then, different illocutionary forces, same perlocutionary effect, or as Hallett (2011, p. 72) puts it: 'apparently conflicting assertions, same reality'.

The recommendation of ministers to member states on the dimension of religions and non-religious convictions within intercultural education attempts to negotiate the conditions for interreligious dialogue in the context of national citizenship. Consider the following:

8. The Committee of Ministers states: that education for democratic citizenship is a factor for social cohesion, mutual understanding, intercultural and inter-religious dialogue, and solidarity.

The central defining characteristic of the non-linguistic context is the principle of 'democratic citizenship' which contributes to many positive things, including social cohesion and inter-religious dialogue. Notwithstanding the fact that the word 'citizenship' connotes republican values which underpin a separation of Church and State, it is not clear at this stage of the document exactly what is meant by democratic citizenship: is it national citizenship as exemplified by national citizenship programmes or is it a putative citizenship of Europe? The document becomes clearer on this point in recommendation 6, which promotes the following attitudes:

9. Recognising that the expression of religious allegiance at school, without ostentation or proselytising, exercised with due respect of others,

public order and human rights, is compatible with a secular society and the respective autonomy of state and religions.

The non-linguistic, macro context here is that of disestablished religion in which matters of faith are subordinated to state legislation. Instead of co-constructed dialogism, we are faced with words such as 'autonomy' and 'compatibility' which suggests that there can be no common ground between religious allegiance and secularism. This lack of dialogue is further illustrated in the following consideration:

10. The Committee of Ministers encourage the member states to promote initial and in-service training for teachers with a view to the objective, balanced teaching of religions as they are today and of religions in history, and to require human rights training for all religious leaders, in particular those with an educational role in contact with young people.

The phrases 'balanced teaching' and 'human rights teaching for religious leaders' generate the unwelcome implied meaning that religious leaders influence young minds through a form of teaching which is not compatible with human rights. Indeed, the dominant teaching style advocated by the document is constrained by the need for 'balance', objectivity, and impartiality. The document suggests a phenomenological approach which fails to fulfil a key notion of inter-cultural/interreligious dialogue I reviewed earlier, namely that participants in inter-religious dialogue should 'bring themselves to that dialogue, most importantly their religious selves' (Knitter, 1985, p. 208). Indeed, the document gives considerable weight to the transmission of factual information about religions. The attendant claim that such instruction will develop mutual understanding and trust seems optimistic and would at best only fulfil the calculus of interpretation.

Since the writing of my 2012 article, France has adopted such a perspective, and has introduced the teaching of some form of religious literacy (the teaching of *le fait religieux* or 'religious fact') by adding largely abstract and historical material to the History and Philosophy curriculum in French secondary schools. The philosopher Debray (2002) admits that the terminology is used for the sake of expediency:

Ne le nions pas: le fait religieux est de bonne diplomatie. L'expression a de l'emploi parce qu'elle est commode et d'une neutralité peu compromettante. Le laïque soupçonneux excusera le religieux par le fait, le croyant réticent excusera le fait parce que religieux. (2002: 171–2)

There's no denying this: the expression 'the teaching of religious fact' is diplomatic. It is used because it is convenient, neutral and hardly incriminating. The disbelieving secularist will excuse the adjective 'religious' because of the word 'fact' and the reticent believer will excuse the word 'fact' because of the adjective 'religious.' (my translation)

Such a didactic and epistemic approach to inter-religious dialogue has not only the effect of privileging those in possession of facts about religion (i.e.

teachers, specialists), but also dangerously turns these practitioners into gate-keepers (see Foucault, 1981) who dictate who can and who cannot enter into a powerful exegetic discourse about faiths.

The purpose of the case study was to explore the notion of inter-religious dialogue from the perspective of pragmatic linguistics and to address the dangers of inclusivist and didactic approaches in some of the texts presented. In this respect, we noted how the adoption of a secular model which claims to be 'the horizon of civilisation' (Quash and Jenkins, 2009, p. 3) marginalises the religious sphere and leads to secularism being perceived as a 'rival form' (p. 3).

12.4   Future Directions

The increase in linguistic analyses of interfaith texts has already produced valuable contributions in such wide-ranging areas as Translation Studies, Intercultural Communication, Dialogism, Discourse Analysis, and Pragmatics. However, an overview of recent studies reveals that a number of issues are not being addressed, which can lead to a lack of coherence in the field.

First, questions that concern the original religious texts in Hebrew, Greek, Arabic, and Aramaic are often written about in English. More attention could be paid to how these ancient languages and the way they are used in a given context affects our ability to engage in dialogue across languages. This is of crucial importance especially when one considers the many possibilities for misunderstanding through the lens of translation and interpretation. Yet, this interpretative dimension has its detractors. Brink-Danan (2015), for example, suggests that a model of 'trans-languaging' which transcends nationalist views about bounded languages may be an alternative to the translation trope. Members of a multifaith society, she argues, do 'effectively' communicate beyond 'translation'. It is not clear, however, from her ethnographic data how divergent truth claims between believers and those of no faith, for example, are to be resolved by an appeal to such a blunt instrument as 'trans-languaging' in English.

As a model for how researchers can approach issues relating to linguistic analyses of inter-religious dialogue, it is useful to consider the work done in fields such as Discourse Analysis. The area has been very successful in applying the methodology to studies of inter-religious utterances. Many questions, however, remain to be answered, namely, how discourse analysis goes about demonstrating that language use has particular social effects, and how conclusions at macro-level can be derived from micro-level analyses. Another recurring problem in this area is one that relates to the dominance of certain types of analysis over others. Discourse Analysis researchers in inter-religious dialogue often do not have much training in Linguistics and seem, as a result, to devote a great deal of time to meta-theoretical reflections (Wijsen, 2013) rather than to empirical analyses of data. What is needed in this area and indeed others such as Scriptural Reasoning is that linguists and theologians work together to analyse data consistently and rigorously across different religious traditions.

Another area that has so far been under-researched is the application of Pragmatics categories to analyses of inter-religious language. Whilst a comprehensive survey of the different aspects of Pragmatics is not possible within such a short space, it may be worth briefly discussing one key component, that of *implicature*. As a starting point, we can use Grice's (1957) foundational definition of *implicature* as what the speaker intends to mean. So, if I say after a meal, 'it didn't make me sick', I can be taken to implicate that the meal was not very good. The application of Gricean implicature has been looked at by Haugh (2008) who astutely observed that recognising speakers' intentions is a messy business. In this respect, he refers to an incident which involves the Mufti of Australia, Sheik TajDin al-Hilali, who in a sermon warned about the dangers of fornication and immodest dress by saying that 'uncovered meat attracts cats'. As Haugh (2008) observed, widely divergent sets of implicatures were drawn by different sections of the Australian population. The Sheik's supporters claimed he 'meant' that Muslim should practise abstinence, while secular feminists interpreted his utterances as implying that women who do not wear the hijab invite rape. Haugh (2008) concluded that a model of communication must go beyond the received view that successful dialogue is based on recovering intentions from speakers. It also involves, he argues, determining what kind of interpretative norms are being used by interactants. Variations between groups of speakers have also been found in their uses of politeness and respect in the context of Politeness Theory (Haugh, 2019). More research of this type applied to inter-religious dialogue would make a significant contribution to our understanding of how dialogue is constructed across languages and cultures.

Finally, relatively little work has been undertaken in analysing spoken interactions between contemporary religious believers in the fields of *Conversation Analysis* or *Discourse Dynamic Approach*. In both areas, it may be shown how dynamic and subject to change speakers' background assumptions are in the context of inter-religious dialogue.

Pragmatic Linguistics has already made many considerable contributions to the study of inter-religious language, and undoubtedly new directions will be taken in the study of authentic interactions between believers from different faith backgrounds, including those of no faith. Analyses of such interactions, possibly by means of corpora, are even more needed now that supra-national institutions like the EU are keen to emphasise convergence between themselves and the religious sphere. By so doing, they risk reducing religious diversity to their own questionable criteria: the complete subordination of faith groups to the secular state and super-state and the introduction of declarative religious teaching in education.

It is to be hoped that the fields of inquiry briefly introduced here will enable us to gain a more thorough understanding of the relationship between those of faith and those of no faith. As was outlined earlier in this chapter, many conflicts originate from a lack of enlightened communication between these, the secular and the religious domains.

12.5   References

Albera, D., & Pénicaud, M. (2017). Uneterresainteetsaturée de sens. In D. Albera & M. Pénicaud (eds.), *Coexistences, Lieux Saints Partagés en Europe et en Méditerranée* (pp. 27–40). Marseilles: Actes Sud.

Austin, J. L. (1988). *How to Do Things with Words*. Oxford: Oxford University Press.

Bakhtin, M. (1981). *The Dialogic Imagination*. Austin: University of Texas Press.

Bhabha, H. K. (2011). Hybridity. *Translation: A Transdisciplinary Journal*, 1, 37–40.

Berman, A. (1984). *L'épreuve de l'étranger*. Paris: Gallimard.

Brink-Dana, M. (2015). Faith in conversation: Translation, translanguaging, and the British God debate. *Journal of Linguistic Anthropology*, 25(2), 173–94.

Burrell, D. (2004). Interfaith perspectives on reconciliation. *New Blackfriars*, 85(995), 44–55.

Clifford, A. (2005). The global horizon of religious pluralism and local dialogue with the religious-other. In T. Tilley (ed.), *New Horizons in Theology* (pp. 162–81). Maryknoll, NY: Orbis.

Debray, R. (2002). Qu'est-ce qu'un fait religieux? *Études*, 397, 169–80.

Ducrot, O. (1984). *Le dire et le dit*. Paris: Editions Minuit.

European Committee of Ministers. (2008). The recommendation of the Committee of Ministers to member states on the dimension of religions and non-religious convictions within intercultural communication adopted at the 1044th meeting of the Ministers' Deputies, 10 December 2008. www.europeanrights.eu/public/atti/dimen sione_religiosa_ing.HTM.

Fairclough, N. (1992). *Discourse and Social Change*. Cambridge: Polity Press.

Foucault, M. (1981). *L'ordre du Discours*. Paris: Gallimard.

Gaudé, J. (2010). Religious Translation. In Y. Gambier & L. Van Doorslaer (eds.), *Handbook of Translation Studies* (pp. 285–93). Amsterdam: John Benjamins Publishing.

Grice, H. P. (1957). Meaning. *The Philosophical Review*, 66(3), 377–88.

Gumperz, J. (1982). *Language and Social Identity*. Cambridge: Cambridge University Press.

Hallett, G. (2011). *Theology within the Bounds of Language: A Methodological Tour*. New York: State University of New York Press.

Haugh, M. (2008). Intention and diverging interpretings of implicature in the 'uncovered meat' sermon. *Intercultural Pragmatics*, 5(2), 201–28.

Haugh, M. (2019). The metapragmatics of consideration in Australian and New Zealand English. In E. Ogierman & P. Garces-Conejos (eds.), *From Speech Acts to Lay Understandings of Politeness* (pp. 1–21). Cambridge: Cambridge University Press.

Hick, J. (1985). *Problems of Religious Pluralism*. Basingstoke: Macmillan.

Huntington, S. P. (1993). Clash of Civilizations. *Foreign Affairs*, 72(3 Summer), 22–49.

Ipgrave, M. (2008). Understanding, affirmation, sharing: Nostra Aetate and an Anglican approach to inter-faith relations. *Journal of Ecumenical Studies*, 43(1), 1–16.

Ipgrave, M. (2014). Remembering the covenant: Judaism in an Anglican theology of interfaith relations. *Anglican Theological Review*, 96(1), 39–55.

Jerome, St. (2004). Letter to Pammachius, trans. Davis, K. In L. Venuti (ed.), *The Translation Studies Reader* (pp. 21–30). London: Routledge.

Lambert, W. E. (1975). Culture and language as factors in learning and education. In A. Wolfgang (ed.), *Education of Immigrant Students*. Toronto: Ontario Institute for Studies in Education.

Lindbeck, G. (1997). The Gospel's uniqueness: Election and untranslatability. *Modern Theology*, 13, 423–50.

Levinson, S.C. (1983). *Pragmatics*. Cambridge: Cambridge University Press.

Knitter, P. (1985). *No Other Name?* London: SCM Press.

Krieger, D. J. (1991). *The New Universalism*. New York: Orbis Books.

Neusner, J. (1991). *Jews and Christians: The Myth of a Common Tradition*. London: SCM Press.

Panikkar, R. (1979). *Myth, Faith and Hermeneutics*. New York: Paulist Press.

Quash, B., & Jenkins, T. (2009). Cambridge Interfaith Programme. www .interfaith.cam.ac.uk/en/resources/papers/cip-academic-profile.

Robinson-Pant, A., & Wolf, A. (2017). *Researching across Languages and Cultures: A Guide to Doing Research Interculturally*. London: Routledge.

Ruparell, T. (2013). Inter-religious dialogue and interstitial theology. In C. Cornille (ed.), *The Wiley-Blackwell Companion to Inter-Religious Dialogue* (pp. 117–32). Chichester: John Wiley & Sons.

Steiner, G. (1998). *After Babel: Aspects of Language and Translation*. Oxford: Oxford University Press.

Thibon, J. J. (2010). Les transformations du dialogue islamo-chrétien: Versl' émergenced'une parole commune dansl'espace public. In E. Dacheux (ed.), *Vivre Ensemble Aujourd' hui: Le lien social dans les démocratiespluriculturelles* (pp. 209–22). Paris: L'Harmattan.

Tillich, P. (1963). *Christianity and the Encounter of the World Religions*. New York: Columbia University Press.

Todorov, T. (1984). *Mikhail Bakhtin: The Dialogical Principle*, trans. W. Godzich. Minneapolis: University of Minnesota Press.

United Nations. (2007). General Assembly session on interreligious dialogue advances values – President' in UN News. https://news.un.org/en/story/2007/10/234912-general-assembly-session-interreligious-dialogue-advances-values-president.

Venuti, L. (1998). *The Scandals of Translation: Towards an Ethics of Difference*. London: Routledge.

Verschueren, J. (2008). Intercultural communication and the challenges of migration. *Language and Intercultural Communication*, 8(1), 21–35.

Weitzman, M. (2001). Judaism. In J. Sawyer & J. Simpson (eds.), *Concise Encyclopedia of Language and Religion* (pp. 68–72). Oxford: Elsevier.

Wetherell, M. (2001). Debates in Discourse Research. In M. Wetherell, S. Taylor & S. Yates (eds.), *Discourse Theory and Practice* (pp. 380–99). Thousands Oaks: SAGE.

Wijsen, F. (2007). *Seeds of Conflict in a Haven of Peace: From Religious Studies to Inter-religious Studies in Africa*. New York: Rodopi.

Wijsen, F. (2013). Discourse Analysis in Religious Studies. *Religion*, 1/43, 1–3.

Winter, (2001). *Qur'an Translations*. In J. Sawyer & J. Simpson (eds.), *Concise Encyclopedia of Language and Religion* (p. 133). Oxford: Elsevier.

Wittgenstein, L. (2009). *Philosophical Investigations*. Translated by G. E. M. Anscombe, P. M. S. Hacker & J. Schulte. Rev. 4th ed. Chichester: Wiley-Blackwell.

Wolf, A. (2012). Intercultural identity and inter-religious dialogue: a holy place to be? *Language and Intercultural Communication*, 12(1), 37–55.

Yule, G., & Brown, G. (1983). *Discourse Analysis*. Cambridge: Cambridge Textbooks in Linguistics.

13   Rituals

Wei-lun Lu and Svitlana Shurma

13.1   Background, History, and Key Terms

Rituals, both religious and non-religious, pervade and sometimes define our everyday lives. While rituals, such as puja, hajj, kathina, or baptism are of the religious character since they are connected with the religious practices across the world, rituals taking place during some sports events, awards, or ceremonies have a secular character. Both secular and religious, rituals are flexible or semi-flexible events functioning as models of human behavior in space and time (Grimes, 1982). These are a "prescribed sequence of verbal and nonverbal acts," having a highly formalized and predictable communication mode (Feuchtwang, 2010). Snoek (2006, pp. 10–12) argues that rituals should be defined through a set of shared characteristics between rituals of different kinds, such as cultural construction, typicality of physical and verbal behavior, space- and time-bound, interactive, symbolic nature, organizing function, etc. Yet, what we will discuss in the chapter is how rituals are connected not just with the performance of certain conventionally prescribed and symbolic actions, but also with formulaic language use. For example, in the Eastern Slavic Orthodox conventions of celebrating Easter, after the participation in the divine service in the church and priest's blessing of the Easter food, it is common to greet others with the phrase *Christ has risen!* and the answer *Truly He is risen* three times. In Hinduism, for instance, Diwali celebration includes the ritualistic greeting *Diwali ki hardik shubhkamnaye* (Heart-felt wishes on the occasion of Diwali). Ritualistic greetings can be found as parts of many other rituals across the globe. Thus, language and actions are firmly tied in the rituals.

One of the main roles of the rituals is to guide cognition (Snoek, 2006). For example, rituals connected with someone's death, such as cremations or burials with the preceding and subsequent traditional practices, "exude vital importance to humans in the quest to make sense of the mysteries surrounding death" (Hoy, 2013, p. 1). Just as any other ritual, death rituals across the world possess a set of cultural and performative characteristics and temporal and spatial requirements. "Whether in a family, friendship circle, nation, or planet, every death introduces some sense of social upheaval; the deliberate cadence of rituals helps to restore balance, reminding all concerned that order will prevail" (Hoy, 2013, p. 11). The actions taken during burials and mourning allow the participants make sense of the death, offer a feeling of safety and facilitate grieving (Giblin and Hug, 2006). For example, night vigils over the dead body in some religious communities are a way of family saying goodbye; ritualistic washing of the dead body in some religions is a way to prepare the soul for the afterlife; prayers, chants, speeches, or eulogies are all praxes that are performed with the aim of accommodating the family (Capone, 2010) of the deceased and prepare the soul of the person who died to what awaits the soul after death according to the shared beliefs.

Linguistic practices are often an important part of death rituals across cultures and religions (Dumitru-Lahaye, 2009). The verbalization of death becomes important for certain elements of rituals and helps the mourners strike a balance in the time of grief. Such formulaic language of ritual is associated with standardized and culturally bound linguistic expression (Weinert, 2010). A formulaic sequence is further defined by Wray (2002, p. 9) as "a sequence, continuous or discontinuous, of words or other meaning elements, which is, or appears to be prefabricated: that is, stored and retrieved whole form memory at the time of use, rather than being subjects to generation or analysis by the language grammar."

Linguistically, formulae are characterized by restrictions in form and distri-bution and compel the reader to choose a pre-formatted word combination within a given context. Such formulae are typically bound to certain language styles, which means that the formulaic language is connected to specific communicative situations. For example, formulae include:

> *My condolences.*
> *My deepest sympathies to you and your family.*
> *I am truly sorry to hear of the loss.*

These phrases are typically bound to communicative situations of mourning, appear on cards or in other messages, or are verbalized during the ritualistic practices connected with mourning and death. Such verbalizations become a part of consistent verbal behavior that accompanies the practices. These formulae are meant to provide solace and accommodate mainly the close relatives of the deceased, yet they still depend on the individual speaker. Given the highly structured nature of ritual, it inevitably involves elements of formulaic language. "Compared to ordinary propositional speech and its almost infinite openness and logic, ritual is far less communicative; it is not logical or propositional but is instead a manifestation of traditional authority" (Feuchtwang, 2010, p. 282).

Traditionally, formulae include fixed phrases, clichés, idiomatic expressions, complex word forms as well "sentence-building frameworks" (Wood, 2002, p. 2) and have even been extended to social routines, narratives, and proverbs

(Weinert, 2010). This fuzziness in defining and identification of formulaic language is problematic because of the semantic and structural diversity of the linguistics sequences which different scholars refer to as "formulae".

Formulaic language can be seen as an indispensable element of speech act(s) associated with a typical situation of communication, or pragmeme. Pragmemes are defined as a "general situation prototype" (Mey, 2001, p. 221) equal to a speech act that is motivated by extra-linguistic context and aims to achieve a certain pragmatic effect. The linguistic shape and pragmatic inferences depend largely on the cultural context and the rules in a society. According to Mey (2001, p. 222), two constituents are important in a pragmeme: text and activity. The activity part involves all sorts of acts, from speech to psychological and physical acts. Assuming that the linguistic behavior is embedded in the human behavior, the textual part, on the other hand, is what carries the speaker's intentions. Therefore, the choice of language formulae, for instance, bears the pragmatic meaning required by the situation or the speakers themselves. The meaning is always context dependent, and extra-linguistic factors cannot be separated from what constitutes a pragmeme. In such an approach, eulogies, for example, can be seen as types of texts along with others, such as sermons, consolations, and so on, within a composite pragmeme of accommodation. The interactive part of the eulogies comes from the type of the speech act and its referentiality, emotions involved, physical acts, and paralanguage; therefore, we claim that eulogy is an act of language use within a general situational prototype executed in a situation of mourning as part of a death ritual that varies depending on the religion of the perished.

The participants in a communicative situation are not just restricted by the conventions, but they can also shape those conventions based on their own intentions, beliefs, wishes, and so on. Communicative cooperation occurs when the intention of the sender, attention of the addresser, and the common socio-cultural knowledge are in balance. This shared knowledge often relies on cognitive scenarios, which are modified in the course of history and changing sociocultural context and reflect how humans view social actions. As cultural models, scenarios help to govern rituals and include "propositional, image-schematic, metaphoric, and metonymic models" (Palmer, 2006, p. 15). Scenarios therefore influence discourse, while formulaic language, though not a speech act, plays an important part in the construal of discourse scenario since it has its specific place and time in the ritual. For example, the greeting *Christ has risen!* in the aforementioned example should be said only after the worshiper has participated in the full ceremony, and this phrase symbolically marks the end of the official church rite and the beginning of the unofficial family rite, if the ritual is kept. At the same time, for less-pious participants it becomes a greeting, a wish, and an act of participation in the celebration of Easter.

The formulaic language in these situations can be understood as pragmatic idioms, or pragmatic units of high conventionality used in standardized situations of communication that fall into conversational routines and situation-bound utterances. Because formulae are conventionally constructed solutions in socially determined situations such as rituals, ritualistic idioms can be referred to the situation-bound utterances, as they become "safe" prefabricated verbalizations that function as "guidelines" of social verbal behavior in typical or ritualized situations. The ritual sets a certain pragmatic property to such formulaic chunks of language. For example, a eulogy at a funeral follows certain rules, since it becomes a way of saying farewell to the deceased. It is a social action that conforms to the norms the ritual prescribes. Thus, it becomes an idiom, or a multi-word formulaic sequence that has a rather fixed form and semantic features and can be treated as "a unit in processing" or "the expression of creative conceptual metaphors" (Espinal and Mateu, 2019). In this chapter, we discuss a particular form of idioms: 成語 *chéngyǔ*, which are four-character lexical constructions that can be found in dictionaries. Such eulogistic idioms are extensively used in pragmemes of accommodation around events of death.

13.2   Key Topics, Questions, and Debates

Like much language around religious discourse, rituals often include metaphorical language and actions. Rituals by engaging its participants into a set of activities such as dance, music, or meditation, appeal to the senses and feelings of those involved. "Mystical interpretations frequently comment on sensation as a source of metaphors for religious experience" (Watts, 2019, p. 2). As a rule, the ritual shifts attention from the senses involved in the ritual to the actions and behaviors, including the verbal ones, often metaphorical in their nature. For example, death rituals in the Christian tradition have an aim of keeping the feelings of the mourners under some degree of control (Capone, 2010). The metaphorical rhetoric helps to accommodate or ease the situation of grief, and typically appears with regard to interpreting the rituals and substitutes the sensations involved (Watts, 2019). Metaphor in death rituals becomes a part of the pragmeme of accommodation (Capone, 2010) as they help to cope with the negative feelings that accompany deaths of the near and dear (Sexton, 1997).

Cognitive Linguistics offers an approach through which the metaphoricity of the language of death can be examined: it sets both the metaphorical speech acts and conceptualizations involved in the speech act production in context. Conceptual metaphor theory (Lakoff and Johnson 1980) offers a framework for analysis of the language of death as it allows us to look at how thought and knowledge about the death is structured in different communities.

Since death rituals are ways to understand and communicate about the act of dying, conceptual metaphors also penetrate the common discourse practices. As death is an unpleasant and painful topic, metaphors, as a means of secondary nomination and a euphemistic resource, make the subject less painful. DEATH acts as the target domain onto which the elements of the source domain related to a more concrete concept are mapped. The source domain is often related to some embodied experience circulating within a culture (Kövecses, 2010), since the knowledge about it makes it easier to explain death. In this way, the community structures the knowledge and offers sense of it. The formulaic language of the ritual reflects the ideas and beliefs circulating in a culture through conceptual metaphors. What becomes the source domains of the culturally bound conceptual metaphors are typical representations of values and knowledge about a given community (Crespo-Fernández, 2013).

Through the analysis of conceptual metaphorical representations, culturally specific interpretations of death can be seen within death rituals. Marín Arrese (1996) and Crespo-Fernández (2013) traced and contrasted the conceptualizations of death in English and Spanish, thus drawing attention to cross-cultural representations and, what is important, differences in cultural representations. The scholars argued that three aspects are significant for the metaphoric language of death: bodily and social experiences as well as cultural constraints. Crespo-Fernández (2013) sums up that it is the cultural context that drives the differences between the conceptual representations. Perhaps, the most comprehensive contrastive study of conceptual mappings within euphemistic death metaphors across six languages of different language groups was conducted by Gathigia et al. (2018). A group of authors identified and examined four conceptual metaphors in Chinese, Farsi, Gikuyu, Russian, Spanish, and Swedish: DEATH IS A JOURNEY, DEATH IS THE END, DEATH IS A REST, and DEATH IS A SUMMONS. They concluded that the DEATH IS A JOURNEY metaphor is present in the languages of the six linguocultures.

Within the study of the language of death functioning in a specific cultural context, a socio-pragmatic approach has been pioneered by Capone (2010) who looks at the language of death as specific speech acts or pragmemes. In his seminal paper, Capone (2010, p. 6) considers death rituals as "prototypical events" having "social intentionality built into them". He places pragmemes in a key position for explaining the formulaic language choices during mourning events and thus steps away from the actual conceptualizations, rather offering an analysis of sociocultural context.

Since rituals are "institutional events" that "enforce interpretation rules" (Capone, 2010, p. 10), agreement on the connotations and meanings of certain sets of words within a given community allows them to become formulae through their recurrent use, entering the community's long-term memory. In fact, it is possible to speak about the "ritual language" or specific utterances that acquire significance in the process of the ritual (Wheelock, 1982, p. 50). The language becomes a part of the multimodal system, where other semiotic systems contribute to, complement, or overlap with the linguistic means (Wheelock, 1982). This claim makes it important to look at the ritual language from cognitive, social, and cultural perspectives.

Socio-pragmatic, sociocultural, and cognitivist approaches to pragmemes have been taken to analyze formulaic language in condolences, euphemisms, eulogies, sympathy cards, and so on in English, German, Italian, Japanese, Chinese, and some other contexts (Parvaresh and Capone, 2017). This research into the cultural aspects of pragmemes has shown the origins of linguistic representations across linguocultures as well as similarities and differences in the conceptualizations, and has challenged the idea of universality in languages and rituals. The linguistic formulas are uttered or exchanged in line with certain procedures of rituals that vary between cultures, communities, and geographies, showing how seeming similarities of conceptual representations might be more complex than they first appear.

13.3   Case Study

The eulogistic idioms that are the focus of this chapter are fixed phrases or elements of formulaic language used at funerals in Taiwan. The phrases are prefabricated and always come in the form of four-characters. In traditional funerals in Taiwan, a mourner presents a white plaque to the family of the deceased (with the white color invoking DEATH in the Taiwanese culture). The plaque typically contains the name of the deceased, information of the mourner (name, affiliation, job title), and the eulogistic idiom of the mourner's own choice (from a conventionalized repertoire of idioms). The semantic content of such eulogistic idioms may reflect the mourner's personal feeling, a general description and praise of the past achievement of the deceased, or the mourner's imagination of the current state of the soul of the deceased.

However, the mourner's choice of the idiom to present cannot be random – instead, the mourner needs to use their discretion in deciding which idiom to use. The reason is that some formulaic expressions contain a specific characterization of a certain profession (such as politicians and teachers, or media workers and legal experts) or of the religion (Buddhists and Christians) of the deceased. Therefore, the choice of the idiom must be based on the actual occupation or the religious belief of the deceased, in order to make the act of delivering the eulogy pragmatically appropriate and acceptable to the family. An inappropriate choice of the eulogistic idiom (such as a Buddhist idiom delivered at a Christian funeral) may be offensive. In traditional funerals in Taiwan, the white plaques are displayed in the funeral hall. After the ceremony, the plaques are incinerated along with the corpse. To reduce the carbon footprint produced as a result of funerals, the Taiwanese government set up an online eulogy request system, where a mourner may apply for a user account and request an idiom to be displayed on the electronic banner in a state-run funeral hall, where the funeral for a deceased known to them is scheduled to take place.

Once the mourner logs onto the eulogy request system, they can select the exact date, the exact venue, and the name of the deceased from a list of scheduled funerals. Once the selection is made, the mourner may proceed to select a predefined category from a pulldown menu that contains a handful of occupations and three religions: Buddhism, Catholic, and Protestant. Once the mourner clicks on one of the characterizations that suits the deceased, the system turns up a selection of idioms that correspond to the religion or the occupation, all included by Taipei Mortuary Services Office from existing lexicographic sources. We focus on the idioms used for the two religions in the system: Buddhism and Christianity. The system presents eight idioms to choose from in the Christian category and fifty-nine idioms in the Buddhist category.

This case study draws on a previous study (Lu, 2017) and shows linguistic analysis of the eulogistic idioms informed by Cognitive Linguistics, in particular conceptual metaphor theory, investigating two religion-specific conceptual metaphors LIFE CYCLE IS ONE SINGLE RETURN JOURNEY (Christian) and LIFE CYCLE IS A REPETITIVE JOURNEY (Buddhist), both being a cultural instantiation of the more schematic LIFE IS A JOURNEY, which has been extensively discussed in the field. We also investigate the metaphor related to end-of-life, DEATH IS REST, and finally orientational metaphors used in the eulogistic idioms in the pragmemes of both religions.

13.3.1   Life as Repetitive Journeys or as a Single Round-Trip

The conceptual domain of JOURNEY has been often cited to relate to that of LIFE, the association of which forms the metaphor LIFE IS A JOURNEY. In addition to that, not only LIFE but also DEATH is conceptualized as a JOURNEY. Based on the aforementioned studies, we may generalize a systematic conceptual metaphor as a first approximation of how LIFE and DEATH are understood, applicable to both religions: LIFE IS A JOURNEY IN THIS WORLD; DEATH IS A JOURNEY FROM THIS WORLD TO THE HEAVENS.

However, Buddhism holds a worldview that the human life cycle is repetitive, where a soul does not perish but will reincarnate indefinitely. Under such rubric, we are able to find an idiom that reflects such worldview, as in (1).

1.   乘   願   再   來
     chéng   *yuàn*   *zài*   *lái*
     ride   wish   again   come
     "(The person will) come again with (great) wishes." (adapted from
     Lu (2017, p. 53)

In example (1), the idiom depicts the motion of an implicit agent, which can be pragmatically identified as the deceased since the idiom is a formulaic lexical construction presented at a funeral. The destination of the motion is towards the speaker (and the hearer), encoded by the verb *lái* 'come', and can be understood to be this world (as opposed to the afterworld). The motion is a journey that is repeated, encoded by the construction *zài* 'again'. All the conceptual pieces prompted by the lexical constructions, when put together, correspond to the Buddhist thinking that a soul may appear in this world again, which is metaphorically understood as another journey to this world. We may, accordingly, formulate another conceptual association between LIFE and JOURNEY as (THE CURRENT) LIFE IS A JOURNEY; NEXT LIFE IS A RETURN JOURNEY TO THIS WORLD. Being analytically sensitive to the lexical cues that invoke the underlying conceptual pattern allows for a newly established conceptual construction that we identified in previous literature. This allows us to come up with a wider metaphorical frame that accommodates our current understanding: LIFE CYCLES ARE REPETITIVE JOURNEYS. In addition to the general metaphor that helps us construe LIFE and DEATH each as a journey, this general conceptual frame sanctions the metaphor DEATH IS A JOURNEY TOWARDS REBIRTH, which is instantiated by example (2).

2.   往   生   極   樂
     wǎng   *shēng*   *jí*   *lè*
     go towards   life   extreme   happy
     "(This person has) gone towards life in the bliss." (adapted from Lu (2017, p. 52)

In example (2), there are lexical prompts that help us identify the conceptual metaphor. First, the PATH of the journey is invoked by the construction *wǎng* 'go towards', with the GOAL of the trajectory being *shēng* 'life'. The phrase *jílè* '(lit.) extreme happiness' has an extended meaning of 'bliss'. In addition, the pragmatic knowledge of the context in which the idiom is used is important, as the fact that the idiom is used at a funeral allows us to identify the deceased as the implicit agent of the motion. Again, we see how the lexical cues, when they appear in a pragmeme, work together to form a coherent conceptual picture that reflects DEATH IS A JOURNEY TOWARDS REBIRTH, a specific cultural instantiation of the highly schematic metaphor LIFE IS A JOURNEY extensively discussed in previous literature. In particular, in the Taiwanese Buddhist pragmeme of death, there exists a most general conceptual frame of LIFE CYCLE IS REPETITIVE JOURNEYS, which entails that (THE CURRENT) LIFE IS

A JOURNEY; NEXT LIFE IS A RETURN JOURNEY TO THIS WORLD. Within such a general frame, each return journey comprises two subparts: LIFE IS A JOURNEY; DEATH IS A JOURNEY TOWARDS REBIRTH. The CIRCLE is a frequent cultural symbol in Taiwanese Buddhist eulogistic idioms, which is invoked by the construction *yuán-mǎn* '(lit.) circle-full; perfect' in the collection of Buddhist idioms. Example (3) illustrates this point.

3. 功   德   圓   滿
    gōng   *dé*   *yuán*   *mǎn*
    feat   virtue   circle   Full
    "(This person led a) full (life like a) circle, having had various achievements."
    (adapted from Lu (2017, p. 54)

This type occurs in three of the fifty-nine Buddhist idioms. The cyclic nature of the Buddhist understanding of LIFE is symbolically associated with the basic geometric fact that the beginning and the end of the shape coincide. In the following, we turn to an analysis of the eulogistic idioms used in a Christian pragmeme of death in Taiwan (that is, the repertoire of idioms that the mourner may choose from in the request system once "Christianity" is chosen). We find that an obvious difference between the Christian and the Buddhist eulogies lies in the type frequency of CIRCLE – remember that it is invoked by 圓滿 *yuán-mǎn* in three Buddhist eulogistic idioms, whereas in the database, we find no lexical item that invokes the same concept in the Christian category. The lack of CIRCLE in Christian eulogistic idioms shows that cyclicity is not part of the conceptual substrate associated with the Christian understanding of LIFE. We also find that in the Christian idioms, there is no occurrence of motion verbs such as 來 *lái* 'come', as in example (1) or 往 *wǎng* 'go toward', as in example (2). The only verb that comes close is 歸 *guī* 'return', which is given in example (4).

4. 息   勞   歸   主
    xí   *láo*   *guī*   *zhǔ*
    rest   toil   return   Lord
    "(This person has) put down (their) hard work (and has) returned to the Lord."

However, the use of 歸 *guī* comes with an important semantic entailment – when one returns to a place, that place is not only the destination of that person's motion but also their origin. There are eight Christian idioms in the eulogy request system in total, two of which contain 歸 *guī*. This fact shows not only that 歸 *guī* is the only verb that instantiates the JOURNEY metaphor but also that RETURN constitutes an important element of the journey, given the high type frequency of 歸 *guī* in the Christian category (two of eight idioms). Based on this reasoning, we may formulate the JOURNEY metaphor as follows: LIFE IS A JOURNEY; DEATH IS A RETURN JOURNEY. No linguistic prompt that may invoke the repetition of journey is found in the collection of Christian idioms.

13.3.2   Death as a Break before the Journey Resumes or as an Eternal Rest

In the Buddhist category, there is one lexical item that invokes REST, which is 歇 *xiē* 'rest' in (5).

5.   歇   即   菩提
     xiē   *Jí*   *pútí*
     rest   LK   bodhi/wisdom
     "(As the deceased is,) rest is the ultimate wisdom."

In the Christian category, there is also one lexical item that invokes REST, which is 息 *xí* 'rest' in example (4). Again, remember that this idiom is a linguistic part of a funeral as a pragmeme of accommodation, so the overarching theme should be DEATH, with the immediate topic being identifiable as the deceased. However, although it seems that in the pragmatic act of helping the family of the deceased accommodate grief, both religions utilize idioms that conceptualize DEATH as REST, there is still a significant difference. If we look up the lexical prompt of the REST metaphor in a corpus, we see that 歇 *xiē* and 息 *xí* actually involve different language formulas that reflect the different nuanced semantic shades that correspond to the different ways LIFE is understood as a JOURNEY in each of the respective religions. In particular, in corpus cognitive linguistics, it is believed that the construal invoked by a construction can be portrayed by the lexical and grammatical company kept by the construction. To apply that notion to our data, what one can easily do is to look up the target word in a platform that contains a sufficiently large and representative language sample, so that we may find the behavioral pattern of the word that allows us to understand the exact meaning of the word. A search in the Buddhist idioms for the verb 歇 *xiē* reveals some of its common collocations and colligations, such as 歇會兒 *xiē-huì-ér* 'break-moment-PRT', 歇口氣 *xiē-kǒu-qì* 'break-CL-breath', 歇一歇 *xiē-yì-xiē* 'break-TENT', 暫歇 *zhàn-xiē* 'temporary-break', which allows us to extrapolate the semantic content of *xiē* being "a *brief* moment off (from an activity)." On the other hand, a search of 息 *xí* does not turn up a similar result – 息 *xí* is used mainly as a noun in Chinese but the search does turn up a usage of it as a verb, as in 奔騰不息 *bēnténg-bù-xí* '(lit.) (the manner of a river running) running-NEG-stop; everlasting'. Another famous instance that contains 息 *xí* can be found in the Chinese version of First Corinthians 13 of the Bible, 愛是永不止息 *ài shì yǒng-bù-zhǐ-xí* '(lit.) love LK forever-NEG-cease-stop; love is everlasting'. From the above collocational behaviour of 息 *xí*, which co-occurs with the negators for the whole phrase to convey an imperfective meaning such as "river running" and "everlasting," this allows us to figure out "termination" as an important part of the conceptual substrate of 息 *xí*. A comparison of the conceptual semantic structures of 歇 *xiē* and 息 *xí* allows us to map the two structures onto the Buddhist and the Christian views on LIFE CYCLE – the Buddhist LIFE CYCLE consists of repetitive journeys, with DEATH being a *short moment off* in between the journeys, whereas the Christian LIFE CYCLE is only one round-trip from heaven to the earth and back to its source, where the journey *terminates*.

Another difference between the religions lies in the type frequency of the REST metaphors. The REST metaphor occurs in the Christian category (prompted by the word 息 *xí*) accounts for three idioms out of the total eight, whereas in the Buddhist category, only one idiom out of a total of fifty-nine contains the REST metaphor (prompted by the word 歇 *xiē*). (Type) frequency wise, this has an important cognitive consequence – the notable difference in ratio (three of eight versus one of fifty-nine) shows that people obviously pay more attention to REST in the Christian pragmeme of accommodation, as people verbalize more about it, conceptually *profile* (Langacker, 2008, p. 61) it more often, thus rendering the concept more cognitively salient in the pragmeme.

Orientational metaphors are found exclusively in the Buddhist pragmeme. In the eulogistic idioms in the pragmeme of accommodation in Taiwan, orientational metaphors occur only in the Buddhist idioms but not in the Christian ones. In the database, we identified two orientational metaphors: one that invokes the vertical dimension and the other that invokes the east–west direction. In Taiwanese Buddhist eulogistic idioms, we find a set of formulae that involves the positive pole of the vertical dimension, lexically instantiated by 上 *shàng* 'up', as in example (6), and 高 *gāo* 'high', as in example (7).

6.   上   生   佛   國
      shàng   *shēng*   *fó*   *guó*
      up   birth   Buddha   country
      "(This person has been) born up in the Buddha's country."

7.   高   登   蓮   品
      gāo   *dēng*   *lián*   *pǐn*
      high   elevate   lotus   category
      "(This person has) risen high to the category of (being pure like a) lotus."

As is obvious in the examples, 上 *shàng* and 高 *gāo* are both lexical items that directly invoke the positive pole of the vertical dimension and are used to describe the positive quality of a person, invoking the conceptual metaphor GOOD IS UP. The second orientation metaphor in the Taiwanese Buddhist death ritual is DEATH IS WEST, instantiated by example (8).

8   化   滿   西   歸
      huà   *mǎn*   *xī*   *guī*
      die   complete   west   return
      "(This person has) died (with his life being) complete (and he has) returned to the west."

The motivation of DEATH IS WEST appears to be religion specific, but it does involve an embodied basis. In trying to explain the motivation of why the Buddhist heaven is in the west, Shì (2017, p. 47) refers to an excerpt by a Buddhist monk, Master Dàochuò (道綽大師) in the sixth century, quoted as example (9).

9.

日	出	處	名	生,
rì	*chū*	*chù*	*míng*	*shēng*
sun	out	LOC	name	birth
沒	處	名	死 . . .	
mò	*chù*	*míng*	*sǐ*	
(sun) set	LOC	name	death	
法藏菩薩	願	成	佛	在
fǎcáng púsà	*yuàn*	*chéng*	*fó*	*zài*
Fǎcáng Bodhisattva	wish	become	Buddha	LOC
西,	悲	接	眾生。	
xī	*bēi*	*jiē*	*zhòngshēng*	
west	sympathy	receive	all creatures	

"The place of sunrise is named birth, sunset death . . . Fǎcáng Bodhisattva (is/was) willing to become a Buddha in the west, in order to receive all creatures with sympathy."

Example (9) shows that as early as the sixth century, Master Dàochuò already related the Buddhist human life cycle to the pattern of sunrise and sunset, where he associated BIRTH with SUNRISE, which directly invokes EAST and DEATH with SUNSET, which invokes WEST. Following on from that, the conceptual extension to couple DEATH with WEST, which is the spatial orientation of the sunset, seems to be natural. In the second half of the passage, it is stated that the location of Fǎcáng Bodhisattva is in the west, and that all creatures are to be received by the bodhisattva in the west after death. The master's preaching not only is consistent with the metaphor DEATH IS A JOURNEY but also fleshes out the detail of the journey by specifying WEST as the DIRECTION of the JOURNEY. Another point to note is the systematic conceptual association between MOVEMENT OF THE SUN and PROGRESSION OF LIFE and between DAY and LIFE by the Buddhist master. What is more, the source concept DAY is not a one-time event but occurs repetitively, and when that is used to reason about LIFE as the target concept, it associates REPETITION with the target concept. Therefore, the Buddhist-specific metaphor of DEATH IS WEST is based on the systematic conceptual mappings between the various elements in the conceptual domain of DAY (as the source domain) and that of LIFE (as the target domain). In addition to that, with a conceptual metaphor theory approach, we are able to relate the Buddhist conceptual pattern DEATH IS WEST to DEATH IS A JOURNEY and LIFE CYCLE IS REPETITIVE JOURNEYS, and are able to assemble the three into a coherent whole that reflects the Buddhist worldview.

In pragmemes of accommodating human death, the linguistic means include lexical instantiations that comply with the conceptual patterns reflecting the worldviews of the religions involved. The most typical examples are the Christian metaphor LIFE CYCLE IS ONE SINGLE RETURN JOURNEY and the Buddhist metaphor LIFE CYCLE IS A REPETITIVE JOURNEY. The REST metaphor is related to how LIFE is conceptualized as a JOURNEY in the religions involved. In particular, in Christian funerals in Taiwan, which contain verbal instantiations of LIFE IS A JOURNEY; DEATH IS A RETURN JOURNEY (based on the belief that the human life cycle is a single return journey to and from the world), the REST metaphor used in the funerals is lexically instantiated by 息 *xí* 'termination'. On the other hand, in Buddhist funerals in Taiwan, the life cycle is considered repetitive, based on (THE CURRENT) LIFE IS A JOURNEY; DEATH IS A JOURNEY TOWARDS REBIRTH; NEXT LIFE IS A RETURN JOURNEY TO THIS WORLD. Under such conceptual rubric, the lexical instantiation of the REST metaphor is 歇 *xiē* 'a brief moment off'. Finally, the exclusive presence of orientational metaphor DEATH IS WEST in Buddhist eulogistic idioms is based on the conceptual mapping between the human life cycle and the movement pattern of the sun, matching BIRTH with SUNRISE and its spatial direction EAST, and DEATH with SUNSET, which is WEST.

Differences between the eulogistic idioms used by the different religious groups at death rituals in Taiwan constitute authentic linguistic evidence that reveals the differences in terms of worldview and how different religious groups reason around an event of death. First, although there is a general overarching metaphor LIFE IS A JOURNEY, we see that, in the pragmeme, each of the two groups has its own religion-specific metaphor that reflects its own understanding of LIFE. Secondly, there is another schematic metaphor related to JOURNEY that is shared by the two groups, which is DEATH IS REST. Each of the two groups uses a distinct set of lexical instantiations in its idioms, which reflects what type of REST is envisaged in relation to the type of JOURNEY that is involved in that particular religion. In addition, Buddhism conceptually relates human life cycle to celestial movement of the sun, which gives rise to the exclusively Buddhist orientational metaphor DEATH IS WEST. The religion-specific conception and reasoning involved in human death rituals is linguistically manifested in the collection of eulogistic idioms used in the pragmemes in each of the religions.

In this study, only Buddhist eulogistic idioms involve the metaphor GOOD IS UP. As a multicultural society, Taiwan has been heavily influenced by Confucianism and (especially Mahāyāna) Buddhism. A central tradition in Confucianism is to extol the virtue and the good deeds of the deceased at a funeral and since Mahāyāna Buddhism shares a lot of similarities and converges with Confucianism in East Asian societies (Fu, 1973), Buddhist eulogistic idioms used in a largely Confucian society have picked up such a cultural practice in a death ritual. Furthermore, although Buddhism is a religion that advocates transcendence of transient phenomena by preaching the rejection of attachment to bodily reasoning patterns, Buddhist doctrine-conveying texts are still full of embodied metaphors (see the analysis of *Heart Sutra* in Lu and Chiang, 2007). In contrast, we may see that the Christian eulogistic idioms used in Taiwan are less conceptually complex and less rich in terms of their semantic content. We believe the main reason is sociocultural, in the sense that Christianity is not the dominant religion in Taiwan, only accounting for a relatively small part of the population (around 4 percent of the population). The demographic fact is reflected in the much lower frequency of the idioms and the lower conceptual complexity compared to the Buddhist eulogistic idioms. Another important reason is historical; Christianity was introduced to Taiwan only a few hundred years ago, with aggressive (Presbyterian) evangelism recorded only as late as 1865, which has left a shorter time span (than Buddhism) for the local development of Christianity and for Christian elements to integrate with local funeral practice. These points, therefore, show the importance of the sociocultural and the historical context in the analysis of religious discourse.

13.4   Future Directions

The previous discussion allows us to see the usefulness of the pragmeme analysis of death rituals conducted through a conceptual metaphor theory approach. Such a Cognitive Linguistic approach to analyzing religious language has been lacking in the field and should be advocated. As we have shown, a cognitive approach to the language of rituals can be useful in the sense that such an approach allows us to use the linguistic constructions that are relevant to certain worldview of a religion and assemble the conceptual pieces invoked by the constructions into a coherent whole. However, in addition to conceptual approaches to metaphor, we believe that there are other Cognitive Linguistic frameworks and research methods that will be equally useful in analyzing language use in rituals. Cognitive Grammar (Langacker, 2008), for instance, may be a good candidate, in the sense that it allows us to explore not only individual lexical expressions but also connected discourse. In the language of rituals, the issue of subjectivity, which is the speaker's role and conceptualization of self in his interaction with the other participants of the ritual, may be an aspect worth looking into. In this connection, sermon has been referred to (though only in passing) as a discourse genre potentially interesting to a Cognitive Grammar approach. The issue of subjectivity, or the way the ritual participants are conceptualized in their verbal exchange, underlies the discourse *viewpoint* (Dancygier, 2012) adopted by the participants of the ritual.

Another discussion that has been going on in Cognitive Linguistics is the limits of the *conceptual metaphor theory*. Though, it is true that a large proportion of our thinking is metaphorical in nature, conceptual metonymy, oxymoron, and antithesis are often kept at the background. Their relationship with conceptual metaphor and their roles in rituals are of no less importance than meanings created through metaphor. If we assume that symbolism is based on the metonymic relations, and rituals are highly symbolic acts, then it opens a new dimension of research not only of the death rituals, but also of the other rituals, such as marriages, coronations, and so on.

In addition to theoretical constructs that may be useful in analyzing the language of rituals, there are various aspects of rituals that can be explored. Note that what we showed in this case study was relatively small; in particular, the linguistic part of death rituals. Therein, we focused only on a highly formulaic type of language usage (i.e. Chinese *chéngyǔ* "four-character idioms"). What we presented was merely one-way verbal communication that the mourner uses to accommodate the family to their loss. In a typical Taiwanese funeral, a representative of the family reads a farewell speech (*jiādiàn wén*) to present their emotions and to give thanks to the mourners, which is another type of one-way verbal communication in a death ritual. Therefore, a comprehensive consideration of the verbal exchanges in different formats in a ritual is desirable. A standard, possibly highly formulaic, text or scripture read at a ritual may also be an important subject of future research.

Note also that language is merely one of the modes of representation (be it written or spoken), and there are certainly other modes of representation (such as visual), so a multimodal analysis of the various dimensions of a ritual, of which the linguistic plays a core part, will be intellectually fruitful. At a funeral, for instance, the language used by the participants is not the only concern; what matters may range from the interior design (such as the display, color, and style) of the funeral hall, the sequence of the various steps of the ceremony, and the body language of the mourners (social distance, posture, etc.), to the physical arrangement of the assembly. Another typical instance can be a burial, where the linguistic representation matters, among numerous others, which may range from the absolute and relative orientation of the coffin, the decoration of the burial site, or whether the corpse is cremated, to the design and layout of the tomb and even the tombstone. Language matters, as well as the other elements of a ritual.

There can also be various research methods for studying language used at a ritual. If the language sample to be studied is already in the written form, a corpus can be built out of it and some keyword or statistical analysis can be conducted to turn up patterns in the sample. The language sample to be studied can be in the spoken form, in which case the researcher might need to record and transcribe the verbal exchanges. If a multimodal analysis is planned, the researcher may need to videotape or to take selective photo shots of the ritual.

Depending on the research tradition of the researcher's field, different methods (or a combination of two or more methods) can be employed.

One more direction that we see as prospective for the development of ritual study is the idea of further testing the universality of metaphor. Kövecses (2010) discusses the issue of universality and cultural variation of conceptual metaphors. Even though research continues to include a greater variety of languages, it is not nearly reaching its completeness. As more and more scholars are getting involved in the intercultural research, we are collecting more information. With the forecasts for stronger globalization, this type of research will also contribute to preserving and documenting of the cultural variations in diachrony, should the ritual get lost and the language or its formulas fall out of use.

And finally, as the term *pragmeme* was addressed in the chapter, we see the future of the ethnolinguistic studies in pursuing a more precise definition of the pragmeme and identification of its elements that can be applied for the study of other rituals, both religious and secular. A question that should be addressed further is how to define and identify the elements of pragmemes when it comes to complex rites of purification or coming of age existing in many religions. These and other questions are only some of the future prospects for the research within the field of rituals and ritualistic language, for linguistics, ethnographers, scholars of cognition, to name just a few.

Contractions Used in the Glosses (Following Leipzig Glossing Rules)

CL: classifier
LOC: locative marker
LK: linker
NEG: negator
PRT: particle
TENT: tentative aspect

13.5   References

Capone, A. (2010). On pragmemes again: Dealing with death. *La linguistique*, 46, 3–21.
Crespo-Fernández, E. (2013). Euphemistic metaphors in English and Spanish epitaphs: A comparative study. *Atlantis*, 35(2), 99–118.
Dancygier, B. (2012). *The Language of Stories: A Cognitive Approach*. Cambridge: Cambridge University Press.
Dumitru-Lahaye, C. (2009). The language of death. In C. D. Bryant & D. L. Peck (eds.), *Encyclopedia of Death & the Human Experience* (pp. 632–5). Thousand Oaks, CA: SAGE.
Espinal, M. T., & Mateu, J. (2019). Idioms and phraseology. In M. Aronoff (ed.), *Oxford Research Encyclopedia of Linguistics*. Oxford: Oxford University Press. https://oxf

ordre.com/linguistics/view/10.1093/acrefore/9780199384655.001.0001/acrefore-97
80199384655-e-51.

Feuchtwang, S. (2010). Ritual and memory. In S. Radstone & B. Schwarz (eds.),
Memory: Histories, Theories, Debates (pp. 281–98). New York: Fordham University
Press.

Fu, C. W. (1973). Morality or beyond: The Neo-Confucian confrontation with
Mahāyāna Buddhism. *Philosophy East and West*, 23(3), 375–96.

Gathigia, M. G., Wang, R., Shen, M. et al. (2018). A cross-linguistic study of metaphors
of death. *Cognitive Linguistic Studies*, 5(2), 359–75.

Giblin, P., & Hug, A. (2006). The psychology of funeral rituals. *Liturgy*, 21(1), 11–19.

Grimes, R. (1982). Defining nascent ritual. *Journal of the American Academy of
Religion*, 50(4), 539–55.

Hoy, W. G. (2013). *Do Funerals Matter? The Purposes and Practices of Death Rituals
in Global Perspective*. New York and London: Routledge.

Kövecses, Z. (2010). *Metaphor: A Practical Introduction*. 2nd ed. Oxford: Oxford
University Press.

Lakoff, G., & Johnson, M. (1980). *Metaphors We Live By*. Chicago, IL: The University
of Chicago Press.

Langacker, W. R. (2008). *Cognitive Grammar: A Basic Introduction*. Oxford: Oxford
University Press.

Lu, L. W. & Chiang, W. (2007). EMPTINESS WE LIVE BY: Metaphors and paradoxes in
Buddhism's Heart Sutra. *Metaphor and Symbol*, 22(4), 331–55.

Lu, W. (2017). Cultural conceptualizations of DEATH in Taiwanese Buddhist and
Christian eulogistic idioms. In F. Sharifian (ed.), *Advances in Cultural Linguistics*
(pp. 49–64). Singapore: Springer.

Marín Arrese, J. I. (1996). To die, to sleep. A contrastive study of metaphors
for death and dying in English and Spanish. *Language Sciences*, 18(1–2), 37–52.

Mey, J. L. (2001). *Pragmatics: An Introduction*. Oxford: Blackwell.

Palmer, G. (2006). When does cognitive linguistics become cultural? Case studies in
Tagalog voice and Shona noun classifiers. In J. Luchjenbroers (ed.), *Cognitive
Linguistics Investigations across Languages, Fields and Philosophical Boundaries*
(pp. 13–46). Amsterdam: John Benjamins.

Parvaresh, V., & Capone, A. (eds.). (2017). *The Pragmeme of Accommodation: The
Case of Interaction around the Event of Death*. New York: Springer.

Sexton, J. (1997). The semantics of death and dying: Metaphor and mortality. *A Review
of General Semantics*, 54(3), 333–45.

Shì, J. 釋見介. (2017). Jílè shìjiè wèihé zài xifāng 極樂世界為何在 「西方」 (Why is
the heaven in the west). *Xiāngguāng zhuāngyán* 香光莊嚴, 127, 46–9.

Snoek, J. A. M. (2006). Defining "rituals." In J. Kreinath, J. A. M. Snoek, &
M. Stausberg (eds.), *Theorizing Rituals: Issues, Topics, Approaches, Concepts* (pp.
3–14). Leiden: Koninklijke Brill NV.

Taipei Mortuary Services Office. (2014). Electronic eulogy request platform. http://w9
.mso.taipei.619 gov.tw/TPFScroll/login.aspx.

Watts, J. W. (2019). Sensation and metaphor in ritual performance: The example of
sacred texts. *Entangled Religions*, 10. https://er.ceres.rub.de/index.php/ER/article/vi
ew/8365/7806.

Weinert, R. (2010). Formulaicity and usage-based language: Linguistics, psycholin-guistic and acquisitional manifestations. In D. Wood (ed.), *Perspectives on Formulaic Language: Acquisition and Communication* (pp. 1–21). London and New York: Continuum.

Wheelock, W. T. (1982). The problem of ritual language: From information to situation. *Journal of the American Academy of Religion*, 50(1), 49–71.

Wood, D. (2002). Formulaic language in acquisition and production: Implications for teaching. *TESL Canada Journal*, 20(1), 1–15.

Wray, A. (2002). *Formulaic Language and the Lexicon*. Cambridge: Cambridge University Press.

14   Metaphor

Aletta G. Dorst

14.1   Background, History, and Key Terms

Religion, faith, belief, conviction – no matter what word we use for it, our relationship with the divine has always been a complicated one. It requires us to worship, trust, and believe in a higher power that we cannot normally see, hear or touch. This intangibility influences the degree to which believers can fully understand the nature of the divine, which, by definition, has no earthly parallel. Research has shown that in both written and spoken texts, from the Bible and Quran (Charteris-Black, 2004) to Quaker pamphlets (Koller, 2017) to religious discussions on YouTube (Pihlaja, 2014), metaphors play an important role in shaping our understanding of the divine and in communicating to others what we believe the role is that religion plays, or should play, in our lives.

Though some may argue that *all* religious language is necessarily metaphorical (see McFague, quoted in Creamer, 2006) since human beings have no direct access to divine reality and therefore cannot understand divine concepts in their own terms, it is clear that many believers interpret religious notions literally rather than metaphorically. In fact, metaphor is in itself a highly complex phenomenon that warrants many different definitions, interpretations, and methods of analysis. In this chapter, I will therefore start by discussing a number of key concepts from contemporary metaphor studies in order to show how these can subsequently be applied in the analysis of how metaphors in language, thought and communication may shape, confirm and challenge our understanding of religion and the divine.

Metaphor has been studied since the time of Aristotle, who is still famously quoted for having said that "the greatest thing by far is to be a master of metaphor. It is the one thing that cannot be learnt from others; and it is also a sign of genius, since a good metaphor implies an intuitive perception of the similarity in dissimilars" (Poetics 22; transl. Bywater, 1940, p. 62). Yet the birth of contemporary metaphor studies starts with the 'cognitive turn' that followed Lakoff and Johnson's (1980) ground-breaking publication *Metaphors We Live By*, in which they set out their cognitive theory of metaphor, now commonly referred to as Conceptual Metaphor Theory.

Conceptual Metaphor Theory (hereafter: CMT) explicitly broke with the tradition of viewing metaphor as a matter of language, as a matter of semantic deviance, and as a matter of creative literary genius – three assumptions that can easily be linked to Aristotle's praise of metaphor quoted previously. In the traditional approach to metaphor, it was believed that the function of metaphors was mainly ornamental and that these instances of decorative language 'trickery' made literary texts more appealing, as readers had to solve a linguistic puzzle before they could understand the text's deeper meaning. Though Aristotle himself did in fact recognize the cognitive potential of metaphor (see Mahon, 1999), and other scholars had already emphasized the cognitive function of metaphor, it was with Lakoff and Johnson's work that the cognitive approach really took flight and launched a sheer avalanche of research on metaphor from different disciplines, including linguistics, psycholinguistics, psychology, anthropology, philosophy, literary studies, education and political sciences.

One of the central tenets in CMT is that the "essence of metaphor is understanding and experiencing one kind of thing in terms of another" (Lakoff and Johnson, 1980, p. 5). More specifically, CMT argues that we understand typically complex, abstract and unfamiliar concepts such as life, death, time, inflation, and democracy in terms of typically more concrete, simple, and familiar concepts that we can experience through our senses – that is, things we can see, feel, hear, touch, taste – such as plants, animals, heat, cold, movement, and containers. We can use our knowledge of the more concrete and familiar *source domain* to understand the more abstract and unfamiliar *target domain*. This process of understanding the target-domain concept in terms of the source-domain concept is called a *cross-domain mapping*, and this mapping is believed to involve a systematic set of *correspondences* between the two domains. For example, we can use our knowledge of the more concrete source domain of fighting in a battle or war to understand the more abstract target domain of a verbal argument between political adversaries. The resulting cross-domain mapping allows us to think about the verbal exchange in terms of 'winning' and 'losing', 'attacking' and 'defending' viewpoints, political 'enemies' and 'allies', and words as 'weapons' and 'traps'. That is, there are systematic correspondences between elements in the source domain – for example, people, actions, objects, aims and outcomes – and elements in the target domain.

This metaphor operates at the level of thought, the level of *conceptual structure*, not merely at the level of linguistic expressions in language. CMT argues that the basis of metaphor lies in our conceptual system, not in language, and that the reason we have metaphorical expressions in our language use is because they are linguistic realizations of underlying conceptual metaphors. As a result of this, metaphorical expressions are not rare or restricted to poetic language but pervasive and systematic in ordinary everyday language, as illustrated by the following examples from Lakoff and Johnson (1980, pp. 7–8; italics in original):

> You're *wasting* my time.
> This gadget will *save* you hours.
> I don't *have* the time to *give* you.
> How do you *spend* your time these days.
> That flat tire *cost* me an hour.
> I've *invested* a lot of time in her.
> I don't *have enough* time to *spare* for that.
> You're *running out of* time.

The italicized expressions all describe the concept of TIME in terms of the concept of MONEY (using small caps to distinguish concepts from words). CMT argues that such systematic and conventional patterns of metaphor in language show that we do not merely *talk* about time in terms of money but that we also *think* of time in terms of money. That is to say, systematic patterns of metaphor in *language* – the metaphorical expressions or *linguistic metaphors* – merely reflect conventional patterns of metaphor in *thought*, so-called *conceptual metaphors*. In CMT, the systematicity in our metaphorical language use is considered to be the direct result of the underlying systematicity in our conceptual system. Because we have a conceptual metaphor TIME IS MONEY in our conceptual system, we also have systematic linguistic realizations of this metaphor in our language.

In addition to what Lakoff and Johnson (1980) call 'structural' metaphors, such as TIME IS MONEY and ARGUMENTATION IS WAR, where our knowledge of the target domain is structured in terms of our knowledge of the source domain, CMT also distinguishes 'orientational' metaphors, which structure "a whole system of concepts with respect to one another" (Lakoff and Johnson, 1980, p. 14) on the basis of spatial orientations such as down-up, in-out, front-back, on-off, and 'ontological' metaphors, which allow us to "understand our experiences in terms of objects and substances" (p. 25). Ontological metaphors allow us to talk about events, actions, activities, and states in terms of discrete entities so that we can "refer to them, categorize them, group them, and quantify then" (p. 25). This is why we can say things like 'Are you *going to* the meeting?', 'He is *in* love' and 'She *put a lot of effort into* this project'. Another class of ontological metaphors is formed by personifications, which allow us to understand our "experiences with nonhuman entities in terms of human motivations, characteristics, and activities" (p. 33), as in 'This *fact argues* against the standard theories' and '*Inflation is eating up* our profits'.

Examples of orientational metaphors are HAPPY IS UP – SAD IS DOWN (e.g. 'My spirits *rose*.'; 'I'm feeling *down*.') and CONSCIOUS IS UP – UNCONSCIOUS

IS DOWN (e.g. 'Wake *up*.'; 'He *fell* asleep.'; 'He's *under* hypnosis.') (p. 14). Lakoff and Johnson argue that orientational metaphors are grounded in our physical experience: our posture is erect when we are happy and healthy and confident, but we slouch and make our bodies small when we are sick or sad or afraid; our bodies are up when we are awake and alive, but down when we are sleeping, sick, or dead. As pointed out by Kövecses (2002), this experiential basis of conceptual metaphors and the notion of the 'embodiment' of meaning is "perhaps *the* central idea of the cognitive linguistic view of metaphor and indeed of the cognitive linguistic view of meaning" (p. 16). Rather than being based on either pre-existing or newly created similarities between the source and target domains, metaphorical mappings derive from our own bodily experiences, and the resulting conceptual metaphors are thus grounded in physical, perceptual, and cultural correlations in our experience.

Given this, it is not hard to see why metaphors would play such a central role in our understanding of religion and the divine, which qualify as abstract, complex target domains par excellence. A CMT-based corpus study of the Bible and Quran by Charteris-Black (2004) demonstrates that these two central holy texts share several conceptual metaphors: "In both texts journey, fire and light and weather metaphors are important and are based on conceptual metaphors such as SPIRITUAL KNOWLEDGE IS LIGHT, GOOD IS LIGHT, DIVINE ANGER IS FIRE and DIVINE PUNISHMENT IS A HOSTILE WEATHER CONDITION" (2004, p. 238). However, he also found a number of striking dissimilarities. For example, metaphors highlighting the power of divine retribution and punishment are more widespread in the Quran, while metaphorical expressions based on the conceptual metaphor SPIRITUAL IS NATURAL are more productive in the Bible. Interestingly, several words from the semantic fields of FOOD, DRINK, and ANIMALS were frequently used metaphorically in the Bible but were much more commonly used in the literal sense in the Quran. These findings thus illustrate that both linguistic metaphor and conceptual metaphor are central notions in the analysis of religious discourse, but we will need additional analytical tools to explain how such metaphors are used in different contexts by different discourse communities.

This section has discussed the main tenets of CMT, which remains the dominant paradigm in metaphor studies to this day. The definition of metaphor as a mapping across conceptual domains is at present, as Steen (2011) emphasizes, "the most productive and best embedded theoretical definition of metaphor" (p. 48). Nevertheless, some of the claims of CMT have been challenged by scholars from varying disciplines, such as psychology, corpus linguistics, and discourse analysis. These critiques will form the basis for the discussion of key topics, questions, and debates in metaphor studies in Section 14.2.

14.2   Key Topics, Questions, and Debates

14.2.1   Metaphor as a Product versus Metaphor as a Process

In Conceptual Metaphor Theory, the presence of conventional conceptual metaphors such as LIFE IS A JOURNEY and ARGUMENT IS WAR is taken as evidence that people understand the target domain in terms of the source domain. Though the distinction between linguistic metaphors in language and conceptual metaphors in thought is useful and indeed essential, it remains a central question in metaphor studies how 'thought' relates to 'understanding', and how 'metaphor understanding' relates to 'metaphor processing'. Psychologists and psycholinguists in particular have warned that the existence of conceptual metaphors cannot be taken as evidence for how metaphorical language is processed by individual language users during on-line comprehension. The metaphors that are identified in the linguistic and conceptual structures of the language system are not necessarily one-to-one reflections of metaphors in the psychological processes of human verbal and cognitive behaviour (e.g. Cameron and Low, 1999; Charteris-Black, 2004; Müller, 2008).

Already in the 1980s, psycholinguistic experiments showed that, as far as our immediate, automatic comprehension of utterances is concerned, understanding metaphorical expressions does not take longer than understanding literal expressions, nor does it require additional cognitive mechanisms. Gibbs (1993), in particular, has emphasized that one common mistake in studies of metaphor has been to confuse the *processes* and the *products* of understanding. Gibbs distinguishes between four main stages in real-time language interpretation, namely comprehension, recognition, interpretation, and appreciation (1993, pp. 255–6). He warns that we cannot infer that people understand an expression such as *Juliet is the sun* metaphorically simply because we can identify the linguistic expression as metaphorical. That is, we cannot draw conclusions about the processes of understanding based on the products of understanding. Importantly, not all metaphor that can be identified at the level of language and thought is necessarily the result of metaphor in on-line processing. Moreover, whether linguistic and conceptual metaphors are processed as metaphors by individuals only concerns short-term discourse processes – production, reception and interaction – that characterize performance; it is an even more complex issue to determine what the relationship is between metaphor and long-term psycholinguistic processes such as language acquisition and attrition.

The fact that many, perhaps even most, metaphorical expressions go unnoticed and are not processed as metaphors leads to what Steen (2008, p. 220) has called "the Paradox of Metaphor". To solve this paradox, Steen proposes a three-dimensional model of metaphor analysis that systematically distinguishes between language, thought and communication, adding communicative function as a third variable in addition to linguistic and conceptual properties. This reintroduces attention to metaphor's context-specific communicative purpose (i.e. divertive, informative, persuasive, etc.) in a particular discourse event and, more importantly, introduces the question whether metaphors are used deliberately or non-deliberately. Though the term 'deliberateness' and Steen's Deliberate Metaphor Theory (2008, 2017) remain a topic of heated debate (see Gibbs, 2015; Müller, 2011), most metaphor analysts working with authentic discourse readily acknowledge that some metaphors play a more important role in achieving the goals of the interlocutors (i.e. persuading, entertaining, explaining) than others.

Within Steen's three-dimensional framework, conventional metaphors in language and thought may still be processed as metaphors (i.e. by comparison) as long as they are used deliberately. Steen argues that a metaphor is used deliberately "when it is expressly meant to change the addressee's perspective on the referent or topic that is the target of the metaphor, by making the addressee look at it from a different conceptual domain or space, which functions as a conceptual source" (2008, p. 222). Non-deliberate metaphors, on the other hand, may be expected to be processed by categorization, as proposed by Glucksberg (2001), or lexical disambiguation, as proposed by Giora (2003). Deliberate metaphors differ from non-deliberate metaphors in being "a relatively conscious discourse strategy" (Steen, 2008, p. 22) involving the conscious re-evaluation (either in production or reception) of the target domain in terms of the source domain. They can be signalled in the discourse in various ways, including word play, extension and elaboration, or explicit signalling using an *A is B* or *A is like B* format. Important to note here is the fact that, within this model, the same metaphorical expressions in language (linguistic metaphors) and the same metaphorical ideas in thought (conceptual metaphors) may be used either deliberately or non-deliberately in communication. The advantage of adopting a three-way model that includes metaphor in communication as an independent level of analysis is that the traditional distinction between metaphor as a rhetorical tool and metaphor as a general tool in language and thought is reinstated without discounting the value in analysing metaphor's linguistic and conceptual properties.

14.2.2   *From Language to Thought and Back Again*

In developing their Conceptual Metaphor Theory, Lakoff and Johnson (1980) were primarily concerned with demonstrating the existence of conceptual metaphors and showing that these conceptual metaphors are systematic and conventional. The metaphorical expressions that they discuss are provided as evidence for the existence of particular conceptual metaphors and are therefore not analysed or discussed in their own right. As a result, the different manifestations of metaphor in authentic discourse did not receive much attention in early CMT-based research. In addition, the examples of metaphorical expressions used by Lakoff and Johnson (1980) were artificially constructed or elicited and collected from personal intuition and experience rather than from authentic discourse. Moreover, these examples were usually presented in isolated sentences rather than in connected stretches of text with a realistic co-text and context. Scholars from disciplines such as discourse studies, communication science, and corpus linguistics have therefore pointed out that the claims made by CMT do not necessarily accurately reflect how metaphor works in authentic language use and the evidence provided for the existence of conceptual metaphors may not be representative of how metaphor really works in practice.

The most systematic investigation of the tenets of CMT in relation to authentic language use has been carried out by Deignan (1999, 2005), who used large electronic corpora (such as the Bank of English) to test whether the main claims and implications of CMT are supported by linguistic evidence from naturally occurring discourse, analysing not only whether and how often particular linguistic realizations of conceptual metaphors occur, but also what in what collocational, syntactic and grammatical patterns. For example, Deignan ran concordances on several lexical items identified by Yu (1995) as being realizations of the conceptual metaphor ANGER IS HEAT, such as "These are *inflammatory* remarks" and "He was *breathing fire*". Deignan's study revealed that some of Yu's linguistic metaphors were indeed frequent in the corpus, while others did not occur at all: *inflammatory* and *smouldering* both occurred regularly in expressions indicating anger, but there was only one single metaphorical instance of *breathe/ed/es/ing fire* in 1,000 citations of *fire*. Such results demonstrate the need to investigate why language users select particular linguistic metaphors out of all theoretically possible linguistic realizations of a conceptual metaphor, and how such choices can be related to their discourse goals, the communicative setting, and their audience's needs and expectations.

Deignan (2005) points out that people often dismiss corpus studies when the outcome strikes them as familiar or trivial, but any "linguistic theory developed without reference to naturally-occurring language data may be elegant and internally consistent, but is simply irrelevant to the task of finding out how language works, because it ignores factual evidence" (p. 88). Her studies show that the analysis of metaphor in naturally occurring discourse poses challenges to some of the central claims of Conceptual Metaphor Theory. Firstly, some of the metaphorical expressions used by cognitive linguists to explain the existence of conceptual metaphors are infrequent or do not even occur at all. Although this does not entail that such conceptual metaphors do not exist or are unimportant, it does indicate that researchers need to refer to corpora if they wish to make any reliable claims about the linguistic realizations. Corpus data also reveal interesting regularities in the collocations and syntactic behaviour of metaphorical expressions, such as that metaphorical expressions often occur in very specific grammatical forms and fixed expressions.

14.2.3   *Authentic Discourse and Reliable Metaphor Identification*

Since Lakoff and Johnson (1980) based their claims for the existence of conceptual metaphors on linguistic examples that they invented or elicited, they had no need to develop an explicit and reliable method to identify metaphorical expressions in naturally occurring discourse. As pointed out in the previous section, this raises issues concerning the reliability and representativeness of the presented linguistic evidence (Deignan, 2005; Semino et al., 2004). However, the more recent focus in metaphor studies on employing authentic data and analysing linguistic metaphor in its natural context has prompted an increased attention on the reliable identification of linguistic metaphor. Deignan (2005) and Semino (2008) both note that metaphor analysts rarely make explicit how they have defined linguistic metaphor and how they have gone about identifying instances in texts. Researchers very often decide whether a particular word or phrase is metaphorical based on their intuitions and knowledge of the language, yet such intuitions do not only vary from individual to individual and from text to text (possibly even from day to day) but also, and even more so, between disciplines and theoretical orientations.

The lack of a precise definition of metaphor and the variability between identification approaches make it almost impossible to compare analyses or statistics, for example, on the frequency or density of metaphorical expressions in particular texts or genres. It also makes it difficult to evaluate claims about the ubiquity of metaphor in language or about the relation between metaphoric language and metaphoric thought. This situation prompted a group of ten metaphor scholars from different academic disciplines to formulate an explicit, reliable and flexible method for the identification of metaphorically used words in spoken and written language, the so-called Metaphor Identification Procedure or MIP (Pragglejaz Group, 2007).

MIP is not concerned with relating the identified metaphorically used words to underlying conceptual metaphors, or with establishing the exact nature of the underlying mappings. MIP should be viewed as "providing a reliable research method for determining whether words in contexts convey metaphorical meaning" (Pragglejaz Group, 2007, p. 2). A procedure such as the MIP can help researchers deal with the identification of individual cases in a consistent and systematic manner. The basic steps of the MIP are as follows (p. 3):

1. Read the entire text–discourse to establish a general understanding of the meaning.
2. Determine the lexical units in the text–discourse.

3. (a) For each lexical unit in the text, establish its meaning in context, that is, how it applies to an entity, relation, or attribute in the situation evoked by the text (contextual meaning). Take into account what comes before and after the lexical unit.

   (b) For each lexical unit, determine if it has a more basic contemporary meaning in other contexts than the one in the given context. For our purposes, basic meanings tend to be

   – More concrete [what they evoke is easier to imagine, see, hear, feel, smell, and taste];

   – Related to bodily action;

   – More precise (as opposed to vague);

   – Historically older;

   Basic meanings are not necessarily the most frequent meanings of the lexical unit.

   (c) If the lexical unit has a more basic current–contemporary meaning in other contexts than the given context, decide whether the contextual meaning contrasts with the basic meaning but can be understood in comparison with it.

4. If yes, mark the lexical unit as metaphorical.

Using these four steps, one can determine whether or not a particular word or expression is used metaphorically. Applying the MIP procedure and concluding that the word 'shepherd' is used metaphorically does not entail that the writer intended it to be metaphorical or that the reader recognized it as metaphorical or understood it metaphorically (i.e. via a cross-domain comparison). Within the MIP framework, the conclusion that a word is metaphorically used simply means that the particular linguistic realization can be analysed as metaphorical in relation to other uses of the same word, and that it therefore has the linguistic potential to be recognized and processed as metaphorical.

The MIP was subsequently further extended and refined by a group of metaphor scholars from the VU University in Amsterdam, the Netherlands, into MIPVU (Steen et al., 2010), which tried to solve a number of issues concerning etymology, word class, and the treatment of multiword units such as polywords, phrasal verbs, and compound nouns. The main difference between MIPVU and MIP is that MIP restricts itself to the identification of metaphorically used words only; that is, linguistic metaphors that involve referential incongruity or indirect meaning. MIPVU, on the other hand, includes not only these *indirect metaphors*, but also two additional types of metaphor, namely *direct metaphor* and *implicit metaphor*. The MIPVU protocol employs the term *metaphor-related words* (MRWs) to encompass all three types of linguistic metaphor.

In the case of direct metaphor, there is no referential incongruity and thus no contrast between the contextual and basic senses of the word being analysed.

Yet an underlying metaphorical comparison is still clearly intended, but evoked via topical incongruity (see Cameron, 2003) and the use of a metaphor-signalling device (see Goatly, 1997). In such cases, the metaphor is thus expressed through 'direct' language, as is the case with similes and metaphorical comparisons: 'He cares for his followers *like a shepherd cares for his flock.*' In this example, the words are not metaphorically used themselves, but through direct reference, they still set up a metaphorical comparison between the leader and his followers on the one hand and a shepherd and his sheep on the other. The third type of metaphor that can be identified using MIPVU is *implicit metaphor*, in which case the lexical unit that is metaphorically used takes the form of a cohesive grammatical or semantic links (such as demonstrative pronouns) that refer back to a linguistic metaphor: 'The shepherd will care for his sheep, and the sheep will follow *him.*' In this case, the word 'him' is not technically metaphorically used, but it replaces an implicit metaphorically used 'shepherd'.

In addition to the problems concerning the identification of linguistic metaphor (i.e. how to decide which words or expressions are related to metaphor), there is also the additional problem of relating the identified linguistic metaphorical expressions to their underlying conceptual metaphors. Many cognitive metaphor scholars maintain a top-down approach, starting from a set of conceptual metaphors they are interested in and then searching through a particular text or selection of texts for linguistic expressions that are consistent with the source and target domains of the conceptual metaphor, so that they can be considered linguistic realizations of the conceptual metaphor under investigation. For example, if a scholar is interested in ANGER IS HEAT, the text(s) will be searched for any words that can be said to belong to the domain of HEAT and/or TEMPERATURE and are used to say something about ANGER/EMOTION. Yet the relationship between individual words and conceptual domains is not self-evident at all; regardless of whether a top-down approach (from conceptual to linguistic) or a bottom-up approach (from linguistic to conceptual) is taken, the problem remains how analysts can reliably relate one to the other and demonstrate that the linguistic expressions are indeed realizations of a particular domain and thus a particular conceptual metaphor.

14.2.4 *Discourse Metaphors, Systematic Metaphors, and Metaphor Scenarios*

One question that has been raised in studies focusing on authentic discourse is how the stable, invariable, and general conceptual metaphors proposed by Conceptual Metaphor Theory can be related to the dynamic, variable, and context-specific metaphors encountered in authentic discourse. Three analytical notions are particularly relevant here, namely *discourse metaphors* (e.g.,

Zinken et al., 2008), *systematic metaphors* (e.g. Cameron and Maslen, 2010), and *metaphor scenarios* (e.g. Musolff, 2004, 2006; Semino, 2008). These three notions allow researchers to bridge the gap between the decontextualized and 'universal' conceptual metaphors proposed by CMT and the highly contextualized and personalized uses of metaphor encountered in natural discourse.

Zinken and colleagues (2008) argue for the presence of discourse metaphors, defined as "relatively stable metaphorical mappings that function as a key framing device within a particular discourse over a certain period of time" (p. 364). Like conceptual metaphors, such discourse metaphors are relatively stable and enduring, and their presence is postulated on the basis of their recurrent presence in discourse. Yet discourse metaphors are argued to be socio-historically specific; as a result, their employment varies across different discourse situations. As Hellsten (2003) points out, discourse metaphors are "robust enough to carry certain implications from one context to another, but at the same time flexible enough to allow for different formulations in different contexts" (n.p.).

Using the metaphor of 'Frankenfood', first coined in 1992, as a case study, Hellsten (2003) shows how this metaphor was used for different purposes by different parties in different discourses: NGOs used the metaphor as a powerful tool to evoke emotions and spur people to take action against the use of genetic manipulation in the production of food. Organization Friends of the Earth then employed the metaphor to launch a campaign against genetically manipulated food, while biotech company Monsanto used it to counter accusations and contradict the information provided by the NGOs, trying to "re-phrase the metaphor" (Hellsten, 2003, n.p.) and take away its negative associations. And newspaper *The Times* employed the same metaphor as a "catchy and concise way of talking about the politicised issue" (Hellsten, 2003, n.p.), drawing the metaphor into the public sphere. Hellsten's analysis shows that the Frankenfood metaphor provided a common ground and shared knowledge base (the Frankenstein myth) across time and discourse settings, but was flexible enough to be used for different communicative goals and allow for different, even opposing, interpretations of the same metaphor by different stakeholders in the underlying political debate.

Another important framework to explain the variability and flexibility of metaphor in discourse is offered by Cameron and colleagues, who consider variability to be the norm rather than the exception and view metaphor as an inherently dynamic phenomenon, emerging in contextualized interaction to form 'metaphor trajectories' and 'systematic metaphors' (Cameron, Low, and Maslen, 2010). Drawing on Complex Systems Theory, Cameron and colleagues take a discourse dynamics approach to metaphor analysis: they trace a metaphor's 'trajectory' throughout a conversation, from the moment it first appears until the moment it leaves the conversation. Once the metaphor's trajectory has been established, Cameron and colleagues analyse how the different interlocutors introduce, reuse, adjust, negotiate, reject, and replace the metaphor in order to achieve their discourse goals. In this approach, metaphor is taken as a "temporary stability emerging from the activity of interconnecting systems of socially-situated language use and cognitive activity" (Cameron et al., 2009, p. 64). As a result, metaphors do not involve decontextualized and fixed mappings but are "processual, emergent, and open to change" (p. 67). Unlike in CMT, this means that the analyst must understand the communicative setting in which the metaphors were used, and how they are integral to the 'discourse activity' performed by the interlocutors.

In this discourse dynamics approach, individual instances of linguistic metaphor are not treated as realizations of underlying conceptual metaphors, but are treated as connected parts of the metaphor's trajectory. By examining the connections between the different parts, the analyst can determine how the interlocutors are developing the metaphor over the course of the discourse activity. The changes and modifications that are made to the metaphors are described by Cameron (2008) in terms of 'metaphor shifting', which can take the form of *metaphor redeployment*, when the same metaphorical expression is used for a different topic; *metaphor development*, when the metaphorical expression is repeated, relexicalized through the use of a synonym or equivalent, expanded, elaborated or exemplified, or contrasted through an antonym; and *metaphor literalization*, when the metaphorical expression becomes literal or metonymic.

Once the trajectory of the metaphors has been traced through the discourse, and the different changes, additions, and developments to the metaphor have been identified, the analyst will be able to establish 'systematic metaphors' (Cameron, Low and Maslen, 2010, p. 127), that is, a system of metaphorical expressions that are semantically related (drawing on the same source domain) and are used to describe a particular topic. The discourse dynamics approach is neither exclusively top-down (going from systematic metaphor to individual instantiations) nor bottom-up (from individual instantiations to systematic metaphor); rather, it "continually moves across levels and timescales of the dynamic systems involved: the micro-level of a particular metaphor, the meso-levels of episodes of talk or topic threads, the macro-level of the conversation as a whole, and the broader socio-cultural level" (Cameron et al., 2009, p. 69). It formulates systematic metaphors based on the trajectories that emerge dynamically in the discourse and then considers how individual instantiations continue to shape and develop the systematic metaphor. Such systematic metaphors may be specific to a single conversation, and tend to be much more specific than conceptual metaphors, such as A RESPONSE TO TERRORISM IS NEGATIVE LABELLING OF MUSLIMS (using small caps in combination with italics to distinguish systematic metaphors from conceptual metaphor) (Cameron, Low, and Maslen, 2010), which was used by Muslim participants of a focus group to describe how the UK authorities responded to terrorism. Cameron, Low, and Maslen (2010) describe such systematic metaphors as "ways of 'framing' the ideas, attitudes and values of discourse participants" (p. 137).

The third useful notion in relating metaphorical expressions to conceptual metaphors is Musolff's (2004, 2006) notion of 'metaphor scenarios'. A scenario can be defined as a narrative elaboration of a conceptual mapping which allows people to "build narrative frames for the assessment of (e.g.) socio-political issues" (Musolff, 2006, p. 36). Such narrative scenarios are rich in the associations and assumptions they evoke about the typical 'actors' in the 'story' and the different 'roles' they play, as well as about typical 'plot twists' and 'endings' they can expect. Once readers recognize the story, they also immediately know how to respond to it, since the story provides them with schema-like knowledge about underlying intentions and motivations, as well as about what would count as 'good' and 'bad' behaviour. For example, if a business merger is described in terms of a marriage, then we know that a happy marriage could involve scenarios such as a honeymoon and children, while an unhappy marriage could lead to fighting, cheating, or even divorce. It is through the scenario that is evoked, rather than the general and abstract conceptual metaphor, A BUSINESS MERGER IS A MARRIAGE (or the even more abstract ontological personification metaphor BUSINESSES ARE PEOPLE), that reveals the particular attitudinal or emotional stance of the writer or speaker on the topic.

Using examples from a bilingual corpus of British and German public debates about the European Union, Musolff (2006) shows how the two datasets share a number of conceptual metaphors, such as THE NATION IS A PERSON, but employ them in very different ways by organizing the source domain into different scenarios that "provide focal points for conceptualizing the target topic", revealing the "particular political dispositions and preferences of the respective national discourse communities" (p. 23). Musolff points out that it is therefore necessary to analyse the texts not only in terms of the source and target domains that are employed, and the conceptual metaphor and basic mapping involved, but also in terms of the culturally and ideologically motivated discourse-dependent scenarios that provide insight into the argumentative point that is being made. While most conceptual metaphors are too general to be argumentative in themselves, the way their linguistic realizations are organized into context-rich scenarios allows us to employ them for specific rhetorical purposes, building narrative frames for the "conceptualization and assessment of socio-political issues and to 'spin out' these narratives into emergent discourse traditions that are characteristic of their respective community" (Musolff, 2006, p. 36). This allows the metaphor analyst to relate the individual linguistic metaphors found in the text, and the way they are combined into meaningful patterns (see Dorst, 2017), to underlying conceptual metaphors.

14.3   Case Study

The case study reported in this section involved a number of group interviews with Dutch Muslim teenagers in which they responded to Christian metaphors while talking about their understanding of Allah and Islam (Dorst and Klop, 2017). The main aim of the study was to establish if and how Dutch Muslim teenagers use metaphors when they talk about their religion and their conceptualization of Allah, and to what extent they would consider the Biblical metaphors for God appropriate descriptions for Allah. For this second part of the research, five principal Biblical metaphors for God were selected, namely GOD AS A KING, FATHER, HUSBAND, MASTER, and JUDGE. As a first step, a corpus search (in English) was carried out of both the Bible and Quran on the keywords *master/king/judge/father/husband* + *God/Allah* to determine whether they involved linguistic realizations of the five selected conceptual metaphors. The search confirmed that these expressions are used as linguistic metaphors for God in the Bible, and also revealed that 'king', 'master', and 'judge' were used as linguistic metaphors for Allah in the Quran; that is, the KING, MASTER, and JUDGE metaphors are not exclusively Christian metaphors. The FATHER and HUSBAND metaphors, on the other hand, occurred only in the Bible. This corpus search therefore led to the hypothesis that the Dutch Muslim teenagers would have more difficulties with the FATHER and HUSBAND metaphors.

The participants in the three group interviews were eight Muslim high school students between the ages of fifteen and eighteen, who attend a Christian high school in the city of Rotterdam in the Netherlands. The school's Theology teacher was asked for advice as to which students were Muslims, as well as which of those students practised their religion seriously. The invited students were interviewed by means of a semi-structured interview, starting with general questions on what their religion means to them, how they experience their belief in Allah, and how they feel about the relationship between Allah and believers. As religion and the divine are notoriously complex and abstract concepts, the participants were expected to use metaphors in their responses to these questions. After these general questions, the teenagers were asked to respond to the five Biblical metaphors, reflect on their meaning and discuss whether they could also be used to talk about Allah. For example, they would be asked whether they thought Allah could be described as a king.

The interviews took about thirty minutes on average and were held in a classroom at the school. They were audio-recorded and then transcribed, after which they were analysed using Dutch MIPVU (Steen et al., 2010), taking only those metaphorical expressions into account that referred to Allah, Muslims, the relationship between Allah and believers, and the participants' faith itself. The identified linguistic metaphors were then grouped and generalized to conceptual metaphors using the electronic version of the *Van Dale*

Groot Woordenboek der Nederlandse Taal to find common terms or phrases in the definitions of the metaphorical expressions that could be used to formulate the 'generalizing' metaphor (i.e. words such as 'serve' and 'lord' were related to the MASTER metaphor, 'rule' to the KING metaphor). In the discussion below, quotes and examples have been translated into English for the sake of readability, though the translation of such expressions is by no means an easy or straightforward matter (as will be discussed in the final section of this chapter).

The results of the interviews showed, first of all, that the Dutch Muslim teenagers used linguistic metaphors spontaneously in their descriptions of Allah, Muslims and the Islamic faith. They described their religion as being their 'starting point' [*uitgangspunt*] (G1) and 'refuge' [*toevlucht*] (G3), and Allah as their 'support' [*steun*] (G1), as "someone who always listens to you and whom you can always ask for forgiveness" (G1). They express their relationship with Allah as a 'bond' [*band*] (G1), as being 'connected' [*verbonden*] (G3), and Allah being 'close' [*dichtbij*] (G3).

Some examples are more elaborate, and reveal the kind of discourse activity that is better captured by Cameron and Maslen's (2010) discourse dynamics approach to metaphor and Musolff's (2004, 2006) notion of scenarios. When Group 1 is discussing the fact that you have to be 'sincere' [*oprecht*] (G1) in practicing your faith, one of the teenagers explains the need for sincerity by referring to the idea of 'penalty points' [*strafpunten*] (G1) being subtracted for bad deeds in order to make clear that it is intention that counts:

And I have also always, ehm, been taught at mosque, ehm, that, for example if I now, ehm, say that, yeah if I go home I'm going to give money to someone poor, I'm going to, ehm, do something good, or I pray, I'm going to do that, then I get, ehm, so to say, points for that, points, but if I, for example, say, ehm, yeah, if I go home now and then I will, I'm just saying something, I'm going to kill someone, and then I don't do it, then Allah does not give penalty points for that. So, what you are saying is not really right actually, if you, say, wear a headscarf and if you do not want that, on the inside, then ... then Allah can still forgive you, do you understand? (G1)

In this case, the interviewer picks up on the metaphor of the penalty points and asks for further explanation of how this works:

Interviewer: And what do you mean by, because I hear you just said, points, but how, ehm, penalty points, pro points, that is a bit new, ehm ...
 Student: In Islam you get, for example, ehm, Judgement Day, when everyone is judged and then it is weighed, so to say, your sins from your good deeds, yeah, your sins and your good deeds, and good deeds, if those are, so to say, higher then you go to Heaven, and if they are not higher then you go to Hell. (G1)

Although Judgement Day came up in all interviews, and several metaphorical expressions occurred that can be related to the JUDGE metaphor, the Muslim teenagers did not use the noun 'judge' [*rechter*] itself. The same was true for the MASTER metaphor, which was only realized through descriptions of believers as 'servants' [*dienaren*], not by comparing Allah directly to a 'master' [*meester*] or 'lord' [*heer*]. This emphasizes Deignan's (2005) point that analysts need to consider authentic data to determine which linguistic realizations are actually used, and that the linguistic realizations may be different from what would be expected or postulated based on the conceptual metaphor alone.

This issue came up even more clearly when the students were asked to respond to the five Biblical metaphors. The Dutch Muslim teenagers used linguistic metaphors realizing ALLAH IS A JUDGE and ALLAH IS A MASTER in their spontaneous responses, and when these metaphors were introduced explicitly by the interviewer, they agreed that they were suitable descriptions of Allah, though they made a point of stressing that Allah is not an *earthly* king or judge: "Judges for example in real life, they are, for example if you do something wrong, like OK wrong, punishment, but Allah can also then forgive you" (G1). There was some doubt and discussion with regard to the metaphor ALLAH IS A KING: this metaphor did not resonate with G1 at all, G2 more or less considered it suitable, but only after some discussion, and G3 found this metaphor suitable in their primary responses. The main problem seemed to be the parallel with 'earthly' kings.

The metaphors ALLAH IS A FATHER and ALLAH IS A HUSBAND, on the other hand, were considered unsuitable by all three groups. Their responses made it very clear that they are familiar with the FATHER metaphor from their knowledge of Christian religion, but both the Quran and their parents explicitly forbid its use:

Student: We see Him as creator, He is simply . . .
Interviewer: It is not allowed right?
Student: No, it is simply not allowed with us . . . it is simply said that He has He does not have children, He has no husband, no wife sorry, no father no mother. He is simply completely different from us. No, it is not allowed with us. (G1)

No, He is my creator, He is my judge, we are His servants. I would not say He is my father, because then you really say, the words alone are ridiculous, that would just be too weak. He is not my father. He made everyone, He made the entire universe, he is not, He does not need a child. He is not someone who makes children. The logic of being a father, that you could never say, because how would you know that? (G2)

Interestingly, this means that the teenagers' frequent use of the linguistic metaphor of 'brothers and sisters' [*broeders en zusters*] can potentially be generalized to MUSLIMS ARE A FAMILY, but the surrounding discourse makes very clear that they cannot be taken as linguistic realizations of an underlying conceptual metaphor ALLAH IS A FATHER. The surrounding discussions may even be taken to suggest that the expression 'brothers and sisters' does not evoke familial connotations for these believers the way it does for Christian believers. It would be interesting to find out if the expressions have closer connections to the idea of 'brothers and sisters in arms', uniting the believers in their fight against a common enemy. The findings suggest that while some of the linguistic metaphors may have clear trajectories in the conversation, and can be grouped into systematic metaphors, perhaps even relatively stable and shared discourse metaphors, they need not result in invariable and universal conceptual metaphors.

The Muslim teenagers' discussions of the Biblical metaphors provide valuable insights into how they interpret common linguistic and conceptual metaphors, how they relate them to their religious experience, and how they draw on the Quran, lessons by their imam and the instructions of their parents to make sense of their religion and what it means to them in everyday life. Their deliberations clearly indicate that the linguistic metaphors found in texts like the Quran and Bible cannot always be related directly to conceptual metaphors, and cannot always be interpreted without considering how believers interact with these texts, since the actual meaning derived from the linguistic expressions appears to be heavily influenced by the believer's personal experience and sociocultural context. While this small study cannot draw any hard and fast conclusions on the nature of religious metaphor, it does help to illustrate some of the points made in contemporary metaphor studies: that we need to distinguish between linguistic and conceptual metaphor, between the products and processes of metaphor, and between our shared conventional and relatively fixed conceptual metaphors on the one hand, and our individualized, dynamic and context-dependent variations on such metaphors on the other.

14.4   Future Directions

Metaphor and religion go hand in hand, given the fact that our religious and spiritual experiences are highly personal, emotional, and abstract. Many chapters in this volume inevitably discuss metaphor as they relate to other topics, most notably *Multimodal Discourse* and *Cognition*. Although a number of valuable studies have already been carried out, a number of important avenues for further research remain open for exploration. More importantly, a number of current imbalances should be pointed out, namely the strong tendency to focus on Christianity, on (sacred) written texts and on English.

Most analyses of metaphor in religious discourse focus on English language data or translate metaphors found in other languages into English to relate them to Lakoff and Johnson's (1980) conceptual metaphors without paying sufficient attention to the effect the process of translation has on the identified metaphors. Unfortunately, it is not uncommon in both publications and conference presentations on metaphor (in any text type) to present only idiomatic English examples without the original language data and any kind of intermediate gloss translation. This is a rather worrying situation, as translations may very well be compatible, but nonetheless skew the data. For example, if an original Dutch text contains the metaphor '*gevecht*', which literally translates into 'fight', the analyst may choose the near-synonym 'battle' to make the example consistent with a WAR metaphor; though the Dutch linguistic metaphor is indeed compatible with this mapping – in Dutch, '*oorlogen*' ['wars'] involve '*vechten*' ['fighting'] and '*gevechten*' ['fights' or 'battles'], the original Dutch linguistic metaphor '*gevecht*' is not as clearly war-related (it may be general fighting, or a sports fight) as the English translation 'battle', which is explicitly war related. Similarly, Dutch '*meester*' means both 'teacher' and 'master'/'lord'. The issue of interpretation in translation is also raised by the *Sacred Texts* chapter, where it is pointed out that most of the 'musts' and 'shoulds' in English Bible translations are the result of the translator's interpretation, since Biblical Hebrew does not have modal verbs. The way translation affects both how believers use metaphors to describe their religious experiences and how researchers analyse religious discourse and present their findings is an essential but as of yet fundamentally underexplored area of research.

The dominance of English and the focus on Christianity in studies of religious metaphor may very well be related. Studies on metaphor in Islam, Judaism, Hinduism, and other spiritual schools of thought may not reach the centre of metaphor scholarship – as published in A-journals and presented at large international conferences – if these researchers are not working with English data or publishing in English. Conversely, Western researchers working on metaphor in religious discourse may simply be focussing on Christianity because they have direct access to written and spoken data by Christians in languages they know. If we consider *Metaphor and the Social World*'s 2017 special issue "Metaphor in Religion and Spirituality" (edited by Pihlaja), we see that it contains six papers, five of which look at Christianity. Only two papers carry out a contrastive analysis between Christianity and Islam (Dorst and Klop; Richardson), one paper looks at online interactions between Christians and Atheists (Pihlaja), and one paper looks at how Ghandi appropriated Christian metaphors into Hinduism (Neary). The sixth paper looks at instructions for meditative practice in Buddhism (Silvestre-López and Navarro i Fernando). As pointed out by Richardson (this volume), there is a great need for more comparative research, as "little work is being done to compare how believers from different religious traditions are thinking about and conceptualizing elements of their experience".

At present, researchers typically look at only one religion, and typically focus on sacred texts (i.e. the Bible, the Quran, the Vedas). As has been made clear throughout this chapter, it is essential not to take the products of metaphor (as found in texts) as evidence for the processes of metaphor (in believers' language production and comprehension). It is also necessary to go beyond abstract and general mappings such as proposed by CMT and look at how metaphors are used dynamically and in context by individuals and social groups. Interestingly, two of the papers in the special issue mentioned earlier look at interviews, and one looks at online discussions: such papers provide valuable insights into how metaphor is used in the dynamic processes of negotiating, accepting, and resisting the meaning of metaphors by actual believers. Online and social-media exchanges (fora, YouTube, Twitter, etc.) are an obvious future interest, as are multimodal religious texts, such as movies, TV documentaries and comics. Such multimodal religious texts have, to my knowledge, not attracted any serious academic attention, while they offer interesting possibilities for both verbal and multimodal metaphor. The need to look at multimodal discourse goes hand in hand with the issue that we need to look at believers who speak widely different languages and belong to widely different cultures than those we may normally study. This is a vital step if the study of metaphor in religion and spirituality wants to become more inclusive and socially relevant. We need a better understanding of what real believers do with metaphors in actual discourse – what these metaphors mean to them and how they adapt and shape the metaphors' meaning in line with their cultural values and expectations, personal experiences, and communicative purposes.

14.5   References

Aristotle (1940). *The art of poetry.* Translated by: I. Bywater. Oxford: Oxford University Press.

Cameron, L. (1999). Identifying and describing metaphor in spoken discourse data. In L. Cameron & G. Low (eds.), *Researching and Applying Metaphor*, pp. 105–32. Cambridge: Cambridge University Press.

Cameron, L. (2003). *Metaphor in Educational Discourse.* London: Continuum.

Cameron, L. (2007). Patterns of metaphor use in reconciliation talk. *Discourse and Society*, 18, 197–222.

Cameron, L. (2008). Metaphor shifting in the dynamics of talk. In M. S. Zanotto, L. Cameron & M. C. Cavalcanti (eds.), *Confronting Metaphor in Use: An Applied Linguistic Approach* (pp. 45–62). Amsterdam: John Benjamins.

Cameron, L., & Low, G. (eds.). (1999). *Researching and Applying Metaphor.* Cambridge: Cambridge University Press.

Cameron, L., & Maslen, R. (2010) (eds.). *Metaphor Analysis: Research practice in Applied Linguistics, Social Sciences and the Humanities.* London: Equinox.

Cameron, L., Maslen, R., & Low, G. (2010). Finding systematicity in metaphor use. In L. Cameron & R. Maslen (eds.), *Metaphor Analysis: Research practice in Applied Linguistics, Social Sciences and the Humanities* (pp. 116–46). London: Equinox.

Cameron, L., Maslen, R., Maule, J., Stratton, P., & Stanley, N. (2009). The discourse dynamics approach to metaphor and metaphor-led discourse analysis. *Metaphor and Symbol*, 24(2), 63–89.

Charteris-Black, J. (2003). Speaking with forked tongue: A comparative study of metaphor and metonymy in English and Malay phraseology. *Metaphor and Symbol*, 18(4), 289–310.

Charteris-Black, J. (2004). *Corpus Approaches to Critical Metaphor Analysis*. London: Palgrave.

Creamer, D. (2006). God doesn't treat his children that way. *Journal of Religion, Disability & Health*, 9(3), 73–84.

Deignan, A. (1999). Corpus-based research into metaphor. In L. Cameron & G. Low (eds.), *Researching and Applying Metaphor* (pp. 177–99). Cambridge: Cambridge University Press.

Deignan, A. (2005). *Metaphor and Corpus Linguistics*. Amsterdam: John Benjamins.

Dorst, A. G. (2017). Textual patterning of metaphor. In E. Semino & Z. Demjen (eds.), *The Routledge Handbook of Metaphor and Language*, (pp. 178–92). Abingdon: Routledge.

Dorst, A. G., & Klop, M. (2017). Not a holy father: Dutch Muslim teenagers' metaphors for Allah. *Metaphor and the Social World*, 7(1), 66–86.

Gibbs, R. W., Jr. (1993). Process and products in making sense of tropes. In A. Ortony (ed.), *Metaphor and Thought* (pp. 252–76). 2nd ed. Cambridge: Cambridge University Press.

Gibbs, R. W., Jr. (2015). Does deliberate metaphor theory have a future? *Journal of Pragmatics*, 90, 77–87.

Giora, R. (2003). *On Our Mind: Salience, Context, and Figurative Language*. Oxford: Oxford University Press.

Glucksberg, S. (2001). *Understanding Figurative Language: From Metaphors to Idioms*. Oxford: Oxford University Press.

Goatly, A. (1997). *The Language of Metaphors*. London: Routledge.

Hellsten, I. (2003). Focus on metaphors: The case of "Frankenfood" on the web. *Journal of Computer-Mediated Communication*, 8(4), n.p.

Koller, V. (2017). The light within: Metaphor consistency in Quaker pamphlets, 1659–2010. *Metaphor and the Social World*, 7(1), 5–25.

Kövecses, Z. (2002). *Metaphor: A Practical Introduction*. Oxford: University Press.

Lakoff, G., & Johnson, M. (1980). *Metaphors We Live By*. University of Chicago Press.

Mahon, J. E. (1999). Getting your sources right: What Aristotle *didn't* say. In L. Cameron & G. Low (eds.), *Researching and Applying Metaphor* (pp. 69–80). Cambridge: Cambridge University Press.

Müller, C. (2008). *Metaphors Dead and Alive, Sleeping and Waking: A Dynamic View*. Chicago: University of Chicago Press.

Müller, C. (2011). Are 'deliberate' metaphors really deliberate? A question of human consciousness and action. *Metaphor and the Social World*, 1(1), 61–66.

Musolff, A. (2004). *Metaphor and Political Discourse: Analogical Reasoning in Debates about Europe*. London: Palgrave.

Musolff, A. (2006). Metaphor scenarios in public discourse. *Metaphor and Symbol*, 21 (1), 23–38.

Ortony, A. (ed.). (1979/1993). *Metaphor and Thought*. Cambridge: Cambridge University Press.

Pihlaja, S. (2014). *Antagonism on YouTube: Metaphor in Online Discourse*. London: Bloomsbury.

Pragglejaz Group (2007). A practical and flexible method for identifying metaphorically used words in discourse. *Metaphor and Symbol*, 23(1), 1–39.

Semino, E. (2008). *Metaphor in Discourse*. Cambridge: Cambridge University Press.

Semino, E., Heywood, J., & Short, M. H. (2004). Methodological problems in the analysis of metaphors in a corpus of conversations about cancer. *Journal of Pragmatics*, 36(7), 1271–94.

Steen, G. J. (2007). *Finding Metaphor in Grammar and Usage: A Methodological Analysis of Theory and Research*. Amsterdam: John Benjamins.

Steen, G. J. (2008). The paradox of metaphor: Why we need a three-dimensional model of metaphor. *Metaphor and Symbol*, 23(4), 213–41.

Steen, G. J. (2011). The contemporary theory of metaphor – Now new and improved! *Review of Cognitive Linguistics*, 9(1), 26–64. DOI 10.1075/ml.9.1.03ste.

Steen, G. J. (2017). Deliberate Metaphor Theory: Basic assumptions, main tenets, urgent issues. *Intercultural Pragmatics*, 14(1), 1–24.

Steen, G. J., Dorst, A. G., Herrmann, J. B., Kaal, A. A., Krennmayr, T., & Pasma, T. (2010). *A Method for Linguistic Metaphor Identification: From MIP to MIPVU*. Amersterdan: John Benjamins.

Yu, N. (1995). Metaphorical expressions of anger and happiness in English and Chinese. *Metaphor and Symbolic Activity*, 10, 59–92.

Zinken, J., Hellsten, I., & Nerlich, B. (2008). Discourse metaphors. In Frank, R.M., Dirven, R., Ziemke, T. & Bernárdez, E. (eds.), *Body, Language and Mind, Vol. 2: Sociocultural Situatedness* (pp. 363–86). Berlin: Mouton De Gruyter.

15   Emotion

Francesco De Toni

15.1   Background, History, and Key Terms

Emotions are a fundamental part of human experience, in general and they play a particularly important role within religious contexts. Emotional life both contributes to the construction of the religious experience and is shaped by religion. On the one hand, religious experience is an emotional experience. Emotions are triggered by individual and collective religious experiences and practices, such as conversions, prayer, and religious rites. On the other hand, religion builds emotional ideologies that affect a wide array of emotional experiences and behaviours. Religion helps to regulate emotions, provides the blueprints (beliefs and rules) that define emotions typical of a creed, and fosters the socialisation of emotions within groups of believers.

Nonetheless, until recently, little attention had been paid to emotions by research on religion. As academic enquiry in the twentieth century favoured a notion of religion as a system of beliefs and behaviours, research steered away from the role of emotions in religious experiences. The perception of emotions as unsuitable for scientific enquiry and a prevailing interest for the role of sacred texts, doctrines, and beliefs on behalf of scholars of religions contributed to the neglect of emotional experiences in religious contexts (Riis and Woodhead, 2010). However, in the last couple of decades, an increasing number of scholars have turned their attention to the role of emotions in the religious experience (Corrigan, 2004, 2007), investigating the multifaceted nature of emotions as physiological, psychological, and sociocultural objects (Roberts, 2007).

Particularly relevant for the analysis of emotions in religious discourse is new research on the sociology and history of emotions, which has cast light on variation in religious emotions across social and cultural groups as well as historical periods. As Roberts (2007, p. 491) has observed, "a person's conceptual framework or worldview or self-understanding also affects his or her emotions", that is, human emotional experiences are susceptible to cultural and historical traditions. In this regard, Riis and Woodhead (2010) have proposed to adopt the notion of *emotional regime* (originally developed by Reddy 2001, with regard to the history of emotions) to describe the normative order for emotions within a given social group.

A similar yet more flexible analytical category is Rosenwein's (2002, 2006) concept of *emotional community*. Unlike emotional regimes, emotional communities do not necessarily imply an external force imposing an emotional normative order; instead, they are "groups in which people adhere to the same norms of emotional expression and value – or devalue – the same or related emotions" (Rosenwein, 2006, p. 2). These communities are usually an aspect of every social group with shared interests and stakes, and each of them is reinforced by ideologies, teachings, and common presuppositions. Rosenwein unsurprisingly identifies religious communities (specifically, mediaeval Christian monastic communities) as typical examples of emotional communities.

Each emotional community is also defined by characteristic discourse and vocabulary, which exert a controlling function over the community members by which they are shared and internalised (Rosenwein, 2006). Thus, as a means for both labelling and sharing emotions, language offers a window on individual and communal emotional experiences in religious contexts. Through the study of the language used to denote and express emotions in religious contexts, we can acquire an understanding of the role of emotions in the religious experience of individuals and communities as well as the effect of religion on emotional life.

This chapter presents a framework for describing and analysing emotional language in religious contexts. The focus is on emotions in religious contexts rather than on emotions in some narrowly defined type of religious language. In fact, the term 'religious language' may suggest that there is a special set of traits in natural languages (e.g. certain words or certain rhetorical or pragmatic structures) that we might regard as typically 'religious' and distinguishable from ordinary language. However, this is not universally true. Although some linguistic traits may be more frequent in the oral and/or written discourse of religious groups than in groups of non-believers, for example, in the use of antiquated vocabulary or the frequency of assertive and commissive speech acts (cf. McNamara and Giordano, 2018), in general, a specific 'religious language' cannot be identified as a collection of distinctive language traits. Instead, the religiosity of the language lies in the context, which we regard as religious because of the participants in the discourse (e.g. believers) and/or the purpose of the discourse (e.g. prayer or predication) (Harrison, 2007). Thus, the framework described in this chapter is not restricted to the emotions in discourse on religion (e.g. scripture) but includes the linguistic expression and representation of emotional experience in religious settings.

Research on emotions and religious language has mainly focused on how emotions in religious contexts are represented and conceptualised through processes of cognition, especially through metaphors. However, approaches that focus on language in its contexts of use can bring analytic attention to how the linguistic representation and expression of emotion are connected to the sociocultural variables that characterise the discourse. Furthermore, as emotions are integral to the context in which they arise, "emotions are always related to somebody and to something"; in this regard, emotion "is not a 'thing' but an embodied stance within the world" (Riis and Woodhead, 2010, p. 208). This consideration allows the analysis of emotion language as a case of evaluative language.

Like cognitive approaches to emotion language, the case study presented in this chapter focuses on lexical structures portraying or expressing emotional experiences (e.g. words like *anger* or *joyful*). However, the framework illustrated in the chapter may also be extended to non-lexical forms of emotional language.

To investigate the relationship between language, emotion and context, categories from *systemic-functional linguistics* (SFL) can be particularly useful. SFL is a social semiotic theory of language founded by Halliday in the 1960s, building on the of ideas of Firth. Firth's (1957) theory of language had highlighted the role of social and cultural context in the emergence of linguistic meaning: according to Firth, linguistic units or 'pieces' construct meaning by the functions they perform in the network of systems that are located at different levels of description of language. The semantic value of words, for instance, is dependent on the context in which they are used. Starting from similar premises to Firth's, Halliday's SFL describes how language functions to create meaning in context of situation, focusing on the study of the systems whereby linguistic functions are realised at each level of linguistic description. Since its foundation, SFL has found application in a wide array of linguistic domains. In fact, Halliday identified 'appliability' as a fundamental property of SLF. In Halliday's (2013, p. 128) words, SFL is a theory that "tackles problems and tries to answer questions" that are raised "not by professional linguists so much as by other people that are somehow concerned with language, whether professionally or otherwise".

One of the most well-established linguistic theories to have branched out of SFL is *appraisal theory*. Established by linguists Martin and White between the 1990s and the 2000s, appraisal theory is a systemic-functional approach to the study of the language of evaluation. The theory provides a theoretical framework to describe the expression of subjectivity of speakers/writers in discourse as they adopt stances towards the material they discuss and their audience (Martin and White, 2005). Emotion is one of the main domains of appraisal. Over the years, a number of studies have adopted and refined appraisal as a framework for studying emotions in discourse. Grounded in the same principle of appliability as SFL, appraisal is thus a useful instrument in the hands of both linguists and non-linguists to analyse emotion in religious discourse.

The analytical power of SFL and appraisal theory is based on the two fundamental concepts of system and function. *Function* denotes a set of related technical meanings in SFL that pertain to the use of language. These include both the extrinsic use of language in its context and the intrinsic organisation of language in different modes of meaning. Functions provide the organisational principles within the language system. *System* is ordering in the *paradigmatic axis* of language, which represents choice within language. A system represents patterns in "what could go instead of what" in language (Halliday and Matthiessen, 2004, p. 22) and it consists of a set of alternative terms (represented by *features*), together with an entry condition specifying the contrast between the alternatives. A system can branch into alternative subsystems, while systems can combine into system networks in a non-mutually exclusive way. In this chapter, systems and system networks are represented with SMALL CAPS.

Two other terms that we will need our analysis are *emotion talk* and *emotional talk*. These terms define an important distinction within the domain of our study. While this distinction is found in various studies on language and emotion, we adopt here the terminology and definitions of Bednarek's (2008) study, which is grounded in appraisal theory. *Emotion talk* is the language *about* emotion, that is, terms that denote emotion, such as *joy*, *hates*, and *angry*, as well as figurative expressions that are lexicalised, like *to have a broken heart*. On the other hand, *emotional talk* is language *as* emotion. This is a heterogeneous class that includes all aspects of linguistic behaviour that conventionally express or signal an emotion. Examples are interjections, evaluative adjectives, metaphors and syntactic markedness.

The notions of emotion talk and emotional talk are not mutually exclusive. In fact, instances of emotion talk (e.g. *happy*) are also instances of emotional talk, when the speaker uses them to express an emotion (e.g. *I am happy*). When it is useful to make these two notions mutually exclusive, we can follow Bednarek in restricting the definition of emotional talk to linguistic behaviour that expresses emotions without explicitly denoting them. Finally, from Bednarek (2008), we also take the terms that refer to two key semantic roles in both emotion talk and emotional talk. The *emoter* is the experiencer of the emotion; it can be either the speaker/writer or another person. The *trigger* is the stimulus of the emotion, which, in the appraisal perspective, is also the object of an evaluation.

15.2   Key Topics, Questions, and Debates

To better understand how the principles of SFL can be applied to the analysis of emotion in religious discourse, this section will introduce several key topics and debates in appraisal theory, with a focus on the practical issues that arise from applying appraisal theory to this area.

15.2.1   *The System Network of* APPRAISAL

The system network of APPRAISAL is divided in to three systems: ATTITUDE, ENGAGEMENT, and as shown in Figure 15.1.

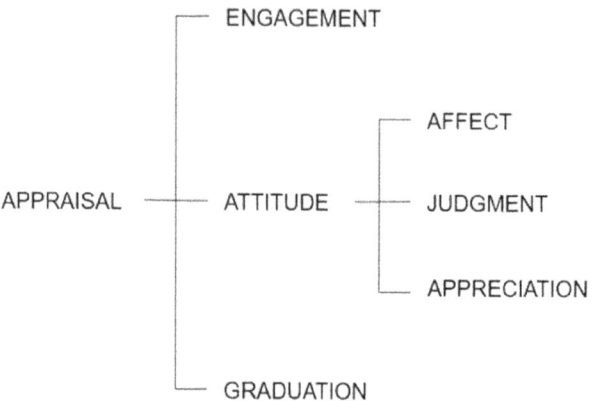

Figure 15.1 The system network of APPRAISAL

ATTITUDE is the system network of the three general classes of evaluation: emotions, ethical/moral evaluations and aesthetic evaluations. It comprises three subsystems, AFFECT is the system of emotions and feelings linguistically realised in the discourse. In Martin and White's (2005, pp. 45–56) framework, AFFECT is further divided into three subsystems:

1. UN/HAPPINESS (emotions concerned with "affairs of the heart": *the monk was sad/happy*).
2. IN/SECURITY (emotions concerned with ecosocial wellbeing: *the monk was anxious/confident*).
3. DIS/SATISFACTION (concerned with the pursuit of goals: *the monk was fed up/absorbed*).

Each of these three systems can have either positive or negative valence (e.g. unhappiness vs happiness). Bednarek (2008) has proposed a modified system of AFFECT (adapted in Figure 15.2), which redefines the existing systems and includes two new systems: DIS/INCLINATION, or emotions that refer to future emotion triggers, rather than present ones, and implies a reference to volition: *the monk desired/refused to leave*; and SURPRISE, which does not: *the monk was*

Figure 15.2 Systems of AFFECT

surprised to see a kangaroo. Unlike the three original systems defined by Martin and White, DIS/INCLINATION and SURPRISE are not characterised by valence. The subclassification of DIS/INCLINATION is based on the polarity between volition and non-volition, whether there is voluntary opposition to something or someone rather than the absence of volition. The separation of SURPRISE from the other classes is based on the absence of a pre-determined subsystem; instead, its valence is exclusively dependent on the context. Surprise can be positive or negative depending on the situation in which it is experienced.

In addition to the aforementioned system of AFFECT, AFFECT can be described through another three non-mutually exclusive subsystems. These subsystems co-occur and combine with each other and with the main system of AFFECT. Of these three systems, the first two are part of Martin and White's (2005) system network of AFFECT, while the third is an original addition by Bednarek (2008).

1. The feelings are construed as directed at or reacting to a specific trigger (*the monk was frightened by the thunder*) or as a general undirected mood with no identifiable cause (*the monk was worried*).
2. The feelings relate to existing triggers or future (imagined or forecast) triggers; this distinction corresponds to the opposition between realis (*the monk disliked leaving*) and irrealis (*the monk feared leaving*).
3. AFFECT can be either overt or covert. Overt affect concerns emotion terms that explicitly label someone's emotional response (*the monk was amazed*). Covert affect concerns emotion terms that, rather than indicating the emotional response to the person experiencing it, refer to events, things or

situations that trigger or can trigger the emotional response (*It was amazing that the bishop was late*; *sadly, they did not receive any letter from you*).

In addition to AFFECT, the system network of ATTITUDE includes two further systems. JUDGEMENT is the system of linguistic resources concerning the expression of moral or ethical evaluation of people's behaviour and character. JUDGEMENT has two main subsystems, each of which can be either positive or negative: judgements of SOCIAL ESTEEM (normality: *normal* vs *odd*; capacity: *clever* vs *stupid*; and tenacity: *brave* vs *coward*) and judgements of SOCIAL SANCTION (veracity: *honest* vs *deceitful*; propriety: *moral* vs *immoral*). APPRECIATION refers to the system of linguistic resources that concerns aesthetic evaluation of the quality of things, processes and situations. As is the case with ATTITUDE and JUDGEMENT, APPRECIATION can be either positive or negative. It comprises three subsystems: REACTION refers to the capacity of something to cause an impact on someone's attention (*captivating* vs *boring*) or an affective reaction of the type like/dislike (*beautiful* vs *ugly*); COMPOSITION concerns perceptions of balance (*symmetrical* vs *uneven*) and complexity (*pure* vs *extravagant*); and VALUATION describes the cognitive assessment of the moral value or usefulness of the evaluated thing (*original* vs *conventional*) (Martin and White, 2005).

The system of AFFECT is the main system for the analysis of the language of emotions. However, the borders between the systems of ATTITUDE are fuzzy. In particular, according to Martin and White (2005), JUDGEMENT and APPRECIATION are institutionalised systems of AFFECT that refer to institutionalised feelings, with JUDGEMENT reworking feelings concerning behaviour and APPRECIATION reworking feelings concerning the value of things. This fuzziness of systems appears particularly applicable to the study of religious discourse, given the frequent interconnection of emotions and moral and aesthetic evaluations in religious contexts, such as "judgments embodied in feelings" (Parish, 2004).

Finally, besides ATTITUDE, APPRAISAL includes two other systems. ENGAGEMENT refers to the different ways in which the speaker/writer can commit towards or align with an utterance. GRADUATION concerns the modification of the intensity of the speaker's engagement or attitude (Martin and White, 2005). While ENGAGEMENT and GRADUATION, unlike ATTITUDE, do not refer to semantic classes of evaluation, they generate different modalities through which evaluation can be expressed.

15.2.2   Degrees of Implicature

As Macken-Horarik and Isaac (2014, p. 86) write, ATTITUDE "works by degrees of implicature." Specifically, ATTITUDE develops along a cline that goes from direct to indirect forms of evaluation (Figure 15.3), in which we can identify three main types of realisation.

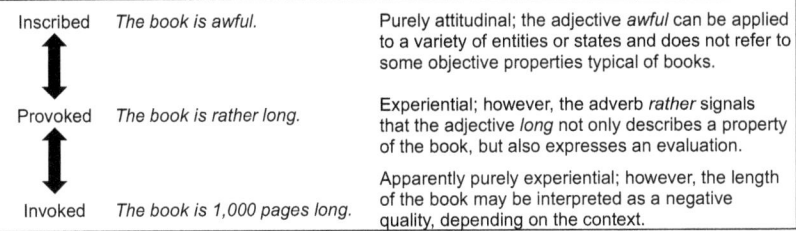

Figure 15.3 The cline of indirectness in expressing ATTITUDE

- *Inscribed* ATTITUDE is explicit evaluation, that is, evaluation realised by recognisable evaluative terms or other linguistic structures.
- *Invoked* ATTITUDE, on the other hand, replaces the explicit evaluation with a non-evaluative (experiential) term or phrase.
- In between these two extremes. we find instances of *provoked* ATTITUDE, in which the discourse is still experiential, but also includes some linguistic structure that signals the presence of an implicit evaluation.

This cline of ATTITUDE, adapted from Thompson (2014, p. 52), applies primarily to the analysis of the *expression* of emotions or emotional talk (in its broader sense), as well as to the analysis of how emotions are elicited in the listener or reader. In fact, the expression and the elicitation of AFFECT require the speaker and the listener to share some background knowledge that allows the listener to recognise *provoked* and *invoked* instances of evaluation.

A different cline of implicitness can be used to describe how AFFECT is *portrayed* in the discourse. Bednarek (2008) proposes a taxonomy of different ways in which emotions can be related through language. The most explicit way to portray emotions is to refer to the emoter's emotions through emotion terms (e.g. *the monk felt happy*) or fixed figurative expressions (e.g. *the monk's heart was broken*) that denote a mental disposition (i.e. through emotion talk). A more implicit way to portray the emotion is to replace terms and expressions denoting a mental disposition with terms denoting the embodied paralinguistic or extra-linguistic manifestation of the emotion; that is, the behavioural surge of emotion (e.g. *the monk smiled*). Terms that do not denote an emotional surge, but still refer to the emoter's behaviour (mental, linguistic, or physical) caused by the emotion, can also portray emotions implicitly (e.g. *the abbot scolded the novice*); in this perspective, emotional talk (e.g. interjections) can be regarded as a way of portraying emotion (especially when the emoter is not the speaker). Finally, the most implicit way to portray emotions is to mention only the trigger, leaving to the listener the work of identifying the elicited emotion. Figure 15.4 is adapted from Bednarek (2008, p. 150) and illustrates emotional portrayal.

Emotions named explicitly	Ways of portraying emotions	Linguistic realisation	Examples
↑	Referring to emoters' emotions	Using mental disposition terms	*anger, love, fear, sadness*
		Using fixed figurative expressions	*to have a broken heart*
	Referring to the emoters' psycho-physiological expression of emotion	Using behavioural surge terms	*cry, tremble*
	Referring to emoters' actions or behaviour	Describing mental, linguistic or physical behaviour	Mental behaviour: *more difficult to talk to, more withdrawn* Linguistic behaviour: • Speech-act terms: *scold, abuse, compliment* • Emotional talk: *wow*, inversions in syntactic order Physical behaviour • Actual: *reward, commit, comfort, flee* • Hypothetical: *I could hit you, I could kiss you*
Emotions inferred from a part of the emotion schema ↓	Referring to causes of emotions	Describing elicitors/ antecedent events	*His brother left for Australia and he hasn't seen him for ten years*

Figure 15.4 The cline of emotion portrayal

These two clines of implicitness are not mutually exclusive, as the first pertains to expressed or elicited emotions and the second to portrayed emotions. Emotion talk can be described by both clines of implicitness, as it is portrayed emotion that can also act as expressed or elicited emotion. On the other hand, emotional talk (in its stricter sense) can also be described by both clines, as it is expressed emotions that can also implicitly portray emotion. Both clines are of particular relevance for the analysis of emotion in religious discourse. First, religious discourse often implies the presence of a certain axiological ground that the speaker and the listener share or negotiate and that involves both moral and aesthetic evaluation. It is against this background that the experiential discourse in religious contexts can become provoked or invoked AFFECT. Second, the portrayal of emotion in religious discourse is often expressed through terms that do not denote mental states. Metaphors and other instances of figurative language are a frequent trait of religious discourse (cf. Dorst in this volume). Furthermore, the connection between rite and emotion in religious contexts causes emotion surges and other behavioural manifestation of emotions to acquire a prominent role in religious discourse, as it is the case, for example, with religious weeping (Ebersole, 2004; Wolfson, 2004).

15.2.3   Prosody and Instantiation

In the framework of APPRAISAL, "choices are relational" (Macken-Horarik and Isaac, 2014, p. 86). ATTITUDE and, more specifically, AFFECT propagate and spread with clusters and patterns of linguistic structures across the discourse. Different instances of ATTITUDE accumulate in a single text, contributing to the construction of the attitudinal meaning of the text. Martin and White (2005) have proposed three possible ways of structuring *prosodies* of ATTITUDE in a text (saturating, intensifying, and dominating), while Bednarek (2008) has developed an approach to the analysis of the prosody of AFFECT. Prosody highlights how multiple choices on behalf of the speaker/writer contribute to the expression of certain attitudinal and emotional positioning. For instance, Malmström (2019) has applied an integrated analysis of AFFECT and other elements of appraisal (e.g. JUDGEMENT) in two preachers' sermons to show how different APPRAISAL profiles express opposite interreligious positions.

The notion of prosody is linked with *instantiation*. According to Martin and White (2005), APPRAISAL can be realised at different levels in a cline of instantiation (i.e. generalisation) that ranges from the language system as a whole and the individual listener/reader's interpretation of the discourse. Between these two extremes, we have intermediate levels of realisation of the language potential; namely, register, text type, and instance. Each of these levels of the general realisation of language is mapped to a level of instantiation of evaluation and is adapted from Thompson (2014, p. 61) in Figure 15.5.

In the same way as the presence of prosody in a single instance (i.e. a single text) produces the attitudinal meaning of the text, the presence of recurring clusters and patterns of ATTITUDE in the same text types and registers produces, respectively, attitudinal stances and keys. When we focus our attention only on AFFECT (emotion), we can talk of affective key and affective stance.

Affective key and affective stance resonate with the idea of emotional communities (including religious communities) as social groups sharing common emotional values, norms, and practices – in our case, linguistic practices. Indeed, as Macken-Horarik and Isaac (2014, p. 87) have noted, in the system of APPRAISAL "choices are institutionally and culturally constrained". However, we must be careful when mapping the sociocultural concept of emotional

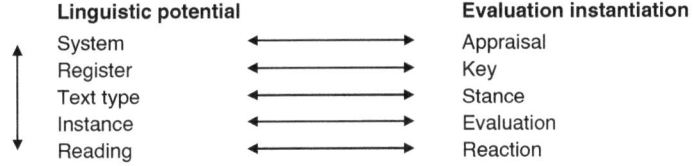

Figure 15.5   The cline of instantiation

community to the linguistic system of APPRAISAL. Key and stance depend on linguistic variables (register and text type) that are likely to be shared across multiple emotional communities. In this regard, comparison of texts from multiple genres and text types would be the ideal approach for identifying evidence of shared emotional values in emotional communities.

15.2.4   Identifying and Systematising AFFECT

One major challenge is that emotions are essentially complex objects (Weigand, 2004). Among the factors determining this complexity, there are:

- the indeterminacy of the concept of emotion (multiple definitions of emotions exists in the psychological literature and different psychological approaches propose different types of emotions);
- the contrast between universalists approaches to emotion (emotions as innate objects shared by all human beings) and sociocultural approaches (emotions as cultural objects that vary across social groups);
- the pervasive presence of emotions at all levels of linguistic realisation, from phonology to pragmatics.

In Martin and White's (2005) original theory of appraisal, the classification of AFFECT is essentially top-down and is based on the semantic opposition between pairs of English terms that act as the prototypical examples of the subsystems of AFFECT. On the other hand, Bednarek's (2008) revised model of AFFECT is more empirically informed and relies on the analysis of the lexico-grammatical and pragmatic properties of emotion talk in a multi-genre corpus of present-day English texts.

Nonetheless, since appraisal theory is built on functional distinctions rather than formal ones, mapping functions to their linguistic forms is an inherent challenge of this approach. First, we need to define what linguistic choices we intend to analyse in the discourse. Analysis of emotion talk (explicitly portrayed and inscribed AFFECT) is usually more straightforward as it can be based on a set of words and phrases that are selected as relevant emotion terms. This is a lexical approach that has also been commonly adopted in research on emotional communities. However, while in qualitative studies the researcher can apply their discernment in determining what terms are to be regarded as instances of AFFECT, in quantitative studies it is usually necessary to have a list of terms to be searched. How to construct such a list is an open question. Semantic databases (such as WordNet and other databases modelled on WordNet) and conceptual dictionaries can be a useful resource to build such lists. However, due to the sensitivity of emotion language to the cultural context, these tools alone may not be sufficient to analyse emotion talk in religious discourse, especially for texts from the past. Specific methodologies and considerations usually need to be developed for each study.

A second challenge is the analysis of implicit portrayal of emotions (e.g. behavioural, including emotional talk) as well as provoked or invoked affect. Compared to identifying inscribed affect, identifying implicit ways of portraying, expressing, or eliciting emotions is considerably more complex, due to their strong dependency from context. Macken-Horakik and Isaac (2014) suggest conducting the analysis of inscribed affect and provoked or invoked affect in sequential steps, so the analysis of provoked or invoked affect can benefit from the insight of the analysis of inscribed affect. However, this may not always be feasible, especially in studies on a large number of texts. This challenge is not exclusive of the SFL approach and is a common obstacle in the analysis of emotion language. In fact, historical research on emotional communities has been almost exclusively limited to emotion talk (Rosenwein, 2008).

Identifying the functions that depend from AFFECT and, more generally, from ATTITUDE is also a challenge in quantitative studies based on appraisal theory, especially as regards emoters and triggers. Different linguistic structures can realise the emoter and the trigger. Sometimes the emoter and the trigger can be derived from the properties (e.g. part of speech) of the linguistic structure portraying, expressing, or eliciting the emotion. For instance, with the verb *to hope*, the emoter is usually the subject of the verb, while the future event that triggers the evaluation is the subordinate clause depending from the verb (e.g. *I hope you will come*). However, in many instances, the mapping between emoters or triggers and their linguistic realisation is less straightforward (i.e. cannot be defined by simple rules). A special case is when the emoter or the trigger are not even linguistically encoded in the sentence; for instance, in the sentence, *there is no hope that he will come*, the emoter of *hope* is not encoded in the sentence and needs to be retrieved from the context.

Finally, a structural challenge in appraisal theory is that the system of APPRAISAL itself (as presented in Figures 15.1 and 15.2) was developed based on semantic oppositions in present-day English. These same oppositions may not prove to be true in different or more specific cultural contexts (including religious contexts) or in other languages. In fact, as Bednarek (2008) modified Martin and White's system of APPRAISAL on the basis of empirical evidence, it is useful to approach the system of APPRAISAL as a research blueprint, which does not necessarily encode linguistic truth in religious discourse(s) and which can be adapted in the light of linguistic evidence. Reviews of the inherent challenges of appraisal theory and a discussion of the methodological approach to appraisal analysis can be found in Macken-Horarik and Isaac (2014). Overall, while the appraisal framework offers a useful set of categories for describing emotion in discourse, the researcher must also reflect on these categories and consider whether they require adaptation based on the linguistic data that are being analysed.

15.3   Case Study

The application of the SFL and appraisal approach to emotions in religious discourse will be presented here in a qualitative analysis of a few examples from the multilingual correspondence of a community of European Catholic missionaries in nineteenth-century Australia. The community belonged to the mission of New Norcia, established by Benedictine monks in 1846 with the purpose of evangelising the Aboriginal people of Western Australia. Correspondence had an essential role in maintaining personal and political ties between the members of the mission and between them and their confreres in Europe. The examples here are drawn from a corpus of 235 letters in Italian and Spanish written by a group of Italian and Spanish missionaries and by their European correspondents in the period 1850–93, plus a group of nine long letters in French written by a French missionary in the years 1846–7. The corpus of letters in Italian and Spanish are preserved in the New Norcia Archives and in other religious archives in Italy (see De Toni, 2020). The letters in French are preserved in the archives of Solesmes Abbey, France, with English translations published in Fonteinne (2014). The examples are characterised by the presence of emotion talk pertaining to the system of UN/HAPPINESS, and they will enable us to examine the interpersonal functions of emotion in the discourse of a religious community. Relevant instances of emotion talk are in **bold** in the excerpts and in the English translations; with few exceptions, original spelling and punctuation have been maintained.

Across all the three languages, directed emotion talk pertaining to UN/HAPPINESS with positive valence (e.g. terms in the semantic field of affection/love) tend to cluster around a recurring trigger, that is, the membership in the monastic community expressed as the relationship with a confrere, a single monastic community and/or the Benedictine order. In some examples, these instances of emotion talk are also instances of emotional talk, that is, expressions of the letter-writer's emotions as represented in the letters. See the following excerpts from two letters written from Western Australia by Brother Léandre Fontainne, former monk of Solesmes Abbey, to Prosper Guéranger, the Abbot of Solemes. The first letter follows an official piece of correspondence that Fonteinne had written to Guéranger.

1. *Elle est donc terminée et close, cette lettre officielle, dans laquelle je ne pouvais dire tout à mon aise à mon bien **aimé** Père. Combien je l'**aime**, combien je **pleure** de ne le plus voir, combien mon âme se trouve toute **désolée** de son éloignement*
    At last it's all finished and sealed that official letter in which I couldn't tell everything to my **beloved** Father, at my ease. How I **love** him, how I **weep** not to be seeing him anymore, how my soul feels completely **desolate** because of his distance.

(L. Fonteinne to P. Guéranger, 14 January 1846, Archives of Solesmes Abbey [ASB], *fonds* Dom Guéranger, *section* Correspondances; ref. 5806 in (Fonteinne, 2014))

2. *Adieu bien **aimé** et tendre Père. Adieu. Ah combien je vous **aime**, je ne puis me lasser de vous le dire. Je vous **aime** tant, je suis si privé de ne vous avoir plus. [. . .] Adieu encore, adieu, adieu. Bénissez votre enfant qui vous **aime** et vous embrasse, mille et mille fois*

   Farewell my **beloved** and tender Father, Farewell. Ah, how much I **love** You, I cannot get tired of telling you so. I **love** you so much and I am so long deprived at not having you anymore. Farewell again, farewell, farewell. Bless your son who **loves** You and who embraces you, one thousand times and one thousand more.

   (L. Fonteinne to P. Guéranger, 16 January 1846, Archives of Solesmes Abbey [ASB], *fonds* Dom Guéranger, Correspondances; ref. 5810)

In both Examples (1) and (2), the degree of implicature is very low. AFFECT is inscribed with the overt emotion term *aimer* 'to love' and both the emoter (*je* 'I'; *votre enfant . . . qui* 'your son . . . who') and the trigger (*le* 'him'; *vous* 'You') are encoded in the sentences. On the other hand, the past participle *aimé* 'loved/beloved' is an example of conventionalised covert emotion term, which syntactically refers to its trigger, leaving the emoter unexpressed and implied.

Emotion terms pertaining to the semantic area of love are also found in the letters in Spanish and Italian, always to denote the feelings between peers or directed from an inferior to a superior (as in a paradigmatic father-son relationship). See the following excerpt, which is from a letter that the founder and Abbot of New Norcia, Bishop Rosendo Salvado, wrote to Fr Venancio Garrido, one his closest collaborators at New Norcia and future Prior of the community. Salvado wrote the letter shortly before Garrido's departure for Ceylon, after the administrator of the diocese of Perth temporarily expelled Garrido from Western Australia for some unknown internal contrasts.

3. *Aqui nadie sabe lo que pasa sobre su marcha de U.[d], pero asi que lo sepan (los hermanos misioneros [. . .]) no me costarà poco travajo el consolarles, ya que del primero al ultimo le **aman** y respectan como Padre, lo que a U.[d] no es desconocido*

   Here nobody knows what is happening regarding your departure, because as soon as they (the missionary confreres [. . .]) know it, it will take me no little effort to console them, since, from the first of them to the last, they **love** and respect You as a Father, which something You do not ignore.

   (R. Salvado to V. Garrido, 24 April 1858, New Norcia Archives [NNA] 2234A-13–034)

The following example, on the other hand, shows a higher degree of implicature. The excerpt is from one of Garrido's reply to Salvado.

4. *. . . por fin ha llegado la hora en que [. . .] debamos poner no solo tierra, sino mar por medio. Esta es bien pequeña diferencia para los que se **aman** de veras en el*

*Señor, de los quales dice S. Bernardo "que no estan menos donde **aman**, que donde animan" lo que seria lo mismo que decir a U. Yllm.a y a la Mission Benedictina de Nueva Nursia que **mi corazon se queda aqui**, mi cuerpo unicamente es obligado a dejarse de la playas de la Australia*

... at last the time has come when [. . .] we have to put not only land, but also the sea between us. There is very little difference for those who truly **love** each other in God, about whom St Bernard says that "they are not less where they love than where they live"; which is the same as to tell Your Grace and the Benedictine Mission of New Norcia that **my heart stays here**, and only my body is forced to leave the beaches of Australia.

(V. Garrido to R. Salvado, 28 July 1858, NNA, 2234A-13–094)

In Example (4), emotion talk is still present, but one of the instances (*mi corazon se queda aqui* 'my heart stays here') is metaphorical (the frequency of the metaphor of the heart for the writer's affection or feelings in the corpus and in nineteenth-century lexicographic sources allows us to regard this as a rather strongly fixed figurative expression). Only this second instance is also emotional talk, the author being encoded as the emoter by the pronoun *mi* 'my'. The other two instances (the second of which is in a quote from Bernard of Clairvaux) do not inscribe emotion; however, the whole period *Esta es . . . animan* (note the evaluation *bien pequeña diferencia* 'very little difference') works as provoked AFFECT, as suggested by the phrase *lo que seria lo mismo* 'which is the same as' connecting it to the instance of invoked AFFECT *mi corazon se queda aqui*.

On the other hand, negative emotion terms in the system of UN/HAPPINESS are recurrently triggered by the separation of the missionaries from their community and from the mission. We can observe this in the next two examples, which are from two letters sent by another member of New Norcia's community, the Italian priest Raffaele Martelli, to Salvado on the occasion of Garrido's departure.

5. *Se v'è cosa che in parte mitighi il mio **dolore** e **sgomento** alla immeritata sorte che è toccata a questo ns. venerato Confratello è la il sentirlo parlare con ferma fiducia di ritorno a questa Missione*

If there is anything that soothes my **pain** and **dismay** at the undeserved fate that has befallen this venerated confrere of ours [Garrido], it is hearing him talking with firm confidence about his return to this Mission.

(R. Martelli to R. Salvado, 19 July 1858, NNA, 2234A-13–358)

6. *Lo stato del nostro animo V. Eccellenza lo può immaginare. Le ultime sue parole al separarci in sulla spiaggia non le dimenticherò facilmente. "Perhaps it is for the good of this Mission". Era profondamente **commosso**. Stringendo le mie nelle sue mani, aggiunse "if it is not for punishment of my sins"*

Your Excellency can imagine what state our souls were in. I will not easily forget his last words when we separated on the beach. "Perhaps it is for the

good of this mission". He was deeply **moved**. Holding my hands in his, he added "if it is not for punishment of my sins".
(R. Martelli to R. Salvado, 28 July 1858, NNA, 2234A-13–363)

In Example (5), the expression of pain is inscribed through emotion talk (*dolore* 'pain/sorrow') triggered by Garrido's departure. On the other hand, in Example (6), the emotion talk (*commosso* 'moved') has the function of portraying the emotions of a third party (Garrido). This combines with an instance of implied portrayed emotion, namely *stringendo le mie nelle sue mani* 'holding my hands in his', which belongs to the second lowest level of implicitness and the second highest level of implicature in Bednarek's cline of emotion portrayal, namely portrayal of behaviour (other than emotional surge) caused by emotion. In this regard, in Example (1) the emotion term *pleur* '(I) weep' expresses negative UN/HAPPINESS through its behavioural surge and intermediate level of implicature.

In all the examples, the instances of emotion talk combine with other emotion terms and/or with other linguistic structures that express emotion or portray emotion, with varying degrees of implicature. This process of saturation of the message with affect contributes to the construction of its interpersonal meaning and facilitates the recognition of the patterns of affect we are analysing here. The overall result is the emergence of an instantiation of the system of AFFECT in which UN/HAPPINESS is frequently associated with the triggers mentioned above.

Further analysis of the corpus in Spanish and Italian also reveals another cluster of emotion talk that cuts across multiple subsystems of AFFECT (with negative and/or positive valence) and is triggered by the letter writers' striving for reducing physical distance with their interlocutors. overall description of the system of AFFECT in this case study is illustrated in Figure 15.6.

This taxonomy, which was driven by the analysis of triggers and emoters, rather than by a top-down categorisation process, represents the affective key of the correspondence analysed as well as a linguistic realisation of the set of norms and values that characterised the correspondents and their confreres as an emotional community. Some of these traits seem to be typical of the Christian monastic and missionary contexts; for example, framing monastic ties as father–son relationships (cf. D'Acunto, 2010), and the expression of

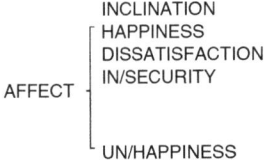

Figure 15.6 AFFECT types in the correspondence in Italian and Spanish

missionary zeal. However, some of the properties of AFFECT in the letters also align with the stylistic conventions of nineteenth-century private letter writing. Thus, AFFECT in each letter depends on both a register-specific affective key and a genre-specific stance.

15.4   Future Directions

The application of appraisal theory to the study of emotion in religious discourse crosses several areas of enquiry in the domain of language and religion. In these areas, the integration of appraisal theory with other linguistic perspectives has the potential to exploit the explanatory power of appraisal and, at the same time, overcome some of the limitation of this theory. Three of these areas are presented below as topics for future research on emotion in religious discourse.

The first area pertains to the role of cognition in emotion discourse. Metaphors are one of the most extensively explored topics in linguistic research on religious discourse, most frequently through the lens of cognitive approaches (Chilton and Kopytowska, 2018). On the other hand, fixed figurative expressions (metaphors, metonymies, etc.) are one of the possible ways to portray emotions and to express them with a relatively low level of implicature; the substitution of mental-disposition emotion terms (e.g. *anger*) with their psycho-physiological manifest-ation (e.g. *to cry*) is also a metonymic process. However, as a social-functional theory of language, appraisal is not concerned with the cognitive processes underlying the functioning of emotion in discourse. Bednarek (2009) has shown that appraisal can be fruitfully integrated with cognitive linguistics to investigate the emotional schemata that organise mental knowledge about emotions. The study of emotion in religious discourse would especially benefit from the application of this integrated approach. An application would be the study of different forms of socially and culturally distributed emotional cognition in religious discourse, leveraging appraisal's focus on interpersonal meaning. For example, this approach could be applied to the study of the interface between emotional stance or key and the "cognitive register" underlying the functioning of certain types of religious discourse, such as prayer (Downes, 2018).

The second area for future research concerns the role of shared emotional norms and values in religious discourse. In this chapter, I have adopted the notion of emotional community to explain the presence of shared linguistic patterns of emotion language (cf. also Rosowsky in this volume). However, religious discourse does not necessarily happen within cohesive emotional communities. Emotions also play a key role in religious discourse between different emotional communities or within what we might call *polyemotional communities*, that is, social communities where multiple emotional values, norms and practices coexist and possibly clash. Examples are online conflictual discourse between believers of different creeds (Pihlaja, 2018; S. Pihlaja in this volume), heretical discourse, and also the discourse in religious missions and proselyting, in general. These are situations in which we would expect a clash of emotional keys or even of systems of APPRAISAL, with possible positive or negative effects on the communication process.

Differences in religious and emotional background knowledge may cause the failure of invoked AFFECT, causing implied AFFECT to be misinterpreted or go unrecognised. Furthermore, rhetorical usage of AFFECT plays a key role in proselyting's and preaching to emotional communities other than one's own or in polyemotional communities. Religious discourse between emotional communities or within polyemotional communities may generate structural changes in the emotional values, norms, and practices of the communities through processes of evaluation and cognition that may call for the cognitive approach to APPRAISAL proposed above. Similarly, the study of the expression and portrayal of AFFECT in texts that testify to change in an individual's or a community's religious values (e.g. conversion narratives) would benefit from integrating appraisal theory and the cognitive-linguistic approach.

The last area of research concerns multilingualism in religious discourse. Appraisal theory was first developed as a descriptive system of the English language. Although studies have applied appraisal to the study of languages other than English, our knowledge of how appraisal works across languages is still limited. Research on emotions in religious discourse would especially benefit from filling this knowledge gap. Besides applications to the translation of sacred texts (Wilson in this volume), a particularly interesting domain of enquiry are the strategies to provoke and invoke religious AFFECT across different languages. The implicatures that determine the successful portrayal or expression of emotions in religious discourse are likely to depend not only on the presence or absence of a shared religious background, but also on the language being used. Combined with the observations presented here on clashing of norms between and within emotional communities, further investigation in this area would benefit both inter-religious and intra-religious communication.

15.5   References

Bednarek, M. (2008). *Emotion Talk across Corpora*. Basingstoke: Palgrave Macmillan.
Bednarek, M. (2009). Emotion talk and emotional talk: Cognitive and discursive perspectives. In H. Pishwa (ed.), Language and Social Cognition. *Expression of the Social Mind* (pp. 395–431). Berlin: Mouton de Gruyter.
Chilton, P., & Kopytowska, M. (eds.). (2018). *Religion, Language and the Human Mind*. Oxford: Oxford University Press.

Corrigan, J. (ed.). (2004). *Religion and Emotion: Approaches and Interpretation.* Oxford: Oxford University Press.

Corrigan, J. (ed.). (2007). *The Oxford Handbook of Religion and Emotion.* Oxford: Oxford University Press.

D'Acunto, N. (2010). *Amicitia monastic*a: considerazioni introduttive. *Reti Medievali Rivista,* 11(1), 123–9.

De Toni, F. (2020). Expressing friendship in letters: Conventionality and sincerity in the multilingual correspondence of nineteenth-century Catholic churchmen. *Multilingua,* 39(1), 33–58.

Downes, W. (2018). Linguistics and the scientific study of religion: Prayer as a cognitive register. In P. Chilton & M. Kopytowska (eds.), *Religion, Language and the Human Mind* (pp. 115–33). Oxford: Oxford University Press.

Ebersole, G. L. (2004). The function of ritual weeping revisited: Affective expression and moral discourse. In J. Corrigan (ed.), *Religion and Emotion: Approaches and Interpretation* (pp. 185–222). Oxford: Oxford University Press.

Firth, J. (1957). *Papers in Linguistics 1934–1951.* Oxford: Oxford University Press.

Fonteinne, L. a. (2014). *The Correspondence of Léandre Fonteinne* (P. Gilet, trans.). Northcote, Victoria, AUS: Morning Star.

Halliday, M. A. K. (2013). Putting linguistic theory to work. In J. J. Wbster (ed.), *The Collected Works of M.A.K. Halliday,* Vol. 11 : *Halliday in the 21st Century* (pp. 127–41). London: Bloomsbury.

Halliday, M. A. K., & Matthiessen, C. M. I. M. (2004). *An Introduction to Functional Grammar.* London: Arnold.

Harrison, V. (2007). Metaphor, religious language, and religious experience. *Sophia,* 46(2), 127–45.

Macken-Horarik, M., & Isaac, A. (2014). Appraising appraisal. In G. Thompson & A. Alba-Juez (eds.), *Evaluation in Context* (pp. 67–92). Amsterdam: John Benjamins.

Malmström, H. (2019). Appraisal, preaching and the religious other: The rhetorical appropriation of interreligious positions in sermonic discourse. *International Journal of Practical Theology,* 22(1), 40–57.

Martin, J. R., & White, P. R. R. (2005). *The Language of Evaluation: Appraisal in English.* Basingstoke/New York: Palgrave Macmillan.

McNamara, P., & Giordano, M. (2018). Cognitive neuroscience and religious language: A working hypothesis. In P. Chilton & M. Kopytowska (eds.), *Religion, Language and the Human Mind* (pp. 115–34). Oxford: Oxford University Press.

Parish, S. M. (2004). The sacred mind: Newar cultural representations of mental life and the production of moral consciousness. In J. Corrigan (ed.), *Religion and Emotion: Approaches and Interpretation* (pp. 149–84). Oxford: Oxford University Press.

Pihlaja, S. (2018). *Religious Talk Online: The Evangelical Discourse of Muslims, Christians, and Atheists* Cambridge: Cambridge University Press.

Reddy, W. M. (2001). *The Navigation of Feeling: A Framework for the History of Emotions.* Cambridge: Cambridge University Press.

Riis, O., & Woodhead, L. (2010). *A Sociology of Religious Emotions.* Oxford: Oxford University Press.

Roberts, R. C. (2007). Emotions research and religious experience. In J. Corrigan (ed.), *The Oxford Handbook of Religion and Emotion* (pp. 490–506). Oxford: Oxford University Press.

Rosenwein, B. H. (2002). Worrying about emotions in history. *American Historical Review*, 107(3), 821–45.

Rosenwein, B. H. (2006). *Emotional Communities in the early Middle Ages*. Ithaca/London: Cornell University Press.

Rosenwein, B. H. (2008). Emotion words. In P. Nagy & D. Boquet (eds.), *Les sujet des émotions au Moyen Âge* (pp. 93–106). Paris: Beauchesne.

Thompson, G. (2014). Affect and emotion, target-value mismatches, and Russain dolls. In G. Thompson & A. Alba-Juez (eds.), *Evaluation in Context* (pp. 47–66). Amsterdam: John Benjamins.

Weigand, E. (2004). Emotions: The simple and the complex. In E. Weigadn (ed.), *Emotion in Dialogic Interaction* (pp. 3–21). Amsterdam/Philadelphia: John Benjamins.

Wolfson, E. R. (2004). Weeping, death, and spiritual ascent in sixteenth-century Jewish mysticism. In J. Corrigan (ed.), *Religion and Emotion: Approaches and Interpretation* (pp. 271–303). Oxford: Oxford University Press.

16　Identity

Helen Ringrow

16.1　Background, History, and Key Terms

Identity plays an important role in religious discourse, particularly the elements of gender, ethnicity, and class in individual and societal contexts. The essence of identity is difficult to pin down and invites a myriad of definitions, but the simplest exposition is that identity is *who we are*, or, as is often more accurately the case, who we are *not*. Who we are (not) may relate to gender, age, sexuality, socioeconomic status, professional affiliation, religious faith, language (including dialect, accent, and first language), disability, politics, race, nationality, and a host of other factors. Through examining historical approaches to identity from a range of diverse traditions, we can track a move from viewing identity as a fixed, inherent component of the self to a more fluid, complex construction which may change over time and according to different social contexts and purposes (Asprey and Lawson, 2018; Joseph, 2004). Crucially for linguists, this newer perspective on identity emphasises that identity is constructed *through language* (Benwell and Stokoe, 2006), and that linguistic analysis can help us to better understand the concept of identity. Any discussion of religious identity should consider, therefore, the role of language in its construction.

　　Religion may provide individuals and communities with a common identity; a shared sense of self based on core beliefs and practices (see *Community* this volume). Jackson and Hogg (2010, p. 632) argue: 'Religious identity describes how a person or group understands, experiences, shapes, and is shaped by the psychological, social, political, and devotional facets of religious belonging or affiliation'. They emphasise that there is not just one discrete theory of religious identity. Instead, the category invites discussion from different perspectives including psychology, sociology, politics, theology, and philosophy (Jackson and Hogg, 2010, p. 632). Analysing identity in religious discourse has indeed tended to cross disciplinary boundaries and theoretical approaches. As such, it is difficult to narrow down what exactly fits into this category. In this chapter, I reference studies which focus on language and/or have implications for language analysis; this leads to discussion of a diverse range of research.

This chapter surveys key research in the field, but due to constraints of space, the development and diversity of the field, and the researcher's own research specialisms, this chapter will provide specific coverage of certain religious traditions in a sample of geographical areas. The case study (Section 16.3) focuses on Latter-day Saint and Evangelical Christian women.

For religious identity, we can consider how speakers use language to *communicate* or *enact* their religious faith (e.g. in everyday conversation; see Joseph 2004 for a range of case studies on this topic) and how religious faith is *represented* by religious groups themselves (e.g. how religious women describe their faith in personal blogs; see the case study in Section 16.3) and by those outside of the faith (e.g. how British newspapers discuss Islam; see, for example, Richardson 2004). Belonging to a faith group can be of increasing or decreasing importance depending on one's current circumstances or stage in life, and faith membership is normally only one element of an individual's overall identity. Religious identities, however salient, often provide the backdrop to our lives and may influence our life decisions, both big and small. As Joseph (2004, p. 172) suggests:

[Religious identities] supply the plot of the stories of our lives, singly and collectively, and are bound up with our deepest beliefs about life, the universe and everything. Moreover, in most cultures ethnic and religious identities are bound up with reproduction, in the sense that they limit who one can marry, whether endogamy or exogamy is the cultural norm.

Religious identities are clearly separate from the state in some parts of the world; elsewhere, religious beliefs significantly shape governmental structures and laws, in addition to cultural norms (Jackson, 2014). Religious identities 'come to life', as it were, through the language we use to talk about them. These religious identities are not necessarily detached from other elements of identity. This leads us to the concept of intersectionality. Intersectionality, primarily attributed to the seminal work of Crenshaw (1989), is crucial to any analysis of identity. This concept refers broadly to how different people can belong to multiple groups. More specifically, intersectionality theory argues that if an individual belongs to more than one marginalised group, this can lead to intensified oppression and/or more than one type of disempowerment. For the purposes of analysing religious discourse in particular, intersectionality considers how religious faith identity overlaps with other aspects of identity such as race, ethnicity, gender, sexuality, disability, age, nationality, profession, marital status, political beliefs, socioeconomic background, and so on. We can consider what advantages or disadvantages multiple group memberships may bring.

How to approach intersectionality in practice, however, is not always very straightforward. Many individuals belong to a range of marginalised group identities that are often a direct result of societal power imbalances. It can therefore be difficult to properly address and analyse how this myriad of subject positions operates simultaneously and holistically (cf. Nash, 2008, p. 4–5). It may, in fact, be impossible for the applied linguistics researcher to appropriately address and consider all aspects of identity in their language analysis, but an increased awareness and sensitivity to the complicated identities most people hold (and their consequences) is an excellent starting point for any linguist exploring language and religious identity (Block and Corona, 2016).

Religious identity can connect people from different backgrounds, but does not necessarily obliterate other aspects of identity difference. For example, Hasidic Jewish women living in Bnei Brak, Tel Aviv, Israel, and those living in Crown Heights, Brooklyn, New York, may share a common religious identity (which could include core beliefs, some of which are manifested through dress and appearance), but to some extent their identity is influenced by their immediate geographical location. The language they use on a daily basis, how they communicate their faith, and whether they face religious discrimination has the potential to be shaped by national identity, family background, political environment, social class, marital status, age, and so on, highlighting both the complexity of religious identity and its intersection with other factors.

16.2   Key Topics, Questions, and Debates

16.2.1   Trends in Linguistic Analysis and Identity Research

Certain trends can be ascertained from surveying the literature on linguistic analysis and identity (see chapter 3 of Joseph 2004 for an excellent overview of relevant research). These trends all have potential applications in the field of religious discourse. For example, language is now seen an important identity element to explore *in and of itself*, and not simply as a communicative or instrumental tool to do other things (although, of course, it also fulfils this role in certain contexts). There is an increased emphasis on how people use and adapt language to carry out 'identity work', including making certain aspects of their identity more salient through the language they use. In keeping with broader trends in linguistics focusing more on reader reception as opposed to text production (Browse, 2018), how people *interpret* different kinds of identities is given increased importance in the literature. For example, if religious social media users are attempting to spread their message online, they must be very aware of how they represent their identity, and how they also tailor their message to the identity of their perceived (and often complicated) target audience (Pihlaja, 2018). Another salient area of growth explores how individuals *self-identify*, especially if this self-identification contrasts with more 'official' (often institutional) identity labels. The *fluid* nature of identity also comes across strongly in more recent linguistic work, moving away from earlier scholarship which viewed identity as somewhat more static. These trends have seen an analysis of a diverse range of identities in different types of data, such as commodified identities in advertising (Benwell and Stokoe, 2006) and institutional identities in organisations (Chun, 2016).

16.2.2   'Sacred' versus 'Secular': Blurred Identity Boundaries

Identity labels are a complex domain for language analysis, especially if these labels are controversial, contested, or hold potentially negative connotations for the reader. Labels to describe religious identity are certainly multifarious and open to interpretation. It is worth considering whether the labels we use are both sufficient and/or reflective of reality. How do labels mark religious identity? What do they tell us about where we draw the boundaries between religious faiths? If, for example, a news article refers to 'the Judeo-Christian tradition', this usage may be an attempt to bring some groups together while potentially shutting others out. This is not always insidious but can sometimes be a deliberate strategy to highlight common ground, or lack thereof, between particular religious (and, often by extension, political) groups. Of relevance here is van Dijk's (1993) work on 'Us/Them' discourses where groups can be linguistically formed through language practices. Building on this idea of Us versus Them, we can consider how adherents of some religious faiths (e.g. Muslims in much mainstream British media) are represented as the 'Other' (cf. Baker et al., 2013). Media texts may foreground religious identity over other aspects, which could be just as relevant: as Gunning and Jackson (2011) point out, 'religious terrorism' is not always inherently 'religious'. If this 'religious' label is employed, we should question why it has been chosen over alternatives. As critical discourse analysis and critical stylistics research argues again and again, language choice is rarely neutral and merits close investigation to ascertain the underlying ideologies (Jeffries, 2010).

Crucially, the labels given to certain groups may not always be their pre-ferred ones or the ones they would choose themselves. *Avowed identity* is the identity we express or highlight to other people; *ascribed identity* is the identity other people give to us or we give to them. These two identity types may not always match (Jackson, 2014). For example, some scholars have argued for the use of the label 'nonliberal' as opposed to 'fundamentalist' religious groups, because the latter can have certain racist, nationalist, and violent connotations which may be inaccurate or inappropriate (Fader, 2009; Mahmood, 2005). Identity labels can change and can also be contested, especially where groups feel labels no longer appropriately reflect them (Caldas-Coulthard and Iedema, 2016). A good example here is the Church of Jesus Christ of Latter-day Saints, which announced in 2018, it would be retiring the monikers 'Mormon' and

'LDS', recommending the original Church title be used. The Church President, Russell M. Nelson, explained:

For much of the world, the Lord's Church is presently disguised as the 'Mormon Church.' But we as members of the Lord's Church know who stands at its head: Jesus Christ Himself [...] I realize with profound regret that we have unwittingly acquiesced in the Lord's restored Church being called by other names, each of which expunges the sacred name of Jesus Christ! (LDS Newsroom, n.d.)

The Church now encourages the use of the full official title wherever possible to (re)emphasise their focus on following Jesus Christ. This revised label, then, is an attempt to reinforce the Church identity, although it may not always match up with how people use these labels in practice.

An oft-rehearsed religious labelling distinction is that of the *secular* versus the *sacred*. However, these labels and the boundaries they attempt to draw are often not so clear-cut. As explained in Fader's study of young Orthodox Jewish girls in Brooklyn, Hasidic Jews in New York conflate and challenge the perceived sacred/secular dichotomy in several ways (Fader, 2009). Hasidic Jewish women in North America must often navigate the 'secular' world and use it to their advantage, such as by working in the 'secular' domain, earning money so that their husbands can focus on their divine calling of Torah study (cf. Fader, 2009, pp. 1–4, 42, 148, 150). As such, 'Hasidic women's authoritative version of religious modernity dismantles an opposition between the secular and the religious that is central to social scientific definitions of the modern' (Fader, 2009, p. 3). Engaging with the secular world is allowed, but this engagement must be 'made to serve Hasidic goals of community building and redemption' (p. 148). What can we comfortably label 'sacred' as opposed to 'secular', then, is not so clear-cut.

16.2.3   *Linguistic Markers of Religious Identity and Community*

In many contexts, language use indexes a particular religious identity. This usage may be a deliberate choice or it may be subconscious. In any case, it is often linked to cultural and regional norms. There may not always be a choice, and some choices have serious social consequences (see Souza, 2010, on linguistic identity markers in a Brazilian Portuguese educational context; see Avni, 2012, on Hebrew-Only language policies in religious schools). Linguistic markers may inform others of both your group membership and your relative status within that group. Young Jewish men, for example, show a certain level of knowledge of Hebrew to demonstrate their bar mitzvah status (Joseph, 2004). Another example is the phrase *inshallah* (God willing) for Arabic speakers across the globe; this expression is extremely commonplace, going beyond a strictly religious expression in many contexts. Clift and Helani (2010), for example, consider the use of *inshallah* to shift the topic of conversation in naturally occurring Levantine Arabic interactions recorded in Syria and in the UK. Language can also mark a certain level of linguistic piety, as when Amish and Menonnite communities (nonliberal Christian sects) often use the (older) King James Version of the Bible, a version they regard as more 'pure' (Joseph, 2004).

Some religious groups, especially those in diaspora who then become a minority in their new home, turn to linguistic purism as a way of marking their identities in a new world, but others do not. Hasidic Jews in North America resolve language gaps 'by the replacing of the forgotten language with the new, changing its orthography and bracketing the innovation with quotation marks' (Fader, 2009, p. 110). Hasidic Jews want to keep their traditions, but they are willing to adapt modern North American English for specific linguistic purposes (Fader, 2009). English, then, takes on a certain Hassidic 'flavour' as an identity marker in diaspora. Rowosky's chapter in this volume (*Community*) discusses these issues in depth.

Digital and non-digital religious communities are a crucial area for linguistic researchers to explore, especially in terms of how language helps construct and maintain such communities, and how language conveys key beliefs and key identity markers. For example, Pihlaja (2018) examines how religious communities are created on YouTube, while Koller (2017) analyses the use of metaphor in Quaker literature. There is an increasing focus in the literature on *computer-mediated* identity creation, although, just like the 'sacred' and the 'secular', the 'offline' and 'online' worlds are not always detached from one another (see *Media* chapter, this volume). A shared religious identity, or at least the perception of a shared religious identity, is paramount to creating and maintaining religious communities both online and off, and in all the intersecting spaces between.

16.2.4   Analysing Religious Identity through Discourse: Ethical Considerations

Ethical considerations are a particularly important issue when researching identity and religious language. One such consideration relates to the researcher's own identity: their religious background, political views, gender, and so on. Beattie (2005, p. 65) argues that the feminist researcher should consider their own position while they often explore the faith of others:

The quest for new ways of understanding what it means to be a gendered human being surely also encompasses the quest for religious identities, communities and practices of faith that affect scholars of religions no less than those they are studying, and this entails a degree of transparency with regard to the scholar's own religious positioning if she is to respect the criteria and ethics of feminist scholarship.

For the feminist researcher, then, it can often be difficult to balance valid critiques of religious faiths with the idea that a 'secular' position is somehow a superior viewing ground, which is not necessarily the case:

The challenge today is to sustain a critical feminist awareness of the complex entanglements of power and vulnerability, oppression and liberation, control and surrender, that are found in all religious institutions and histories, but to avoid the dangerous illusion that the secular marks a domain from which to study such spiritual, social and historical complexities, without participating in their struggles or being affected by their consequences (Beattie, 2005, p. 77).

For Fader (2009), researching young Hasidic Jewish women in New York, the women she is writing about share her city as fellow New Yorkers, even though they do not necessarily share her political and religious beliefs. Fader emphasises the importance of considering her multiple identities: she is an anthropologist as well as a Jewish New Yorker; at certain times, one identity may take more salience over the other, or one identity may be more appropriate to foreground over the other.

For all researchers of religion, language, and identity, how harm of research participants can be avoided is a crucial consideration. This question is a complicated one. Defining harm is difficult and context-dependent. Critical discourse analysis often suggests calling out oppression and inequalities through our analysis, which may or may not extend to religious value systems regarded as problematic by the researcher. It is not always clear how to appropriately critique groups if we do not share their value systems, and equally so if we *do* share their value systems. There are no easy answers here. What constitutes ethical research practice may also need revising in line with technological developments, especially as the boundary between what is off or online is increasingly blurred and people increasingly navigate new technologies (Mackenzie, 2017).

16.3   Case Study

'Mommy' and modest fashion blogs written by those who identify as women from North American Evangelical Christian and Church of Jesus Christ of Latter-day Saint backgrounds provide a range of data where we can explore identity and religious community, something my own research has analysed (Ringrow, 2020a, 2020b). Motherhood and lifestyle blogging has found a comfortable home within these religious groups or, alternatively, these religious groups have made motherhood and lifestyle blogs their comfortable home (Lopez, 2009; Morrison, 2011). This may be because of how (despite some theological differences between the two) these faiths emphasise the divine calling of womanhood and motherhood as key female identities.

Blogging enables those who identify as religious women and mothers to share their experiences with other women who may or may not belong to their immediate faith communities or socioeconomic classes, in addition to generating income through their blogs through sponsorship deals (Hunter, 2016). These blogs are often viewed as acceptable ways to connect with other women and to represent their faith groups online.

My research has looked at the presence of metaphor (following Lakoff and Johnson, 2003 and Charteris-Black, 2004) in religious modest fashion blogs, analysing twelve biography posts from a range of Latter-day Saint and Evangelical Christian women. These women explicitly identify as members of faith communities. In sharing their daily lives online with their social media followers, they also assume the role of 'microcelebrity', an 'ordinary' person famous via the Internet (Jerslev, 2016). Common themes in these blogs are looking 'fun', fashionable and modern without sacrificing personal modesty standards. Bloggers share information on their outfit choices (both everyday and occasion wear) and modesty 'hacks' (e.g. layering a t-shirt under a strapless dress; turning old jeans into shorts; wearing dresses over trousers, etc.).

A recurring metaphor found in these modest fashion blogs is: LIFE IS A WORK OF ART, which encapsulates the 'sub' metaphors: GOD IS AN ARTIST/DESIGNER and WOMEN ARE DRAWINGS/CREATIONS. The use of this metaphor helps here to foreground women's identity as a divine gendered creation. Some examples include:

1. God himself created and prepared your body especially for you! [*Modest Goddess*]
2. A truly liberated female is one who knows her worth in God's eyes and views her body as a handcrafted masterpiece designed by God for His glory. [*Girl Defined*]
3. God designed you as a beautiful masterpiece and His plans for you are far greater than anything our raunch [*sic*] culture has to offer. [*Girl Defined*]
4. I write about the importance of modesty because I believe that one of the ways we show respect for ourselves and our Father in Heaven who made us, [*sic*] is by clothing our bodies both respectfully and beautifully. [*Modest Goddess*] (Ringrow, 2020a)

The use of metaphors suggests a 'counter-cultural' narrative in which society at large does not place value on this aspect of female identity, but religious faiths do. If, as these metaphorical expressions emphasise, women are viewed as God's special creations, then modest fashion plays a role in appropriately highlighting and responding to this particular identity construction. If women's bodies are indeed 'handcrafted masterpieces', 'created' and 'designed by God' for spiritual purposes, then outer clothing should reflect this inner worth by 'respectfully and beautifully' dressing the body. Gender and identity are intrinsically linked in this specific religious context where there exist clearly prescribed and differentiated roles and behaviour for women and men, often drawing on scriptural justifications for these claims. Metaphors in these blogs may emphasise that women and men are created to be fundamentally different, and show how religious adherents might view women's bodies differently than the broader social context of North America.

In addition to modest fashion blogs, religious motherhood blogs also represent a certain kind of identity for women through the language they use. My research has provided a discourse analysis of extracts from three Latter-day Saint and three Evangelical Christian blogs, identifying key metaphors of motherhood. The data is comprised of sixty blog entries: ten entries each from three Latter-day Saint bloggers: *Love Taza*, *Hey Natalie Jean* (previously *Nat the Fat Rat*), and *The Daybook Blog*, and ten blog entries each from three Evangelical Christian bloggers: *The Humbled Homemaker*, *Momastery*, and *The Purposeful Mom*. These blogs represent a sample of popular North American Latter-day Saint and Evangelical Christian mommy blogs (although it is worth noting that *Hey Natalie Jean* and *Momastery* are arguably now more liberal than their counterparts listed here).

A recurring metaphor found in the modest fashion blogs analysed is that of MOTHERHOOD IS A JOB, which foregrounds the work of mothering and puts mothers and children in the following roles: MOTHERS ARE BOSSES/CEOS and CHILDREN ARE EMPLOYEES/SUBORDINATES. The following examples are taken from the data:

1. If I set up a fun Pinterest activity with my boys and start to micromanage, then I probably need to stop and do a heart check. [*The Humbled Homemaker*]
2. My hardest job and my proudest accomplishments. My loves, my lights and my whole life, right there, contained in those two little souls. Lucky, lucky me. [*The Daybook Blog*]
3. Brandon [her husband] goes off to work and i don't feel jealous of his importance or his title. i rather respect his sacrifice all the more, because i had that life once and i hated it. it was not for me. this right here, this is the promotion. and huck's [her son] not the boss, like some might think. i'm the boss. i'm more than the boss [*Hey Natalie Jean*; lack of capitalisation follows the original post] (Ringrow, 2020b)

In these religious contexts, women are called to be mothers, and this debate fits into broader cultural discussions around women working outside/inside the home; arguably, the 'work' of motherhood is not always a metaphor. Religious bloggers who fit into the identity of stay-at-home moms, however, use these metaphors to help affirm their choices and to highlight the work that they do. In the last example, the blogger identities herself as 'the boss' and indeed 'more than the boss', responding to critics' suggestions that she is a kind of 'pushover' parent who lets her son do whatever he wants. Crucially, the MOTHERHOOD IS A JOB metaphor reinforces the value of parenting as labour, regardless if a blogger has any other work in addition to being a mother.

With both religious motherhood and religious modest fashion blogs, there is diversity of belief and practice even within the same groups; religious identity is complicated and the categories of belonging and the connotations of these categories differ depending on who is ascribing them, both in the contexts in which they are used and when researchers speak about individuals and their beliefs. Further reader reception work could help to ascertain critical responses to the blogs. Indeed, fans and critics of religious motherhood and modest fashion blogs (and those who assume both roles) may challenge or critique religious identity, especially if perceived as inauthentic or hypocritical (see Browse, 2018, on responses to (in)authenticity in political discourse). For example, religious motherhood bloggers are often praised by their followers and fans for being a good example of a young Evangelical Christian or Latter-day Saint mother in contemporary society, while they are often critiqued on internet snark sites (notably, GOMI: Get Off My Internets) for being hypocritical or inconsistent in how they seem to approach their faith, how they show their children on their blogs, and their sponsorship deals. For example, in the following extracts from GOMI posters on the public Mommy Bloggers Forum, users comment on what they regard as over-monetisation of blogger children and repetitive content:

January 29, 2017 – 9:48 am

It's more, like – Naomi, we don't need to see every damn thing the kids do. Pick and choose. Filter it to the special stuff, because if you post everything saying it's special, then nothing is special. They are kids doing kid things, which is getting boring because none of them are cute anymore. It becomes no different than someone posting photos of their lunch every day – who cares?

February 1, 2017 – 1:07 pm

Eleanor's birthday post creeped me out. I can't place my finger on why, exactly, but maybe it's just that Naomi is SO ATTACHED to her kids?
It's sad.
They're all she's got. They are literally her source of income.

February 29, 2016 – 3:33 pm

Agreed, the house is gorgeous. Having a sponsored post almost exclusively promoted by your baby daughter wearing just her diaper is gross though.

September 13, 2018 – 12:56 pm

The new blog post really made me laugh. Shut the f**k up Naomi. The first thing you did was update your profile to include "twin mama" and now you say you don't want to refer to them as "the twins"???

> I love how this bitch talks about not wanting to mess up their children's so [*sic*] esteem. YOUR CHILDREN ARE YOUR F*CKING CAREER! You exploit them for trips to Rome and Spain and wherever else the f**k you want to go.

Blogger identities can be contested in terms of how outwardly religious/ observant they may appear to be, for example, not wearing something deemed 'modest' enough or which suggests they are not wearing their Latter-day Saint religious garments under their clothes. This criticism often highlights presupposed assumptions about what is acceptable for women who profess to fit into certain identity categories:

June 19, 2013 – 3:33 pm

I feel like Amber will use the "I'm wearing a swimsuit underneath" or "Spending a day at the pool/beach" excuse any time she can just so she has an "excuse" to not wear her garments. It just gets annoying. I know, I know, no one's perfect, but you made vows to God in the temple to wear your garments, so the least you can do is I don't know, wear them from time to time.

August 4, 2017 – 3:05 pm

You can see part of her nipple in her most recent workoutwear post on Instagram (not sure how to post pics here) such modest.

May 5, 2017 – 11:57 am

I wore that exact embroidered denim jumper to my kindergarten graduation. It looks like she stole that dress out of Isla's closet. And those shoes from her Grandpa. Her fashion sense sucks so badly. Hire a professional stylist please Rach!
PS isn't that dress too short for garments?

The language (and imagery) of technologically mediated communication is situated and understood in relation to social and cultural contexts, including our 'frames' of how a person who believes X or subscribes to Y is expected to behave. We might consider how blogs 'index the self' (Fader, 2017) in addition to their faith group, and how women communicate their faith and how others respond to them. Metaphor analysis can illuminate how women draw on often-commonplace metaphors to put forward their views on their religious identity. In addition to describing their emphasis on modesty, the actual clothing (including head coverings) they wear can be considered an 'embodied language' (Fader, 2009). Clothing can convey religious identity just as much (if not more so) as language, and this kind of embodied religious communication may also cross religious divides, as women from a range of different faith traditions often advocate some form of modest fashion.

16.4   Future Directions

With new(er) and emerging religious identities come opportunities for exploring the language used. Three such groups of new religious identities include Hasidic Hipsters, Mormon Feminism, and the Stay-at-Home Daughters movement. Within these new identities, we often see increased specific intersections between religion and class, ethnicity, and/or gender. The role of language in these emerging intersectional identities offers potential for linguistic analysts to further investigate the relationship between individual identity and religion. This type of linguistic analysis could help better explore the complexities of multiple integrated identities.

This kind of intersectionality can be seen, for example, in 'Hasidic Hipsters', the term given to young(er) Jews in North America who combine Orthodox Jewish beliefs and style with contemporary trends. This might include combining Jewish principles of modesty with contemporary fashion or combining Jewish spiritual lyrics with contemporary music (Schmitz, 2016). Fader's (2009) work explores arguably *non*-hipster Hasidic Jewish women in Brooklyn, but these women still want to retain their religious beliefs vis-à-vis 'the embodied discipline of modesty' and look 'good' according to current North American fashion. Hasidic Hipsters may take this idea even further by engaging with very contemporary trends of dress, food, music, and so on, which again challenges the distinction between the material and the sacred (Fader, 2009). Analysing, for example, the song lyrics of Hasidic Hipster music could provide more detail on how this 'identity work' is done.

Mormon Feminism (Brooks, Steenblik, and Wheelwright, 2015) represents another example of identity work examining more than one identity category, as a social religious movement advocating for gender equality within the Church of Jesus Christ of Latter-day Saints. This is a Church that has traditionally prescribed separate roles and domains for men and women, and a Church in which only men can hold the Priesthood (positions of power and authority within the faith). To the best of my knowledge, this group has not yet revised their name based on the official Church guidelines mentioned earlier. Linguistic analysis of, for example, online discussion groups and blogs hosted by Mormon feminists would provide more information on how they linguistically negotiate some quite complicated issues of gender, spirituality, power, and identity (Leamaster and Einwohner, 2018).

The Stay-At-Home-Daughters (SAHDs) movement can be categorised as a nonliberal Biblical patriarchal faction. Its broad tenet is that girls and women belong to their father until they get married, when they will then belong to their husband. In the interim, they stay at home under the 'headship' of their father and prepare to be a wife and mother, often by doing housework and caring for younger siblings; university education and careers outside the home are generally discouraged. Some SAHDs have public social media accounts where they both discuss and justify their lifestyles to an 'outside' audience (i.e. those who do not share their identity), in addition to encouraging and advising other young women who are in similar positions. Again, how they frame their identity in these online contexts, and how their identities may be contested by others (for example, in reader comments responding to their YouTube videos and their blogs) would provide materials for the potential researcher investigating online religious identity construction. This work would also fit into broader stylistic trends on the importance of reader reception work (Browse, 2018).

Emerging distinctive religious identities may therefore provide the opportunity for rich datasets to analyse, especially in terms of (1) labelling self, (2) labelling others, and (3) considering intersectionality. Of course, as noted previously in this chapter, consideration of ethics is paramount in how researchers approach these groups – especially if these groups lack support or recognition. There are also careful discussions to be had around advocating for groups of which you are not a member.

As the concept of identity is arguably multidisciplinary, linguistic research into identity has a long tradition of integrating approaches from adjacent disciplines. In addition, therefore, to (critical) discourse analysis, sociolinguistics, conversation analysis, and stylistics, researchers have paid attention to theories and methods from philosophy, sociology, ethnography, and anthropology. For example, in my own research on modest fashion blogs written by Evangelical Christian and Latter-day Saint women, I draw on methods from cognitive linguistics (such as conceptual approaches to metaphor) and interpret results in light of relevant research from sociology, anthropology, media studies, religious studies, etc., as well as extant research in linguistics. In practical terms for the researcher, this may involve gaining (more) familiarity with a discipline different to one's own and/or a discipline in which one has received no formal training. It takes work to understand and engage with topics, theories, and methods from other fields, and to do this well – but the results and discussion should be a more in-depth, multifaceted discussion of your chosen data. As Asprey and Lawson (2018, p. 22) rightly point out, 'the integration of insights from a variety of analytical and theoretical perspectives will not only allow us to investigate how language is part of identity construction/production, but also how language is bound up with other aspects of being'. Considering these different aspects of being is important within and across faith groups (and faith groups themselves are, of course, not homogenous entities).

A further potential for research in the field of religion and linguistic identity is that of transgender identity in religious contexts. Many religious faiths have traditionally been predominantly cisgendered spaces, and much official spiritual leadership has not always been supportive of trans rights. This lack of support has material (as well as symbolic) and potentially harmful consequences for transgender individuals and their wider social networks within these faith groups (Shah, 2016; Sumerau, Mathers, and Cragun, 2018). Religious faiths are under increasing pressure to provide statements on their position on trans members of their faith, and analysing this documentation and subsequent reader response (including from interfaith trans advocacy groups) could add to our understanding of the intersection between religious identity and gender identity. Interfaith dialogue should also be a key consideration here in identity research going forward. How language constructs and reflects religious identity is of increasing importance in a world that is in some ways more interconnected than ever before, and yet at the same time more literal and metaphorical borders are being erected.

16.5   References

Asprey, E. & Lawson, R. (2018). English and social identity. In P. Seargeant, A. Hewings & S. Pihlaja (eds.) *The Routledge Handbook of English Language Studies* (pp. 212–25). London: Routledge.

Avni, S. (2012). "Hebrew-only language policy in religious education". *Language Policy*, *11*(2), 69–188.

Baker, P. Gabrielatos, C., & McEnery. T. (2013). *Discourse Analysis and Media Attitudes: The Representation of Islam in the British Press*. Cambridge: Cambridge University Press.

Beattie, T. (2005). Religious identity and the ethics of representation: the study of religion and gender in the secular academy. In U. King, and T. Beattie (eds.), *Gender, Religion and Diversity: Cross-cultural perspectives* (pp. 65–78). London: Continuum.

Benwell, B. & Stokoe, E. (2006). *Discourse and Identity*. Edinburgh: Edinburgh University Press.

Block, D. & Corona, V. (2016). Intersectionality in language and identity research. In S. Preece (ed.), *The Routledge Handbook of Language and Identity*. London: Routledge.

Brooks, J., Hunt Steenlik, R., & Wheelwright, H. (2015). *Mormon Feminism: Essential Writings*. New York: Oxford University Press.

Browse, S. (2018). *Cognitive Rhetoric*. Amsterdam: John Benjamins.

Caldas-Coulthard, C., & Iedema, R. (eds.). (2016). *Identity Trouble: Critical Discourse and Contested Identities*. London: Springer.

Charteris-Black, J. (2004). *Corpus Approaches to Critical Metaphor Analysis*. Basingstoke: Palgrave Macmillan.

Chun, C. (2016). Exploring neoliberal language, discourses and identities. In S. Preece. (ed.) *The Routledge Handbook of Language and Identity* (pp. 558–71). London: Routledge.

Clift, R., & Helani, F. (2010). *Inshallah:* Religious invocations in Arabic topic transition. *Language in Society*, *39*, 357–82.

Crenshaw, K. (1989). Demarginalizing the Intersection of Race and Sex: A Black Feminist Critique of Antidiscrimination Doctrine, Feminist Theory and Antiracist Politics. University of Chicago Legal Forum, Article 8.

Fader, A. (2009). *Mitzvah Girls: Bringing up the Next Generation of Hasidic Jews in Brooklyn*. Princeton: Princeton University Press.

Fader, A. (2017). The counterpublic of the J(ewish) Blogosphere: gendered language and the mediation of religious doubt among ultra-Orthodox Jews in New York. *Journal of the Royal Anthropological Institute*, *23*(4), 727–47.

Gunning, J. & Jackson, R. (2011). 'What's so "religious" about "religious terrorism"?' *Critical Studies on Terrorism*, 4, 369–88.

Hunter, A. (2016). 'Monetizing the mommy: Mommy blogs and the audience commodity'. *Information, Communication & Society*, *19*(9),1306–20.

Jackson, J. (2014). *Introducing Language and Intercultural Communication*. London: Routledge.

Jackson, R. L. and Hogg, M. A. (2010). Religious identity. In R. Jackson (ed.), *Encyclopedia of identity* (pp. 632–36). Thousand Oaks, CA: SAGE.

Jeffries, L. (2010). *Critical Stylistics*. London: Palgrave.

Jerslev, A. (2016). In the Time of the Microcelebrity: Celebrification and the YouTuber Zoella. *International Journal of Communication*, *10*, 5233–51.

Joseph, J. (2004). *Language and Identity: National, Ethnic, Religious*. Basingstoke: Palgrave Macmillan.

Koller, V. (2017). 'The light within': metaphor consistency in Quaker pamphlets, 1659–2010. *Metaphor and the Social World*, *7*(1), 5–25.

Lakoff, G. & Johnson, M. (2003). *Metaphors We Live By*. 2nd ed. Chicago: University of Chicago Press.

LDS Newsroom. (n.d.). President Nelson Stresses Importance of Jesus Christ in Church Name: 'It Is His Church'. https://newsroom.churchofjesuschrist.org/article/presi dent-nelson-stresses-importance-of-jesus-christ-church-name.

Leamaster, R. J., & Einwohner, R. L. (2018). 'I'm not your stereotypical Mormon girl': Mormon women's gendered resistance'. *Review of Religious Research*, *60*(2), 161–81.

Lopez L. K. (2009). The radical act of 'mommy blogging': Redefining motherhood through the blogosphere. *New Media & Society*. *11*(5), 729–47.

Mackenzie, J. (2017). 'Can we have a child exchange?' Constructing and subverting the 'good mother' through play in Mumsnet Talk. *Discourse & Society*. *28*(3), 296–312.

Mahmood, S. (2005). *Politics of Piety: The Islamic Revival and the Feminist Subject*. Princeton: Princeton University Press.

Morrison, A. (2011). 'Suffused by feeling and affect': The intimate public of personal mommy blogging. *Biography*, *34*(1), 37–55.

Nash, J. (2008). Re-thinking intersectionality. *Feminist Review*, *89*, 1–15.

Pihlaja, S. (2018). *Religious Talk Online*. Cambridge: Cambridge University Press.

Richardson, J. (2004). *(Mis)Representing Islam: The Racism and Rhetoric of the Broadsheet Press*. Amsterdam: John Benjamins.

Ringrow, H. (2020a). 'Beautiful masterpieces': Metaphors of the female body in modest fashion blogs. In H. Ringrow and S. Pihlaja (eds.), *Contemporary Media Stylistics* (pp. 15–34). London: Bloomsbury.

Ringrow, H. (2020b). 'I can feel myself being squeezed and stretched, moulded and grown, and expanded in my capacity to love loudly and profoundly': Metaphor and religion in motherhood blogs. In J. Mackenzie & S. Zhao (eds.), Special issue on motherhood online. *Discourse, Context & Media*.

Schmitz, M. (2016). Between the hipsters and the Hasids. *First Things: A Monthly Journal of Religion and Public Life*, *261*, 72–4.

Shah, S. (2016). Constructing an alternative pedagogy of Islam: the experiences of lesbian, gay, bisexual, and transgender Muslims. *Journal of Beliefs & Values*, *37*(3), 308–19.

Souza, A. (2010). Language choices and identity negotiations in a Brazilian Portuguese community school. In V. Lytra & P. Martin (eds.), *Sites of Multilingualism: Complementary Schools in Britain Today* (pp. 97–107). London: Trentham.

Sumerau, J. E., Mathers, L. A., & Cragun, R. T. (2018). Incorporating transgender experience toward a more inclusive gender lens in the sociology of religion. *Sociology of Religion*, *79*(4), 425–48.

van Dijk, T.A. (1993). *Elite Discourse and Racism*. Thousand Oaks, CA: SAGE.

17 Cognition

Peter Richardson

17.1 Background, History, and Key Terms

This chapter rests upon two central premises: first, trying to explore the way religious adherents conceptualize their beliefs is valuable; and second, the analysis of language is one way to uncover and track such conceptualizations. Religion has been a fundamental component of human society for thousands of years. In its many diverse forms, it continues to provide communities with a shared identity and set of values, a common purpose, and rich frameworks of meaning. However, it can also contribute to conflict and tension within many societies. The same religion may be a source of harmony and unconditional kindness in one form or context, and the source of conflict and discrimination in another. One factor that determines the difference is the way people think about or construe their beliefs. They may, for example, choose to foreground one aspect over another, represent complex elements in simplified, binary terms, compare one thing in terms of another, or view relationships and experiences as underpinned by particular opposing forces. These are all cognitive operations that can significantly change how religious adherents think about and subsequently practice their faith. These operations are also detectable in the language that believers use across a variety of situations and contexts. By identifying and tracking how they evolve across different texts and discourse streams, it should be possible to develop a rich picture of how individuals and communities view their beliefs and the world around them.

I will draw on some of the key aspects of *Cognitive Linguistics* to provide a rigorous framework for exploring the relationship between language, cognition, and thought. Cognitive Linguistics is an approach to language that first developed in the late 1970s and early 1980s as a response to the view that language ability is modular, innate, and disconnected from the general cognitive operations of the human mind. It began with a small group of key figures, such as Ronald Langacker, Leonard Talmy, Charles Fillmore, and George Lakoff, and focused mainly on the close relationship between grammar, meaning, and general cognition, in addition to the importance of notions such as idealized cognitive models and conceptual metaphor. However, over time it has expanded into a collection of approaches and frameworks that are now more than just a response to a particular theory of language acquisition. What connects the different strands of this multifaceted approach is that they all focus on exploring what is happening beneath language at the level of the concept.

Before I begin to introduce some of the key terms, it will be useful to focus the discussion around an authentic extract of religious language. Jeff Wilson's (2009, p. 183–4) collection of stories and personal experiences related to Jodo Shinshu Buddhism contains one particularly colourful retelling of a well-known account ideal for this purpose. It revolves around a *myokonin*, an adherent of Jodo Shinshu Buddhism who often lacked education or wealth but was known to be unusually devout.

Extract 1. Shoma and the Priest

At one time, an illiterate *myokonin* named Shoma who did manual labour for a living was staying at a Jodo Shinshu temple. The priest had been reading one of the Pure Land Sutras and had a thought, which he expressed out loud: "What is the meaning of the phrase 'Amida's compassion embraces all beings, forsaking none?'"

Shoma jumped up, flung his arms wide, and began speaking in a loud voice. The priest thought Shoma had gone crazy and went running away. Shoma raced after him, close behind. They ran back and forth in the worship hall, the priest's robes flapping like a giant black crow trying to raise itself into the air. Finally the priest ducked down a corridor and hid himself in a closet.

Shoma came pounding down the hallway and stopped outside the closet. "Priest, I am here!" he shouted. Then he threw the closet door open and stood there with his arms outstretched. In a booming voice he said, "This is the meaning of the phrase, 'embracing all beings, forsaking none!'"

The priest laughed and said joyfully, "Now I understand. That which never lets me go, despite all my desperate attempts to escape or deny it – that is the meaning of embracing all beings and forsaking none."

As we read through this story, we notice that each term can be situated within specific networks of background information, which are available to different degrees and in ever-developing forms in different people's minds. The term *Jodo Shinshu* may not be familiar to many of the readers of this chapter, but others may immediately situate the term within their knowledge of Buddhism in general and Mahayanna Buddhism in Japan in particular. Within this body of knowledge, they may also be making connections with other terms occurring within the extract, such as *myokonin*, *temple*, *priest*, *the Pure Land Sutras*, and *Amida*. Some of these words will connect to more general conceptions. For example, the word *temple* can connect to schematic information relating to religious buildings in general, while also connecting to more specific conceptions of a Jodo Shinshu temple in particular. One of the key terms used in Cognitive

Linguistics is the notion of *conceptual domains*, which refers to these networks of background information where knowledge is stored and organized in our minds (Langacker, 1987). These domains are often written in small capital letters to mark them as referring to mental concepts, rather than an instance of language. For example, Christians understand a reference to *Matthew's gospel* by drawing on a BIBLE conceptual domain, which in turn connects to a more abstract SACRED TEXT domain.

Another closely related term in Cognitive Linguistics is the idea of *frames*. First used by the sociologist Erving Goffman (1974), they describe how people use language to frame what they are saying in a way that is intended to produce a particular interpretation or effect. Fillmore (1982) later incorporated the notion of frames into his theory of *frame semantics*, using it to describe how a particular lexical unit activates a whole body of stored knowledge accumulated through past experiences. Despite significant overlap between the notions of frames and domains, they are often used for different purposes. For example, the former are often used in discourse analysis to describe how a particular frame produces a specific perspective or construes an event in a certain way. See the sample analysis in Section 17.3 to further explore the use of frames to develop specific perspectives.

Religious language draws on many abstract, metaphysical domains and frames. However, when we examine these, we find that many aspects of these abstract networks of knowledge are rooted in more physical, *embodied* domains. By embodied, I mean domains that reflect the fact that our minds are an intrinsic part of our physical human bodies (Lakoff and Johnson, 1999). Basic aspects of being human, such as seeing and feeling heat and cold, therefore become crucial elements in the way we think about things. They cannot be separated from how we think about the world.

In the case of the Shoma extract, the story illustrates the meaning of Amida's commitment to honour his vow to enable all beings to be reborn in the Pure Land. The story's author could have offered a complex, highly abstract explanation, but instead the meaning is expressed through words describing physical action like *embrace, running, raced, pounding,* and *arms outstretched*. These words not only involve bodily actions but also can have quite emotive and visceral associations, and bring us to another key term used in Cognitive Linguistics that is crucial to the study of religious language: *embodied cognition*. This is the idea that our minds are intrinsically connected to our human bodies, which are in turn intrinsically connected to the physical environment around us. Religious language is constrained and influenced to various degrees by the nature of the relationship between our bodies and our environment, and all human beings generally share these embodied experiences.

17.2   Key Topics, Questions, and Debates

17.2.1   Conceptual Metaphor & Metonymy

Within Cognitive Linguistics, Lakoff and Johnson (1999) developed the idea that metaphor was pervasive in human language and that it was also a key element in structuring the way we think. They argued that many metaphors involve a mapping across two conceptual domains – a *source* and *target domain* – that became established within a culture and, in the case of some metaphors, across cultures. Many of these mappings are connected to our shared experience of having a human body and pursuing typical human goals, which is why they can appear in some form across multiple languages.

Returning to the Shoma story, consider the statement, "Amida's compassion embraces all beings, forsaking none." The word *embrace* connects to a familiar physical action, although metaphorical mappings do not just involve applying all the elements of the source domain (the concept of embracing someone) to the target domain. Embracing someone can carry numerous entailments depending on different cultural contexts and situations. For example, it can be something we do when we meet someone we haven't seen for a long time, saying goodbye, congratulating someone, or expressing affection or acceptance. Careful attention therefore needs to be paid both to the immediate context in which the metaphor occurs and our background knowledge of Jodo Shinshu Buddhism in general and Wilson's take on it. If we consider its occurrence with "forsaking none" and "never lets me go, despite all my desperate attempts to escape", the focus appears to be a determination to physically hold everybody with the commitment to never abandon them. This fits with other examples of Amida's commitment in Wilson's (2009) book, such as "for as long as we live … we are floating on the ocean of grace" and those who trust in Amida being "grasped, never to be abandoned". We can connect all these occurrences under a single conceptual metaphor: BEING SAVED IS BEING HELD AND NEVER RELEASED. The mapping is written in capitalized letters to mark it out as an underpinning conceptual metaphor, rather than a quote of a metaphor occurring in a text. The first part identifies the usually more abstract target domain and the second part the more physical source domain. For more details about conceptual metaphor and its relationship to the study of metaphor outside of Cognitive Linguistics, please see the *Metaphor* chapter in this volume.

We have so far looked at how conceptual metaphor makes use of a cross-domain mapping process to view one thing in terms of another, such as in the case of BEING SAVED IS BEING HELD AND NEVER BEING RELEASED. However, my analysis of *embrace* has so far failed to consider an important element of that sentence: the subject performing the embrace. In the text, it is not Amida that embraces all human beings but Amida's *compassion*. We can approach this in two ways: either as an example of Amida's compassion being personified as Amida himself, or we can view his compassion as a key, salient characteristic that is being used here to stand for or represent Amida. To rephrase these two options using more technical terminology, we can view Amida's compassion here as either an example of metaphor (and *personification*, in particular) or as a TRAIT FOR PERSON *metonymy* (see Littlemore, 2015, p. 107, for a more in-depth discussion of personification and metonymy). However, given the emphasis that Wilson (2009) often places on this particular trait of Amida, the latter appears preferable.

The story of Shoma highlights the sometimes close and even blurred relationship between metaphor and metonymy, but an important difference between them is that conceptual metonymy involves one salient aspect of a domain standing for another aspect of the same domain rather than a comparative mapping across two domains (Kövecses, 2002). A key term that comes up often in the metonymy literature is *contiguity*. What this means is that if two elements are closely associated with each other, and are not simply being compared to each other, then it is likely that a metonymic relationship is present.

The aforementioned TRAIT FOR PERSON example is one member of a broader category of metonymy: PART FOR WHOLE. Two types of metonymy that are especially common in religious language are PART FOR WHOLE and WHOLE FOR PART relationships. One example of the former is the representation of people as *souls* in this sentence from the *Catholic Herald*, "I've become convinced that each missionary is called for a chance meeting with just one lost soul" (Phillips, 2019). In this example, the salient characteristic that the author is interested in is the perceived part of a human being that survives death and enters either hell or heaven. An example of WHOLE FOR PART metonymy is the use of *America* in this statement by a *Christian Post* reporter summarizing a talk given by the theologian Norman Geisler, "America has paid a heavy price for abandoning God" (Zaimov, 2016). In this example, America appears to include everybody in America despite the fact that the author presumably does not view himself or those committed members of his American Christian audience as abandoning God. Metonymy serves as a shortcut, allowing believers to use one or two words to refer to a specific idea or conception of something. However, it can also have a negative function in that it sometimes provides users with the capability to implicitly assert or assume the reality of a controversial, exaggerated, or simplified way of thinking.

Cognitive linguists often ask how particular conceptual metaphors originated, and for some cross-domain mappings, particular metonymies may have been a precondition. In the case of the figurative understanding of light, Kövecses (2011) argues that because light is a crucial ingredient of life as we know it, it is likely that light and life became associated with each other as a

LIGHT FOR LIFE metonymy. This then provides the basis for the conceptual metaphor mapping LIFE IS LIGHT, which itself relates to religious metaphors like GOD IS LIGHT and FAITH IS LIGHT (Kövecses, 2011, p. 332). It is possible to follow a similar process of reasoning with the related conceptual metaphor KNOWING IS SEEING or UNDERSTANDING IS SEEING. Seeing a physical object is one step in a process of understanding it, so KNOWING IS SEEING could have developed out of an association between these two elements. We could then describe this in metonymic terms as an association established through an embodied PRECONDITION FOR RESULTING EVENT/ACTION metonymy (Kövecses, 2002, p. 158). We could follow similar logic with other highly productive religious metaphors. For example, the development of SPIRITUAL KNOWLEDGE IS LIGHT may have been partly influenced by the association of understanding sacred texts while reading them by candlelight (Charteris-Black, 2017).

When it comes to practical methodologies for identifying metonymy in text, no single, widely accepted framework exists. One possible framework (evaluated in more detail by Littlemore 2015) is Biernacka's (2013, p. 117) adaption of the *Metaphor Identification Procedure*, known as MIP (Pragglejaz, 2007), discussed in the chapter on *Metaphor* in this volume. This procedure begins with similar steps to MIP in terms of first reading the text in order to establish its overall meaning and mark out lexical units. The next step involves identifying metonymic lexical units based on first determining their immediate and wider contextual meaning, and then establishing whether it has a more basic meaning in other contexts than the one being considered. If this is found to be the case, "determine if they are connected by contiguity, defined as a relation of adjacency and closeness comprising not only spatial contact but also temporal proximity, causal relations and part–whole relations" (Biernacka, 2013, p. 117). The final step is to check forwards and backwards to determine how far this particular instance of metonymy extends.

After establishing the number and type of occurrences of metonymy, we can group them together according to type and look for patterns in the text as a whole. The relationship between metonymy and metaphor usage in the text can then be investigated, in addition to areas of overlap where both may be present to some degree, or where it may be difficult to establish precisely whether the relationship is one of contiguity or comparison. The analysis of a conversation between two religious believers in the case study in this chapter provides an example of how this framework is applied to an authentic text.

17.2.2 *Conceptual Blending*

In terms of the Shoma extract, I have already examined the statement, "Amida's compassion embraces all beings, forsaking none" (Wilson, 2009) from the perspective of metaphor and metonymy. However, the precise relationship between Shoma chasing the terrified priest and this statement deserves more focus because the actions are an analogy designed to further explain the metaphorical components of the statement (which were themselves attempts to describe Amida's actions and commitment). They therefore cannot be analysed as a straightforward mapping between a source and a target domain. How certain elements of Shoma's actions relate to the statement is not immediately clear, such as the fact that the priest initially construes his behaviour as frightening. What we naturally end up doing as we read this passage is attempting to integrate Shoma's actions with Amida's action of embracing and never forsaking and then trying to determine what unique elements emerge. We will therefore now move on to a consideration of the notion of conceptual blending.

Fauconnier and Turner's (2002) *Conceptual Blending Theory* (CBT) attempts to provide a rigorous analytic framework to explain instances in language that require the integration of two or more concepts. Their theory argues that at least four mental spaces are required for us to process examples involving the integration of two concepts: two input spaces, one generic space, and one blended space. The generic space is where the various elements of the two input spaces are connected, and the blended space details the elements that emerge, along with the elaborations that appear because of running the blend.

To illustrate exactly how this works, let us consider the case of Shoma and Amida's actions as a conceptual blend in more detail. As we see in Figure 17.1, we can view Shoma's act of chasing the priest as the first input space with Amida's action of embracing all and forsaking no one as a second input space. Shoma's open arms and Amida's embrace can be matched in the generic space as a commitment to accept, which in the blend becomes Amida's initial acceptance of all living beings and his commitment to bring them to the Pure Land. Shoma's act of doggedly chasing the priest and Amida's commitment to forsake no one can also be matched in the generic space as a commitment to never withdraw acceptance regardless of the response. The blend therefore consists of Amida's commitment to not just accept all living beings, but also to ensure that they all finally reach the Pure Land.

The most complex part of the blend is the priest's initial response of fear and his attempt to escape. In order to match this with the second input space, we need to draw on our background knowledge of Amida's acceptance and the nature of people's *ego-self* or *self-power* (terms commonly used in Jodo Shinshu to describe individual intention) in Wilson's (2009) book as a whole. Wilson (2009) argues that it is impossible (or at least extremely difficult) for people to get to the Pure Land through their own efforts and self-discipline. This is because the ego-self naturally finds it very difficult to let go of its attachment to itself and its own desires. We can therefore match the priest's response to the nature of the ego-self in the generic space as acceptance being initially resisted, which in the blend becomes the initial resistance of living beings to the compassion of Amida. Finally, the priest's laughter at the end of the story can be matched to Wilson's (2009) explanation that eventually all living beings will be happy to reside in the Pure Land, and from there achieve enlightenment. However, we are still left with a key element of disanalogy when we run the blend. This relates to the fact that at the beginning, the priest does not just resist Shoma's attempt to embrace him, but understandably resists him based on his extreme and threatening behaviour (his sudden gesture and raised voice). When readers run the blend, we will either discard this elaboration, perhaps putting it down to a detail added for comic effect, or incorporate it as a unique emergent structure. If so, this would add an extra layer of insight into Amida's actions, where, from the egoistic perspective of those being embraced, the compassion of Amida could initially be experienced as something that appears dangerous and harmful.

The scope of CBT and its focus on the emergent elements of the blend have made it an increasingly popular approach in recent analyses of religious texts.

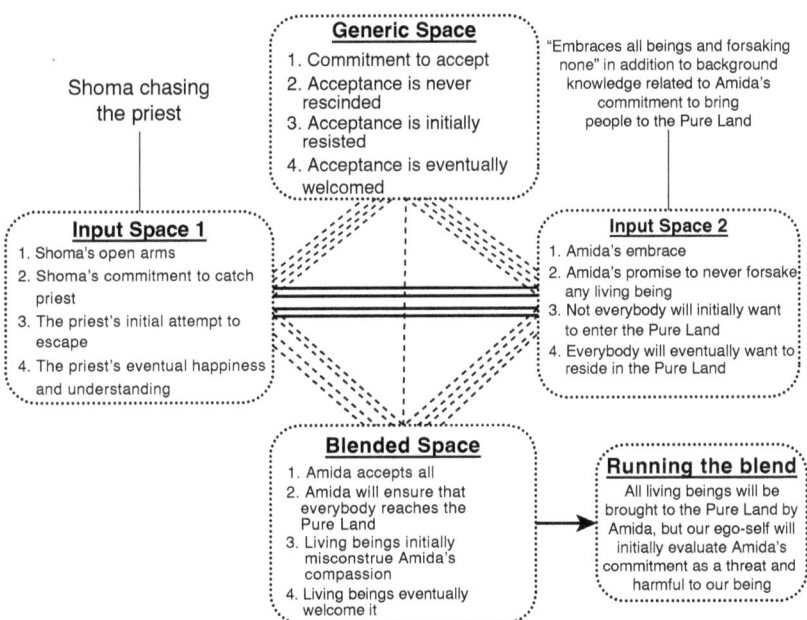

Figure 17.1 Conceptual blending in the Jodo Shinshu *myokonin* story

One initial indication of its popularity is the number of studies that draw on this type of analysis. For example, in Howe and Green's (2014) edited volume focusing on the application of Cognitive Linguistics to Biblical Studies, five of the eleven studies draw on the CBT framework. Another indicator is the wide range of texts that have been analysed using this framework, from verses in the Bible such as John 14:6 (Kövecses, 2011) to the analysis of Christians and demons and their relation to the inner warfare of the self in the sixteenth-century classic, *Unseen Warfare* (Antović, 2018).

Another example of the variety of religious texts CBT has been applied to is Charteris-Black's (2017) analysis of fire frames in the *Upanishads*, a key body of texts in Hinduism produced around the sixth century BCE. He explores how the human body and soul are blended with the concept of fire in the text. For example, the input space of physical and spiritual needs is connected in the generic space with a fire's requirement for fuel, giving us the notion of creation. Conceptualizing desire as the fuel for a fire then emerges from the blend, resulting in the frames LUST IS FIRE and even WOMEN ARE FIRE. For example, Charteris-Black (2017, p. 121) also discusses examples in the text where men are passively construed as "straw" being consumed by their desires for attractively dressed women (who are themselves figuratively represented as fire). However, this lust can then itself be burned away by a commitment to acquire divine knowledge. This is based on the blending of language and spiritual expression with the notion that sparks produce fire. The emergent conceptualization of language and spirit as fire results in descriptions situated in frames such as PURIFICATION IS FIRE.

Conceptual Blending Theory is therefore a useful approach when focusing in on important elements emerging from an integration of two mental spaces. However, the theory has been criticized for lacking empirical support in its claims about what is happening inside our minds, and it also fails to fully explore how the content of emergent structures may, in some cases, vary depending on the individual or belief community. In addition, continuing our discussion of the fire frames, what conceptual blending does not provide here is a framework for exploring the tug-of-war relationship between desire and divine knowledge. As we have seen, fire is being conceptualized as both a negatively evaluated creative force and a positively evaluated destructive force. These two types are construed as existing in a competing relationship with each other, with lust having a force tendency to reject divine knowledge and spread unchecked, while divine knowledge displays a force tendency related to eradicating lust (Charteris-Black, 2017, p. 121). These points take us beyond the purview of CBT into the domain of force dynamics.

17.2.3   Force Dynamics

Talmy's (2000) notion of force dynamics posits that some examples of language are underpinned by a relationship of two opposing forces, where one eventually overcomes the other. We have briefly mentioned the example of competing forces in the fire frames of the Hindu Upanishad texts, but let us look in more detail at the force-dynamic relationship in our story of Shoma.

We've already noted that Jodo Shinshu includes the belief that our egos and determination to rely on self power make it almost impossible for us to achieve enlightenment by our own efforts. An additional element that emerges in the Shoma and Amida blend is that human beings will initially misconstrue the actions of Amida as a threat. From a force-dynamic perspective, we can view Amida's embrace of all living creatures (represented by Shoma attempting to catch the priest) and the ego's commitment to self power (represented by the priest's reaction) as two competing forces: an *antagonist* and an *agonist* respectively. When the focus is only on the physical movement dynamics of the story, we would view it simply as Shoma trying to catch up with the priest. However, if we view it from the theological perspective of bringing or moving people to the Pure Land, Shoma's intention (as the antagonist) is to overcome the priest's force tendency (as the agonist) to resist that movement. This force tendency to remain at rest is marked with a black circle in Figure 17.2. The competing force dynamic is resolved when the antagonist's stronger force tendency (marked with a "+" symbol in the diagram below) successfully overcomes the force tendency of the agonist. In terms of the Jodo Shinshu belief system, that is when living beings are accepted by Amida and begin to move towards the Pure Land.

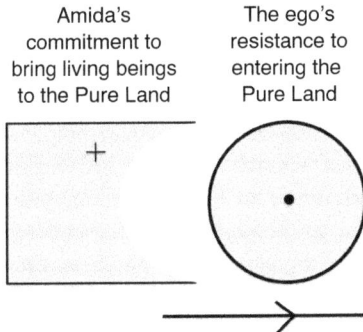

Figure 17.2   Force dynamics in "Amida embraces all, forsaking none"

Religious language is often underpinned by force-dynamic relationships. One reason for this is that certain forms of religious belief are construed as high-cost practices that involve struggle and doing something that is initially seen as difficult or unnatural. We see this, for example, in the use of sinful disobedience and the work of the devil as counter forces in Christian and Muslim language, or the pull to become attached to our desires in Buddhist language (Richardson and Nagashima, 2018). Once again, a close analysis of these force tendencies across multiple discourse streams allows us to explore in depth how believers conceptualize the tug-of-war of their daily experience.

One final contribution of force dynamics is that it provides a framework for exploring the outer boundaries of religious experience. Mystical texts related to Judaism, Christianity, and Islam, and many descriptions of the later stages of Buddhist and Hindu practice describe the idea of a final dissolution of any form of force dynamics (Kowalewski, 2018; Silvestre-López, 2016). This sometimes takes the form of divine union between the believer and God, the dissolution of the self (and therefore the extinguishing of the counter force of desire), or a non-dualistic realization that the existence of agents and patients, agonists and antagonists were an illusion. However, without initially drawing on force dynamics in some form, producing an extended text or stretch of discourse is impossible. Texts that detail these kinds of experiences must develop a way to shift from talking about the competing relationships between entities and the dissolution of those relationships (Richardson and Mueller, 2019). A framework for analysing force dynamics is invaluable for tracking those shifts, allowing us to explore their significance for how believers perceive an ultimate meaning and its dissolution.

17.3   Case Study

Having introduced many of the key topics relating to the application of Cognitive Linguistics to religious language, I will now explore how some of them can be practically applied to a brief analysis of a conversation between a Muslim and a Christian arranged at the University of Birmingham (UK) about how they are certain their beliefs are correct. The extract below is from a recorded conversation between Diya, a female Indian Christian in her 20s living and studying in the UK, and Tanvi, an Ibadhi Muslim student in her 20s from Oman also studying in the UK (both names are pseudonyms). The meeting began with an activity where the participants had to share why they thought the other participant was certain about their beliefs. They were then encouraged to share their answers and discuss them.

In this particular extract from their conversation, Tanvi's two turns take up 120 words with Diya's two turns totalling 128 words. Using MIP, I identified three metaphorical units in Tanvi's language and one instance of metonymy. In Diya's language, I identified thirteen metaphorical units.

When analysing interactions, it is important to emphasize the occasioned nature of the discourse. Tanvi's two turns in the extract consolidate and develop an earlier point she made that Christianity is "unfair" because it is essentially based on someone being punished for someone else's wrongdoing, "it doesn't make much sense to me that someone like Jesus would be blamed or punished for my, for my sins, it's just unfair." Throughout the discussion, she stresses the importance of the believer's responsibility and God's willingness to support and guide those who commit themselves to following God's commands. Her statements here need to be situated within that goal of providing a practical explanation of how she believes a good relationship with God can be maintained or damaged by an individual's commitment or lack thereof. The extract begins with Tanvi discussing the importance of following God's commands by focusing on a fictional example of a woman who called herself a Muslim but chose not to wear the hijab.

Extract 2. A good Muslim

1 **Tanvi:** hmm well I'm not saying I'm a better Muslim
2   but I have a better relationship with God because I am wearing hijab and she is not
3   but again it is not up to me to say she is going
4   definitely going to hell because she is not wearing hijab
5   it's not up to me
6   but these instructions are really important, you know
7   well I mean
8   a Muslim who doesn't pray five times a day
9   his salvation is really in danger
10 **Diya:** that's scary
11 that's really scary I think
12 **Tanvi:** I think it's scary
13 but Islam is very important
14 like we have this loving merciful God
15 he is the merciful
16 but again it's not good to underestimate his power
17 And

Tanvi's focus is on maintaining a good relationship with God by being obedient to what God requires. Her explanation attempts to strike a careful balance between human responsibility and God's authority by initially emphasizing the agency of the believer in deciding whether to observe God's commandments or not. When she does explicitly mention God in response to Diya's labelling of her description as "scary … really scary", she only implicitly refers to his supporting and punitive agency in reference to his mercy and power. The description of God simply as "the merciful" works as a CHARACTERISTIC FOR

PERSON metonymy and emphasizes her point that a true understanding of God requires an appreciation of the balance between these two potential forms of agency. This can also be viewed in force-dynamic terms as the two opposing forces of divine mercy and the divine power to judge with the overcoming force being dependent on the obedience of an individual and his or her willingness to submit to the will of God.

Diya's interjection and use of the term "scary" sets up the beginning of her counter conceptualization of what she views to be a good relationship with God. It allows her to subtly develop an implied construal of Tanvi's relationship with God as one of fear (which Tanvi attempted to counter by stressing the love and mercy of God as well as his power in her response). Diya says:

Extract 3. My faith is freedom

18 what really sticks out for me in my faith is freedom
19   and hmm
20 how it says in the Bible the truth will set you free
21 what I believe is that truth in my faith obviously is the fact that I have been set free
      by the Spirit
22 and I'm no longer who I used to be
23 no longer bound by the things that you know
24 bound by the laziness that I used to have
25 like not wanting to pray in the morning
26 you enjoy it in a sense because you have that better relationship
27 like you said
28 a relationship with God
29 and when the Son of Man sets you free
30 you will be free indeed right?
31 so I am free indeed

In Extract (3), Diya stresses the notion of freedom, setting up a contrast between Tanvi's emphasis on human responsibility (which depends on freedom) and Diya's own belief that all non-Christians are deprived of freedom (because of the impact of original sin). She is also setting up a second contrast between Tanvi's statement that a Muslim's salvation would be in danger if they didn't pray five times a day and her own claim that she prays in the morning because she enjoys it (as a result of being set free). The use of *freedom* was identified as metaphorical here because Tanvi's language connects to John 8:34–36 which refers to non-Christians as slaves of sin:

[34] Jesus answered them, Truly, truly, I say to you, everyone who practices sin is a slave to sin. [35] The slave does not remain in the house forever; the son remains forever. [36] So if the Son sets you free, you will be free indeed. (English Standard Version)

Diya is therefore not just referring to an abstract sense of freedom, but specifically to the metaphor scenario encompassed by BEING A NON-CHRISTIAN

IS BEING A SLAVE OF SIN and BEING A CHRISTIAN IS BEING FREED FROM THE SLAVERY OF SIN. Her references to being formerly bound by behaviour she perceives as bad can then be viewed as an elaboration on this SLAVERY frame, which implicitly competes with Tanvi's RESPONSIBILITY frame. This notion of being liberated is represented through eight separate metaphorical occurrences, so it is clearly central to Diya's argument here. It is also associated with the divine agency patterns of the Spirit setting her free and then the Son of Man setting her free – both key persons and acts associated with the Christian Trinity, a doctrine that Tanvi would not adhere to. There is a clear contrast here in force-dynamic terms between Tanvi and Diya's conceptualizations of God's interaction with people. As we saw, the main force-dynamic focus in Tanvi's language is between God's mercy and his power to judge, with the stronger force tendency being dependent on the key element of human responsibility. In contrast, the force-dynamic relationship for Diya is between the binding nature of sin (for example, the compulsion to be lazy) and the stronger, emancipating force tendency of the Son of Man. In this conservative Christian dynamic between two competing powers (Richardson and Nagashima, 2018), what is noticeably absent in this particular stretch of discourse is any force being exerted by human responsibility.

There are two moments where Diya appears to be interested in establishing common ground in terms of the two belief systems. The first is her sharing of the term *relationship with God,* marked by "like you said" in line 27 of Extract (3), and the second is her use of "right" in line 30. The word *right* is usually used in this way to mark an argument or a statement that is likely to elicit agreement from both participants in the discourse. However, Tanvi's detailed development of her SLAVERY frame for people not saved by Jesus Christ makes it clear that she is operating within a binary worldview with no grey areas. The use of *right* should therefore be understood in the sense that Diya believes she is correcting Tanvi's understanding of the term *relationship with God* and Tanvi should realize that what she is asserting is obviously correct.

In Pihlaja's (2018, p. 152) analysis of the language of two well-known evangelists on social media, the Muslim John Fontain and the Christian Joshua Feuerstein, he draws the following conclusion:

For those interested in the state of interreligious dialogue, this book does not offer an especially positive picture. Users were observed positioning themselves and others in fairly predictable storylines, some that have been told again and again both online and offline. John Fontain and Joshua Feuerstein are civil with one another, but a closer look at what they are saying shows limited critical engagement.

This conclusion can be equally applied to this present dialogue. The analysis of frames, metaphor, metonymy, and force dynamics reveals a tug-of-war between these two participants in terms of who can establish the dominant conceptualization through their explanations. In addition, the analysis of these underlying conceptualizations brings into sharp relief the gulf between the two positions. It allows us to precisely map where the differences exist, where the points of potential conflict and tension exist, and what underpins them. This analysis of what lies beneath the surface of the discussion also adds to our appreciation of the complexity and richness of the dialogue. The importance of the fact that two people with such divergent beliefs and backgrounds could come together and engage in such a careful conversation should not be underestimated.

17.4   Future Directions

The increase in cognitive linguistic analyses of religious texts has already produced valuable contributions in areas such as metaphor, metonymy, conceptual blending, agency, and force dynamics. However, an overview of recent studies demonstrates some gaps and some developing imbalances.

First, many of the analyses are written in English and therefore involve the listing of conceptual metaphors, metonymies, and blends in English, and yet the texts themselves are often in another language. In many cases, not enough focus is given to how particular conceptualizations are affected when they are expressed in English rather than the original source language. One of the core premises of Cognitive Linguistics is that our language determines the way we think about the world, and yet this insight is sometimes not given the weight it deserves. As a model for how researchers should approach issues relating to language difference in cognitive linguistic analyses, it is useful to consider the work done in fields such as Biblical Studies. For example, Howe and Green's (2014) edited collection of studies consistently and rigorously integrate issues relating to the unique properties of classical Hebrew and Greek into cognitive linguistic analyses written in English.

An imbalance is developing in terms of the majority of studies involving non-comparative analyses of sacred or classic religious texts. There is no question that previous studies cover an impressive variety of religious traditions, and yet, with a few exceptions (for example, see Charteris-Black, 2004; 2017), little work is being done to compare how believers from different religious traditions are thinking about and conceptualizing elements of their experience. At some level, this situation is inevitable in that specialists in various areas will understandably choose to focus exclusively on those areas: Bible scholars will want to study the Bible, scholars of the Koran will focus on the Koran, and researchers with expertise in Buddhism will tend to keep to Buddhist texts. However, what is also needed is a growing number of cognitive linguistic researchers who are able to analyse data that spans different religious traditions and investigate shared, schematic similarities and unique aspects.

Another developing imbalance relates to the popularity of certain types of analyses over others. Cognitive linguistic analyses of religious language have tended to predominantly focus on Conceptual Metaphor Theory and Conceptual Blending Theory with some focus on metonymy and force dynamics. One area that has so far been under-represented is the application of *cognitive grammar* to analyses of religious language. This is all the more noticeable because of the quite extensive progress that has been made in applying aspects of cognitive grammar to a cognitive linguistic *Critical Discourse Analysis* framework for examining political speeches and media articles (for example, Hart, 2015). Space does not permit an exhaustive survey of the different aspects of cognitive grammar, but it is worth briefly discussing one key component: *attention*. This aspect relates to Langacker's (1987) notion of *profiling*, where a language user focuses attention on a specific part of an utterance while backgrounding other elements. Hart (2015), for example, discusses the following news report related to reports of the Koran being burned by NATO soldiers:

Seven killed in Afghanistan Koran burning protests [headline]
Seven people were killed today in clashes between Afghan security forces and protestors demonstrating against the burning of Muslim holy books at a NATO military base. (Independent online, 22.02.2012)

Hart (2015) argues that the agentless passive construction "were killed" has the effect of backgrounding the role of the Afghan security forces in the deaths of the protestors. In addition, the nominalization in the use of "the burning of ... " involves a summary scanning mode which backgrounds the agents involved in the action.

We are beginning to see the application of profiling and a focus on the entailments of activating particular conceptual domains to fields such as Biblical Studies. However, the number of studies is limited compared to those that draw on Conceptual Metaphor Theory and Conceptual Blending Theory. One key example is Van Wolde's (2014) analysis of the Hebrew words for 'outcry' and 'city gates' in the context of the Sodom and Gomorrah story. This study demonstrates how a rigorous application of cognitive grammar can challenge traditional interpretations of Biblical stories. This is achieved by establishing the entailments of a particular word in a specific context by analysing multiple previous instances and then uncovering patterns detailing which aspects of particular domains are being profiled. Van Wolde (2014) has clearly demonstrated the value of applying this aspect of Cognitive Linguistics, but there is room for more studies to further explore the value of its application to the study of religious language.

A second under-represented area of Cognitive Linguistics is *Deictic Space Theory*. This theory examines how we experience and construct reality as an

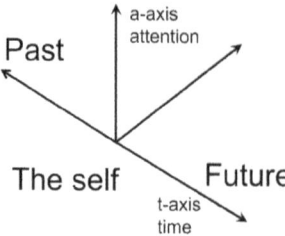

Figure 17.3 Deictic space

extension of conceptual space around the self. For the purposes of analysing language, the current self is positioned as the point of intersection for three axes. The first is the a-axis, which relates to the degree of focus or attention that is being given to a relevant entity in the participant's environment, and the second is the t-axis, which extends in two directions and relates to how a participant is conceptualizing an event or entity in terms of its location in the past or the future. The final m-axis relates to modality and the degree to which an entity is perceived as real, true, and present (see Figure 17.3).

In one of the few studies that applies Deictic Space theory to the analysis of religious language, Chilton (2018) analyses a detailed description of the ritual structure of the Roman Catholic Tridentine mass. The analysis demonstrates how the combination of language, smells, sounds, and performance systematically shifts the perception of a distant historical event into a moment where the believer conceptualizes Jesus' body and blood as something that is in the centre of their attention, present, and real. The study concludes by arguing that the sophisticated doctrine of transubstantiation (the bread and wine literally being transformed into the body and blood of Jesus) was an attempted rationalization that resulted from people's experiences rather than an idea that framed their experiences from the beginning.

The under-representation of analyses relating to cognitive grammar, Deictic Space Theory, and Text World Theory also connects to one final avenue for future research. Very little work is being done in analysing interactions between contemporary religious believers and applying the growing influence of dynamic systems theory. Usage-based approaches emphasizing the fluid and dynamic nature of language have become well established in cognitive linguistic theory (for example, Gibbs and Cruz, 2012). In addition, their usefulness in analysing the occasioned and fluid use of religious language in conversations and social media posts has been repeatedly demonstrated by analyses rooted in the Discourse Dynamic Approach and applications of Positioning Theory (for example, Pihlaja, 2018). These types of studies have an important practical application to areas such as religious dialogue in that they allow researchers to track how individuals dynamically react to each other's ideas and beliefs in real time. Cognitive Linguistics should be especially suited to contribute to this type of analysis because of its focus on how discourse participants conceptualize meaning, which makes it ideal for tracking shifts in ways of thinking and attitudes.

Components of cognitive grammar and Deictic Space Theory could become especially valuable in studies of interaction. For example, studies could examine how the use of profiling shifts over the course of a conversation and across different conversations with different participants and contexts. The notion of usage-based, dynamic shifts in attention, modality, and immediacy are also built into the fabric of Deictic Space Theory, making it an ideal framework for the analysis of interactions. Cognitive Linguistics has already made significant contributions to the study of religious language, but scope remains for many more advances, especially in relation to comparative studies and interactions between believers from different belief communities. Contributions in these areas may also have significant practical applications to important areas relating to religious dialogue and conflict management.

17.5   References

Antović, M. (2018). Waging war against oneself: A conceptual blend at the heart of Christian ascetic practice. In P. Chilton & M. Kopytowska (eds.), *Religion, Language, and the Human Mind* (pp. 386–406). Oxford: Oxford University Press.

Biernacka, E. (2013). The role of metonymy in political discourse. Unpublished PhD thesis, Milton Keynes: The Open University.

Charteris-Black, J. (2004). *Corpus Approaches to Critical Metaphor Analysis.* Basingstoke: Palgrave Macmillan.

Charteris-Black, J. (2017). *Fire Metaphors: Discourses of Awe and Authority.* London: Bloomsbury.

Chilton, P. (2018). Hoc est corpus: Deixis and the integration of ritual space. In P. Chilton & M. Kopytowska (eds.), *Religion, Language, and the Human Mind* (pp. 407–36). Oxford: Oxford University Press.

Fauconnier, G., & Turner, M. (2002). *The Way We Think: Conceptual Blending and the Mind's Hidden Complexities.* New York: Basic Books.

Fillmore, C. (1982). Frame semantics. In Linguistics Society of Korea (eds.), *Linguistics in the Morning Calm* (pp. 111–37). Seoul: Hanshin Publishing Co.

Gibbs, Jr., R. W., & Santa Cruz, M. J. (2012). Temporal unfolding of conceptual metaphoric experience. *Metaphor and Symbol, 27*(4), 299–311.

Goffman, E. (1974). *Frame Analysis: An Essay on the organization of experience.* London: Harper and Row.

Hart, C. (2015). Cognitive linguistics and critical discourse analysis. In E. Dabrowska & D. Divjak (eds.), *Handbook of Cognitive Linguistics.* Berlin: Mouton De Gruyter.

Howe, B., & Green, J. B. (eds.). (2014). *Cognitive Linguistic Explorations in Biblical Studies.* Berlin: De Gruyter.

Kowalewski, H. (2018). Snakes, leaves, and poisoned arrows: Metaphors of emotion in early Buddhism. In P. Chilton & M. Kopytowska (eds.), *Religion, Language, and the Human Mind* (pp. 210–28). Oxford: Oxford University Press.

Kövecses, Z. (2002). *Metaphor: A Practical Introduction.* Oxford: Oxford University Press.

Kövecses, Z. (2011). The biblical story retold: A cognitive linguistic perspective. In M. Brdar, S. T. Gries & M. Z. Fuchs (eds.), *Cognitive Linguistics: Convergence and Expansion* (pp. 325–53). Amsterdam: John Benjamins.

Lakoff, G., & Johnson, M. (1999). *Philosophy in the Flesh: The Embodied Mind and Its Challenge to Western Thought.* New York: Basic Books.

Langacker, R. W. (1987). *Foundations of Cognitive Grammar.* Stanford: Stanford University Press.

Littlemore, J. (2015). *Metonymy: Hidden Shortcuts in Language, Thought, and Communication.* Cambridge: Cambridge University Press.

Philips, F. (2019). Meet the evangelists saving souls in Wall Street. *Catholic Herald.* https://catholicherald.co.uk/commentandblogs/2019/05/13/meet-the-evangelists-saving-souls-in-wall-street/.

Pihlaja, S. (2018). *Religious Talk Online: The Evangelical Discourse of Muslims, Christians, and Atheists.* Cambridge: Cambridge University Press.

Pragglejaz Group. (2007). MIP: A method for identifying metaphorically used words in discourse. *Metaphor and Symbol, 22*(1), 1–39.

Richardson, P. & Mueller, C. (2019). Moving yet being still: Exploring source domain reversal and force in explanations of enlightenment. *Language and Cognition,* 11, 310–39.

Richardson, P., & Nagashima, M. (2018). Perceptions of danger and co-occurring metaphors in Buddhist dhamma talks and Christian sermons. *Cognitive Linguistic Studies,* 5(1), 133–54.

Silvestre-López, A. J. (2016). The discourse of mindfulness: What language reveals about the mindfulness experience. In P. Ordóñez-López & N. Edo-Marzá (eds.), *New Insights into the Analysis of Medical Discourse in Professional, Academic and popular Settings* (pp. 173–98). Bristol: Multilingual Matters.

Talmy, L. (2000). *Toward a Cognitive Semantics.* Cambridge: MIT Press.

Van Wolde, E. (2014). Cognitive grammar at work in Sodom and Gomorrah. In B. Howe, & J. B. Green (eds.), *Cognitive Linguistic Explorations in Biblical Studies* (pp. 193–223). Berlin: De Gruyter.

Wilson, J. (2009). *Buddhism of the Heart: Reflections on Shin Buddhism and Inner Togetherness.* Somerville: Wisdom Publications.

Zaimov, S. (2016). Theologian Norman Geisler explains how America abandoned God, and what it can do to reclaim His favor. www.christianpost.com/news/theologian-norman-geisler-explains-how-america-abandoned-god-what-it-can-do-reclaim-his-favor.html, www.christianpost.com/news/theologian-norman-geisler-explains-how-america-abandoned-god-what-it-can-do-reclaim-his-favor.html.

18   Sacred Texts

Karolien Vermeulen

18.1   Background, History, and Key Terms

Sacred texts are at the heart of religious discourse. They form the condensation and canonization of the discourse of a particular group of people at a specific place and point in time. Simultaneously, they are the starting point for new religious discourse based upon these. As history shows us, such new discourses can appear anywhere and can be produced by anyone, from the pope in the Vatican to the child playing with the nativity set at home, and from the atheist having a conversation with his Muslim friend to the Mormon mommy blogger. The sacred text is both an end point and a starting point of conversation.

The analysis of the language of sacred texts offers insight into the experiential world of religion. As simple as this sounds, this formulation of the chapter's topic brings to the fore some of the key terms crucial to the study of sacred texts. They have to do with: (1) what texts are, (2) what determines their sacrality, (3) what languages they come in, (4) who creates them, and finally (5) who reads them.

When mentioning *texts* in a context of religious discourse, one primarily refers to the written version of a collection of words that were originally transmitted *orally*. Such is true for the Hebrew Bible, but also for the Qur'an in Islam, and the Pali canon in Buddhism. All religious traditions have prophets or sages hearing words of the deity or leading character of the religion. What is more, even when written down, these texts kept some of their orality through communal reading practices. During mass, a priest or lecturer reads to the audience from the gospel, for example. It is not as if everybody is taking a minute for themselves to go through the chapter in silence. Sacred text is to be heard (Graham, 2010; Niditch, 1996). However, because of its written and canonized form, the form of the text is *fixed* (contrary to its initial form that was far more fluid, even when written down). When reading *sūrah* x from the Qur'an, one is not going to freely create a text on the spot, but a person will give you the words as they occur in an authoritative form of the text. Furthermore, sacred texts may come in a single book volume, but the best way to describe them is as a *florilegium*; that is, a collection of diverse stories. The Hebrew

Bible is a particularly good example because it includes narrative, but also poetry, wisdom sayings, legislative texts and songs, among others. Some of the material goes back as far as the tenth century BCE, while other pieces are from the second century BCE. There are stories written in Judah, while others were produced in Babylonia. All of these different pieces have been brought together, amended and edited over a long period of time. The text most people refer to is this final product, called the Hebrew Bible, also known as the Old Testament.

The reason for the formal rigourousness of sacred texts has to do with the words' presumed divinity. Texts are *sacred text* when their words are considered to not only be *about* God, but also *of* God. They are divine revelation, put into the mouth of a prophet or sage. Allah's word was revealed to Muhammed, Moses was given God's word at Mount Sinai, and the Vedas contain revelations of ancient sages, credited to Brahma. Even in Buddhism, where no personal god exists, the Pali canon is considered sacred, containing the words of Buddha. Because the texts are considered God's word (or that of another spiritual figure), nothing can be changed. The rabbinic tradition says, you should not add or subtract, every letter counts. Hence, when the Hebrew text of the Bible, which is a consonantal text, was eventually vocalized in the process of transmission (in order to protect its interpretation), the Masoretes, the group of people who took care of it, developed a system that did not touch the letters in the manuscript. Instead, they added a set of dots and accents above and below the consonants. If they did not agree with a certain word, they did not cross it out or replace it, but added a little circle above the word that referred the reader to the margin where a change was suggested.

This practice tells a lot about two other key elements for understanding the discourse of sacred texts: the *author* and the *reader*, or rather *authors* and *readers*. Both should be understood as plural and indefinite rather than singular and definite. Even though the texts themselves and their believers attribute authorship of the text to God, or to his prophets or human substitutes on earth, the texts themselves are written by people. They may be in languages that are dead or scarcely used, such as Biblical Hebrew, Old Church Slavonic, or Sanskrit, but these languages remain human nevertheless. As Paul Chilton and Monika Kypotowska (2018) have argued, this creates the paradoxical status of language, and in extension sacred text, in religious theory. The divine being stands, by definition, beyond such human means, and yet, simultaneously, the only tool available to speak about the divine are these very texts and the language that gives rise to them. Most of the sacred texts of the current-day religions originate from a time before writing as the individual expression of a single person. Especially when it comes to religion, writers were a sort of medium serving a deity, not the equivalent of rock stars.

While authorship is often plural and anonymous due to the transmission process and different ideas about authors, *readership* is plural primarily because of the diversity among readers. Traditionally, religious scholarship pays a lot of attention to the original readership of a sacred text. A good amount of biblical research, for example, aims at reconstructing this audience and their interpretation of the text. However, the biblical text has been read by many more people since it first came into being. All of these readers had an understanding of the text. Some subfields of biblical studies have conducted research on these different audiences, resulting in fields such as biblical interpretation history, reception history, and more recently various fields that pay attention to voices in the text different from the dominant ideology, such as feminist studies, postcolonial studies, ecocriticism, and queer studies.

A last key term to mention in this section is *source language*. This refers to the original language of the sacred text. Because these languages lost their role as vernacular after a while, as far as they ever were, sacred texts were translated into other languages (see *Translation* this volume). Thus, many people have read the Old and New Testament only in English or German. And several Buddhists may only know the Pali canon in a Chinese translation. For some traditions, such as Islam, the source language is so crucial to the text's status that translations, even though they exist, are an issue of debate. Although they are used, they do not have the same *authority* as the original text. Note that such was also the case when the Septuagint, the Greek translation of the Hebrew Bible, was first presented to the public in the second century BCE. Practical cannot always compete with sacred.

Every single study of religion somehow touches upon sacred texts, so that one could say that almost every scholar of religion has at some point studied these texts. Yet, at the same time, very few studies actually focus on the language of the text as their main topic. Language and text are often a means to come to a reconstruction of the historical context, the social context, the composition history of a text, its (theological) meaning for a particular group of people, and the narrative construed (as literature, law, ideology, etc.). Two strands of research have been consistently interested in sacred texts for their language: *philology* or *linguistics* and *rhetorical studies*. Both focus on a different aspect of sacred-text-as-religious-discourse.

In *philology*, the study of language is at the heart of studying a text. One should not forget that it is texts, such as the Vedas and the Hebrew Bible, that have given rise to the first grammatical treatises, of Classical Sanskrit by Panini (fourth century BCE) and of Biblical Hebrew by Saadya Gaon (tenth century CE). In the old days, philology was the starting point for any kind of analysis of sacred text, including language, textual and extra-textual context. Over the years, philology has lost its momentum as other approaches gained popularity as well as funding (think of the cognitive turn and the spatial turn in the 1970s and 1980s, and most recently, the digital turn). What is more, linguistics, initially the term used for the study of language proper (and often applied for modern, spoken languages), has taken over much of the research domains traditionally covered by philologists (Pollock, 2009). For the current discussion, it suffices to say that either term works with regard to sacred texts as long as the focus remains on language, its peculiarities, and possibilities to express religious beliefs and practices. It goes without saying that the study of these features is invaluable to understand any of a sacred text's functions.

Rhetorical studies pay attention to one particular function, the persuasive one (see *Rhetoric* in this volume). Given that sacred texts are ideological in nature, they all showcase persuasive techniques in order to justify the claims made and assure readers of the sacred status of the text. In biblical studies, one sees a clear divide between Old Testament and New Testament studies when it comes to this approach. Rhetorical criticism in the former plays only a minor role, considered to be a subdiscipline of a literary approach to the text. Starting as a promising method with James Muilenburg's presidential address in 1968 (published 1969), it turned into a study of literary or rhetorical devices, with minor visibility. In New Testament studies, on the contrary, rhetorical studies are more numerous and influential, with groundbreaking work done by George Kennedy (1984) and Vernon Robbins (2009). This difference may partially be explained by the fact that the New Testament shares the Greek language with the Greco-Roman rhetorical tradition and is written in its cultural shadows. For the Hebrew Bible/Old Testament both language and context were different.

In the contemporary context, two or perhaps three fields of research seem to focus primarily on the discourse of sacred texts: *philology*, in its re-emerging form as a crossover of linguistics with an interest in literature, its context, and use (Couey and James, 2018, Vayntrub, 2019); *cognitive linguistics*, focusing primarily, though not uniquely, on metaphor as explained in the chapters by Richardson and Dorst (see *Metaphor* and *Cognition* in this volume) (Howe and Green, 2014); and *cognitive stylistics*, drawing on cognitive-linguistic concepts in order to explain what happens when we read sacred texts (Vermeulen and Hayes, forthcoming). Whereas two of the three approaches are new or renewed versions of older approaches, they all build upon previous scholarship. They take into account sensitivities that span across different subfields with language as their common denominator. All of these necessarily work with source texts. Given the unequal amount of research done on different sacred texts, I have limited this state of the art to the field of Hebrew Bible studies. Nevertheless, given the similarities on other matters, research on other sacred texts, such as the Vedas or the Qur'an, eventually may evolve in a similar direction. After all, the approaches reviewed in this chapter are those most closely related to the nature of language, itself a product of human beings. All sacred texts share these features, regardless of their specific context, use, and history of scholarship and interpretation.

18.2   Key Topics, Questions, and Debates

A quick look at a university library shows how many questions scholars have asked with regard to sacred texts. A great number of these questions are very specific, focused on a particular text, and often a specific section of that text. Monographs discussing a few verses of the biblical text, for example, form no exception. Nevertheless, there are a set of key topics that recur in most studies on the discourse of sacred texts. To illustrate this, consider the following example from the Hebrew Bible, from the Book of Nahum (3:4–5),

> [4] Because of the many harlotries of the harlot,
> the charming mistress of sorcery,
> who sells nations by her harlotries
> and peoples by her sorcery,
>
> [5] I am going to deal with you –
> declares the LORD of hosts.
> I will lift up your skirts over your face
> and I will show your nakedness to nations
> and your shame to kingdoms.

The prophet Nahum is uttering a prophecy of God against Nineveh, the capital of the Assyrian empire, one of the enemies of the Israelites in the Hebrew Bible. The prophecy envisions the city as a woman, more in particular, as a harlot and a sorceress. In response to the city's willful exposure, God will expose her without her approval. The passage imagines a reversal of fates: the powerful will become powerless. It draws on the conceptual metaphor THE CITY IS A WOMAN to develop a discourse on the relationship between God, the city, and the other nations. Three key issues play in this passage. First, what does it mean? Is the biblical God a rapist? Or are there other meanings to be considered? Second, does the translation do justice to the original text? Does the English 'harlot' catch what the Hebrew *zonah* is saying? Third, how should we read this? And did the ancient readers read this differently?

18.2.1   *The Meaning versus a Meaning*

One of the oldest and most crucial questions with regard to sacred texts is: what does it mean? Meaning is what drives reading. For sacred texts, meaning is often equated with *the* meaning. Being divinely inspired, these texts are considered to have one particular meaning, the one intended by the deity. A lot of scholarship and debates, inside as well as outside academia, centre around finding this unique, original meaning. As time goes by, the separation in time and space between text and interpreter makes it more challenging for current-day audiences to uncover such a meaning. What is more, this same passing of years shows that, regardless of what was intended initially, sacred texts are open to interpretation. Various readers understand the text differently. The history of interpretation of, for example, the Hebrew Bible reveals that there are many possible meanings. For texts, such as the Hebrew Bible or the Qur'an, language assists in this position, because Semitic languages with their consonantal script are, by definition, more polysemous than languages that spell out all their consonants and vowels, such as Greek or Sanskrit. In addition, people have often considered the language of sacred texts to be *figurative, allegorical or symbolic*, as such adding a layer of meaning on top of the literal reading of the text. Think of Philo's allegorical reading of the biblical text as a way to bridge Judaism and classical philosophy.

For the Nahum passage, scholars soon resorted to a metaphorical reading. The prophet uses the image of a violated woman to express the city's imagined conquest. Hence, God is not a rapist, but a warrior taking over the space of the enemy. However, not all readers buy into this interpretation, which underestimates the impact of the literal reading. The reason why the metaphor works is precisely because readers can and do picture a harassed woman. As I will discuss below, separating between a literal and a metaphorical reading has become more difficult for current-day readers, which has resulted in alternative readings of the passage. What does it mean when Nahum says the above words? Is it about God, as the traditional interpretation goes? Or is it about males shaming other males? Or do we have to deal with *pornoprophecy*, where the female body is on display for the male eye? (O'Brien, 2009). All of these meanings have been drawn from the same text.

18.2.2   *Translatability*

Translation is interpretation. Translation is making choices. By definition, a translation is a more-or-less-text; it never equals the original 100 per cent. For most texts, this does not form a major problem. However, for a sacred text it does. We are dealing with divine words and revelation. This revelation should be translated as it was meant, that is, precisely as what it means in the original text. Hence, translators have a difficult task ahead when working on sacred texts. They have to translate the *meaning*, preferably also the *form*, and where possible, even the *ambiguities* (Barnes, 2011; Şerban, 2006). A translation, such as the Jewish Publication Society of America Version (JPS) for the Hebrew Bible, does this by including footnotes at the bottom of the page, to signal other readings. In addition, translating *idioms* may pose a problem. Many of the Bible translations come across as archaic or written in a strange form of English (or German or . . .).

This has to do, among others, with the fact that the Old Testament itself was written in a *stylized* form of the vernacular. In other words, nobody was really speaking the kind of Hebrew you find in the biblical text. Another reason for turning to a more *formal register* when translating the text has to do with its sacred nature. This is not just a random piece of writing but the word of God. Such requires a special register of language. Furthermore, the stiff English in translations has to do with a tendency to stay as close as possible to the original language structures, even when those sound really awkward in English. On top of that, one often tried to translate the same Hebrew word consistently with the same English word, as if the Hebrew *yad*, always meant 'hand' and not also 'power' (metaphorically) or the whole person (through metonymy).

Most translations of Nahum speak of 'harlots' and 'uncovering nakedness', very polite words for what is actually said in Hebrew. Feminist scholars in particular have problematized such renderings. The city is not called a harlot – some readers may not even know the word – but a plain old whore. She is not uncovered like some extraordinary present, but her clothes are ripped off, showing her genitals. But even if translators would have chosen a more to-the-point rendering, the passage contains too much information to put in a simple translation. The metaphor THE CITY IS A WOMAN runs throughout the biblical corpus as one of the mental models to envision and consequently talk about cities. In Nahum, this city is Nineveh, but elsewhere, it is Jerusalem, Samaria, Damascus, or Babylon. Not only the image but also the precise setting and even wording (of 'uncovering nakedness') appears elsewhere in the prophets. There is an intertextual dialogue going on, a game with adopting and adapting language within the biblical corpus. For Nineveh the Hebrew *zonah* becomes 'harlot', for Jerusalem more often 'adulteress'. Translations as such make a distinction the biblical text itself does not make. The latter uses the word *zonah* for illegitimate relationships and plays with cultic (where the word 'harlot' belongs) and familial realms (where 'adulteress' fits) (Vermeulen, 2020). The Nahum example shows precisely what is at stake in translating sacred texts and how difficult it is to find the balance between literal and metaphorical, archaic and understandable, one meaning and many meanings.

18.2.3   *Reading and Rereading*

Sacred texts are read and reread, by the same individuals as well as by people through the ages. Upon a first reading, people notice different things than when rereading later. Reader knowledge is not only built during the reading process but also brought along for rereadings of the same text. In many religions, the sacred text is read yearly, following a preset order. Whereas the text itself never changes, the interpretation of it does. Things may have changed in the world at large, or in the smaller world of the individual believer. Resultantly, every reading is a new reading. Nevertheless, the so-called original reading forms the focus of a lot of scholarship. Considered the closest to the text, scholars draw upon a reconstruction of its context in their quest for the meaning of the text. This meaning consequently is placed along readings that are produced nowadays, in contexts that greatly to significantly differ from that of the original readership. Such *rereadings* are inherent to the changing times (e.g. Sardan, 2011). They show the vitality of a religion and its ability to recontextualize its sacred texts. However, sometimes these readings are not just new interpretations for new times. They become *counterreadings*, that openly distinguish themselves from earlier interpretations which are deemed problematic if not completely wrong. Counterreadings are combative and simultaneously protective of the sacred text. They go against the text's discourse on the one hand, but offer a reading considered acceptable on the other hand. Ultimately, the goal of readings, rereadings, and counterreadings is the same: to make sense of the sacred discourse in a particular context.

The city-woman of Nahum has been the subject of quite a few counterreadings in the last decades (e.g. O'Brien, 2009). Whereas its metaphorical interpretation was sufficient for a long period of time, the changes in the position both of women and with regard to violence, and especially in combination, have redrawn the interpretive landscape. In an age of #MeToo, it is no longer enough to state that rape is a biblical metaphor for city conquest. What is more, the image resonates so strongly with modern-day sensitivities that discussions on Nahum's discourse often seem to be about women rather than about cities. Although scholars are aware of the metaphor on a theoretical level, their actual reading of the text seems to dismiss that knowledge. The metaphor has become dysfunctional. Yet, despite these problems with the image of the city-as-woman, researchers and other readers alike are still capable of producing valuable interpretations of the Nahum text in the end. Reading sacred texts may be challenging at times: Nobody intends to defend the rape image in Nahum. However, it is there and people work with what they have to make sense of it, as the world in which the text is read changes. They will not, as happens with a lot of non-sacred classics, adapt to accommodate modern concerns. Rather, they will read, reread and, if necessary, counterread the text and its discourse as it stands.

18.3   Case Study

As pointed out already, sacred texts are considered to be of and about the divine, or more generally the spiritual. This double focus also appears with regard to spiritual experience as something told of in the text as well as experienced by readers of these texts. *Spiritual experience* is generally defined as "the experience of a break-through . . . a movement from the mundane to the supermundane dimension" (Lauster, 2016, p. 17). The experience is individual, temporary, and real and unreal at the same time. It lingers between "fairy-objects" and "fact-objects" as Yvonne Sherwood (2016, p. 33) has argued for religious experiences in general. Given the very nature of spiritual experience, it seems almost impossible to verbalize it, let alone reveal any linguistic structure that all expressions of such experiences may share. Nevertheless people have always tried to put these events into words. Also the Hebrew Bible relates various stories of characters encountering the divine.

In the following case study, I will analyse three such biblical stories (Hagar in the desert, Moses and the burning bush, and Jonah in the fish), looking at the linguistics behind the spiritual experience. My analysis is *cognitive-stylistic* in nature, to refer back to the above-mentioned scholarly approaches to sacred text. I will track the linguistic cues for the reader in the text, providing the JPS English *translation* for convenience but with Hebrew in parentheses to show what is happening in the *source text*. I will show that spiritual experience is spatially constructed and conceived, creating a "sense of place", that is, an "affective bond between people and place or setting" (Tuan, 1990 [1974], p. 4) with religious significance. Although the stories differ in many ways (different writers, historical context, narratological setting, gender and origin of the characters, . . .), they apply the same linguistic toolbox and spatial layout to present the spiritual experience as a utopian or mythical space.

18.3.1   *Hagar in the Desert*

Because Abraham and his wife Sara cannot conceive, Sara offers her handmaid Hagar to start a family. Hagar gives birth to a son, Ishmael (Genesis 16). Later on, against all odds, also Sara will have a son, Isaac (Gen 21: 1–3). For reasons unmentioned although imaginable (jealousy towards Hagar and her son, concern for her own son's future), Sara asks Abraham to send away Hagar and Ishmael. Abraham is not eager to do so and consults with God who assures him he will take care of Ishmael under all circumstances (Gen 21: 9–13).

[14] Early next morning Abraham took some bread and a skin of water . . . together with the child, and **sent her away** (וישלחה). And she wandered about **in the wilderness** (במדבר) of Beer-sheba.

[15] When the water was gone from the skin, **she left (BH: threw)** (ותשלך) the child **under** (תחת) one of the bushes

[16] and went and **sat down** (ותשב) at a distance, a bowshot away, for she thought, "Let me not look on as the child dies." And **sitting** (ותשב) thus afar, **she lifted up** (ותשא) her voice and wept.

[17] God heard the cry of the boy, and a messenger of God called to Hagar **from heaven** (מין השמים) and said to her, "What troubles you, Hagar? Fear not, for God has heeded the cry of the boy where he is.

[18] **Get up (קומי), lift up (שאי)** the boy and hold him by the hand, for **I will make a great (גדול)** nation of him."

[19] Then God opened her eyes and she saw a well of water (באר מים).

After a first spatial movement away from the household and the centre of life into the desert and loneliness, the story continues in the desert, arid by definition literally and conceptually. Hagar puts down the child (*down*) under a bush and sits herself down (*down*) a little further. Consequently she lifts up her voice (*up*) and weeps. God hears the crying of the boy and sends a messenger. The messenger encourages Hagar to get up (*up*) and pick up the child (*up*). The initial double downward movement is countered by a double upward movement. The passage concludes with the promise that God will make the boy grow up (*up*). Consequently, Hagar sees a well of water and the water saves mother and child.

A combination of *motion verbs* and *directional prepositions* creates the space of the spiritual experience. This space is characterized by a going-up-through-going-down. This movement is physically contradictory: it is impossible to go up if you go down. Nevertheless this is how the space is conceived. Given the circumstances, an encounter with the divine, may be exactly why the space is unusual in terms of directionality, as if the writers of the text, necessarily bound by the possibilities of human language and thinking, had to find a way out of the embodied nature of language into the incorporeal realm of the supernatural. The space of the meeting can be deemed *mythical* as defined by Yi-Fu Tuan (1977, p. 99), "an intellectual construct ... differ[s][ent] from pragmatic and scientifically conceived spaces in that it ignores the logic of exclusion and contradiction". Finally, the space also resembles *utopian* spatial constructs. It is both a better place and a no-place (More, 2016: 123), "a literary artefact[s] which generate[s] cognitive estrangement between the world described in the text and the world of the author" (Uhlenbruch, 2015: 13). The desert is an unpleasant place; nevertheless, it holds a promising future for Hagar and Ishmael. At the same time, the desert and water are, normally speaking, mutually exclusive. In the story of Hagar and Ishmael they are not.

To sum up, Hagar's spiritual experience is spatially constructed by means of motion verbs, directional prepositions and spatial locations. The space is characterized by a trajectory up-through-down, which is not only *literally* present in the motions of the characters, but also *metaphorically* in their emotional world. Hagar is not just sitting down after having put down the child; she is giving up hope to live, depressed by the thought of her son's death. The spiritual experience is a way out of her impasse and creates a better place for her son and herself. This place plays with the logic of the physical world, merging opposite directions (up and down) and mutually exclusive spatial features (such as water and desert). The proposed reading is a *rereading*, applying new frameworks (cognitive-stylistics) as well as new foci (spatial, a minor female character). Due to the latter, one may also consider it a *counterreading* to some extent.

18.3.2   Moses and the Burning Bush

In Exodus 3, God calls Moses to free his people from the slavery in Egypt and to lead them to the Promised Land. The episode of his call starts with the burning bush that appears to Moses when he is shepherding the flock of his father-in-law on mount Horeb.

[1] Now Moses, tending the flock of his father-in-law Jethro, drove the flock into **the wilderness** (המדבר), and came to Horeb, the **mountain** (הר) of God.

[2] A messenger of the LORD appeared to him in a blazing fire **out of a bush** (מתוך הסנה). He gazed, and there was a bush all aflame, yet the bush was not consumed.

[3] Moses said, "I must **turn aside** (אסרה) to look at this **marvellous sight** (מראה גדול); why doesn't the bush burn up?"

[4] . . . God called to him out of the bush

[5] "Do not come closer. **Remove** (של) your sandals **from your feet** (מעל רגליך), for **the place on which** (עליו) you stand is holy ground . . ."

[7] And the LORD said, "I have seen well the plight of my people in Egypt and have heard their outcry . . .

[8] **I have come down** (וארד) to rescue them from the Egyptians and to **bring them out** (והעלתו) **of that land** (מן הארץ ההוא) **to a good and spacious land** (אל ארץ), a land flowing with milk and honey . . ."

Here as well, the experience requires a removal from the central space of living to a more isolated and empty space, the desert. Moses is already on higher ground (*up*) when he meets with God, partially bridging the spatial gap between the human and the divine realm, even though he is unaware himself until the messenger appears to him in the burning bush. This bush draws Moses's attention because it burns without being consumed. It defies the laws of physics. It is part of a *mythical* space in which God can meet with men. Although Moses cannot understand the space in its dimensions, he deems it גדול, "marvellous," "great" (*up*) when facing it. Conceptually, the space is associated with good things through its orientation (Lakoff & Johnson, 2003 [1980]), and thus a good-place, a *eu-topia*. The story continues with the messenger asking Moses to remove his sandals (*down*). Various explanations, mostly anthropological and/or religious, have been given to this request (ancient Near Eastern habit, no touching of holy ground with dirt, being smaller without shoes). From a purely spatial perspective the function is quite simple: it is a downward movement, helping to shape the spiritual experience of the character. When Moses takes off his sandals, he has to lower himself (*down*). God's message continues the spatial discourse: I, God, have come down (*down*) to Egypt to bring up (*up*) my people to a good land. Moses will make the same spatial journey, being the medium through which God will free the Israelites. For Moses, this movement will be *literal* (geographically speaking Israel is on a higher altitude than Egypt), for the Israelites, it will also be *metaphorical*. Their oppression (*down*) by the

Egyptians will end and they will be free to worship their God again (*up*) in the Promised Land.

Similar to Hagar's story, the experience is characterized by a spatial pattern of up-through-down. This pattern is present in the language of the text through the use of *motion verbs* and *spatial locations and adjectives*. With these linguistic tools, the *writers* create a space that follows a logic different from reality. It can hold burning bushes that are not consumed by fire and downward movements that lead you upward. The space is *mythical* and marvellous; above all, it is *good*. Moses has his spiritual experience, the Israelites' one is ahead. The presented spatial *rereading* does not need to rely on chemistry to explain the burning bush. Rather, it draws on language and its capacity to imagine the impossible.

Note that even nowadays, the spatial language has been kept to speak of Jews moving to Israel. They make '*aliyah*', literally 'an upgoing'. In modern-day Hebrew, Israel is still the high ground, the good place, to which people migrate from a lower space. While the immigrants may not necessarily experience the move as spiritual (although many will in one way or another), the language used to speak of it does evoke the upgoing of the Israelites in Exodus and their preceding oppression in Egypt.

18.3.3   Jonah in the Fish

A last example is drawn from the book of Jonah. The prophet Jonah must go to Nineveh to prophesy its end. Rather than doing so, he turns the other direction on a journey downward (*down*): down to the harbour, into the ship, on its floor, in a deep sleep, in the water, and finally in the fish (Jonah 1). Most scholars connect the movement to the spiritual crisis of Jonah, thus reading the *literal* movement *metaphorically*. In chapter 2, this crisis turns into a spiritual experience.

2:1 The LORD provided a huge fish to swallow Jonah and Jonah remained **in the fish's belly** (במעי).

³ **From the belly of Sheol** (ומבטן שאול) I cried out, and you heard my voice

⁴ **you cast** (ותשליכני) me **into the depths** (מצולה), **into the heart of the sea** (בלבב ימים), the floods engulfed me; all your breakers and billows **swept over me** (עלי עברו).

⁶ The waters closed in over me, the deep (תהום) engulfed me.

⁷ **I sank** (ירדתי) **to the base of the mountains** (לקצבי הרים); the bars of the earth closed upon me forever. Yet **you brought my life up from the pit** (ותעל משחת), o LORD my God!

Inside the fish, at the bottom of the sea, when Jonah cannot sink any further, he meets God. Jonah's psalm, which holds between a prayer of distress and thanksgiving, describes exactly that experience. It starts with emphasizing the downward path which Jonah took: the belly, Sheol, the depths, the heart of the sea, the deep, the base. It leads him up to God, or rather it is God who lifts Jonah up (*up*). Similar to the previous stories, the space created by the narrative and its language resembles *mythical* and *utopian* places. The story creates a range of questions about how one can stay alive after being eaten by a giant fish; who else was there to witness Jonah's experience and to testify to the fish's existence; and where exactly is that special fishly space where Jonah met God. Rationally speaking, the answer would be nowhere (hence, *ou-topia*) or only in a story (hence, the label fiction and myth for the Jonah narrative). Nevertheless, Jonah is in a good place (*eu-topia*) and thankful to God in chapter 2. Jonah's spiritual experience follows the up-through-down trajectory of the other two stories. This journey neatly fits in the larger directional construction of the book as a whole, read as a metaphorical tale of Jonah's inner state of mind.

The presented analysis *rereads* the passage in Jonah 2 as a textual representation of a spiritual experience (rather than only a step in Jonah's emotional journey). This experience is created for the reader by means of *spatial indicators*, primarily of the deep, and by means of *motion verbs*. Jonah's descent to the bottom of the world leads him up, to a better although unlikely world in which he will not die inside the fish but will have the opportunity to be a faithful servant of God.

Whereas spiritual experiences are individual encounters with the supernatural, out of the reach of the general laws of this world, the stories about them are not. They depict spiritual experiences as spatial; they have a directionality describing an unusual journey that leads you up by means of descending. The pathway is created with language's typical means to evoke space: motion verbs, directional and locational prepositions, and spatial vocabulary for particular locations, such as the desert or a mountain. Because of human language and its embodied nature, these are the tools at disposal (Tan, 2016, p. 217). Even the supermundane has to be described by human means. At the same time, it is exactly by means of language, and more in particular by defying its logic, that spiritual experiences are related. The spaces draw on contradictions and oppositions: up and down, desert and well, burning bush and living bush, and death in a fish and alive in a fish. These spaces resemble mythical spaces as well as utopian spaces in their double definition of both good place and no-place. Meeting God is a super-experience that plays by rules different from the ones of this world. By defining that experience in the analysed stories as a spatial construct that both follows the rules of language and violates the referential logic behind it, the reader gets to experience himself or herself exactly what is at stake in these spiritual encounters: "a movement from the mundane to the supermundane dimension" (Lauster, 2016, p. 17).

18.4   Future Directions

Whereas the so-called anti-historicist interpretive approaches are still popular, the study of sacred texts seems to turn again more frequently to text-based and especially language-based methodologies. Philology may be making a comeback, accompanied by the rise of cognitively inspired linguistic and stylistic analyses. These approaches, no doubt, will have to compete with an ever-growing array of methods that do not have language as their focus; however, they may be their perfect partners in the end.

One such partnership should intend to be *cross-disciplinary*, going in preferably two directions: *cross-religious* and *cross-linguistic*, since each of the sacred texts comes with a specific language. As mentioned in other chapters in this volume, the study of religion, and therefore also of sacred texts of those religious traditions, tends to be a specialist business. It requires the knowledge of particular languages and particular contexts in which those texts were created. Rather than looking for people with skills in more than one field, cooperation should be established that brings together specialists of the different sacred texts. It would allow to work on questions, such as comparing the discourse in the Hebrew Bible and the Qur'an or the Vedas, investigating which features that they share, linguistically calling for a category or even a prototype of sacred text, or whether 'sacred' is mainly an attribute that is imposed upon the text, regardless of its language. Analysis could also look for similarities around spiritual experience by investigating, for example, if the Pali canon also constructs this experience as a spatial utopia that defies the logic of physical movements.

Another partnership should be set up between scholars of sacred text on the one hand and *media studies specialists* on the other. Some general studies have been conducted on the impact of digitalization and the Internet on, for example, Bible reading. The notion of canon seems to be affected, since the Internet contains so much more than the Bible and readers no longer hold a physical book in their hands that holds the word of God. Online reading is fragmentary and ephemeral (Siker, 2017), but the effect of this reading on the text and whether it makes a difference for readers in terms of meaning production could be further investigated, looking, for example, at whether Jonah's experience in the fish results in another meaning for the text when read in a digital form. Rereading may also differ in digital and non-digital contexts, such as whether the digital sacred text is read or rather listened to or viewed. Meaning construal work could also be affected, with the addition of background knowledge with hyperlinks, adding knowledge many readers do not have when reading a sacred text on paper.

A third collaboration requires specialists on the *source text* and on different *translations* of the text. They should focus on similarities and dissimilarities in discourse, not just singular words or idioms. For example, how spiritual experience is construed similarly in translations of the Hebrew Bible and where there are differences, whether they are the result of linguistic constraints or rather instigated by text-external differences. Such construal may change as the world around the readers of the sacred text changes. The interpretation history of the city-woman in the Hebrew Bible, for example, shows that this context greatly determines the meaning of the image. It would be, in particular, interesting to do this kind of comparative research for discourse on key concepts within the specific religions, such as on the temple in the Hebrew Bible, or the *nirwanah* in Buddhism.

Finally, scholarship on sacred texts tends to overlook *real readers*. It focuses on an intended reader, either ancient or more contemporary. However, this reader is mostly a mental construct. Actual readers are rarely consulted. Even when analyses are presented from a female perspective, to just name one example, the only real reader involved in these studies is the scholar conducting the research and identifying herself or himself as representing the interpretation of female readers, as a group. In order to gain further insight in religious discourse, *reader response studies* should supplement the existing studies looking at how real readers understand this discourse and which cues they pick up. In the three stories from the Bible on spiritual experience, for example, do believers sympathize with the characters or are they preconditioned to read the story by the fact that Hagar is the non-official wife of Abraham and Jonah the prophet who forfeits his task? Understanding what ultimately determines their reading experience, and eventual spiritual experience could shed light on how meaning emerges.

In terms of specific frameworks or approaches, two additional ones with potential have been mentioned in between the lines in this final section: *Text World Theory* and *Prototype Theory*. Both fall within the broader category of cognitive approaches to language. Text Wordl Theory (TWT) pays attention to reading as an interaction between linguistic cues in the text and a reader in a particular context with certain knowledge. Sacred texts would be ideal material to analyse in such a way. What is more, it may further Text World Theory itself as well since it is developed with English in mind. Given the broad variety of source languages found for sacred text, the application of TWT will go hand in hand with a further refinement or adaptation where needed. An important concept in TWT is world-switching. TWT states that a reader construes a new text-world when a shift in time and/or place occurs in the text. For example, when someone relates a dream or what she would like for her birthday present. Some of these world-switches create modal worlds, meaning that they express a desire (boulomaic), an obligation (deontic), or a belief (epistemic). They are marked linguistically with modal verbs, such as 'want' (boulomaic), 'must' (deontic), and 'suppose' (epistemic) as well as modal adverbs, such as 'hopefully' (boulomaic) or 'perhaps' (epistemic). In addition, they make use of constructions with the verb 'to be', such as 'it is good to' (boulomaic) or 'it is forbidden to' (deontic) (Gavins, 2007). Yet, how does this work in a language that scarcely marks modality? Biblical Hebrew, for example, does not have modal verbs. Much of the 'musts' and 'shoulds' in the English translation are the result of interpretation, not of rendering a linguistic structure that is actually traceable in the source text. Nevertheless, the framework offers a lot of opportunities for analysing the discourse in sacred texts.

And so does Prototype Theory, especially with regard to the big question of what determines the sacrality of a text, from a discourse point of view. Prototype Theory is a theory about cognitive categorization. It looks for so-called prototypes, the best examples of a category. With regard to the prototype 'sacred text', the closer a text comes to the prototype, the more likely it deserves the label 'sacred text', the further away, the less likely (e.g. Lakoff, 1987; Rosch, 1978). In addition to the prototype of sacred text as a whole, one can also consider other important categories through a prototype lens, such as prophetic discourse, divine discourse, discourse of prayer, of revelation, etc. Here again, one should take into account the peculiarities of the source texts, without superimposing preset ideas about these categories. Such is exactly what philologists nowadays are aiming at: to describe sacred texts on their own terms, rather than on those of a later time and place. It is letting the text speak for itself first, and only then have it engage with the many possible frameworks that come with specific questions. It is through understanding the discourse that we will understand the text. And it is through understanding the text that we will be able of having meaningful conversations about it. Language is the beginning of sacred text, as the Gospel of John states, but it surely is the end as well.

18.5   References

Barnes, R. (2011). Translating the sacred. In K. Malmkjaer & K. Windle (eds.), *The Oxford Handbook of Translation* (pp. 37–54). Oxford: Oxford University Press.

Chilton, P., & Kopytowska, M. (2018). *Religion, Language, and the Human Mind.* Oxford: Oxford University Press.

Couey, J. B., & James, E. T. (2018). *Biblical Poetry and the Art of Close Reading.* Cambridge: Cambridge University Press.

Gavins, J. (2007). *Text World Theory: An Introduction.* Edinburgh: Edinburgh University Press.

Graham, W. (2010). *Islamic and Comparative Religious Studies: Selected Writings.* London: Routledge.

Howe, B., & Green, J. B. (2014). *Cognitive Linguistic Explorations in Biblical Studies.* Berlin: de Gruyter.

Kennedy, G. (1984). *New Testament Interpretation through Rhetorical Criticism. Studies in Religion.* Chapel Hill: University of North Carolina Press.

Lakoff, G. (1987). *Women, Fire and Dangerous Things: What Categories Reveal about the Mind*. Chicago: University of Chicago Press.

Lakoff, G., & Johnson M. (2003 [1980]). *Metaphors We Live By*. 2nd ed. Chicago: University of Chicago Press.

Lauster, J. (2016). How to do transcendence with words? The problem of articulation in religious experience. In T. Hardtke, U. Schmiedel & T. Tan (eds.), *Religious Experience Revisited: Expressing the Inexpressible* (pp. 15–29). Studies in Theology and Religion 21. Boston: Brill.

More, T. (2016). *Utopia*. G. M. Logan (ed.). Trans. R. M. Adams. Cambridge Texts in the History of Political Thought. 3rd ed. Cambridge: Cambridge University Press.

Muilenburg, J. (1969). Form Criticism and Beyond. *Journal of Biblical Literature*, 88(1), 1–18.

Niditch, S. (1996). *Oral World and Written Word: Ancient Israelite Literature*. Library of Ancient Israel. Louisville: Westminster John Knox Press.

O'Brien, J. M. (2009). *Nahum*. 2nd ed. Sheffield: Phoenix Press.

Pollock, S. (2009). Future philology? The fate of a soft science in a hard world. *Critical Inquiry*, 35(4), 931–61.

Robbins, V. (2009). *The Invention of Christian Discourse*. Rhetoric of Religious Antiquity Series 1. Blandford Forum: Deo Pub.

Rosch, E. (1978). Principles of categorization. In E. Rosch & B. Lloyd (eds.), *Cognition and Categorization* (pp. 27–48). Hillsdale: Lawrence Erlbaum.

Sardan, Z. (2011). *Reading the Qur'an: The Contemporary Relevance of the Sacred Text of Islam*. Oxford: Oxford University Press.

Şerban, A. (2006). Translation and genre: Sacred texts. In K. Brown (ed.), *Encyclopedia of Language and Linguistics* (pp. 47–53). 2nd ed. London: Elsevier.

Sherwood, Y. (2016). Modern trials and tests of "experience": Plastic commonplace and managed exception. In T. Hardtke, U. Schmiedel & T. Tan (eds.), *Religious Experience Revisited: Expressing the Inexpressible* (pp. 30–56). Studies in Theology and Religion 21. Boston: Brill.

Siker, J. S. (2017). *Liquid Scripture: The Bible in a Digital World*. Minneapolis: Fortress Press.

Tan, T. (2016). The corporeality of religious experience: Embodied cognition in religious practices. In T. Hardtke, U. Schmiedel & T. Tan (eds.), *Religious Experience Revisited: Expressing the Inexpressible* (pp. 207–26). Boston: Brill.

Tuan, Y.-F. (1977). *Space and Place: The Perspective of Experience*. 8th printing 2014. Minneapolis: University of Minnesota Press.

Tuan, Y.-F. (1990 [1974]). *Topophilia: A Study of Environmental Perception, Attitudes, and Values*. New York: Columbia University Press.

Uhlenbruch, F. (2015). *The Nowhere Bible: Utopia, Dystopia, Science Fiction*. Studies of the Bible and Its Reception 4. Berlin: De Gruyter.

Vayntrub, J. (2019). *Beyond Orality: Biblical Poetry on Its Own Terms*. The Ancient Word. New York: Routledge.

Vermeulen, K. (2020). *Conceptualizing Biblical Cities*. Cham: Palgrave McMillan.

Vermeulen, K., & E. Hayes. (Forthcoming). *How to Read the Bible*. Grand Rapids: Eerdmans.

19   Ecology

Mariana Roccia

19.1   Background, History, and Key Terms

The way the natural environment is portrayed in religious terms is crucial for determining the nature of the interactions that individuals will have with the environment. The field of eco-theology, in its broadest sense, attempts to describe and analyse how environmental concerns can also engage with a deep theological reflection that may lead to practical changes. Whilst extensive research has been conducted to establish common threads between ecology and theology, the connections between language use within these particular fields remain largely unexplored. Alexander (2009), for instance, urges scholars that interdisciplinary research within discourse studies is crucial to the understanding of eco-logical issues. By blending linguistic techniques and cognitive theories into an ecological linguistic framework, Ecolinguistics offers the possibility of revealing how linguistic features can convey positive attitudes towards the environment and develop positive discourses that are informed by various theological strands.

As Fill and Penz (2018) note, the term *Ecolinguistics* is highly nuanced and encompasses a multiplicity of understandings that scholars have been associating with the field over the years. Its origins can be traced back to the mid-1960s when linguists Florence and Carl Voegelin first used it to refer to the connections between language and ecology in their research about indigenous languages in North America. However, it was only after linguist Einar Haugen's talk in 1970 that the field of "language ecology" emerged. The Haugean approach informed scholars' research in the fields of endangered languages, language contact, and multilingualism to name a few. Ecolinguistics continued to be primarily concerned with these topics until the early 90s when Michael Halliday's presentation at the 1990 AILA conference introduced another novel strand. In his talk, Halliday broadly claimed that environmental issues also concern applied linguistics and suggested exploring the connections between language use and its impact on the wider ecological context.

Consequently, much of the contemporary use of the term Ecolinguistics relates to the explorations of the role language plays in the interactions between humans and their surroundings, and the positioning of humankind within larger ecosystems not merely as part of social systems. In doing so, Ecolinguistics draws from cognitive theories, discourse analysis, and linguistic techniques to reveal language patterns that convey destructive or environmentally friendly practices (Stibbe, 2015).

In this regard, Ecolinguistics owes much of its success to Critical Discourse Analysis (CDA) for deconstructing dominant discourses that promote antienvironmental practices. However, some scholars believe that critiquing is only the first step in a much more ambitious venture and that there is a need to rethink the focus. Martin (2004) offers what he calls a 'complementary perspective' to the well-established field of CDA, namely one that emphasizes the search for inspiring texts and discourses which he calls Positive Discourse Analysis. He argues that whilst extensive research has been conducted in CDA, Positive Discourse Analysis (PDA) remains a relatively unexplored area though its contribution is much needed. Holding that CDA's focus is on the 'negative' discursive features may be unfair, but rather ultimately to reveal how discourse channels oppressive power relationships. Likewise, Ecolinguistics has traditionally focused on the hegemonic power relationships that human groups exercise over ecological systems whilst sometimes overlooking the range of existing constructive discourses. Therefore, this approach aligns well with the role Ecolinguistics plays in searching for stories that inspire beneficial interactions (Stibbe, 2018).

Researchers can use an ecological philosophy, or *ecosophy* (Naess, 1995) to judge whether stories are beneficial or not. Based on his ecosophy, Stibbe (2015, p.16) judges stories as positive if they "value and celebrate the lives and wellbeing of all species, promote human wellbeing, call for a reduction of consumption, and promote redistribution of resources". In sum, ecolinguistic PDA will involve identifying features of language in a chosen corpus which convey particular stories. Once identified, these stories are then compared against the analyst's ecosophy. If both are aligned, then the discourse is considered a positive one (Stibbe, 2018).

The ecolinguistic framework followed by this study identifies eight types of STORIES, that is, mental models in the minds of individuals or shared across the minds of multiple individuals in a society: *ideology, framing, metaphor, evaluation, identity, conviction, erasure,* and *salience* (Stibbe, 2015). Since these stories function at the level of personal and social cognition (Van Dijk, 2009) they cannot be accessed directly. Therefore, a range of linguistic and cognitive theories are deployed to reveal the patterns of language in the stories and whether they align to the ecosophy leading the study.

The concepts of framing, salience, and re-minding can be particularly useful in analysing language in relation to environmental concerns. Broadly speaking, frames are cognitive structures that guide our perception of reality (see *Cognition* in this volume). *Framing* is a useful tool for enacting social change. For Lakoff (2010), the ENVIRONMENT frame has historically been conceived within the Euro-Western tradition as nature being independent from human existence. However, the continuous crossover with other critical areas, such as economics, health, and security, to name a few, blurs the scope of what is an environmental issue and what is not. In short, environmental issues are everyone's responsibility (Corbett, 2006) and a conscious effort should be made to erase inadequate frames and build background frames that enable not only a more holistic understanding of the environment but also encourage individual political engagement. In this regard, doctrinal statements like official statements by the pope offer "a communication system that allows for sufficient spread over the population, sufficient repetition, and sufficient trust in the messengers" (Lakoff, 2010, p. 72) whilst drawing on various sources from key religious figures to scientific accounts.

Salience, or the "story in people's minds that an area of life is important or worthy of attention" (Stibbe, 2015, p. 162), can also be a useful feature to examine. By analysing the different levels of transitivity, metaphors, and abstractions, it is possible to reveal, for instance, how environmental campaigns advocate the protection of a specific area by giving salience to its local species. In a similar vein, the concept of re-minding focuses on the erasure of an area in a discourse or a text by explicitly drawing the attention to its reconsideration. As Stibbe (2015) notes, whilst these concepts are often used in visual analysis, researchers can also observe features in written texts that produce a concrete and intense linguistic representation of a particular area deserving attention, such as in the previous example. The relevance for pursuing an analysis of this kind lies in the possibility of encouraging not only a cognitive but also a behavioural transformation. The activation of concrete imagery in the discourse – as opposed to abstract nominalizations – creates a more vivid representation which encourages the protection of those groups or individuals foregrounded in the discourse.

19.2   Key Topics, Questions, and Debates

In recent years, Ecolinguistics has received some major attention from scholars working at the intersection of critical discourse studies and media. No extensive studies have applied an ecolinguistic approach to religious texts to date, although the relationship between religion and the environment has been a major scholarly area of interest, especially in connection to Catholicism (Conradie et al., 2014).

With a lasting account of conflicting interpretations regarding nature and the environment, the Catholic Church is yet to develop a homogenous stance on this topic. Its position is perhaps better understood in terms of *Christianities* (Wolf & Gjerris, 2009), a label which seems more suited to encompass the multiplicity of views. In this regard, eco-theology originates in response to the pressing environmental threats and pursues to engage the Christian traditions to play an active role in the response.

White Jr.'s (1967) influential essay "The Historical Roots of Our Ecologic Crisis" is a useful starting point for unravelling the articulation of environmental concerns and religion. White postulates that one of the main causes of the environmental crisis stems from the techno-scientific paradigm promoted from the Christian Western European tradition. He observes that humanity's dependence on science and technology to subdue nature is now turning against us, and these will not be able to provide all the responses to the environmental damage that was an increasing concern in the 1960s. There is historical evidence that the passages in Genesis 1:26–28 (Holy Bible ESV, 2013) ("Let us make mankind in our image, in our likeness, so that they may rule over the fish in the sea and the birds in the sky, over the livestock and all the wild animals, [a] and over all the creatures that move along the ground") began to be interpreted in North-Western Europe in the Middle Ages as a means to legitimize human domination of nature.

Today, some biblical scholars interpret these passages as mandating stewardship, that is, the protecting and keeping of the earth because it is God's creation, in line with God's instruction to Adam in Genesis 2:15 (Kearns, 2004). Similar notions can be found in other religions. In Islam, for instance, the word *ayat* is used in the Holy Qu'ran to refer to the signs of God's creation and 'nature', a notion for which there is no specific word in the Qu'ran (Khalid, 2002). In this regard, there is an emphasis in the Islamic tradition that humankind must act as *khalifahs,* that is, protectors and guardians of God's creation. This understanding arises from the four Islamic principles governing human behaviour: the unity principle, the notion that we all united in creation; the creation principle, the purity in which all things are created; the balance principle, the notion that there is a natural order in creation; and finally, the responsibility principle or *khalifa*, by which humankind has the moral responsibility to protect all of God's creation. Interconnectedness is also one of the key tenets of Buddhism. For Buddhists, nature is seen as having a mutually interdependent relationship with humans; thus, protecting the natural environment means protecting oneself.

White (1967, p. 6) concludes his essay by stating: "Since the roots of our trouble are so largely religious, the remedy must also be essentially religious, whether we call it that or not. We must rethink and refeel our nature and destiny". As for Christianity's contribution to the response, White's claim that the Franciscan tradition may offer some significant answers resonates with the current Pope's views regarding environmental and social issues. But responses may also come from secular and religious activist groups. Kearns (2004) groups Christian ecological activism into three rough categories she calls 'ethics': Christian stewardship, eco-justice, and Creation spirituality. The first ethic refers to the role Christians have in protecting God's creation as stewards by following a close reading of the Bible in these terms. As Kearns notes, *Christian stewards* counteract more conservative anti-environmental and anti-pantheist strands. Pope John Paul II became an advocate of steward-ship as seen in his interventions in the early 90s (See Pope John Paul II, 1990: *The Ecological Crisis: A Common Responsibility*).

Eco-justice Christians, on the other hand, see environmental issues as social issues which often affect oppressed minorities such as the poor, women, children, and indigenous communities, often in developing countries. Deeply influenced by the doctrine of Jesus and the Social Gospel, eco-justice advocates believe and actively seek to remedy sociopolitical inequity. The emergence of the liberation theology movement in Latin America takes on board many of the concerns regarding social injustice and environmental issues, which are being reconsidered by the current Pope. The third category, *Creation spirituality*, sees humankind as just one of many components of a larger universal project. Advocates of this movement are less orthodox in their views since the Bible is only one of many sources of inspiration and understanding of the universe. This often entails performing ritual practices that incorporate the sacred to daily life (Kearns, 2004).

A number of international networks and social activist groups have emerged in recent years with the aim of linking religion and environmental awareness. The Global Catholic Climate Change Movement (2017), for instance, addresses social, ethical, and environmental issues regarding climate change. In this regard, religious environmental discourse provides a rich and dynamic arena for debates that ultimately also seek to accomplish practical changes. A notable example of how these disciplines can contribute is seen in the 2015 joint report by the CAFOD, Islamic Relief, Tearfund, and Christian Aid organizations. In this project, Christian and Muslim leaders remodelled com-plex biomedical reports on the Ebola epidemic to communicate more effective messages that could truly provide relief. Projects like these illustrate how talk about environmental problems among people of different religions can motiv-ate genuine practical action.

Considering the role of religious institutions in religious belief and practice, doctrinal statements like Papal encyclicals which specifically address environ-mental concerns are particularly important in influencing approaches to the environment among believers. Papal encyclicals are didactic letters primarily directed to the clergy – but also to people in general – which give salience to a moral issue worthy of exhaustive consideration. In doing so, the encyclical becomes a site of struggle whereby the pope oscillates between a fraternal and paternal tone: "paternal in the pope's insistence that his ruling is binding and should not be questioned; fraternal in his request for assistance from the bishops in conveying the encyclical to the laity" (Jamieson, 1975, p. 407). However, as Gramsci (1971) further notes, this feature is perhaps unsurprising when considering the overall institutional role the Catholic Church has historically played in advocating societal change:

> The strength of religions, and of the Catholic church in particular, has lain, and still lies, in the fact that they feel very strongly the need for the doctrinal unity of the whole mass of the faithful and strive to ensure that the higher intellectual stratum does not get separated from the lower. The Roman church has always been the most vigorous in the struggle to prevent the "official" formation of two religions, one for the "intellectuals" and the other for the "simple souls." (Gramsci, 1971, p. 634)

The encyclical genre embodies, then, the discursive challenges faced by religious leaders in addressing not only a disparate audience, but also a moral issue with multiple layers of complexity. What is more, "The trick of an encyclical is to produce policy novelty, while couching this novelty in terms of a tradition that is ancient and ontologically secure" (Monagle, 2017, p. 2). This statement strongly resonates with what Miller (2010) defines as 'antecedent genre', that is, a genre that relies on the near or distant past to assist in the understanding of a new situation. For Jamieson (1975), nonetheless, conceiving the encyclical as an antecedent genre has its disadvantages: in invoking statements made by their predecessors, the popes not only sustain their arguments but also incorporate the generic constraints accumulated in the Church's historicity.

Francis' encyclical *Laudato si'* (2015) is an exemplary document, but unusual in addressing a wider audience aiming at secular and non-secular audiences as noted by various scholars (Deane-Drummond, 2016). Presumably, Pope Francis' Jesuit background plays a significant role in his degree of openness to other voices by connecting often dissimilar discourses in an ecumenical text:

> The Jesuits have undoubtedly been the major architects of this equilibrium, and in order to preserve it they have given the Church a progressive forward movement which has tended to allow the demands of science and philosophy to be to a certain extent satisfied. (Gramsci, 1971, p. 635)

In this regard, how Francis criticizes modernity, whilst drawing on ecological science, is remarkable, clearly distancing himself in that respect from former 'antimodernist encyclicals' (Latour, 2016). Given the large outreach of the Catholic Church in promoting beneficial interactions, examining how *Laudato si'* (2015) discusses environmental discourse compared to previous statements, and what strands of eco-theology they draw on, may show how the church and believers come to think and act with regard to the environment.

19.3   Case Study

To illustrate the benefits of using linguistic analysis of eco-theological texts, I will present a case study qualitative analysis of five papal documents (Table 19.1) produced by different popes and available in English at the official Vatican website (The Holy See).

With Pope Francis' encyclical *Laudato si'* (2015) at the centre of the study, four more documents are considered within the sample: *Caritas in Veritate* (Benedict XVI, 2009), *Redemptor Hominis* (John Paul II, 1979), *Octogesima Adveniens* (Paul VI, 1971), and *Pacem in Terris* (John XXIII, 1963), each of which Francis explicitly references in *Laudato si'* (2015). The intertextual connections drawn by Pope Francis reveal the linguistic patterns that provide good examples of positive discourse towards the environment and show how the papal discourse has evolved over the years in their treatment of environmental issues.

Corpus linguistics techniques (following McEnery and Hardie, 2012) were used for analysing the data, looking specifically at patterns of collocations with words related to the environment. After identifying these patterns, close reading and qualitative analysis of lexical segments containing frames and other patterns provided the possibility to identify where positive messages about human interaction with and in the 'environment' and 'nature' were present. When collocation patterns could be identified, a thematic procedure was followed with the concordance lines which enabled corpora to be examined under both eco-theological constructs and ecolinguistic devices that were used to convey a positive discourse. Various studies have suggested that Pope Francis engages with Leonardo Boff's (1997) works in connection to liberation theology and in his choice of name to honour St. Francis of Assisi, Patron Saint

Table 19.1 *Select papal documents*

Document	Author	Date	Word count	Genre
Laudato Si'	Pope Francis	24 May 2015	40,567	Encyclical Letter
Caritas in Veritate	Pope Benedict XVI	29 June 2009	30,445	Encyclical Letter
Redemptor Hominis	Pope John Paul II	4 March 1979	23,306	Encyclical Letter
Octogesima Adveniens	Pope Paul VI	14 May 1971	11,392	Apostolic Letter
Pacem in Terris	Pope John XXIII	11 April 1963	15,907	Encyclical Letter

of Ecology. The case study and methods therefore focused on search terms around the environment which might reveal how *Laudato si'* shared the language of liberation theology and the extent to which it represented a more bio-inclusive view of ethical relationships with the environment. I will show some key examples that illustrate the opportunities for analysing theological corpora in the light of ecolinguistic techniques and its articulation with eco-theology and the field of environmental ethics.

19.3.1 'Environment' in Laudato si' (2015)

The item 'environment' occurs ninety-one times in the corpus and using a Mutual Information score and a cut off point for collocates (following Brezina, McEnery, and Wattam, 2015) to calculate the strength of the colloca-tion (that is, how often the pair is observed together compared to the times the pair can be observed separately), twenty-one items were identified for future analysis. Although the search throws a high frequency of function words due to the small scale of the sampled document (see Table 19.2), a closer examination to the lexical words provides some linguistic evidence of the discourse around this specific item.

The concordance lines in Table 19.3 show that 'Natural' appears as a predominant left collocate and often qualified as a 'collective good', 'the patrimony of humanity' and ultimately everyone's responsibility (§95). Francis relies on drawing intertextual links with the other popes to sustain his argu-ment, namely Pope John Paul II's encyclical *Redemptor Hominis* (1979) and Benedict XVI's *Caritas in Veritate* (2009) to emphasize the lack of long-term concern towards the natural environment. More specifically, in the first two

Table 19.2 *Top ten collocates with* 'environment' *in* Laudato si' *(2015)*

Collocate	Freq (coll.)	Freq (corpus)
Natural	9	29
Concern	5	34
Development	6	55
On	16	202
More	6	105
The	124	2,453
Human	10	199
They	5	120
For	18	464
Our	9	259

Table 19.3 *Concordance lines for 'natural' in* Laudato si' *(2015)*

1	see no other meaning in their **natural**	environment	than what serves for immediate use and
2	asked us to recognise that the **natural**	environment	has been gravely damaged by our irresponsible
3	and inalienable responsibility to preserve its country's	environment	and **natural** resources, without capitulating to spurious
4	arise. V.GLOBAL INEQUALITY 48. The human	environment	and the **natural** environment deteriorate together; we
5	48. The human environment and the **natural**	environment	deteriorate together; we cannot adequately combat
6	effects on human dignity and the **natural**	environment	Here we see how environmental deterioration and
7	credit, insurance, and markets." [77]95. The **natural**	environment	is a collective good, the patrimony of
8	brothers and sisters and for the **natural**	environment	These attitudes also attune us to the
9	the common good and to defend the	environment	Whether **natural** or urban. Some, for example,

concordance lines in Table 19.3, Francis refers to Pope John Paul II's encyclical by emphasizing the often-misleading assumption that human beings frequently 'see no other meaning in their natural environment that what serves for immediate consumption' (§5). Similarly, Pope Francis articulates Benedict XVI's notion of detrimental growth 'to recognise that the natural environment has been gravely damaged by our irresponsible behaviour.'

As seen in this table, Francis' overall use of these collocates highlights the complexity of relationships arising from the terminology in so far, the natural and the social environments are intertwined. Moreover, what stands out from Table 19.3 is not only a strong emphasis on our reliance on nature, but also humanity's role as an active agent in its deterioration.

In this regard, examining the use of the adjective 'human' may disclose further information regarding Francis' holistic advocacy. 'Human' collocates eleven times with 'environment' and often as the antithesis of 'natural'. Examples from the concordance lines for this item follow in Table 19.4.

Once again, it can be drawn from Table 19.4 Francis' strong emphasis to understand the interdependence of both natural and human environments: "The human environment and the natural environment deteriorate together" (§48) in as much that "we cannot adequately combat environmental degradation unless we attend the causes related to human and social degradation" (§48). In these examples, Francis draws on scientific accounts to maintain that inadequate distribution of resources and inadequate acknowledgement of environmental justice issues in the global agenda are to be blamed. The emphasis on the poor as the most afflicted group undergoing environmental degradation in this section strongly resonates with the works of Gutiérrez (1988) and Boff (1997, p. 1) on liberation theology: 'The logic that exploits the classes and subjects people to the interests of a few rich and powerful countries is the same as the logic that devastates the Earth and plunders its wealth, showing no solidarity with the rest of the humankind and future generations.'

Table 19.4 *Extract from the concordance lines for 'human' in* Laudato si'
(2015)

1	human ecology". [6] The destruction of the **human**	environment	is extremely serious, not only because of God
2	arise. V. GLOBAL INEQUALITY 48. The **human**	environment	and the natural environment deteriorate together; we
3	48. The **human** environment and the natural	environment	deteriorate together; we cannot adequately combat env..
4	effects on **human** dignity and the natural	environment	Here we see how environmental deterioration and
5	heal our relationship with nature and the	environment	without healing all fundamental human relationships.
6	a society's institutions has consequences for the	environment	and the quality of **human** life. "Every
7	life can light up a seemingly undesirable	environment	At times a commendable **human** ecology is

Liberation theology is primarily concerned with the struggles of the oppressed and not necessarily with the ecological devastation of the environment. However, since 'the poor and the oppressed belong to nature and their situation is objectively an ecological aggression" (Boff, 2014 p. 321), the intimate relationship between the two is used to reinforce one another. Perhaps more importantly, this theology sets off from other traditions in recognizing political involvement as crucial for achieving true liberation, a position strongly rejected by Pope Benedict XVI.

19.3.2   *'Nature' in* Caritas in Veritate *(2009)*

Pope Francis' predecessor, Benedict XVI, was elected Supreme Pontiff on 19 April 2005, and resigned in 2013. He is a renowned theologian and strong advocate for preserving the traditional views of the Catholic teaching. Following his appointment by Pope John Paul II in the early 80s as Prefect of the Congregation for the Doctrine of the Faith, he severely condemned unorthodox views within the Church. It was precisely during his time as Prefect that Leonardo Boff was suspended for his communist tendencies and his strong criticism against the hierarchical impositions of the Church.

Caritas in Veritate (2009) is Pope Benedict XVI's third encyclical. The document largely dwells on the topic of love as instrumental in addressing social issues connected with economic development. The concordance lines in Table 19.5 illustrate the lexical item 'nature'.

What stands out is that 'nature' is often portrayed as an active participant: 'Nature expresses a design of love and truth'; 'Nature speaks to us of the Creator (cf. Rom 1:20) and his love for humanity'; 'Nature is at our disposal not as "a heap of scattered refuse" [116], but as a gift of the Creator' (§48). Giving salience to this item is crucial for promoting its protection; nonetheless, Benedict XVI is careful not to align such claims with pantheistic understandings as illustrated in the following example: 'But it should also

Table 19.5 *Extract from the concordance lines for 'nature' in* Caritas in Veritate *(2009)*

1	nature as the fruit of God's creation.	Nature	expresses a design of love and truth.
2	God as the setting for our life.	Nature	speaks to us of the Creator (cf.
3	1:19–20). Thus it too is a "vocation" [115].	Nature	is at our disposal not as "a
4	is contrary to authentic development to view	nature	as something more important than the human
5	new pantheism–human salvation cannot come from	nature	alone, understood in a purely naturalistic sense
6	which aims at total technical dominion over	nature	because the natural environment is more than
7	a result of these distorted notions. Reducing	nature	merely to a collection of contingent data
8	encouraging activity that fails to respect human	nature	itself. Our nature, constituted not only by
9	fails to respect human nature itself. Our	nature	constituted not only by matter but also
10	beings legitimately exercise a responsible stewardship over	nature	in order to protect it, to enjoy
11	live with dignity, through the help of	nature	itself-God's gift to children-and
12	deterioration in turn upsets relations in society.	Nature	especially in our time, is so integrated

be stressed that it is contrary to authentic development to view nature as something more important than the human person. This position leads to attitudes of neo-paganism or a new pantheism – human salvation cannot come from nature alone, understood in a purely naturalistic sense' (§48). Although the Catholic teaching takes great pains to reject animism – a stance which has misleadingly been interpreted by many as a license to exploit nature – Benedict XVI warns, 'it is also necessary to reject the opposite position, which aims at total technical dominion over nature, because the natural environment is more than raw material to be manipulated at our pleasure' (§48). What is more, Benedict XVI forbears a responsible use of nature 'to satisfy our legitimate needs, material or otherwise, while respecting the intrinsic balance of creation. If this vision is lost, we end up either considering nature an untouchable taboo or, on the contrary, abusing it' (§48). His call for responsible stewardship is a response to the consequences of development and the cultural processes that shape self-destructive behaviours which impact on the environment, a concern which was also taken on board by his predecessor, Pope John Paul II.

19.3.3   *'Nature' and 'Environment' in* Redemptor Hominis *(1979)*

Pope John Paul II began his papacy in 1978 and lasted nearly thirty years until his death in 2005, making him one of the longest-serving popes. His first encyclical, *Redemptor Hominis* (1979) was released shortly after his election as Supreme Pontiff. Unlike later documents in his papacy, which strongly suggest an evolution from a conservative standpoint to a more eco-centric position, *Redemptor Hominis* (1979) is not primarily concerned with environmental issues but rather with the relationship of man and Christ facing the millennium. Accordingly, a search for the items 'nature' (9) (see Table 19.6)

Table 19.6 *Concordance lines for 'nature' in* Redemptor Hominis (1979)

1	joined with the awareness of her own	nature	and certainty of her own truth, of
2	disfigured ever since the first sin. Human	nature	by the very fact that is was
3	environment, alienate him in his relations with	nature	and remove him from nature. Man often
4	relations with nature and remove him from	nature	Man often seems to see no other
5	Creator's will that man should communicate with	nature	As an intelligent and noble "master" and
6	former. They fit in with the dialectal	nature	of human knowledge and even more with
7	the Church lives more profoundly her own	nature	and mission by penetrating into the depths
8	must persevere in fidelity to her own	nature	which involves the prophetic mission that comes
9	vocation, as is demanded by the indissoluble	nature	Of the sacramental institution of marriage. Priests

Table 19.7 *Concordance lines for 'environment' in* Redemptor Hominis *(1979)*

1	the threat of pollution of the natural	environment	in areas of rapid industrialization, or the
2	with them a threat to man's natural	environment	alienate him in his relations with nature
3	see no other meaning in his natural	environment	than what serves for immediate use and
4	and energy resources, and compromising the geophysical	environment	these structures unceasingly make the areas of

and 'environment' (4) (see Table 19.7) and yielded a low frequency of occurrence with only three instances referring to the natural world as seen in the examples in bold.

The data in these tables largely stems from the section entitled *Redemption as a new creation* which dwells on the impact of human activity on the environment. The following paragraph expands on the concordance lines in Table 19.7:

It is enough to recall certain phenomena, such as the threat of pollution of the natural environment in areas of rapid industrialization, or the armed conflicts continually breaking out over and over again, or the prospectives [*sic*] of self-destruction through the use of atomic, hydrogen, neutron and similar weapons, or the lack of respect for the life of the unborn. (§8)

In this example, Pope John Paul II relies on *re-minding* to draw attention to a relevant area of life which has been erased from the discourse and shall be brought back into consideration (Stibbe, 2015). In addition, the use of concrete lexical items relating to the use of nuclear power and superordinate items such as 'industrialization', 'armed conflicts', and 'weapons' activates the WAR frame in the recipient's mind, hence reiterating the Pope's concern that this is an area of urgent attention.

A similar situation can be observed where the concordance lines from Table 19.7 are expanded:

At the same time, exploitation of the earth not only for industrial but also for military purposes and the uncontrolled development of technology outside the framework of a long-range authentically humanistic plan often bring with them a threat to man's natural environment, alienate him in his relations with nature and remove him from nature. Man often seems to see no other meaning in his natural environment than what serves for immediate use and consumption. (§15)

In this paragraph, by giving salience to the role of humanity in relation to superordinate levels of human activity, namely 'exploitation', 'industrial and military purposes', and 'technology', the Pope brings into consideration the long-term effects of such actions on the environment and how they are being disregarded. Man's role in protecting the environment is being challenged by self-destructive patterns as seen in the choice of appraising items, that is, lexical items that evaluate an area of life as positive or negative: 'Man should communicate with nature as an intelligent and noble "master" and "guardian", and not as a heedless "exploiter" and "destroyer"' (§15). The lexical choices give salience to man's role as 'a steward of creation' in alignment with the notion of 'till and keep the earth' as seen in Gen 2:15. At the same time, it echoes Genesis 1 in affirming the biblical notion of human dominion whilst stressing that this passage does not entail ruthless exploitation; thus, distinctly aligning himself with the *Christian stewardship* ethic proposed by Kearns (2004).

19.3.4   'Nature' and 'Environment' in Pope Paul VI's Octogesima Adveniens (1971)

Deeply concerned with the struggles faced by industrial societies, Pope Paul VI released the Apostolic Letter *Octogesima Adveniens* in 1971 advocating for the Christian social responsibility to be exercised first at the local level and to then aim at the larger global scale (Social Spirituality, 2011). Consequently, the document touches largely on the effects of development on the environment, more specifically, with the plundering of natural resources. The following concordance lines illustrate uses of 'nature' and 'environment' (see Tables 19.8 and 19.9).

In a similar vein as Pope John Paul II's encyclical, the analysis of the concordance lines in terms of the use of the items 'nature' (14) and 'environment' (4) suggest a discursive approach geared towards the *re-minding* of such impact on the environment as seen in the following example taken from the previous concordance lines:

Table 19.8 *Concordance lines for 'nature' in* Octogesima Adveniens *(1971)*

1	which springs from his innermost being. Ambiguous	Nature	of progress 41. This better knowledge of
2	his activity. Having rationally endeavoured to control	nature	(7) is he not now becoming the
3	not in the face of a hostile	Nature	which it has taken him centuries to
4	responsibility is basic demand of man's	Nature	a concrete exercise of his freedom
5	himself in face of the demands of	Nature	and of social constraints; progress was the
6	aware that by an ill-considered exploitation of	nature	he risks destroying it and becoming in
7	on technological research and the transformation of	nature	industrialization constantly goes forward, giving proof of
8	own way and rising above their particular	nature	the concrete demands of the Christian faith
9	this way demands of a directly political	nature	When it is a question of public
10	subject to changes, even of a profound	Nature	Besides, who can deny that those movements,
11	more fundamental doubt is raised. Having subdued	Nature	by using reason, man now finds
12	own ways, those ultimate convictions on the	Nature	origin and end of man and society,
13	"Neither can false philosophical teachings regarding the	Nature	origin and destiny of the universe and
14	as definitive and inherent in the very	Nature	of man. These sciences are a condition

Table 19.9 *Concordance lines for 'environment' in Octogesima Adveniens (1971)*

1	they permit an adjustment of the human	environment	which better avoids the proletarianism and crowding
2	orderly civil progress is based (15). The	environment	21. While the horizon of man is
3	this degradation. Not only is the material	environment	becoming a permanent menace-pollution and refuse,
4	longer under man's control, thus creating an	environment	for tomorrow which may well be intolerable.

Man is suddenly becoming aware that by an ill-considered exploitation of nature he risks destroying it and becoming in his turn the victim of this degradation. Not only is the material environment becoming a permanent menace – pollution and refuse, new illness and absolute destructive capacity – but the human framework is no longer under man's control, thus creating an environment for tomorrow which may well be intolerable. This is a wide-ranging social problem which concerns the entire human family. The Christian must turn to these new perceptions in order to take on responsibility, together with the rest of men, for a destiny which from now on is shared by all. (§21)

What is interesting about this paragraph is that the focus is not on giving salience to the environment, but rather on the prospect of nature turning against humanity due to reckless management. Therefore, the item 'nature' undergoes a process of activation, in discursive terms, whilst 'man' becomes a passive agent subdued to the growing whims of manufactured goods as seen in the following examples: 'It can thus rightly be asked if, in spite of all his conquests, man is not turning back against himself the results of his activity. Having rationally endeavoured to control nature, (7) is he not now becoming the slave of the objects which he makes?' (§ 9). Human activity is creating an

'intolerable' environment which not only entails the destruction of the immediate physical surroundings, but also the development of tools which diminish
humanity's ability to reason: 'Having subdued nature by using his reason, man
now finds that he himself is as it were imprisoned within his own rationality; he
in turn becomes the object of science' (§38). In Pope Paul VI's view, the human
sciences subject humanity to a reductionist understanding of our behaviour
with the danger of imposing societal models that manipulate desires, behaviours, and values which may challenge religious views and moral understandings. In a similar vein as his predecessor, Pope John XXIII, Pope Paul VI's
encyclical conveys the concerns around the far-reaching consequences of
human activity and its impact on the environment.

19.3.5   'Nature' and 'Environment' in Pope John XXIII's Pacem in Terris *(1963)*

Pacem in Terris (1963) was Pope John XXIII's last-ever encyclical. The
document had significant influence at the time since it was formulated in
response to the Cuban missile crisis, the erection of the Berlin Wall, and the
development of the United Nations. Pope John XXIII's focus lies on the
collective and individual obligation of nations to protect civil rights.
Accordingly, a search for the items 'nature' and 'environment' yielded thirty-
one and one instances respectively (see Tables 19.10 and 19.11. Only the top 23
items which are relevant to the analysis were included in Table 19.10.).

The term 'nature' is predominantly used to ascribe qualities or with reference
to a specific phenomenon, often highlighting rights and duties which could
usefully attain the common good. The following examples expanded from
Table 19.10 yield further evidence of the use of frame activation: '[Man's] His
is a nature, that is, endowed with intelligence and free will. As such he has rights
and duties, which together flow as a direct consequence from his nature. These
rights and duties are universal and inviolable, and therefore altogether inalienable' (p. 2); 'For the common good, since it is intimately bound up with human
nature, can never exist fully and completely unless the human person is taken
into account at all times. Thus, attention must be paid to the basic nature of the
common good and what it is that brings it about' (p. 39); 'We must add,
therefore, that it is in the nature of the common good that every single citizen
has the right to share in it – although in different ways, depending on his tasks,
merits and circumstances' (p. 6). In the examples from these concordance lines,
lexical items such as 'duties', 'rights', 'universal', 'inalienable', 'inviolable',
'citizen', 'governs', 'regulate', 'relations', 'law', and 'institutions' immediately
prompt the law frame in the reader. This is further reinforced in the following
sections: 'The same law of nature that governs the life and conduct of individuals
must also regulate the relations of political communities with one another' (p. 9);

Table 19.10 *Extract from the concordance lines for 'environment' in* Pacem in Terris (1963)

1	living beings and in the forces of	nature	is the plain lesson which the progress
2	the universe has inscribed them in man's	nature	and that is where we must look
3	is truly a person. His is a	nature	that is, endowed with intelligence and free
4	flow as a direct consequence from his	nature	These rights and duties are universal and
5	Pius XII expressed it in these terms:	Nature	imposes work upon man as a duty,
6	21. As a further consequence of man's	nature	he has the right to the private
7	Meeting and Association 23. Men are by	nature	social, and consequently they have the right
8	Collaboration 31. Since men are social by	nature	they must live together and consult each
9	in human society is wholly incorporeal in	nature	Its foundation is truth, and it must
10	the true God- a personal God transcending human	nature	They recognise that their relationship with God
11	wisdom." (29) God has created men social by	nature	and a society cannot "hold together unless
12	than society itself, has its source in	nature	and consequently has God for its author." (30)
13	passing of such laws undermines the very	nature	of authority and results in shameful abuse.
14	therefore, the authorities must obviously respect its	nature	and at the same time adjust their
15	it is intimately bound in human	nature	can never exist fully and completely unless
16	attention must be paid to the basic	nature	of the common good and what it
17	add, therefore, that it is in the	nature	of the common good that every single
18	that it is in keeping with human	nature	for the State to be given a
19	be of so ambiguous and explosive a	nature	that they are not susceptible of being
20	they have a clear idea of the	nature	and limits of their own legitimate spheres
21	cooperation, and freedom. The same law of	nature	that governs the life and conduct of
22	which is revealed in the order of	nature	by the Creator Himself, and engraved indelibly
23	inviolable principle that all States are by	nature	equal in dignity. Each of them accordingly

Table 19.11 *Concordance lines for 'environment' in* Pacem in Terris (1963)

1	their own homes, settling in a strange	environment	and forming new social contacts. The Problem

'We would remind such people that it is the law of nature that all things must be of gradual growth. If there is to be any improvement in human institutions, the work must be done slowly and deliberately from within' (p. 18). It would be useful at this point to introduce the concept of 'natural law', a notion that has greatly informed Western political theory and practice by regulating the state's scope of action (cf. Northcott, 1996). Consequently, societies adopt values and principles that enable them to live harmoniously in a community, but this does not necessarily entail safeguarding the ecological systems. With the threat of imminent nuclear war, Pope John XXIII's message attempts to convey the importance of following the rules of nature for the common good of humanity. Nonetheless, the emphasis given in the encyclical to the notion of 'natural law' appears to be consistent with the liberal humanistic tradition previously mentioned rather than distinctly ecological.

To conclude, all the sampled documents broadly delve into environmental issues though with various degrees of depth and perspectives. In this regard, the ecolinguistic analysis deploys the various strategies used by the popes. There is a marked preference towards salience, re-minding, and framing, presumably to reinforce the urgency that such issues deserve in the production of positive discourses. In the sampled documents, this is achieved in various ways: Pope John XXIII relies on framing to activate the natural law frame, whilst Pope Paul VI is concerned with the re-minding of the devastating consequences of technological advances and the risk of nature turning against us. In the context of the looming development of weapons of mass destruction, Pope John Paul II relies on re-minding and salience to foreground areas of life which would otherwise be erased by human activity, particularly due to overexploitation and conflict. On the other hand, Pope Benedict XVI gives salience to protecting the environment, whilst being careful not to align with pantheism.

Papal encyclicals are intended to reflect on a current topic deserving ethical and moral attention, and *Laudato si'* (2015) has been pivotal in redressing the Vatican's position apropos of eco-social issues. Critical to understanding the text then are the works of other popes and theologians that feed into the encyclical and produce a more nuanced understanding of the position of the church in regard to pro-environmental discourses. Although *Laudato si'* (2015) does negotiate with various and often dissonant stances, it also uniquely achieves a balance in endorsing former papal discourses at the same time it recognizes more progressive stances, such as liberation theology, a theology formerly rejected by Pope Benedict XVI and John Paul II. In doing so, Francis' encyclical incorporates Kearns' three ethics seamlessly: from recognizing the notion of stewardship to promoting the common good of the marginalized – both in terms of the human and the environment – on the assumption that all creatures have intrinsic value in their relationship with God.

19.4   Future Directions

With the growing concerns around climate change and a renewed interest by the faiths to engage in questions of inequality and eco-justice, exploring how the different religions refer to the environment is a key point in helping the conversation move forward. Notably, the UN has recognized the role of religious leaders in ensuring the attainment of the Sustainable Development Goals since "through their teachings and practices they manifest the core beliefs and with them the core values of their tradition, using language which is accessible and value filled such as compassion or love or trust" (ARC & UNDP, 2015:19). Therefore, the power of the faiths in channelling key environmental messages should not be underestimated: they provide an important lens for appraising the values and norms which will ultimately frame our actions. It appears then that

Ecolinguistics within the field of religious studies has the potential not only for revealing inspiring discourses but also *enabling* action. However, apart from Le Vasseur's (2018) explorations at the interface of religious studies and Ecolinguistics in the context of Genesis 1:26–28, no other extensive studies have attempted to scrutinize eco-theological corpora using an ecolinguistic approach. Although his study focused on the Judeo-Christian tradition, Le Vasseur (2018, p. 431), urges scholars to apply this approach to "all forms of religious discourses"; a call which Fill and Penz (2018) also voice with regard to Positive Discourse Analysis in the same volume.

Examining faith-based initiatives and their outreach also appears to be a promising starting point for a sustained long-term commitment in terms of environmental awareness and Ecolinguistics can help achieve this by (1) deploying the methodological tools that reveal stories which are unhelpful and that sustain the logic of domination over the natural environment and the social groups associated to them; (2) identifying positive stories which can promote behaviours that can be broadly understood as respectful of the various ecological systems; (3) promoting those positive discourses and trusting they can encourage people to act accordingly; and (4) informing how religious leaders can communicate their environmental messages more effectively.

Firstly, in terms of methodology, using an ecolinguistic approach will assist in promoting interdisciplinary exchanges between the field of religious studies and the wider field of the environmental humanities, by deploying a framework that can be adapted to various texts and contexts. The use of corpus methods, for instance, can help in collecting relevant linguistic data to facilitate understanding how conversations about environmental issues spread across the different traditions and how these patterns have changed over time. One of the challenges of undertaking this type of linguistic analysis is bearing in mind the immediate textual and historical context, as well as the intertextual links amongst the documents (Prozesky, 1976). Whilst this may appear limiting at first, it has the potential for providing a more comprehensive picture of how religions' view of ecology can have an impact on pro-environmental attitudes. This task will become a true interdisciplinary endeavour which, if done adequately, can be an interesting methodological contribution to the comparative study of religious texts.

Secondly, Ecolinguistics not only reveals but also searches for inspiring discourses that have the potential for informing our worldviews. Therefore, applying the relatively novel approach of PDA to religious texts appears to be a promising field to test in parallel to CDA. A further step will entail taking an activist role and promoting those inspiring discourses. In this regard, further empirical research is essential for realistically addressing the social dimension of how those discourses are perceived, treated, and enacted in the public and private spheres, such as the impact of the positive discourse of *Laudato si'* (2015) within Catholic and secular communities.

Finally, a more ambitious task for Ecolinguistics could involve helping religious leaders communicate their message in ways that can be relatable to both believers and non-believers. This will involve conducting in-depth comparative analyses of their discourses and teaching them how they can become more sensitive to understanding and identifying key linguistic patterns, such as the ones introduced in this chapter. This would strengthen the impact of their work insofar as Ecolinguistics will help them communicate complex and often distressing environmental messages whilst embedding their faith's underlying ethos.

19.5   References

Alexander, R. (2009). *Framing Discourse on the Environment: A Critical Discourse Approach*. London, New York: Routledge.

ARC & UNDP. (2015). *Faith in the Future: The Faiths and the Sustainable Development Goals. The Bristol Commitments*. Ipswich: The Alliance of Religions and Conservation and the United Nations Development Program.

Boff, L. (1997). *Cry of the Earth, Cry of the Poor*. Maryknoll, NY: Orbis Books.

Boff, L. (2014). Liberation theology and ecology: Rivals or partners, Leonardo Boff (1997). In R. Bohannon (ed.), *Religions and environments* (pp. 319–28). London: Bloomsbury.

Brezina, V., McEnery, T., & Wattam, S. (2015). Collocations in context: A new perspective on collocation networks. *International Journal of Corpus Linguistics*, 20(2), 139–73.

Conradie, E., Bergmann, S., Deane-Drummond, C., & Edwards, D (eds.). (2014). *Christian Faith and the Earth: Current Paths and Emerging Horizons in Ecotheology*. London, New York: Bloomsbury T&T Clark.

Corbett, J. (2006). *Communicating Nature: How We Create and Understand Environmental Messages*. Washington, DC: Island Press.

Deane-Drummond, C. (2016). Pope Francis: Priest and prophet in the anthropocene. *Environmental Humanities*, 8(2), 256–62.

Fill, A., & Penz, H. (eds.). (2018). *The Routledge Handbook of Ecolinguistics*. New York, London: Routledge.

Gramsci, A. (1971). *Selections from the Prison Notebooks*. London: ElecBook.

Gutiérrez, G. (1988). *A Theology of Liberation: History, Politics and Salvation*. New York: Orbis Books.

Holy Bible: English Standard Version (ESV) Anglicised Compact Edition. (2013). London: Harper Collins.

Jamieson, K. H. (1975). Antecedent genre as rhetorical constraint. *Quarterly Journal of Speech*, 61, 406–15.

Kearns, L. (2004). The context of eco-theology. In G. Jones (ed.), *The Blackwell Companion to Modern Theology* (pp. 466–84). New York: Blackwell.

Khalid, F. M. (2002). Islam and the environment. *Encyclopedia of Global Environmental Change*, 5, 332–9.

Lakoff, G. (2010). Why it matters how we frame the environment. *Environmental Communication*, 4(1), 70–81.

Latour, B. (2016). The immense cry channeled by Pope Francis. *Environmental Humanities*, 8(2), 251–5.

LeVasseur, T. (2018). Religion, language and ecology. In A. F. Fill & H. Penz (eds.), *The Routledge Handbook of Ecolinguistics* (pp. 420–33). New York & London: Routledge.

Martin, J. (2004). Positive discourse analysis: Solidarity and change. *Revista Canaria de Estudios Ingleses*, 49, 179–200.

McEnery, T., & Hardie, A. (2012). *Corpus Linguistics: Method, Theory and Practice*. Cambridge: Cambridge University Press.

Miller, C. (2010). Antecedent Genre. https://genreacrossborders.org/gxb-glossary/ante cedent-genre.

Monagle, C. (2017). The Politics of extra/ordinary time: Encyclical thinking. *Cogent Arts & Humanities*, 4(1) 1390918.

Naess, A. (1995). The shallow and the long range, deep ecology movement. In A. Drengson & Y. Inoue (eds.), *The Deep Ecology Movement: An Introductory Anthology* (pp. 3–10). Berkley: North Atlantic Books.

Northcott, M. S. (1996). *The Environment and Christian Ethics*. Cambridge: Cambridge University Press.

Pope John Paul II. (1990). *The Ecological Crisis: A Common Responsibility*. www .catholicculture.org/culture/library/view.cfm?id=5439.

Prozesky, M. H. (1976). Context and variety in religious language. *Scottish Journal of Theology*, 29(3), 201–13.

Social Spirituality. (2011). Octogesima Adveniens – A Call to Action. https://social-spirituality.net/octogesima-adveniens-a-call-to-action/.

Stibbe, A. (2015). *Ecolinguistics: Language, Ecology and the Stories We Live By*. London & New York: Routledge.

Stibbe, A. (2018). Positive discourse analysis: Rethinking human ecological relation-ships. In A. F. Fill & H. Penz (eds.), *The Routledge Handbook of Ecolinguistics* (pp. 165–78). New York & London: Routledge.

The Global Catholic Climate Movement. https://catholicclimatemovement.global/.

The Holy See. www.vatican.va/content/vatican/en.html.

Van Dijk, T. (2009). *Society and Discourse: How Social Contexts Influence Text and Talk*. Cambridge & New York: Cambridge University Press.

White, L. (1967). The historical roots of our ecologic crisis. *Science*, 155(3767), 1203–7.

Wolf, J., & Gjerris, M. (2009). A religious perspective on climate change. *Studia Theologica*, 63(2), 119–39.

20   Conclusion

David Crystal

This book was conceived and partly written BC (before coronavirus), and partly during the crisis (evidenced by mentions in the chapters on *Interaction, Institutions,* and *Education*), and will be read PCE (Post-COVID Era) in a world that is already being described as a 'new normal'. If this proves to be the case, then many of the insights into religious discourse presented in this book will provide a basis for the new interpretations that will one day prove to be necessary.

Linguistics is used to 'new normals'. Indeed, a recurring theme in this book is the way linguistic paradigms of enquiry have shifted over relatively short periods of time, from diachronic to synchronic in the early decades of the twentieth century, from formal structure to social context in the later decades, and from description to explanation as the new millennium approached and the field of pragmatics added a fresh perspective to the study of discourse. This latter topic is especially important. It comes to the fore in Lu and Shurma's chapter on *Rituals,* with its use of the notion of pragmemes to throw light on the choice of language formulae in rituals, but it surfaces in several other chapters:

- in relation to gesture (Turner, *Multimodality*): 'gestures ... serve pragmatic functions, highlighting key areas of the message and direct the hearer's attention to particular elements that the speaker deems important';
- in relation to translation (Wilson): 'an understanding of translation is only as good as the linguistic and pragmatic theory in which it is embedded';
- in relation to inter-religious dialogue (Wolf): 'Another area that has so far been under-researched is the application of Pragmatics categories to analyses of inter-religious language'.

It lurks beneath the surface in the others, even though they may not explicitly use the term. All the writers in this book invite us, in one way or another, to ask the question 'Why is religious language the way it is?'; and pragmatics, as a branch of linguistics, evolved to focus on exactly that.

As with every other theoretical concept addressed in this book, pragmatics has several definitions. Mine is as follows (Crystal, 2020, and elsewhere): 'the study of the choices people make when they use language in particular situations, the reasons for those choices, and the effects that those choices convey'.

This definition helps to explain the many approaches to be found within the subject. The content listings of any two textbooks on pragmatics can look very different: some focus on a description of the choices themselves (as in stylistics), some on the reasons (as in psycholinguistics, with such notions as intention and relevance prominent), and some on the effects (relating formal features to such social variables as age, gender, role, class, and occupation). The notion of situation has also to be explicated, for it includes synchronic and diachronic (historical) dimensions, the latter involving change that is both long term (such as, in the present context, the differences between the English of the King James Bible and that of the present day) and short term (such as the switch from Latin to the vernacular in Roman Catholic liturgy in the second half of the twentieth century).

The study of religious discourse within linguistics hovers somewhat uncertainly above all these facets, and its character has changed over the years, reflecting the academic fashions of the time. In the 1960s, the focus was descriptive: what formal features identify religious language? A generation later and the focus had shifted to the social function of these features. I reflect this shift myself in two papers on the language of liturgy in Roman Catholic and Anglican settings, one written in 1964, called 'A liturgical language in a linguistic perspective' and one 25 years later called 'A liturgical language in a sociolinguistic perspective' (see References). In the first, the focus was solely on the syntax (word order), morphology (word structure), lexicon, phonology (sound system), and graphology (orthographic system) of the genre. In the second, the focus was on the functions that these features convey, using the kinds of categories that today are very familiar (and reflected in some of the chapter headings in this book): to convey information, signal identity, express emotion, initiate changes of state (performatives), sanction historical traditions, facilitate thought, maintain community rapport, and provide aesthetic appreciation. In the interim, of course, the formal features had themselves changed, with new translations and liturgical practices altering the norms in both denominations.

There is plenty to describe in religious discourse, for the phonology (especially the prosody: Hammond, 2015), grammar, and lexicon of this variety makes it one of the most distinctive in any language, as is evident when samples from different genres are stylistically compared (as in Crystal and Davy, 1969). Such descriptions, however, have inevitably been partial and selective, exploring only certain kinds of texts, or certain time periods. Also, most of the published accounts in those days focused on English, with only occasional reference to other languages. Rare indeed to see a description of religious discourse in a language from outside the Indo-European family (an exception is the collection of papers in Samarin (1976), where we find Telugu, Hebrew, Zuni, and other languages comfortably co-existing).

Those days? These limitations are still being felt, as illustrated by comments in the present book:

- on the study of sacred texts (Vermeulen): 'very few studies actually focus on the language of the text as their main topic';
- in the context of trans-languaging (Wolf): 'questions that concern the original religious texts in Hebrew, Greek, Arabic, and Aramaic are often written about in English. More attention could be paid to how these ancient languages and the way they are used in a given context affects our ability to engage in dialogue across languages';
- in relation to conceptual metaphor (Richardson): 'not enough focus is given to how particular conceptualizations are affected when they are expressed in English rather than the original source language'.

The dominance of English is clearly a concern, voiced in several contributions, such as Dorst:

> it is not uncommon in both publications and conference presentations on metaphor (in any text type) to present only idiomatic English examples without the original language data and any kind of intermediate gloss translation ... Studies on metaphor in Islam, Judaism, Hinduism and other spiritual schools of thought may not reach the centre of metaphor scholarship – as published in A-journals and presented at large international conferences – if these researchers are not working with English data or publishing in English.

When it comes to 'future directions', a stronger comparative linguistic presence in the study of religious discourse has to be a priority. But even within English, there is evidently much to be done by way of description. A comparative stylistic perspective is needed here too, as illustrated in Wilson: 'the translator of religious discourse needs to focus on how religious language works, which will involve investigation into how religious language differs from other kinds of language use'. It is inherent in the notion of diglossia, addressed in Rosowsky's chapter on *Community*, where we encounter different varieties of English whose linguistic relationship warrants further investigation (the devil lies in the detail – here, what is involved in 'might vary slightly'): 'in Anglican English-speaking congregations, a particular religious register of Standard English arguably prevails in sermons, hymns and in other domain-specific genres. This register's linguistic proximity to Standard English might vary slightly from one context to another but no one experiences it as an incomprehensible or alien variety'. It is there again in Turner, which argues for a multimodal analysis of ritual: 'how spiritual belief is conveyed, not only linguistically but through a conjunction of other modes such as movement, gesture, posture, sound, and image'. It also has a diachronic dimension, as pointed out in Warner in relation to the notion of

interdiscursivity: 'the construction of meaning does not happen in isolation but in relation to prior texts and the ever-evolving social influences of
culture and ideology'.

Above all, hypotheses about religious discourse need to be tested – not
only by the use of case studies, well illustrated in this collection, but by
the use of corpora. In a sense, corpora have always been with us – any
collection of sacred texts can be viewed as a corpus – but the kinds of
corpus now routinely available in linguistics allow fresh kinds of investigation, as seen in several chapters of this book: the use of keywords (S.
Pihlaja) or collocations (Lu and Shurma, Richardson), and above all in
Dorst, where we see how a theoretical notion (conceptual metaphor) can
be tested against a corpus of actual discourse. The author concludes: 'We
need a better understanding of what real believers do with metaphors in
actual discourse – what these metaphors mean to them and how they
adapt and shape the metaphors' meaning in line with their cultural values
and expectations, personal experiences and communicative purposes'.
The role of a corpus is critical here. Individual intuitions can generate
hypotheses a-plenty, but only a present-day corpus can test them. (That
temporal adjective is important: early twentieth-century corpora contained only a few million words, whereas corpora such as the Bank of
English mentioned in Chapter 14 have billions.) And the testing needs to
be global, especially when we are dealing with a domain of usage that
claims universal relevance. Corpora such as the Corpus of Web-based
English (GloWbE) will prove to be increasingly valuable in this connection (for a site giving details of corpora see the references: Mark
Davies).

It would be satisfying if a study of an aspect of religious discourse could be
called definitive. But the ever-present fact of language change militates
against any such naivety. Experience teaches us that whatever religious
discourse was like last year, it is likely to be different this year and to be
different again next. This is a theme introduced at the very beginning of this
book (Warner): 'religion is very much a dynamic entity, and it is always
changing through the ways that people experience it ... Neither religion nor
interaction are static entities, and this fact is what makes them both fascinating and challenging to study.' The point is taken up in other chapters, such as
Rosowsky, where the notion of a 'linguistic repertoire' is challenged 'by
conditions of rapid change in patterns of human mobility and modes of
communication (including electronic ones)'. This chapter also draws our
attention to an especially intriguing aspect of change: 'the growing use of
English for devotional purposes, leading to an even greater variety of discursive interactions, modes and genres through which young people negotiate
their religious and linguistic identities'. Once upon a time, linguistic change

was thought to be a relatively slow-moving process. Not any more. The Internet has seen to that.

Online communication is another 'new normal'. Whether we call it 'electronic' (as in Rosowsky), 'computer-mediated' (as in relation to identity creation in Ringrow), 'digital' (as in B. Pihlaja), or by some other name – Netspeak, Cyberspeak, Netlish ... – the fact is that the arrival of this new medium of discourse has changed everything. From a world where language study focused routinely on only two major mediums of linguistic communication, speech and writing (I say 'routinely' so as not to forget the study of sign languages), within one generation we encounter a third, and the emergence of a new area of research, Internet linguistics (Crystal, 2011). Online discourse is different, in that it blends the two traditional modes (as when we *write* emails, but talk about having an email *conversation*) and offers novel communicative techniques (such as hypertext linking) and opportunities (email, texting, social media ...). It's not an exaggeration to say that all previous linguistic generalizations, based on analyses of traditional speech and writing, have to be re-examined to see whether they hold up in online situations. In some domains, there is little evident change (many Web pages are like any traditional piece of writing); in others, there is a more radical shift, as in the new conventions that characterize short-messaging services (such as texting abbreviations and Twitter hashtags). New stylistic varieties have emerged, such as blogging and instant messaging, and we see new trends in spelling, capitalization, and punctuation, along with a great deal of new vocabulary. And – as more than one Internet article has been headed – 'we ain't seen nothin' yet', for the online medium has hitherto been predominantly graphic, and we have yet to see the flowering and the linguistic consequences for discourse of 'voice over the Internet'.

All of this is being sensed by several contributors to this book. In Chapter 6, we read of 'the proliferation of rhetorical contact by a wider variety of rhetors on and via internet'; in Chapter 7, of the Internet as an 'agent of change ... where the translation of religious discourse flourishes', especially with the increased availability of major texts and online translation tools; and in Chapter 16, in relation to identity, where digital religious communities are seen alongside non-digital communities as 'a key area for linguistic researchers to explore, especially in terms of how language helps construct and maintain such communities, and how language conveys key beliefs and key identity markers'. These communities were once viewed as fairly stable, but in Chapter 3, we are given a different view, prompting the rethinking of linguistic repertoire as 'tied to membership in relatively stable speech communities': 'Instead, global conditions of migration and new communication technologies may allow (or constrain) participants in moving between various more or less short-term group formations across the lifespan.' In Chapter 18, our attention is directed to sacred texts, where, despite the 'fragmentary and ephemeral' character of online reading, there are likely to be effects in terms of meaning production that need investigation, 'looking, for example, whether Jonah's experience in the fish results in another meaning for the text when read in a digital form'. The comparative issue arises again: 'Rereading may also differ in digital and non-digital contexts, such as whether the digital sacred text is read or rather listened too or viewed. Meaning construal work could also be affected, with the addition of background knowledge with hyperlinks, adding knowledge many readers do not have when reading a sacred text on paper.'

Also noted is the arrival of the cellphone (Rosowsky): 'the now ubiquitous use of the mobile phone to access, download and store liturgical language resources ... allowing for liturgical language practice to be supported in an ever-increasing range of contexts and situations'. The point is explored in detail in the chapter on *Media* (S. Pihlaja), where the contributor points out that religious believers 'now read their sacred texts on their phones, with apps providing them with personalised devotional readings or alerting them to the call to prayer or guiding them through mediation practices'. A very important point follows: 'Seeing a clear delineation between a person's online and offline religious practices has become increasingly difficult and there is little reason to believe that in the short to medium term, the integration of technology in the day-to-day interaction of religious believers is likely to become less pronounced.' The conclusion is inescapable:

The analysis of media texts and the processes of mediatisation must therefore be central to any study of religious discourse, at least in understanding the contexts of interaction. As mobile technologies continue to proliferate and become increasingly integrated into the social world, the processes by which they change, manipulate, and adapt to individuals must be at the forefront of religious discourse analysis.

It is indeed going to be a brave new world, which has such media in it. It is not simply that the use of electronic technologies is becoming routine – as Rosowsky puts it, 'a regular part of some acquisition practices with software, data projectors and iPads mediating the liturgical languages of various faiths'. Rather, there has been a shift: 'the move from the communal experience to the individual one. Traditional liturgical language practices have centred on communal rituals and ceremonies. The move to an online religion experience has often resulted in a more private experience.' Just as fundamental is the view we read in Lytra concerning 'the increased significance of digital technologies in sustaining and transforming language use and in creating new religious practices and identity options'. We are encountering 'the development of more individualised forms of religious expression and the concomitant fragmentation of traditional religious authority', a development that raises questions regarding 'what might count as authentic religious practice in the twenty-first century' (Lytra, *Ethnography*). In the Post-COVID Era, as one might now say.

PCE. This is where I came in. COVID-19 is a perfect illustration of the rapidity with which the process of social, and thus linguistic, change can happen. It is already anticipated in Gao and Thondhlana, in the context of faith in education, where the writer suggests that one result of the crisis could be that religion 'may play a more pronounced role in people's lives'. Already, by June 2020, there were reports of shifts in behaviour as a result of the move to online events. In the world of literary festivals, for example, the Hay Festival, held every year in the small town of Hay-on-Wye in Wales, usually attracts a physical audience of several thousand, but online for the first time, as a result of lockdown, the audience was around half a million. Priests and ministers streaming services were also reporting an unexpected increase in daily attendance – something for which there was clear evidence in the attendance analytics – and articles were being written about the development of creative thinking to promote what is being called 'home liturgy' (as in Lamb, 2020). Communities have found new ways of coming together using such technologies as Zoom, with traditional liturgical practices, such as homilies, prayer groups, and hymn-singing, being given a novel online incarnation. I found myself engaged in just such a development, as a consequence of places of worship being in lockdown, that would have been inconceivable just three months before: constructing a website for an audio reading of liturgical texts (www.lectionaryreadings.com). The consequences for religious discourse are unpredictable and have yet to be explored. But it is already possible to see some of the linguistic issues.

Anyone who has taken part in a conversation or discussion group online will already have had experience of some of these issues. The crucial factor is the lack of simultaneous feedback – the listener vocalizations (*mhm, yeah, huh?*), body movements, and facial expressions that form an essential part of face-to-face conversation. Without these to give speakers a sense of how the interaction is going, they feel isolated and their speech is affected as a consequence. In a one-to-one interaction, such as via Skype, unpredictable time-lag alters the dynamic, leading to uncertain pauses and overlapping speech. In a multi-participant setting, such as a Zoom room with gallery view, a speaker cannot maintain eye contact with the people in the various screens, turn-taking cues are either absent or need to be established artificially by the host (such as: if you want to speak, raise your hand), and there is the ever-present visual distraction of idiosyncratic movements and interruptions in the home settings – even auditory distractions, at times, if the participants' microphones aren't muted. To use a term from sociolinguistics, there is no *accommodation* – the feature of behavioural interaction that describes the way participants in a conversation influence each other (sharing accents, gestures, stances, choice of dress, and so on). Discourse situations involving unison speech – as when a congregation unites to speak a prayer – are especially affected.

An ethnographic study of the new situations, along the lines of the one reported in Chapter 3, would be of particular interest. In a setting where there is dialogue, what should the leader of worship do? Leave a pause for the isolated home participant to give the expected response? And if so, how long a pause? Speak the response aloud? And if so, at what speed? Play a recording of the response made by a reader? The issue is especially problematic for speakers who rely on vocal response, such as the formulae that elicit listener affirmations (*Amen! Alleluia!*) in some spontaneous sermons (Rosenberg, 1970). Correspondingly, in such settings how should isolated listener/viewers respond? In response to a greeting, such as 'The Lord be with you', what should they do? Say the response ('And with our spirit') out loud? Think it without vocalization? Ignore it? Some ministers say the response on behalf of the congregation. Some utter only the longer responses, leaving the short one-liners to 'speak for themselves'. There is great diversity of practice – inevitable in a new and rapidly evolving situation – and the long-term effects are not at all clear.

The same issues arise in relation to nonverbal behaviour (Chapter 5): if the celebrant gives a blessing, or some other gesture that would normally elicit a reaction from the participants (such as a bow, or the sign of the cross), how does the isolated viewer behave? And if a viewer intends to take part in an online service, what preparations would be made? As pointed out in Chapter 6, 'the material world remains a mediating force in any religious practice, organizing adherents' language use'. So which aspects of that world are to be replicated in the home environment? And does the substitution of these affect the nature of the religious experience? Will they stand or kneel as required? Will they position their body relative to the east? Will they make use of icons? And, to take an example that has been given linguistic expression in the neologism *upperwear* (that part of the clothing that can be seen on screen), will viewers 'dress up' for the occasion in the same way as they would when attending the event in person? One writer reported her experience (Jones, 2020):

I wouldn't go to church in my PJs but, I must confess, I've sometimes been to a virtual Mass wearing them. And, just as I'd pause the livestreamed Coriolanus from the National Theatre, mid-act, to put the kettle on, I do the same at Sunday Mass. Some sermons, I've found, are better with a strong coffee in your hand.

But I did get dressed, and even put on lipstick, to attend the papal weekday Mass . . .

An extreme case is what to do at the point in a service if a congregation is asked to exchange a 'sign of peace', or some similar act of solidarity with the community. Before lockdown, when the coronavirus risk was becoming evident, people were already being advised not to shake hands or kiss, but to use some other gesture, such as a socially distanced namaste – a replacement that has been given a lot of publicity due to its increased use in political and other settings. What does an isolated viewer actually do, if the celebrant initiates it? Or will awareness of the problem mean that this kind of interaction is to be omitted? And if omitted, what is the effect on the viewer's overall sense of participation in the event? The closure of places of worship means that activities involving physical contact (such as the taking of communion, the use of water, or the sharing of an object such as a candle) are impossible – and even when these places reopen, there will be measures in place to maintain some sort of physical distancing, at least for the immediate future. What happens to the discourse at such moments? Discourse creativity can be the result. Traditional formulations may need to be adapted, or new prayers composed, to give participants a sense of presence in the truncated service.

The point is especially relevant when we consider the way these issues relate to young people, especially in religious situations where the average age of the worshippers is high. How is this generational gap to be bridged? The online encounter with religion will not in itself present young people with a problem, for this is their world. They are well used to an environment where the screen is central and books or other written texts are marginal. The problem is a pragmatic one: how to present religious discourse in such a way that it is intelligible and appealing. And who is to take responsibility for devising these fresh approaches? The senior members of a faith community are typically not in the best position to advise, for they grew up in a pre-Internet era, and for many, the new technology is alien. For them, books and traditional written texts are central and the screen is marginal. There may even be antagonism to the new medium – or to the language used within it, just as there was in the early 2000s, when text messaging received a largely negative response in the media (Crystal, 2008). And indeed there are challenging problems in working out ways in which the screen can be incorporated into situations of worship without disturbing the sanctity of the events. But the problems have to be faced, for they are not going to go away. The observation in Lytra applies: 'if as educators we wish to honour all children's languages, literacies, heritages and histories and we are committed to supporting and sustaining inclusive and pluralistic peda-gogies then more attention needs to be given to children's religious practices and identities'. This now has to include a respect for their use of digital communication.

In a PCE world, everyone may find themselves becoming increasingly dependent on digital technology as a means of maintaining communication among a dispersed community or one which has been locked down. It will not be enough to explore what happens in public places of worship. As the editor says in his introduction to this book: 'Everyday interaction, where institutional discourse is worked out and used in real life, is harder to track and trace, but its position within religious belief is essential for understanding how religions emerge, develop, and change over time.' In the case of digital technology, there are well recognized issues of how to obtain reliable data without contravening considerations of privacy. We need much more information about the ways in which this technology can be used to best effect in the various domains of religious discourse in these circumstances, and – even more important – about the attitudes of worshippers to this technology. Although it's good to see moves in this direction (Pihlaja, 2018, Rosowsky, 2017), I sense a sequel, one day: *Analysing Online Religious Discourse*. I think that will probably solve it.

References

Crystal, D. (1964). A liturgical language in a linguistic perspective. *New Blackfriars*, 148–56.

Crystal, D. (1990). A liturgical language in a sociolinguistic perspective. In D. & R.C. D. Jasper (eds.), *Language and the Worship of the Church* (pp. 120–46). Basingstoke: Macmillan.

Crystal, D. (2008). *Txtng: The Gr8 Db8*. Oxford: Oxford University Press.

Crystal, D. (2011). *Internet Linguistics*. Abingdon: Routledge.

Crystal, D. (2020). *Let's Talk: How English Conversation Works*. Oxford: Oxford University Press.

Crystal, D., & Davy, D. (1969). *Investigating English Style*. Harlow: Longman.

Davies, M. English Corpora. www.english-corpora.org.

Hammond, C. (2015). *The Sound of the Liturgy*. London: SPCK.

Jones, E. (2020). 'Have Mass, will travel'. *The Tablet*, 6 June, 18–19.

Lamb, C. (2020). Post-Covid Catholicism. *The Tablet*, 30 May, 8–9.

Pihlaja, S. (2018). *Religious Talk Online: the Evangelical Discourse of Christians, Muslims, and Atheists*. Cambridge: Cambridge University Press.

Rosenberg, B. A. (1970). The formulaic quality of spontaneous sermons. *Journal of American Folklore*, 83, 3–20.

Rosowsky, A. (2017). *Faith and Language Practices in Digital Spaces*. Bristol: Multilingual Matters.

Samarin, W. J. (ed.). (1976). *Language in Religious Practice*. Rowley, MA: Newbury House.

Key Terms

For EU product safety concerns, contact us at Calle de José Abascal, 56–1°,
28003 Madrid, Spain or eugpsr@cambridge.org.

www.ingramcontent.com/pod-product-compliance
Ingram Content Group UK Ltd.
Pitfield, Milton Keynes, MK11 3LW, UK
UKHW020432240426

470322UK00017B/479